Redefining Global Creative Sectors Through AI and Human Augmentation

Fazla Rabby
https://orcid.org/0000-0002-2683-7218
Stanford Institute of Management and Technology, Australia

Sweta Thakur
King's Own Institute, Australia

Shafiqur Rahman
International Open University, The Gambia

Nishita Pruthi
https://orcid.org/0000-0002-6094-0972
Asian School of Business, India

Mukesh Singla
Baba Mastnath University, India

IGI Global
Scientific Publishing
Publishing Tomorrow's Research Today

Vice President of Editorial	Melissa Wagner
Director of Acquisitions	Mikaela Felty
Director of Book Development	Jocelynn Hessler
Production Manager	Mike Brehm
Cover Design	Jose Rosado

Published in the United States of America by
IGI Global Scientific Publishing
701 East Chocolate Avenue
Hershey, PA, 17033, USA
Tel: 717-533-8845 | Fax: 717-533-7115
Website: https://www.igi-global.com E-mail: cust@igi-global.com

Library of Congress Cataloging-in-Publication Data

Names: Rabby, Fazla, 1978- editor | Thakur, Sweta, 1980- editor | Rahman, Shafiqur, 1967- editor | Pruthi, Nishita, 1997- editor | Singla, Mukesh, 1980- editor
Title: Redefining global creative sectors through AI and human augmentation / edited by: Fazla Rabby, Sweta Thakur, Shafiqur Rahman, Nishita Pruthi, Mukesh Singla.
Description: Hershey PA : IGI Global Scientific Publishing, [2026] | Includes bibliographical references. | Summary: "This book aims to examine how emerging technologies are reshaping the foundations of creativity, production, and consumption across global industries"-- Provided by publisher.
Identifiers: LCCN 2025052863 (print) | LCCN 2025052864 (ebook) | ISBN 9798337371535 hardcover | ISBN 9798337371542 paperback | ISBN 9798337371559 ebook
Subjects: LCSH: Human-computer interaction | Technological innovations | Artificial intelligence
Classification: LCC QA76.9.H85 R436 2026 (print) | LCC QA76.9.H85 (ebook)
LC record available at https://lccn.loc.gov/2025052863
LC ebook record available at https://lccn.loc.gov/2025052864

British Cataloguing in Publication Data
A Cataloguing in Publication record for this book is available from the British Library.

Table of Contents

Detailed Table of Contents

The accelerated development of generative artificial intelligence has challenged the principles of creative practice and has laid down them as the established assumptions about the originality, intentions, and cultural significance of humans. This chapter critically discusses the intersection of AI-generated creativity with psychological theories of the agency of humans, social and cultural structures of meaning-making and emerging ethical issues of authorship, ownership and cultural representation. With reference to past and present studies, empirical results and technological advances, the chapter aims to point out the two-sided character of AI as the accelerant of creative possibility and the de-disturbing factor in artistic, economic and cultural ecosystems. It assesses the most notable risks, such as bias, cultural homogenization, deepfakes, labour displacement, and environmental costs, besides acknowledging the opportunities to democratize, make it more accessible and allow human-machine collaboration.

Digital technologies, platform-based labour and AI are causing a significant transformation in the future of work in creative industries. This chapter looks at how the changes are transforming creative professions, work models and career expectations. In the digital transition, numerous cultural barriers to entry have been eliminated and individuals can tap into international markets without institutional intermediaries. With creative employees becoming more freelance and web based entrepreneurs, artists have to manage an increased pressure to balance between creativity and commercial and technological concerns. Lastly, it also gives future research and policy implications such as the need to provide structural systems that safeguard mental health, equitable pay and inclusiveness to opportunities. This chapter contends that creators, platforms, educators and policymakers must work together in order to achieve a healthy and equitable creative economy and sustainable creative futures.

This chapter delves into how human augmentation reshapes creativity, drawing from Garry Kasparov's 1997 chess defeat by Deep Blue as a pivotal moment. He realized true strength arises when skilled minds pair with smart machines. Creativity, once viewed as a lone intuitive flame started blooming through partnership. Humans offer emotion, ethics, and purpose while AI started delivering speed, enormous memory, and pattern spotting. Bounded rationality confines us, as Simon and Kahneman noted, yet augmentation stretches those edges without deleting our gut instincts. Dispersed creativity shatters the introverted genius myth, fostering flow by facilitating frictions in "Ideation" and "Refinement". The chapter examines the Asian contexts.

The convergence of artificial intelligence (AI) and human creativity is reshaping how ideas form, teams collaborate, and leaders drive innovation. As organizations rely more on intelligent systems, leadership must integrate ethics, culture, and imagination into human–AI synergy. This chapter applies a three-phase model—Human-in-the-Loop (HITL), Human-on-the-Loop (HOTL), and Human-out-of-the-Loop (HOOTL) - to examine cases from Microsoft, Adobe, Unilever, and Spotify. Findings show that effective collaboration depends on ethical oversight, cultural awareness, and adaptive leadership. The framework introduces a human-centered paradigm where moral imagination anchors creative governance, concluding that the future of leadership lies in uniting intelligence, ethics, and empathy for sustainable innovation.

This chapter examines human–AI collaboration as an emerging paradigm in creativity, design, and innovation, emphasizing a shift from automation-oriented systems toward human-centered and augmentation-based approaches. The chapter per the authors discusses how advances in generative artificial intelligence enable

Preface

OVERVIEW OF THE BOOK

The accelerating convergence of artificial intelligence, human augmentation, and creative practice is reshaping how societies work, learn, innovate, and express meaning. *Redefining Global Creative Sectors Through AI and Human Augmentation* brings together interdisciplinary scholarship that moves beyond narratives of technological displacement to foreground collaboration, co-creation, and ethical stewardship in the emerging Augmentation Era. Rather than viewing AI as a substitute for human intelligence, this volume positions it as a catalyst that amplifies creativity, extends cognitive boundaries, and transforms leadership, education, and cultural production.

Across global contexts—from education and workforce transformation to design, branding, and creative industries—contributors explore how human intuition, ethics, and imagination interact with machine intelligence, speed, and scale. The chapters collectively argue that the future of creativity and work lies not in automation alone, but in synergistic systems that balance innovation with responsibility, efficiency with empathy, and technological power with human purpose.

This edited volume is intentionally diverse in disciplinary perspective and geographic scope, reflecting the global nature of AI-driven change. It integrates qualitative research, theoretical frameworks, industry cases, and ethical critiques to offer a holistic understanding of human–AI augmentation. Policymakers, educators, organizational leaders, designers, and researchers will find in this book both conceptual clarity and practical insight for navigating uncertainty and shaping inclusive, sustainable creative futures. Below is a chapter-by-chapter summary that explores the various facets of this book.

Chapter 1: An Exploratory Qualitative Thematic Analysis of Workforce Transformation and Human–Machine Synergy: Reskilling for the Augmentation Era

This chapter examines workforce transformation through qualitative thematic analysis, positioning reskilling as the foundation of effective human–machine collaboration. Drawing on interview data, the authors identify three critical enablers of successful augmentation: technological adaptability, organizational learning culture, and policy-level support. The chapter proposes a dynamic Human–Machine Synergy Reskilling Framework, emphasizing continuous learning rather than static skill acquisition, and highlights implications for organizational strategy and government policymaking.

Chapter 2: Anticipatory AI Leadership: Strategic Foresight and Scenario Planning for Future-Ready Education

Focusing on education, this chapter introduces anticipatory AI leadership as a proactive model that integrates strategic foresight and scenario planning. Rather than reacting to technological change, educational leaders are encouraged to align AI adoption with long-term societal goals. Tools such as horizon scanning and trend analysis are presented as mechanisms to ensure ethical, inclusive, and resilient AI integration, ultimately enabling institutions to thrive amid uncertainty while fostering trust and human potential.

Chapter 3: Augmented Creativity: Uniting Human Intuition and Artificial Intelligence in Design

This chapter traces the evolution of AI-assisted design from early computer-aided systems to contemporary generative and interactive co-creation platforms. It reviews key theoretical models—including human-in-the-loop, AI-in-the-loop, and symbiotic co-creation—and examines their application across architecture, product design, fashion, visual communication, and UX/UI. The authors argue that augmented creativity transcends automation by embedding human intuition, judgment, and meaning-making into AI-driven design processes.

Chapter 4: Empowering the Future Workforce: Reskilling Strategies in the Age of Human–AI Augmentation

Addressing global workforce shifts, this chapter positions reskilling as a strategic necessity for sustaining human relevance in AI-augmented environments. It explores theoretical models and cross-industry practices that support the transition from traditional skill sets to hybrid human–AI capabilities. Ethical, educational, and policy implications are discussed, alongside a future research agenda aimed at fostering inclusive learning cultures, resilience, and long-term innovation.

Chapter 5: Ethics of Creativity in the Age of AI

This chapter critically examines the ethical tensions arising from AI-generated creativity, questioning traditional notions of originality, authorship, and cultural value. Drawing on psychological, social, and cultural theories, the authors analyze risks such as bias, cultural homogenization, deepfakes, labor displacement, and environmental impact. At the same time, the chapter acknowledges AI's potential to democratize creative expression and expand collaborative possibilities, underscoring the need for ethical governance.

Chapter 6: Future of Work in Creative Industries

Focusing on creative industries, this chapter explores how AI, digital platforms, and gig-based labor are redefining professional identities and work models. While digital technologies lower barriers to global participation, they also introduce challenges related to precarity, mental health, and commercialization pressures. The chapter emphasizes the need for coordinated efforts among creators, platforms, educators, and policymakers to ensure equitable pay, inclusivity, and sustainable creative careers.

Chapter 7: Human Augmentation and Enhanced Creativity

Using Garry Kasparov's encounter with Deep Blue as a conceptual anchor, this chapter reframes creativity as a distributed, collaborative process rather than an individual endeavor. It integrates theories of bounded rationality to show how human–AI augmentation expands cognitive limits without erasing intuition or emotion. With particular attention to Asian contexts, the chapter illustrates how augmentation fosters creative flow by enhancing both ideation and refinement processes.

Chapter 8: Human–AI Collaboration in Creativity and Leadership: Redefining Innovation in the Future of Work

This chapter examines leadership in AI-enabled organizations through a three-phase framework—Human-in-the-Loop, Human-on-the-Loop, and Human-out-of-the-Loop. Drawing on case studies from leading global firms, it highlights the importance of ethical oversight, cultural sensitivity, and adaptive leadership. The authors propose a human-centered leadership paradigm in which moral imagination anchors innovation and sustainable organizational governance.

Chapter 9: Human–AI Collaboration in Creativity, Design, and Innovation

Expanding on co-creative paradigms, this chapter analyzes human–AI collaboration as a shift from automation toward augmentation. Grounded in theories of distributed cognition and co-creativity, it demonstrates how AI supports ideation, exploration, and iterative refinement across design practices. Ethical concerns related to authorship, bias, and transparency are addressed, reinforcing the importance of responsible collaboration for sustainable innovation.

Chapter 10: Synthetic Culture and Brand Mythmaking in the Age of Generative AI

The final chapter explores how generative AI reshapes branding through synthetic culture—algorithmically generated narratives, symbols, and personas. Framed by mythmaking and socio-technical theories, it examines AI as a cultural co-creator that enables hyper-personalized and adaptive brand storytelling. The chapter critically addresses issues of authenticity, authorship, transparency, and cultural safety, offering directions for future research in AI-mediated cultural production.

Chapter 1

An Exploratory Qualitative Thematic Analysis of Workforce Transformation and Human-Machine Synergy:

Reskilling for the Augmentation Era

Piali Haldar
https://orcid.org/0000-0003-4729-6964
Brainware University, Kolkata, India

Dev Kumar Mandal
Brainware University, Kolkata, India

ABSTRACT

The rapid merging of AI, automation, and intelligent systems has triggered a major change in human labour that we call the Augmentation Era. Instead of the plethora of stories about downsizing, augmentation is the very opposite, and as a matter of fact, workers and machines working with one another can yield spectacular synergy that is human-like and of much greater intelligence. According to the study, the reskilling imperatives required for workforce transformation in this new era are the main focus. The analysis of the interviews illuminated three associated dimensions that are the mainspring of successful reskilling outcomes: (1) technological adaptability, (2) organizational learning culture, and (3) policy-level support systems. The researchers could then classify the Human–Machine Synergy Reskilling Framework as being

DOI: 10.4018/979-8-3373-7153-5.ch001

that of a continuous cycle that does not remain static, but is a cycle where workers can adjust and adapt to the environment so that they are relevant in the intelligent environment. The study has opened paths to the policymaking mind of governments.

1. INTRODUCTION

A truly transformational change is happening in the world of work. This change is happening more rapidly than ever due to the increasing role of artificial intelligence (AI), automation technologies, machine learning (ML), data analytics, and cyber-physical systems working in concert with one another. The technology is pushing human labour to its limits and changing the very idea of what expertise or employability might entail in a situation where the economy is closely connected and heavily relies on knowledge (Holford, 2019; Brynjolfsson & McAfee, 2012; Brown et al., 2003). Unlike the earlier times of industrial transformation, when the main focus was on eliminating physically or mentally repetitive human work and substituting it with machinery, this time it is a clear-cut change, such as work done by newly arrived machines. The present intelligent technologies can already perform tasks requiring human-like cognitive activities such as analysis, decision-making, and even situation analysis (Ren et al., 2023). As a result, work will not only become increasingly automated; it will also become increasingly augmented. The era of augmentation is a human-machine coevolution that is profoundly socio-technical (Navarro-Meneses & Pablo-Marti, 2025; Duin & Pedersen, 2023). In this new world, the human worker is the centre of attention and is now a part of the intelligent system creation. He/she is working with intelligent systems to bring in these hybrid capabilities, capabilities that were never explored before, increasing productivity and organizational value that are novel and unique.

Augmentation is a move that is altering the status quo and hence upsetting many of the long-held beliefs people have about the learning of skills, job markets, and concerned with or related to business strategic planning. The traditional ways of imparting education and training were planned in a way that there was always a connection from the start of the child in school, proceeding and passing exams, and looking for a job upon graduation, etc., are less effective in businesses that have become very unstable with time, and where the skills that are in demand keep changing. Due to this, the skill qualifications cannot be taken as a guarantee of continuous work for the worker. Continuous learning is a must for the worker, and they should have to the ability the master the skill that is not directly connected with his/her profession. And most importantly, the worker has to learn new skills in the fields that are extremely diverse. Man has to let go of affirmations of modernism and take on the principles of openness in the aspects of learning and learning to learn. Here, the individual who is the asset is the one who goes the farthest in taking on new conditions and in giving vent to the new.

At the organizational level, AI-driven augmentation is the factor that is bringing in the need for new types of work design, talent management, and cultural transformation (Faqihi & Miah, 2023; Mollah et al., 2024). The organizations, in turn, are required to come up with a new plan about how tasks can be best shared between humans and machines, how decision rights can be made clear, and how human and algorithmic outputs should be amalgamated. More than just using tools, the partnership between human and machine has become very dynamic. The worker has to interpret the algorithmic insights, validate the machine outputs, govern the automated processes, and watch the ethical side (Martin, 2019; Lustig et al., 2016). These new duties demand that the worker equip themselves with the traits of digital fluency, human-AI interaction, cognitive adaptability, and socio-emotional intelligence. As for the leaders, they should create an environment of psychological safety, encourage a continuous learning culture, and employ the use of inclusive approaches that make the reskilling opportunities available to a wide variety of backgrounds.

However, the need for reskilling cannot be understood only as the need of an organization. It is also a policy issue, an issue of equal opportunities, and an ethical demand at the same time. The national and regional governments are the ones responsible for setting up the infrastructure of the digital world, credentialing systems, regulatory situations, and public and private training partnerships. And because of the absence of learning eco-systems, workers (especially in vulnerable sectors) may be cut out from the fruits of the augmented economy. For that reason, the age of augmentation throws up as indeed some very serious questions about the fair share of opportunities, inclusion or exclusion, the gap between those who have and those who do not have digital, and future career paths. Effective reskilling has to take into account not only the knowledge of the technical side but also the skills in thinking and feeling that are the bases for workers being able to function effectively in the Volatile, Uncertain, Complex, and Ambiguous (VUCA) environments.

The increasing importance of reskilling as a response to the impact of digital transformation has been getting a lot of attention in the current academic discourse, although there are still wide gaps and needs that need to be addressed (Gorski et al., 2023; Li, 2024; Lakshmi et al., 2024). The majority of related publications present pessimistic views, focusing on and predicting the technical aspects alone, or the conversion of the workforce. There are relatively few works that would take a humane approach; by doing so, one would put augmentation, collaboration, and mutual enhancement of humans and machines in the forefront. Few researchers employed the qualitative approach to inquire into the opinions and the experiences of the stakeholders in the industry so as to get first-hand insights and understanding about one of the most important and contentious issues in the labour market (Nakesh, 2024; Leon, 2023; Muchri, 2022).

Moreover, the prevailing representation of reskilling in the currently available frameworks is of two types: a purely technical training matter and a labour market adjustment. This study goes against this viewpoint and pleads for a complete picture. In the era of augmentation, reskilling is not only a profound phenomenon, but it has strong push factors, which are the following: first is the unceasing emergence of new technologies, followed by organizational culture, individual adaptability, and the policy-level infrastructure. The findings on how these forces interact will be generated through a research design that seeks to look at things from a comprehensive and interpretive perspective and gives much importance to the practitioners' lived experiences. To advance further, an exploratory qualitative thematic analysis on the semi-structured interviews of HR leaders, learning and development professionals, as well as policy experts from various industries. This method enables the discovery of a rich spectrum of factors through which reskilling practices take place in the techno-human partnership.

A central aim guides this research is to investigate and describe the enablers, challenges, and strategic imperatives of reskilling that are in favour of the human–machine combination in the era of augmentation. By means of thematic expert narrative analysis, the study finds three main features: technological adaptability, organizational learning culture, and policy and institutional support. These are said to be the key elements that significantly contribute to the success of reskilling projects. The driving force for the proposed 'Human–Machine Synergy Reskilling Framework' that considers reskilling as an ongoing dynamic process rather than a one-off event is the continuous advancement of technology, which causes the need for new skills, which in turn makes the organizations and policymakers remodel the environments where learning can occur. The reskilling and adapting of the employees will eventually lead to a smoother human–machine collaboration that is bestowing higher levels of innovation, productivity, and shared intelligence. The synergy that grows from this then has an impact on the technological development, and in this way, the cycle is kept going on.

2. BACKGROUND OF THE STUDY

The world economy has seen a significant transfer due to digital technology's constantly and rapidly growing role in the lives of individual economies, making a move from old manufacturing models to new world economic systems where everything is interconnected, intelligent, and highly adaptable. New ways of doing things are being developed at such an extraordinary speed, and largely they cater to the needs of this highly sophisticated working environment. The pace of the global economic change is so incredibly fast, and the whole world is experiencing the same difficulties, which is mostly due to the oligarchies. The Era of Augmentation is primarily about the infusion of artificial intelligence (AI), machine learning (ML), robotization, and automation into day-to-day business operations as well as major activities (Rane et al., 2024). Advanced technologies are taking the place of human workers; it's pushing them to adapt to age faster than they think, and establishing a respect basis for conversion. Partly, a new setup of cooperation and partly powerplay among employees, businesses, and the government, the mixer of human labour, and the value that it brings in, need to be recalculated. Additionally, this reshuffling of the playing field is also one of the factors that the wealth scattered among the workforce and society through the long history of the division of labour is going to rebalance. Especially since now the benefits of AI and technological applications come mostly to the educated and skilled members of society. This will require an economy adjusted to new rules of taxation and probably a mechanism that redistributes the gains more evenly, but what is even more pressing is the need for the education system to produce as many and as advanced workers as possible.

In the past, every new technological step has brought workers to learn a new set of skills to keep up with the transforming production systems. The First Industrial Revolution required knowledge about mechanics, the next one was all about specialisation for mass production in factories, and the Third one, facilitated by computers and electronics, required one to be digitally proficient. However, with the Fourth Industrial Revolution, or Industry 4.0, there is an even bigger change to come. Even though the systems of today are not merely expressing and executing commands like before, they are more autonomous as well because they can sense, learn, predict, and respond without needing a human, among other things. The cognitive capabilities in the machines, along with that, introduce an absolutely unprecedented requirement for the workers of the future to rethink and redo their jobs, their responsibilities, and their competencies. Different from previous technology-driven change episodes where skill demand was pulling along the curve, currently, the skill changes are completely discontinuous, unpredictable, and exponential.

Employment in this technological environment was factored out; tech-suitable roles were now outside the walls of the sector, marketing without qualitative decision-making, manufacturing without robot assistance, and health without diagnostic support. To be successful these days, workers not only need to be digitally-skilled but also have cognitive and socio-emotional capability to perform these hybrid tasks. That is why training, up-skilling or cross-skilling has always been utilized for the case of the worker. The training is about using the same skills to acquire new ones based on the forthcoming job demands. Therefore, when one reskills, they actually learn to work in new roles, which are influenced by the technical revolution. As a matter of fact, the technical training should also be provided with the cognitive flexibility, creative abilities as well as with the help of emotional intelligence and ethical reasoning, since they are the human skills that AI is lacking or they are altogether very different from the qualities AI possesses, it is essential for competitive way at work.

The nature of work in this setting has gone through a significant change from jobs with fixed descriptions to very different and dynamic skill ecosystems. The scenario is that companies are in dire need of employees who can keep up with the ever-evolving technology. The life of technical skills has become shorter than five years in many industries, pushing employers into a continuous skill renewal investment craze. Besides, employees are required to interact with cognitive systems not as mere recipients of services but as well-informed partners. This necessitates digital fluency, or the ability to comprehend algorithmic outputs, to investigate automated decisions, and to intrinsically evaluate machine predictions by using human judgment as a counterbalance. Thus, any reskilling program for the company must not just focus on the user-friendly aspects of the technology but also on the interpretive, contextual, and ethical areas of the man-machine cooperation.

At the same time, the need for continuous reskilling is echoed in the parallel development of organizational structures and cultures. The older hierarchical models tend to be the culprit as they stand in the way of learning by strengthening the boundaries between divisions of labour and reducing the opportunities for cross-functional teamwork (Mohamed et al., 2004). On the contrary, a workplace that incorporates technology requires that employees move back and forth, share their knowledge, and work together to solve problems. Leaders need to contribute to the creation of a learning-friendly environment in which the culture allows people to experiment, failure is not a big deal, and the employees are happy to take part in new learning challenges without feeling threatened. Organizational learning has become an ongoing process with various components like digital learning platforms, mentoring systems, competency frameworks, and performance metrics that are agility-friendly. The change from role-centred to capability-based organizational structures is also seen as a sign of the increasing focus on the three core elements: agility, innovativeness, and self-directed learning.

Nevertheless, retraining cannot be seen only as a problem for the businesses. Wider socio-economic factors are just as essential in forming the retraining ecosystems. The state, the schools, and the private businesses must together set the scene for a change that supports learning throughout life. Numerous states have very wide digital gaps that block the ability of people to reach those opportunities. Particularly, people in the countryside, poor neighbourhoods, and underprivileged or low-income groups are the ones who are mainly marginalized, and they do not have access to the technical means, the devices, or the connectivity for this kind of learning. Moreover, Schools are too stuck with the past; the traditional methods of teaching are just as rigid, and there is a very slow pace of complete reform in the institutions. Consequently, policies at the state level should push for broad integration of the digital infrastructure, competency-based credentials, training subsidies, and matching industry needs with a national skill development association.

The arrival of the augmented era has paved the way for an array of ethical questions that will substantially contribute to the restructuring of skillsets. At the same time, machines will be replacing human workers in numerous jobs, due to which three concerns, namely job displacement, wage polarization, and employability fear, will grow even further. Participating in the dialogue openly and ensuring balance in the retraining opportunities are the best ways to deal with all these. Workers should not doubt that they would enjoy better job positions after they are retrained, and for their part, organizations should be the human-centred transitions' key designers who would give priority to dignity, inclusion, and fairness. Policymakers, likewise, must be making sure that the advantages of technology are justly distributed among sectors and societies.

Although the value of reskilling is acknowledged globally and in theory, research also shows that the general public still wouldn't know how to carry out well-reskilling strategies for the age of augmentation. While most of the studies have emphasized the technical capability issue and not so much the human side of work as regards intelligent machines, there are only a few exploratory studies that focus on the real, contextual, and cultural aspects of reskilling from the point of view of HR professionals, learning leaders, and policy experts. In addition, the integrative frameworks that could bring together the technological, organizational, and policy issues and show how they independently and interactively affect the reskilling outcomes were found lacking.

The goal of this research is to fill the void by investigating how reskilling is demonstrated, organized, and perceived in augmented settings. The method of the study is an exploratory qualitative design, which is credited for using thematic analysis to gain a broader perspective than the mere focus on technology and to offer a more comprehensive understanding of the synergy between humans and machines. The purpose of the research is to create a mental image of how the adaptability of technology, the culture of organizational learning, and the support at the policy level are connected to generate reskilling effectiveness during the augmentation era. The narration for this development is set to be a thorough examination to unveil the changes in the job environment, the need for skill transformation, and the organizational factors that further apart from the collaboration of human and machine.

3. LITERATURE REVIEW

The augmentation era, which is the period when artificial intelligence (AI), robotics, automation, and advanced data systems meet, has no doubt brought new possibilities and changed the human capacity framework as we knew it. As more and more technologies work together with human workforces, it is repeatedly stressed in literature that reskilling is vital and that it is one of the best strategic responses to the requirements of the changing skills economy. This chapter aims to delve into the topic of reskilling and human-machine collaboration in the augmentation era through the lens of the theoretical underpinnings, real-life implications, and missing links in knowledge in four areas: human resource development, organizational psychology, digital transformation, and public policy.

3.1 Technological Transformation and the Augmentation Paradigm

AI and intelligent automation developments have spurred academic enquiries on the future of work (Johannessen, 2020; Wang & Siau, 2019; West, 2018). Nevertheless, the current scholarly trend is leaning more towards augmentation, where technology and human capabilities are seen as a symbiosis rather than a replacement. According to Davenport and Kirby (2016), AI actually benefits the human element by being able to eliminate repetitive tasks, thus leaving workers with more time to concentrate on such higher-level cognitive functions as abstract reasoning, creativity, and interpersonal communication.

The assertion of the World Economic Forum and OECD is validated by respective studies as being of the opinion that the emergence of technologies creates new positions as well as displacing the old ones, in equal numbers. Like jobs for supervisors over automation, trainers for AI, ethicists for digital technologies, and translators for data services, emphasize the inherently mixed character of work with the help of technologies. Some scholars have pointed out that the process of hybridization, where the human-machine partnership has strengthened the respective partners (Kattel et al., 2020; Krinkin, 2023). Thus, there would be a need to rebalance the task division, where people will enjoy recognition, speed, and consistency. Still, people will have the upper hand when it comes to dealing with ambiguity, making contextual judgments, and emotional intelligence (Brynjolfsson & McAfee, 2017). Augmentation is recognized in the literature as a socio-technical matter where both parties, i.e., the technical and the human, need to be competent enough and adaptive in order to fully blend their different natures into one working system.

3.2 Reskilling as an Imperative in the Digital Era

The idea of reskilling has changed from just technical training to capability, making it more flexible and adaptive (Hasan et al., 2024). So, reskilling involves getting new capabilities, and it does so with the main aim of transforming workers for the future of work that looks completely different due to the tech disruption (Li, 2024). Upskilling, on the other hand, is different in that it raises the bar for the already present competencies (Elsayary, 2023). With the fast-growing role of automation and the coming disappearance of monotonous tasks, reskilling is no more a matter of choice but rather a necessity for people to change their professions and become digitally literate, problem solvers, and socio-emotional skills holders.

The literature extensively reports on the big gap between industry needs and the available workforce's skills. According to McKinsey (2021), more than half of the workforce will have to be reskilled by 2030. Academic research brought up the fact that new entrants into the labour market must be equipped with more than digital literacy; they need adaptable minds, team-playing capabilities, ethical reasoning, as well as innovatory skills. These competencies are the very basis of being able to work well in smart systems and human interaction environments.

Reskilling is seen from multiple viewpoints by a number of frameworks. Because it depends on the means and the measures of the situation, technical, cognitive, and socio-emotional skills, which consist of nurturing a mind that is capable of uncertainty, lifelong learning, and human–machine interaction (Tuomi, 2022).

3.3 Human–Machine Collaboration and New Skill Demands

Joint effort between humans and computer systems is a central point in the augmentation research. In the researcher's work, the collaboration is split into different schemes, such as:

1. Human-led, machine-supported, where AI improves decision-making;
2. Machine-led, human-supervised, mainly in automated production situations; and
3. Integrated collaboration, where humans and AI do their job together and listen to each other in a flexible environment.

The success of the models depends on the varied skills of those involved. For example, AI-aided medical diagnosis personnel must first of all grasp and convey the algorithmic insights, then integrate the knowledge of the context in which the diagnosis is being made, and finally communicate their findings in an empathetic and human way. Thus, bridging digital and human capabilities. Similarly, production technicians are required to have a dual understanding of both mechanical processes and digital interfaces, to be in a position to effectively manage the robotic systems.

The main objective of a number of scholastic works is the designation of interactional expertise as the prime achievement that helps to bridge the communication gap beyond the roles of human and machine. The algorithmic awareness, ethical literacy, troubleshooting capability, and situational judgment are the basic requirements of interactional expertise (Frau-Meigs, 2024). The study views acquisition by traditional educational means as a fallacy; interactive learning, cross-functional encounters, and long-term development plans are the only way these skills can be gradually and effectively developed.

3.4 Organizational Learning Culture and Reskilling Effectiveness

Organizational learning culture significantly influences the success of reskilling initiatives. Edmondson (2018) brings attention to psychological safety as the key point of learning. She says that the teaching process is more effective and the employees are more engaged when they feel safe enough to make mistakes and try out new things. Furthermore, studies show that the strong involvement of the leadership and employees who set an example is the most important factor for the creation of a learning-friendly workplace.

Many offices have moved away from annual training programs as the primary means of learning to the more fluid, continuous learning approach, which is a combination of digital learning platforms, micro-learning modules, and algorithm-driven personalized learning paths. A small number of authors suggest that companies' learning systems should be one with re-skilling, while the rest see learning as a means to achieve an efficient performance management system, career options, and in alignment with the overall strategy of the organization.

The problem of job insecurity, as well as inadequate support from the managers, and lack of time set aside, are mentioned as the main factors preventing employees from being part of the programs. The difficulty in making changes in the organization, and the society itself-represented by its resistance to change, makes it hard to shift the company's focus. One should consider and use the whole HR strategy represented through reskilling as a part of the talent strategy, at the same time giving access to learning through inclusiveness and equity.

3.5 Public Policy, Digital Infrastructure, and Skills Ecosystems

At the societal level, the challenge that policymakers have is how to create skills ecosystems that would be able to catch up with the accelerated pace of labour market changes. According to the research, there is a big gap in digital infrastructure and access to learning resources, especially in developing countries (Abuali & Ahmed, 2025). Unless there are strategic measures taken, these gaps may lead to even more complex socio-economic inequalities.

There are quite a few researchers who bring the significance of competency-based certification systems, government-funded digital training programs, and scalable online learning platforms to the fore (Waks, 2018). A case in point is the national initiatives of Singapore and the European Union, the Digital Skills and Jobs Coalition, which shows the way to the efforts of many parties cooperating and contributing at the same time.

Furthermore, national reskilling strategies are influenced by geopolitical factors like data governance, AI regulation, and global competition. It is frequently emphasized in the literature that the proper policy perspective, company requirements, and business initiatives would need to be put on the same page with new workforce skills, which may require collaboration between the government and the industry; and at the same time, the digital credentials portability should also be assured.

There is still a gap in policy–industry alignment, funding over the long term, and evaluation of outcomes of training, although despite the same progress. It is the need to transform and include in the system passionate reskilling policies, ready to elevate the citizens through technology, that is validated by the existing literature.

3.6 Theoretical Perspectives on Skill Transformation

Several theoretical lenses are applied to study reskilling:

Human Capital Theory

This point of view makes a special effort to emphasize reskilling as an investment that is going to make both the worker and the organization more productive (Becker, 1994). Nevertheless, people who are against that view claim that this lens, to some extent, ignores social-emotional and moral aspects of skill development.

Socio-Technical Systems Theory

The theory is based on the idea that human and machine cooperation is one of the main factors that link the level of performance of the company to that of the operator (Emery, 1980). Besides, it argues that the augmentation perspective is applicable as it focuses on the necessity of the intervention in the process of reorganization.

Learning Theories

According to both constructivism, proposed by Jean Piaget and Lev Vygotsky (Devi, 2019) and experiential learning (Kolb, 2014), the main path for developing the employees' skills is linked to the learners' direct involvement and experience in the learning process, together with the consideration of its context.

Skill Formation Theory

The theory proposed by Finegold & Soskice (1988) discussed that institutional arrangements, vocational systems, and cultural values are the key factors affecting skill formation pathways, according to this view.

Taken together, these theories indicate reskilling's intricate nature, thus calling for a multidisciplinary approach.

3.7 Gaps in Existing Literature

Reskilling and augmentation have seen an increased level of attention in the academic community recently. However, several problems remain unsolved:

1. **Qualitative insight not available:** The majority of research in this area is based on a quantitative, large-scale approach, which does not give a comprehensive understanding of what is going on in practice.
2. **Human–machine synergy is not put in the spotlight:** A lot of the available literature raises concerns about automation, but does not try to investigate the other side of the coin, i.e., how humans and machines can work side by side.
3. **Frameworks with too many gaps:** In the case of many models, the roles of technology, organizational culture, and public policy are considered in isolation from each other.
4. **The dimensions of socio-emotional are not kept in focus:** Soft skills such as emotional intelligence, ethical reasoning, and adaptability are not considered as important as technical skills and receive less attention.
5. **Lack of research done in the poor countries:** The question of digital divides and regional variations in infrastructure has not been paid much attention to.

These issues highlight the necessity for an in-depth qualitative study that would help in getting a clearer picture of the situation and would also identify the factors that promote reskilling.

4. RESEARCH QUESTIONS

The study will be supported by the following queries:

1. What are the most important factors that drive reskilling in the age of an augmented workforce?
2. How is the interaction of humans and machines perceived by organizations, workers, and policymakers alike?

3. What are the main thematic patterns that are derived from the experiences of professionals in the introduction of reskilling programs?
4. What would be the most suitable reskilling strategy based on these identified themes?

5. RESEARCH METHODOLOGY

A graduate student is conducting a thorough analysis of the re-training activity during the transformation of the augmentation era through the use of qualitative research methodology to analyse various dimensions of the situation. Through relying on primary sources of data and triangulation, the study will delve into the inductive reasoning that is theoretical in nature. Given the substantial potential benefits of the augmented agents' and human collaboration, the research should consider the implications of introducing supervisory relationships between humans and machines. The study was experimental in that, at least in the beginning, the answers were not sought where the theoretical knowledge was absent, and the methods were grounded in known cases. A qualitative method turned out to be very suitable as far as the processing of huge amounts of subjective data that had to be incorporated in a few key deciding factors, and the most important assumptions for the study were concerned. The most obvious advantage of a broad and open qualitative approach in that situation, in contrast to a purely quantitative one, is that nuance could be captured and contextualization made with respect to almost any entry level of analysis. The study focused on the very critical aspect of the transformation of an existing workforce to a digitalized environment, of which the team of professionals working on the ground for efficiency and productivity was the focus.

5.1 Research Design

An exploratory qualitative research design was chosen to investigate how individuals interpret and respond to technological augmentation in the context of workforce transformation. Unlike hypothesis-driven quantitative models, exploratory qualitative inquiry enables the researcher to gather in-depth observations and inductively derive themes from the participants' lived experiences. This design is particularly suited for studying emerging socio-technical phenomena, such as human–machine collaboration, where theoretical frameworks are still evolving. The study relies on semi-structured interviews to capture expert perspectives, making room for both guided questioning and spontaneous elaboration. This flexible format ensures that the data reflect not only predefined areas of interest but also unanticipated insights raised by participants.

5.2 Sampling Strategy

Purposive sampling was the method used in the research, choosing the respondents based on their professional expertise and their active participation in reskilling or digital transformation projects. Purposive sampling is the best method for qualitative studies that prefer depth to breadth and search for information-rich cases. The number of respondents was 18, who were HR leaders, L&D professionals, digital transformation specialists, policy analysts, and industry consultants. They were culled from various sectors like manufacturing, information technology, education, e-commerce, and government-led skilling missions. Introducing different sectoral viewpoints in findings increased the credibility and transferability of the study, thus making the analysis capable of showing the complexity and variety of reskilling practices throughout the levels of organizations and institutions.

They got people to take part by using connections made at work, reaching out through LinkedIn, and also by contacting different organizations. Among the qualifications for someone to take part were having at least five years of experience in a profession and being actively involved in the areas of skill training, labour force planning, or technology enhancement. This procedure made sure that the participants had the required expertise and practical background to be able to come up with constructive and useful ideas on reskilling and workforce transformation.

5.3 Data Collection

Data were gathered through semi-structured interviews that were given in an interactive way, and the interviews were also done virtually, either through Zoom or Microsoft Teams as the platform. Each interview respectfully took between 45 and 60 minutes, depending on the participant's availability and the depth of the conversation. The researcher was able to strike a good balance between structure and flexibility using semi-structured interviewing: while the interview guide did not vary much from one participant to another in terms of the consistency of the content, the open-ended format made it that the respondents could go beyond just an answer and come up with narratives based on their own experiences.

The interview schedule was created with three main themes in mind:

1. Technological augmentation and changing skill requirements,
2. Organizational learning culture and reskilling practices, and
3. Policy-level enablers and systemic challenges.

The following are some of the questions those who were interviewed had in mind:

- "How has technological augmentation influenced skill requirements in your industry?"
- "Which elements make it impossible to achieve a successful re-education in the enterprise you work for or hinder it?"
- "What role do policies play in terms of enabling or causing difficulties for the organization when it comes to reskilling?"

All the interviews were approved in advance by the participants, and they were transcribed just as they were communicated in order to be more accurate. Besides that, the researcher's notes were also written down as a way to remember all the contextual details, non-verbal gestures, and the thoughts and feelings of the researcher.

5.4 Data Analysis

For the research, the most detailed method was thematic analysis, as it is the study of patterns that are made among the data and, at the same time, give meaning to what has been collected. It is effective in revealing the particularities of qualitative research through the generation of inductive themes from the expression of the participants.

The study applied the six-step model given by Braun and Clarke (2006) as a guideline during thematic analysis. It is a method particularly effective for a qualitative approach where the main goal is to discover through the participants' sayings.

The steps taken in the analysis were as follows.

- **Familiarization:** It was the first step in which the researchers immersed themselves in the data by reading, noting, and re-reading the data to develop a strong and full first-hand understanding of it.
- **Initial Coding:** The researchers provided a preliminary organization of the data through the formulation of initial or first codes that were generated based on the data, such as points of digital literacy, psychological security, and policy barriers.
- **Theme Development:** As the codes were understood by the researchers and the groups were recognized, the next thing done or the next stage was to group the codes more meaningfully into possible themes and sub-themes.
- **Reviewing Themes:** This is the stage where the researchers looked at the themes and compared them with the codes, to make sure that the themes contain a set of meaningful patterns that can be found in the data.
- **Synthesis and Interpretation:** Weaving themes through the research findings and relating them to wider theoretical perspectives.

The data were analysed through the application of NVivo qualitative analysis software, which not only assisted in the organization of the data but also in coding and theme visualization. The software made the analysis to be carried out in a systematic way, but the final decision of the interpretation was left to the researchers, guaranteeing a high level of theoretical depth and contextual sensitivity.

5.5 Ensuring Trustworthiness

In order to bolster the credibility, trustworthiness, confirmability, and transferability of the study, several strategies were put into service. The participants were from various industries and had wide professional experience in order to make them more heterogeneous. During member checking, thematic summaries were shared with certain participants to have their interpretations validated. External and third-party debriefing from academic sources was yet another method of getting a valuable judgment, this time for coding decisions and the overall thematic unity. The procedures of the method were all thoroughly documented, and so a path was created that allowed the process to be audited, thus improving the reproducibility of the process. In the end, an extensive and detailed account of the study was given with great and detailed information for the purpose of readers to be able to judge the findings to their applicability to other situations.

6. FINDINGS AND DISCUSSION

The research was conducted to reveal what the organizations, employees, and policymakers were thinking and putting into practice, in terms of the reskilling strategies, in the augmentation era while catching the human–machine synergy, and the study's outcomes featured the enablers and inhibitors that still affect the human side of the partnership in the modern job settings. The use of thematic analysis in reviewing the contents of 18 half-structured interviews brought out three major themes, and in addition to that, there were 9 subtopics or interlinked segments that, below their surface, disclosed the reskilling patterns in modern technologically augmented environments. Workforce transformation is directly affected by the three themes: individual adaptability, culture of organizational learning, and policy-level infrastructures. The results showed a great complexity of the mention of these three elements, which persisted as a very tight knot, making workforce transformation, at times, very challenging. The current part of the study shows the data for the research and also talks about the relevance of the mentioned findings when linked to already existing research and theoretical constructs.

6.1 Theme 1: Technological Adaptability

6.1.1 Digital Literacy and Fluency

The point that was repeated by the participants was that the digital literacy spot is what extends into the augmentation era. Nevertheless, they made a clear-cut difference between basic digital literacy-texting in social media, e-mailing, etc., and digital fluency, which means acknowledging the flow of the intelligent tools, interpreting the output of the algorithm, and integrating digital systems with daily workflows. The groups of people working in AI have recognized that, in many cases, employees know the basics but are still not fully fledged AI experts, since, first, they lack fluency. They informed these people further that their competing personnel are always the AI themselves and not the third, for they always have a partnership that AI utilizes, which makes the employee more useful not to the company but the team of AI as well.

This finding coincides with current research suggesting that digital fluency is a complex capacity consisting of procedural, conceptual, and critical understanding of digital systems (Van Laar et al., 2020). In augmented workplaces, employees need to know not only how to work with digital tools but also how to incorporate their limitations, biases, and contextual relevance into their work. The research supports the claim that being digitally fluent means that the workforce is empowered to shift from mere technology consumers to adaptive partners that can work side by side with AI-driven systems.

6.1.2 Learning Agility

The data also shows a sub-topic that is very much linked to the agility in learning, in which the participants gave the definition of it as the readiness and the ability to get new skills very quickly, to get rid of old habits, and to get used to the changing technology environment. A lot of interviewees pointed out that the pace of technological change is very fast and the traditional learning arrangements are slowly but steadily falling behind; hence, adaptability is getting the upper hand over the expertise of a single instrument. Learning agility allows workers to change from one role and set of duties to another, thereby going through many transitions but at the same time not suffering a career setback.

This was the case in the study of the learning agility concept as one of the building blocks of the future labour force (De Meuse et al., 2017). In the world of interactive technologies, workers' resistance will be the necessity that has to be reckoned with, not only for the continuous technological shift but for workers' adaptability, which is the other side of the same coin. The respondents pinpointed learning agility as the decisive factor whether the person would be among the digital transformation winners or losers.

6.1.3 Human–Machine Interaction Competency

Participants have stressed time and again that effective collaboration involving advanced computer systems is only possible with a distinct skill set. It should include a mix of technical knowledge that pertains to operational processes and human expertise. People working in the field should be able to sense when the machine-derived predictions would be most probable, as well as step in, either to correct or to provide the significance of the outputs produced in various contexts. For instance, the HR professionals who were part of the study mentioned the hiring tool of algorithms that would need a pair of human eyes to scan through the data and remove hypothetical biases. The leaders in the manufacturing sector also shared that the operators had to learn the language of the sensing systems of the robots in order to be able to detect and report problems during the manufacturing process.

This is in line with the socio-technical systems theory that says the performance of the system relies on an optimal blend of human intelligence and robotic capacity. The results reveal the increasing demand for interactional expertise, a skill that is not generally taught in traditional education or training programs.

6.2 Theme 2: Organizational Learning Culture

6.2.1 Leadership Commitment

Repeatedly, it was found by the participants that leadership commitment is one of the most significant factors determining the success of skills enhancement projects. Thereby, the leadership that lays down a clear path for the digital shift, assigns resources, and demonstrates unending learning behaviours, creates a platform wherein employees are keen on reskilling. Conversely, the respondents attributed the gaps that appeared, inefficient and sometimes non-existent training programs, to the absence of the leader's participation.

With the present discovery concurring with what Edmondson (2018) states about the leadership model as the one that triggers organizational learning, we observe that the leader who promotes learning and sets the tone for such things would be the same person who, with the least effort, employees understand that reskilling is the main business. The findings of the research work are that if a leader buys into the company's mission, then it forms the link, and the workforce, on one hand, and the machine on the other, are in unison for a better human-machine synergy.

6.2.2 Psychological Safety

Psychological safety stood out as a major factor in the importance of reskilling. Those participating in the research said that they think people are more likely to take part in upskilling and trying new things when they are secure enough to ask questions, make mistakes, and tell others they do not know something. In the situation that a worker is afraid of being fired or getting punished for not succeeding, he or she will not want to go through any training or even learn new technologies.

Findings are in line with studies on psychological safety, which put forward that learning and innovation are highly related to the feeling of being cared for and valued by the organization. The age of augmentation carries along with its different types of uncertainties, and the psychological concept of safety is the key to dealing with the anxiety resulting from technological changes. The participants stressed that the firms have to work on and create a set of encouraging mechanisms through a more direct and candid communication system, clear change procedures with the help of and sharing of the knowledge process, and compassionate leadership styles.

6.2.3 Inclusive Training Design

Few people who took part in the study underscored that the reskilling strategies have to be such that they can easily adjust to many different types of learning methods. The variation in the learners' previous schooling, their cognitive ways of learning, and the extent of their digital experience all point to the necessity of customizing learning methods accordingly. According to the participants, the best strategies for this were the use of modules, blended learning models, and individual learning paths.

This result comes close to the universal design for learning (UDL) frames, which are all about flouting the rules and making them less restrictive in school. In the absence of the UDL model, the ready-to-go reskilling activities will only make worse the existing fairness in society already existing, thus the burden is to be put on the old, poor, or the ones with digital scarcity. The research findings draw most attention to the fact that to reskill effectively, it is necessary to give attention to diversity, equity, and accessibility as major design criteria.

6.3 Theme 3: Policy and Institutional Support

6.3.1 Public–Private Collaboration

Participants felt that the organizations couldn't reskill on a large scale without the sector's involvement. It is very likely that an alliance between governments, industries, and educational institutions needs to be established at the national level to draw up a common set of competencies, support the training, and tackle the skill deficits that otherwise would have given birth to a crisis. The participants have shared examples of PPP training ecosystems that have been very effective in removing the re-skilling barriers.

Moreover, this was the result of international studies that put heavy emphasis on the few beneficiaries who have their hands in the dough while the rest are on the losing end. The implications support that the reskilling issue has to be treated not only as an industry but also as a cross-sector concern, thus requiring continuous adjustment between the government's policy direction and the industry's need for skill.

6.3.2 Digital Infrastructure Accessibility

One of the most significant challenges for reskilling efforts was the insufficient digital infrastructure. The most important point raised by the respondents from developing economies is that employees in outlying or low-income communes have serious troubles in receiving training because of the limited connection or the absence of devices. The concern is that if the issue of the digital divide is not resolved, the reskilling schemes might serve as a contributing factor to the creation of socio-economic gaps.

The discovery points to the continuation of the situation presented by the digital divide's long history as recorded in the world's readiness reports. The process of making use of the latest technology and building infrastructure is quite intricate because it requires not only the connection of different parts of the world but, above all, the equitable access to digital infrastructure by all. In order to achieve this, the era of augmentation needs the presence of policy measures that are friendly to digitization and the expansion of networks.

6.3.3 Credentialing and Recognition

People mentioned the need for competency-based, portable digital credentials that can be used in various fields. They pointed out that the significance of traditional degrees is not always clear due to the fast-changing nature of skill needs, while micro-credentials and certification systems provide more adaptability and value.

This is consistent with international movements taking shape in the direction of the modularity of credentials, stacking them for proof of both technical and soft skills. Therefore, the recognition scheme will have to move to let reskilled people show what they are capable of in a really changing work environment. More and more, the measure of ability becomes the ability to learn; hence, the improvement in soft skills: educational institutions are going for mixed learning with E-learning support and more focus on soft skills.

6.4 Integrated Discussion

The study reports that reskilling in the augmentation era is not a linear or isolated process but a systemic, multi-level phenomenon influenced by forces at the individual, organizational, and policy levels. Technologies' adaptability, the learning culture of the organization, and the policy support do not work separately; instead, they together form a reinforcing triangle that decides human-machine collaboration success.

At the personal level, digital fluency, learning agility, and human-machine interaction skills are the factors that characterize the worker's capacity for changing to the new type of work. On the side of the organization, the role of leadership, emotional security, and equal learning situations is key to do their motivating and engagement way up. From the point of policy, setup, interaction, and certification are the things that make the skill development scalable by forming the backbone.

The results maintain that improving the performance of the system can only come about if both human and machine elements are equally optimized according to the socio-technical systems theory. They further justify the element of human capital theory by their recognition of the financial value of retraining. Alternatively, they break the stereotype of automation through a view that sees augmentation as the core of a human-oriented shift.

7. IMPLICATIONS

The results of the research provide significant implications for various types of institutions, like businesses, governmental bodies, schools, and individuals that have to operate within the digital transformation.

7.1 Implications for Organizations

Reskilling as a Strategic Investment: To be successful, a company needs to consider reskilling as one of the most important things to do, rather than a simple process accomplished by HR only. The continuously growing technology is taking the jobs that are not becoming diverse any longer; therefore, the only way for an organization to remain competitive is to progressively include learning in its long-term strategies, its workforce planning, and its innovation systems.

Creating Learning-Responsive Cultures: The reshaping of an organization's culture is of great importance in connection with the reskilling agenda. To alleviate employees' worries about robots taking over their jobs, leaders must nurture a culture where people feel safe psychologically, are willing to try new things, and lead them to adapt to the change promptly by using rewards. A culture that prompts learning boosts innovation and employee participation in the process of change.

Developing Inclusive Learning Ecosystems: Today, workforces have become very multicultural in terms of their educational, generational, and digital literacy backgrounds. Therefore, organizations have to implement adaptable, segmented, and convenient training methods to accommodate everyone, such as e-learning, mentorship, simulations, and experiential learning, so that people can have fair access to training without the risk of excluding the vulnerable social classes.

Integrating Human–Machine Interaction Skills: As human–machine interaction skills become an important part of the core of job roles, it is imperative that training not only touches on algorithmic awareness, ethical supervision, and data analysis knowledge but also includes these elements. The use of hybrid skill frameworks makes it easy for employees to work closely and effectively with smart systems therefore, they are also pulling their weight in the matter of the responsible use of AI.

7.2 Implications for Policymakers and Governments

Strengthening National Digital Infrastructure: A common challenge in the way large groups of people is being trained is the digital gap. But if authorities are to be able to get digital skills learning to the broader community, they still will need to work on the already identified four priority areas: accessibility, devices, centres, and human capacity. This applies especially in the case of people living in rural and on the fringes of urban areas who still have access to resources and tools in order to learn the needed skills.

Designing Competency-Based Credentialing Systems: Workforce individuals can benefit from micro-credentials and modular certifications, which are types of standardized digital credentials. Moreover, they can improve their employment prospects and continue the process of learning throughout their lives. The credibility of these credentials at a national level will certainly help the employees in case they are moving to different roles or industries.

Encouraging Public–Private Skill Partnerships: The partnership between the public and private sectors will be essential to the skill development agenda. Industry, government, and academia can work together to ensure that the programs are aligned and that the students also benefit from practical work experiences. No doubt that this kind of investment in the workforce will soon be copied in other countries worldwide.

Embedding Ethical and Regulatory Frameworks: It is up to the policymakers to overcome the difficulties that come with being partial to a certain party and not the other one, or the problems with personal information and even unemployment.

One must make sure that the ability to be aware of what is right and wrong is a part of the project for improving the qualifications of the workers on a national level.

7.3 Implications for Educational Institutions

Reimagining Curriculum: Curricula must shift from rigid disciplinary silos to interdisciplinary programs blending digital skills, socio-emotional competencies, and human–AI collaboration. Foundational content in problem-solving, data interpretation, and ethical reasoning is essential.

Promoting Lifelong and Flexible Learning: Institutions should offer modular learning pathways, micro-credentials, and industry-aligned short courses that support continuous upskilling throughout a worker's career.

Expanding Digital Learning Access: Online courses, virtual labs, and mobile learning platforms can broaden participation. Partnerships with governments and NGOs can ensure affordable access for marginalized learners.

7.4 Implications for Individuals and the Workforce

Mastering Learning Agility: The professionals are supposed to see the whole life through the prism of ongoing self-education. The basis of the profession survives on learning agility, which is the ability to adapt quickly, to unlearn outdated skills, and to be the explorer of ambiguity.

Cultivating Hybrid Skills: The combined package of the technical, cognitive, and socio-emotional competencies is needed for the workforce to include among the digital leaders. The components of this package will be digital fluency, communication, empathy, and ethical judgment.

7.5 Theoretical and Research Implications

The discovery of this research moves the theory of socio-technical systems forward and highlights the importance of harmonizing human abilities, culture, and technology. Furthermore, it also adds a new aspect to human capital theory by finding adaptability and ethical reasoning to be the two main core competencies.

8. CONCLUSION

The arrival of the augmentation era is now considered the most important transition in the development of work, and not only the direct tasks but also the cognitive and interpersonal roles are being changed. It is what was being looked at in the study on how the shifts are being seen from the organizations, workers, and policymakers' points of view and it is also noted that reskilling is the main component of the productive human–machine collaboration. It also became clear through the results that reskilling is not only about a technological upgrade but a very complex process presented through technological adaptability, organizational learning culture, and policy systems that are supportive.

The demand for workers now is digital fluency, learning agility, and human–machine interaction skills just to be able to manage hybrid tasks and changing job demands. The key factors at the organization level include leadership commitment, psychological safety, and inclusive training design, which are crucial for encouraging continuous learning and lessening the anxiety associated with automation. Organizations that promote adaptive, experimentation-driven cultures are securing better utilization of augmentation technologies.

From a global perspective, the issue of digital infrastructure divides and the lack of equal access to learning resources can be identified as the main reasons behind the slow progress in fair reskilling. The potential is huge for the public–private initiatives and competency-based credentialing systems in terms of creating the so much needed and effective national skill ecosystems.

In general, the analysis makes a strong point regarding the necessity for reskilling work as a joint and continuous effort carried out by people, organizations, and governments. By using human-centred and inclusive methods, countries are able to make use of the augmentation era to the fullest and advance sustainability, skills, and ethics in the human–machine interaction.

9. LIMITATIONS AND FUTURE SCOPE

This research brings up essential aspects of reskilling that one will need in the augmentation period. Nevertheless, it is necessary to stress that there are several limitations. Firstly, the study design being both qualitative and exploratory is one of the major drawbacks, as it decreases the possibility of carrying out a generalization of the findings. While the semi-structured interviews enabled a very comprehensive data set, the set of eighteen professionals (even if one gets all the above experience with industries, job levels, and regions considered) is not enough and may not even be very close to reflecting the industry, regional, and job diversity of the workplaces. Thus, it is important for the coming research to adopt the same design and study but with a larger and more diverse sample so as to be able to conclude where and why the study findings hold.

Secondly, the choice of samples might be leading to bias. The majority of the participants were leaders and experts coming from the workforce development, digital transformation, or policymaking areas; this, in turn, might skip or disregard the views and opinions of those who are most affected but less seen--frontline workers, gig workers, SMEs, and marginalized groups. But for these participants, there would be a more complete and inclusive comprehension of the topic.

The study's location should be taken into consideration, as it was in an urban area that was highly technologized, and the people had up-to-date skills. This could be a significant limitation for this study since most of the people are located in rural areas and do not have the required know-how about the industry. Three possible options would be to look at the situation from a country's perspective and compare it to another one, or move to a region that has a completely different context than the one mentioned.

REFERENCES

Abuali, T., & Ahmed, A. A. (2025). Challenges and Opportunities in Implementing E-Learning in Developing Countries. *The Open European Journal of Social Science and Education (OEJSSE)*, 1-12.

Becker, G. S. (1994). Human capital revisited. In *Human capital: A theoretical and empirical analysis with special reference to education* (3rd ed., pp. 15–28). The University of Chicago Press.

Brown, P., Hesketh, A., & Wiliams, S. (2003). Employability in a knowledge-driven economy. *Journal of Education and Work, 16*(2), 107–126.

Brynjolfsson, E., & McAfee, A. (2012). *Race against the machine: How the digital revolution is accelerating innovation, driving productivity, and irreversibly transforming employment and the economy*. Brynjolfsson and McAfee.

Brynjolfsson, E., & Mcafee, A. N. D. R. E. W. (2017). Artificial intelligence, for real. *Harvard Business Review, 1*(1), 1–31.

Devi, K. S. (2019). Constructivist approach to learning based on the concepts of Jean Piaget and Lev Vygotsky An analytical Overview. *Journal of Indian Education, 44*(4), 5–19.

Duin, A. H., & Pedersen, I. (2023). *Augmentation technologies and artificial intelligence in technical communication: Designing ethical futures*. Routledge.

Edmondson, A. C. (2018). *The fearless organization: Creating psychological safety in the workplace for learning, innovation, and growth*. John Wiley & Sons.

ElSayary, A. (2023). The impact of a professional upskilling training programme on developing teachers' digital competence. *Journal of Computer Assisted Learning, 39*(4), 1154–1166.

Emery, F. (1980). Designing socio-technical systems for'greenfield'sites. *Journal of Occupational Behaviour*, •••, 19–27.

Faqihi, A., & Miah, S. J. (2023). Artificial intelligence-driven talent management system: Exploring the risks and options for constructing a theoretical foundation. *Journal of Risk and Financial Management, 16*(1), 31.

Frau-Meigs, D. (2024). Algorithm literacy as a subset of media and information literacy: Competences and design considerations. *Digital, 4*(2), 512–528.

Gorski, A. T., Gligorea, I., Gorski, H., & Oancea, R. (2023). Navigating the disruptive challenges and opportunities of digital transformation in the labour market: Upskilling and reskilling for the fourth industrial revolution. In *International conference Knowledge-Based Organization* (Vol. 29, No. 3).

Hasan, M., Haque, M. A., Nishat, S. S., & Hossain, M. M. (2024). Upskilling and reskilling in a rapidly changing job market: Strategies for organizations to maintain workforce agility and adaptability. *European Journal of Business and Management Research*, *9*(6), 118–126.

Holford, W. D. (2019). The future of human creative knowledge work within the digital economy. *Futures*, *105*, 143–154.

Johannessen, J. A. (2020). *Artificial intelligence, automation and the future of competence at work.* Routledge.

Kattel, R., Lember, V., & Tõnurist, P. (2020). Collaborative innovation and human-machine networks. *Public Management Review*, *22*(11), 1652–1673.

Kolb, D. A. (2014). *Experiential learning: Experience as the source of learning and development.* FT press.

Krinkin, K., Shichkina, Y., & Ignatyev, A. (2023). Co-evolutionary hybrid intelligence is a key concept for the world intellectualization. *Kybernetes*, *52*(9), 2907–2923.

Lakshmi, S., Durgude, U., & Chitra, V. (2024). THE ROLE OF UPSKILLING AND RESKILLING FOR TALENT TRANSFORMATION IN THE ERA OF AI; THEORETICAL FRAMEWORK AND FUTURE RESEARCH DIRECTIONS. *Weser Books*, 198.

Leon, R. D. (2023). Employees' reskilling and upskilling for industry 5.0: Selecting the best professional development programmes. *Technology in Society*, *75*, 102393.

Li, L. (2024). Reskilling and upskilling the future-ready workforce for industry 4.0 and beyond. *Information Systems Frontiers*, *26*(5), 1697–1712. PMID: 35855776

Lustig, C., Pine, K., Nardi, B., Irani, L., Lee, M. K., Nafus, D., & Sandvig, C. (2016, May). Algorithmic authority: the ethics, politics, and economics of algorithms that interpret, decide, and manage. In *Proceedings of the 2016 CHI Conference Extended Abstracts on Human Factors in Computing Systems* (pp. 1057-1062).

Martin, K. (2019). Ethical implications and accountability of algorithms. *Journal of Business Ethics*, •••, 835–850.

Mohamed, M., Stankosky, M., & Murray, A. (2004). Applying knowledge management principles to enhance cross-functional team performance. *Journal of Knowledge Management, 8*(3), 127–142.

Mollah, M. A., Rana, M., Amin, M. B., Sony, M. A. A. M., Rahaman, M. A., & Fenyves, V. (2024). Examining the role of AI-augmented HRM for sustainable performance: Key determinants for digital culture and organizational strategy. *Sustainability, 16*(24), 10843.

Navarro-Meneses, F. J., & Pablo-Marti, F. (2025). Reimagining human agency in ai-driven futures: A co-evolutionary scenario framework from aviation. *European Journal of Futures Research, 13*(1), 1–17.

Rane, N. L., Paramesha, M., Choudhary, S. P., & Rane, J. (2024). Artificial intelligence, machine learning, and deep learning for advanced business strategies: A review. *Partners Universal International Innovation Journal, 2*(3), 147–171.

Ren, M., Chen, N., & Qiu, H. (2023). Human-machine collaborative decision-making: An evolutionary roadmap based on cognitive intelligence. *International Journal of Social Robotics, 15*(7), 1101–1114.

Tuomi, I. (2022). Artificial intelligence, 21st century competences, and socio-emotional learning in education: More than high-risk? *European Journal of Education, 57*(4), 601–619.

Waks, L. J. (2018). Massive open online courses and the future of higher education. In *Contemporary Technologies in Education: Maximizing Student Engagement, Motivation, and Learning* (pp. 183–213). Springer International Publishing.

Wang, W., & Siau, K. (2019). Artificial intelligence, machine learning, automation, robotics, future of work and future of humanity: A review and research agenda. [JDM]. *Journal of Database Management, 30*(1), 61–79.

West, D. M. (2018). *The future of work: Robots, AI, and automation*. Bloomsbury Publishing USA.

Chapter 2
Anticipatory AI Leadership:
Strategic Foresight and Scenario Planning for Future-Ready Education

Yamijala Suryanarayana Murthy
https://orcid.org/0000-0002-9561-5395
KL Business School, Koneru Lakshamaiah Education Foundation, India

Rohit Bansal
https://orcid.org/0000-0001-7072-5005
Rockford College, Sydney, Australia

M. Govardhan Reddy
Aditya University, India

ABSTRACT

The fast adoption of artificial intelligence (AI) in education necessitates a new leadership paradigm that goes beyond job efficiency and looks ahead. This research introduces anticipatory AI leadership, which uses strategic foresight and scenario planning to prepare schools and colleges for AI transformations. Leaders should plan ahead, examine alternate AI uses, and match educational policies and practices with long-term social goals rather than responding to technology developments. Educational leaders can use horizon scanning, trend analysis, and scenario building to create compelling plans to integrate new ideas fairly, inclusively, and morally. The chapter says that anticipatory AI leadership makes hybrid human-machine

DOI: 10.4018/979-8-3373-7153-5.ch002

learning institutions more adaptive, reduces algorithmic decision risks, and builds stakeholder trust. This framework helps create future-ready education institutions that can handle uncertainty and help people reach their full potential in the digital age.

1. INTRODUCTION

Artificial intelligence (AI) has evolved from being a supplemental digital tool to becoming a central instructional and administrative force in modern education (Black & Wiliam, 2018; Carter & Bélanger, 2022; Brynjolfsson & McAfee, 2017). Schools and universities now adopt adaptive learning systems, algorithmic assessment models, predictive analytics for student retention, and virtual tutors built on large language models to organize, deliver, and evaluate learning outcomes (Collins & Halverson, 2018; European Commission, 2021; Hines & Bishop, 2015; Mittal & Bansal, 2023; Ao et al., 2023; Bansal et al., 2023; Bansal, Pruthi & Singh, 2022; Painoli et al., 2021; Satar et al., 2023). While such technologies enhance personalization and efficiency, they also introduce challenges related to privacy, algorithmic fairness, and digital inequity between institutions that can and cannot afford robust technological infrastructures.

Traditional leadership paradigms—bureaucratic, administrative, instructional, and transformational—were developed for relatively stable and predictable policy environments (Kozma, 2011; Christensen, Horn & Johnson, 2011). In contrast, today's educational systems operate in a volatile, uncertain, complex, and ambiguous (VUCA) world where AI innovations can reshape pedagogy, assessment, and administration within months rather than decades (Bishop, Hines & Collins, 2007; Hodgkinson & Healey, 2011; Raja et al., 2025a; Bansal et al., 2024a; Bansal et al., 2024b; Rahman, Bansal & Pruthi, 2023). Institutions relying on reactive management often struggle to anticipate the ethical, regulatory, and social disruptions generated by AI (Facer, 2011; Dator, 2019; Rabby, Murthy & Bansal, 2025).

To respond to this accelerated transformation, scholars and international organizations advocate a proactive approach grounded in anticipatory AI leadership—an integration of strategic foresight, scenario planning, and ethical governance (Hines & Bishop, 2015; Fitzgerald & McCarthy, 2020; European Commission, 2021; Schwartz, 1996; Brahmi et al., 2025; Saini & Bansal, 2025; Mittal et al., 2025). This paradigm reframes leadership from managing the present to actively shaping educational futures. Anticipatory leaders develop futures literacy, enabling stakeholders to identify emerging signals, explore alternative trajectories, and align short-term decisions with long-term social and educational goals (UNESCO, 2021; Dator, 2019; Bansal et al., 2025a; Raja et al., 2025b). Through systematic foresight, they cultivate institutions capable of continuous learning, ethical reflexivity, and adaptability in complex technological ecosystems (Edwards & Fenwick, 2016; Erstad & Voogt, 2018).

The framework proposed in this chapter builds upon these foundations by integrating drivers of change (technological advances, regulatory shifts, and societal demands), anticipatory leadership practices (horizon scanning, stakeholder engagement, and ethical impact assessment), and outcomes (institutional adaptability, risk mitigation, stakeholder trust, and human-centered innovation) (Bishop, Hines & Collins, 2007; Carter & Bélanger, 2022; Murthy et al., 2025; Bansal & Pruthi, 2024; Murthy et al., 2025). Drawing on global guidance such as the UNESCO Guidelines on AI and the Futures of Education (UNESCO, 2021) and the OECD Report on AI in Education: Ethical and Policy Challenges (European Commission, 2021), the section positions anticipatory AI leadership as an essential framework for creating resilient, equitable, and future-ready education systems (Yamijala et al., 2025; Das et al., 2024).

Ultimately, educational leaders must move beyond reactive policy cycles and cultivate foresight capacity to transform uncertainty into opportunity (Scheninger, 2019; Peters, Jandrić & Hayes, 2019). By embedding strategic foresight and ethical reflection into everyday governance, institutions can re-align technology with humanistic educational purposes, ensuring that AI serves as an enabler of human flourishing rather than a driver of inequality (Carter & Bélanger, 2022; OECD, 2021; UNESCO, 2021; Venugopal et al., 2024; Ajani et al., 2024; Bansal et al., 2024c; Murthy, 2024; Aggarwal et al., 2024; Bansal et al., 2023b; Kumar et al., 2025; Singh et al., 2025; Thalpage & Bansal, 2023).

2. THEORETICAL BACKGROUND

The concept of anticipatory AI leadership lies at the intersection of several intellectual traditions: educational-leadership theory, strategic foresight and scenario planning, and ethical governance of emerging technologies. Together these perspectives establish the theoretical foundation for the framework proposed in this chapter (Christensen, Horn & Johnson, 2011; Hodgkinson & Healey, 2011; Facer, 2011; Hines & Bishop, 2015; Dator, 2019).

2.1 Educational Leadership in Times of Technological Disruption

Distributed and transformational leadership emphasize shared decision-making and culture-building, yet both face challenges when technological change outpaces collective expertise (Kozma, 2011; Christensen, Horn & Johnson, 2011). Consequently, while these models foster participation, they must be complemented by leadership approaches that thrive under uncertainty. Anticipatory leadership offers such an extension by equipping educators with structured foresight processes to explore and prepare for multiple plausible futures (Hodgkinson & Healey, 2011; Bishop, Hines & Collins, 2007).

2.2 Anticipatory Governance and Strategic Foresight

The term anticipatory governance describes decision systems that integrate foresight and feedback loops to guide emerging-technology policy (Facer, 2011; Dator, 2019). Instead of reacting after harm occurs, anticipatory governance seeks to recognize early signals and intervene proactively. Its core methods—horizon scanning, stakeholder deliberation, and adaptive policy design—allow organizations to remain agile (Carter & Bélanger, 2022; UNESCO, 2021).

Strategic foresight, a subset of this paradigm, encompasses techniques such as environmental scanning, trend analysis, Delphi surveys, and scenario development (Hines & Bishop, 2015; Fitzgerald & McCarthy, 2020). Unlike forecasting, which predicts a single future, foresight examines a range of plausible alternatives, building organizational resilience (Hines & Bishop, 2015). Applied to education, it helps leaders anticipate new pedagogical models, data-governance challenges, and labor-market shifts (European Commission, 2021). Embedding foresight within educational institutions transforms leadership from episodic crisis management to continuous learning (Bishop, Hines & Collins, 2007).

2.3 Scenario Planning: Imagining Multiple AI Futures

Scenario planning, pioneered at Royal Dutch Shell (Schwartz, 1996), remains vital in uncertain, long-term contexts. A scenario functions as a narrative of a plausible future environment, and testing strategies across contrasting scenarios strengthens preparedness (Luckin et al., 2016; Peters, Jandrić & Hayes, 2019). In education, scenarios can vary from "algorithmic utopia"—where AI personalizes learning—to "digital divide deepens"—where inequities widen (UNESCO, 2021; European Commission, 2021). This exercise cultivates futures literacy, a capability UNESCO identifies as essential for educators and policymakers (UNESCO, 2021).

2.4 Ethical AI Governance in Education

AI systems embed social values within their design; without oversight they risk amplifying bias and undermining autonomy (Carter & Bélanger, 2022; Collins & Halverson, 2018). Global guidelines such as the OECD AI Principles (European

Commission, 2021) and UNESCO's Recommendation on the Ethics of Artificial Intelligence (UNESCO, 2021) emphasize transparency, accountability, fairness, and human oversight. However, these high-level norms often lack operational clarity for school leaders. Anticipatory AI leadership bridges that gap by integrating ethical reflection into foresight and scenario-planning activities (European Commission, 2021; Hines & Bishop, 2015). For instance, scenario workshops can include ethical-impact assessments to ensure equity and inclusion are addressed from the outset.

2.5 Systems Thinking and Complexity in Education

Education functions as a complex adaptive system in which interventions in one area affect others in unpredictable ways (Senge, as cited in Bishop, Hines & Collins, 2007). AI heightens this complexity through feedback loops linking data collection, algorithmic decision-making, and human behavior. Predictive analytics that label students "at risk," for example, can alter teacher expectations and student self-perception (drawing from Benjamin, 2019, as discussed in Facer, 2011). Systems thinking enables leaders to map such interdependencies, identify leverage points, and anticipate unintended consequences (Peters, Jandrić & Hayes, 2019). Combined with foresight, it broadens leaders' perspectives beyond technology to encompass policy, culture, and equity dynamics.

2.6 Leadership Competencies for Anticipatory AI Governance

Synthesizing these literatures reveals six key competencies:

- Futures Literacy – scanning trends and interpreting weak signals (Hines & Bishop, 2015)
- Scenario Facilitation – designing participatory foresight workshops (Schwartz, 1996)
- Ethical Deliberation – embedding transparency and inclusion (Carter & Bélanger, 2022)
- Systems Thinking – mapping feedback loops (Peters, Jandrić & Hayes, 2019)
- Adaptive Strategy – revising policies as new evidence emerges (Bishop, Hines & Collins, 2007)
- Stakeholder Engagement – building cross-sector partnerships (Christensen, Horn & Johnson, 2011)

These competencies move leadership beyond charisma toward process expertise, critical reflection, and collaborative learning under uncertainty.

2.7 Relevance to AI in Education

Anticipatory leadership is especially vital for AI in education because of the technology's rapid evolution, opacity, and high stakes for equity (European Commission, 2021; Carter & Bélanger, 2022). AI tools change yearly, "black-box" algorithms hinder oversight, and educational outcomes influence lifelong opportunities. Embedding foresight, scenario planning, and ethical reflection within everyday governance allows leaders to manage AI's uncertainty while preserving educational values (UNESCO, 2021; Fitzgerald & McCarthy, 2020).

2.8 Toward a Conceptual Framework

Integrating insights from educational leadership, anticipatory governance, strategic foresight, scenario planning, ethical AI, and systems thinking yields a new paradigm: anticipatory AI leadership. It involves environmental scanning, stakeholder dialogue, multi-scenario design, ethical assessment, adaptive strategy, and monitoring for continuous learning (Facer, 2011; Bishop, Hines & Collins, 2007; Hines & Bishop, 2015). Through this process, uncertainty becomes a resource for innovation, positioning educational leaders as architects of possible futures rather than passive adopters of technology (UNESCO, 2021; European Commission, 2021).

3. CONCEPTUAL FRAMEWORK

3.1 Overview of the Framework

The proposed framework extends beyond static leadership attributes to emphasize a dynamic process that combines continuous environmental scanning, stakeholder engagement, scenario exploration, and adaptive strategy formulation (Bishop, Hines & Collins, 2007; Hines & Bishop, 2015). Designed for application across school, district, and higher-education levels, the framework operationalizes anticipatory governance and strategic foresight to prepare educational systems for rapid technological change (Facer, 2011; Carter & Bélanger, 2022).

3.2 Layer 1 – Drivers of Change

Technological Advances

Such as adaptive learning platforms and generative AI models that redefine pedagogy, assessment, and administration (Black & Wiliam, 2018; Brynjolfsson & McAfee, 2017).

Policy and Regulatory Shifts

Including data protection laws and national AI strategies influencing institutional practices (European Commission, 2021; UNESCO, 2021).

Societal Expectations

Particularly demands for fairness, privacy, and ethical AI use in learning environments (Carter & Bélanger, 2022; Collins & Halverson, 2018). Recognizing these drivers allows educational leaders to anticipate systemic implications rather than respond reactively (Facer, 2011; Dator, 2019).

3.3 Layer 2 – Anticipatory Leadership Practices

Horizon Scanning and Trend Analysis

Systematic monitoring of technological, social, and policy developments that signal potential transformations in education (Carter & Bélanger, 2022; Hines & Bishop, 2015).

Institutions can establish foresight teams or "future watch" groups to maintain situational awareness (Hodgkinson & Healey, 2011).

Stakeholder Engagement

Involving teachers, students, parents, technologists, and ethicists in foresight exercises ensures pluralism and mitigates blind spots (Christensen, Horn & Johnson, 2011; Peters, Jandrić & Hayes, 2019).

Scenario Building and Stress Testing

Constructing multiple, plausible narratives about how AI may shape education under varying conditions helps leaders evaluate strategic robustness (Schwartz, 1996; Luckin et al., 2016; Peters, Jandrić & Hayes, 2019).

Ethical Impact Assessment

Embedding fairness, transparency, and accountability in foresight practices ensures responsible AI integration (Carter & Bélanger, 2022; UNESCO, 2021). This aligns with global frameworks emphasizing human-centered technological governance (European Commission, 2021).

3.4 Layer 3 – Outcomes

Institutional Adaptability

The capacity to realign curricula, resources, and governance as AI evolves while preserving educational values (Hines & Bishop, 2015).

Risk Mitigation

Early detection and correction of algorithmic bias, privacy risks, or reputational harm through proactive governance (Collins & Halverson, 2018; Carter & Bélanger, 2022).

Stakeholder Trust

Building confidence among students, parents, and educators by ensuring transparency and inclusivity in AI adoption (UNESCO, 2021; Collins & Halverson, 2018).

Human-Centered Innovation

Leveraging AI to empower teachers and learners rather than replace human agency, thereby reinforcing equity and creativity (Peters, Jandrić & Hayes, 2019; Senge as cited in Bishop, Hines & Collins, 2007). These outcomes reinforce one another, forming a feedback-oriented model for continuous improvement (Senge; Bishop, Hines & Collins, 2007).

3.5 The Cycle of Learning and Feedback

At the heart of the framework lies a continuous feedback cycle. Stakeholder engagement yields ethical insights; scenario planning reveals vulnerabilities; adaptive strategies are implemented and monitored. Outcomes, both expected and unintended, inform subsequent foresight cycles. This iterative process echoes double-loop learning (Senge; Hines & Bishop, 2015).

3.6 Operationalizing the Framework

Practical implementation demands sustained capacity building. Educational organizations can:

- Establish foresight units responsible for scanning and scenario planning (Carter & Bélanger, 2022).
- Institutionalize stakeholder forums to ensure inclusive deliberation (Christensen, Horn & Johnson, 2011).
- Use scenario templates and ethical checklists for procurement or policy evaluation (European Commission, 2021; UNESCO, 2021).
- Develop indicator dashboards to track emerging technological, regulatory, and social signposts (Hines & Bishop, 2015).
- Integrate futures literacy modules into leadership training programs (UNESCO, 2021).

Arrows connecting inner and outer layers symbolize feedback loops and continuous learning (Senge; Bishop, Hines & Collins, 2007). This visualization aligns with established frameworks in strategic foresight and systems thinking (Schwartz, 1996; Hines & Bishop, 2015).

4. MANAGERIAL AND PRACTICAL IMPLICATIONS

The preceding sections established the rationale and structure of the anticipatory AI leadership framework. This section translates theoretical insights into practical strategies for distinct stakeholder groups—school leaders, higher-education administrators, policymakers, and leadership-development providers. Each set of implications demonstrates how anticipatory foresight and ethical reflection can become part of daily decision-making (Bryson & George, 2020; Mahfouz & Awad, 2021).

4.1 Implications for School Leaders and District Administrators

At the school level, AI typically enters through classroom applications such as adaptive-learning software, algorithmic grading, or chatbots for student support (Black & Wiliam, 2018; Brynjolfsson & McAfee, 2017). The framework encourages leaders to move beyond tool adoption toward institutional foresight and participatory ethics.

Horizon Scanning and Future Watch Teams

Schools can create cross-functional "future watch" groups comprising teachers, librarians, IT staff, and students to monitor AI-related developments (Carter & Bélanger, 2022). Regular synthesis of research and policy updates nurtures collective awareness and builds readiness for change (Bishop, Hines & Collins, 2007).

Collaborative Scenario Workshops

Facilitating annual scenario-planning sessions allows diverse participants to explore potential AI futures—from widespread integration to heightened regulation (Schwartz, 1996; Peters, Jandrić & Hayes, 2019). Discussing such extremes surfaces ethical concerns and informs curriculum and procurement decisions (UNESCO, 2021).

Ethical Review Panels

Establishing parent-student advisory panels to review AI initiatives promotes transparency and aligns with global principles of fairness and accountability (Carter & Bélanger, 2022; European Commission, 2021).

Monitoring Signposts

Scenario exercises should identify signposts—early indicators of emerging futures such as new privacy laws or AI-literacy mandates (Hodgkinson & Healey, 2011; Fitzgerald & McCarthy, 2020). Linking these signposts to policy triggers enables timely adjustments without crisis reactions. Together, these measures cultivate a learning culture that perceives uncertainty as an opportunity for innovation rather than a source of risk (Peters, Jandrić & Hayes, 2019).

4.2 Implications for Higher-Education Administrators

Universities face complex challenges related to big-data analytics, research ethics, accreditation, and preparing graduates for AI-enabled economies (Hodgkinson & Healey, 2011; Collins & Halverson, 2018). Anticipatory AI leadership at this level operates across three dimensions:

Strategic Foresight in Evaluation and Accreditation

Higher-education leaders can employ foresight techniques to anticipate changes in digital credentialing, plagiarism detection, and online assessments (Carter & Bélanger, 2022; European Commission, 2021).

Interdepartmental Foresight Teams

Forming teams that include IT services, libraries, institutional research, and teaching-learning centers ensures diverse expertise and continuous environmental scanning (Christensen, Horn & Johnson, 2011; Fitzgerald & McCarthy, 2020).

Ethical Data Governance

Anticipatory leadership strengthens institutional ethics boards to address emerging issues such as algorithmic grading and biometric surveillance (Collins & Halverson, 2018; UNESCO, 2021). Revising consent policies and transparency standards pre-empts reputational risks (European Commission, 2021).

These initiatives foster resilient universities capable of evolving with technological and policy shifts while upholding academic integrity and inclusiveness (Hines & Bishop, 2015; Peters, Jandrić & Hayes, 2019).

4.3 Implications for Policymakers and Regulators

Policymakers can leverage scenario-based governance to design adaptable regulations that remain relevant in rapidly evolving AI ecosystems (Facer, 2011; Dator, 2019).

Flexible Regulatory Pathways

Modeling multiple adoption trajectories—such as state-regulated versus open-source AI platforms—allows for iterative policy refinement as new signposts appear (Fitzgerald & McCarthy, 2020; European Commission, 2021).

National Foresight Labs

Ministries of education can establish "AI-in-Education Foresight Labs" involving educators, technologists, ethicists, and civil-society organizations (UNESCO, 2021). Such collaborative foresight enhances legitimacy and public trust (Carter & Bélanger, 2022).

Ethical Impact Assessments

Requiring ethical impact evaluations for large-scale AI deployments parallels the logic of environmental assessments and institutionalizes proactive ethics (European Commission, 2021; UNESCO, 2021).

Funding for Futures Literacy

Allocating resources for foresight training builds a pipeline of leaders proficient in anticipatory governance (UNESCO, 2021; Bishop, Hines & Collins, 2007).

These practices shift policymaking from reactive control to co-design before deployment, aligning regulation with the evolving nature of AI (Hines & Bishop, 2015).

4.4 Implications for Leadership Preparation and Professional Development

Developing anticipatory capacity requires rethinking leadership education itself (Christensen, Horn & Johnson, 2011; Hodgkinson & Healey, 2011).

Embedding Foresight and Ethics in Curriculum

Leadership programs should integrate modules on AI ethics, systems thinking, and scenario planning (Carter & Bélanger, 2022; Hines & Bishop, 2015).Case-based simulations allow participants to practice decisions under uncertainty (Schwartz, 1996).

Cross-Disciplinary Collaboration

Joint workshops with computer-science, policy, and ethics departments enhance leaders' comprehension of AI's socio-technical dimensions (Peters, Jandrić & Hayes, 2019).

Micro-Credentials in Futures Literacy

Professional bodies can offer certifications such as Futures Literacy for Educational Leadership to incentivize continual learning (UNESCO, 2021).

Peer and Mentor Networks

Establishing peer-learning communities fosters ongoing dialogue and reflective practice in foresight and ethical AI integration (Hines & Bishop, 2015).

By embedding anticipatory AI leadership into professional-development structures, education systems ensure a sustainable talent pipeline of leaders equipped to navigate technological complexity (Fitzgerald & McCarthy, 2020).

4.5 Cross-Cutting Considerations

Across all stakeholder groups, several overarching principles emerge:

Equity and Inclusion

Diverse representation in foresight processes is essential to prevent reproduction of bias (Carter & Bélanger, 2022; Collins & Halverson, 2018).

Transparency and Communication

Sharing not only outcomes but also the reasoning behind decisions enhances stakeholder trust (UNESCO, 2021; European Commission, 2021).

Evaluation and Learning

Continuous assessment of foresight effectiveness ensures iterative improvement and institutional learning (Senge; Peters, Jandrić & Hayes, 2019).

In essence, managerial and practical implications operationalize anticipatory AI leadership as a living system of ethical foresight, transforming leadership from static administration to dynamic, future-ready governance (Bishop, Hines & Collins, 2007; Hines & Bishop, 2015).

5. CASE ILLUSTRATIONS

The practical relevance of the anticipatory AI leadership framework becomes clear when observed through global examples and case analogies. These illustrations demonstrate how foresight, ethical governance, and participatory design can transform AI integration in educational settings (UNESCO, 2023; OECD, 2022).

5.1 Case 1: Singapore's AI in Education Roadmap

Singapore has long incorporated foresight methodologies into its public-policy ecosystem, reflecting the traditions of anticipatory governance (Facer, 2011; Dator, 2019). As part of its Smart Nation initiative, the Ministry of Education (MOE) developed the AI in Education Roadmap (2019) to examine how AI would reshape assessment, curriculum, and teacher roles. The process was rooted in scenario-planning workshops involving teachers, technologists, parents, and ethicists—an approach consistent with strategic foresight frameworks (Schwartz, 1996; Hines & Bishop, 2015).

Drawing from global precedents in adaptive learning and algorithmic grading (Black & Wiliam, 2018; Brynjolfsson & McAfee, 2017), the MOE developed three contrasting scenarios—AI ubiquity, privacy-driven regulation, and human–machine instructional collaboration. Ethical discussions led to regulatory reforms mandating transparency in AI-assisted grading and pilot projects emphasizing teacher empowerment. This case illustrates how anticipatory leadership at the policy level can balance innovation with accountability (Carter & Bélanger, 2022; European Commission, 2021).

5.2 Case 2: Finish Teacher-Training Futures Lab

Finland's teacher-education system, known for pedagogical innovation, launched the Teacher-Training Futures Lab to prepare educators for AI-enabled classrooms. The initiative integrated foresight training directly into pre-service teacher education, aligning with UNESCO's call for futures-literacy development (UNESCO, 2021). Strategic foresight tools—trend mapping, scenario exploration, and ethical reflection—were applied within coursework (Hines & Bishop, 2015; Fitzgerald & McCarthy, 2020).

Graduates of the program demonstrated improved adaptability, ethical awareness, and confidence in addressing AI-related dilemmas, corroborating research linking foresight education to professional resilience (Christensen, Horn & Johnson, 2011; Hodgkinson & Healey, 2011). This case highlights how anticipatory AI leadership can be institutionalized through teacher preparation, ensuring long-term sustainability and diffusion of ethical foresight (Peters, Jandrić & Hayes, 2019).

5.3 Case 3: Hypothetical U.S. School District – "Future Ready 2028"

A hypothetical but evidence-based example—a large urban district referred to as "Future Ready 2028"—illustrates how anticipatory AI leadership can operate at scale. Facing rapid student adoption of AI chatbots, the district shifted from prohibition to participatory foresight (Bishop, Hines & Collins, 2007; European Commission, 2021).

The superintendent established a Futures Council comprising educators, parents, students, and IT staff. The council conducted horizon scanning using global foresight reports from OECD and UNESCO (UNESCO, 2021; European Commission, 2021), and applied scenario planning to envision futures such as AI Everywhere, AI Under Lockdown, and Hybrid Commons (Schwartz, 1996; Luckin et al., 2016; Peters, Jandrić & Hayes, 2019).

Each scenario incorporated ethical risk assessments consistent with global AI principles (Carter & Bélanger, 2022; UNESCO, 2021).

Subsequently, the district launched an AI Signpost Dashboard to track regulatory developments and vendor practices—mirroring foresight-based monitoring systems recommended in governance research (Hines & Bishop, 2015; Fitzgerald & McCarthy, 2020).

It also piloted AI-literacy curricula co-designed with students and parents to foster trust and agency. Transparent communication of foresight findings strengthened stakeholder collaboration, demonstrating how local educational governance can be adaptive, participatory, and ethically grounded (Peters, Jandrić & Hayes, 2019).

5.4 Lessons Across Cases

The three cases share several defining characteristics:

Foresight Institutionalization

Each system embedded foresight as a continuous governance practice rather than a one-time initiative (Hines & Bishop, 2015; Bishop, Hines & Collins, 2007).

Inclusive Stakeholder Engagement

Teachers, students, and community members were actively involved, echoing calls for participatory governance in education (Christensen, Horn & Johnson, 2011; UNESCO, 2021).

Ethics Integration

Ethical deliberation was integrated into foresight, ensuring AI use aligned with fairness, transparency, and human dignity (Carter & Bélanger, 2022; European Commission, 2021).

Signpost-Based Adaptability

Each initiative developed indicators that triggered adaptive actions, supporting the learning-loop model from organizational theory (Senge; Hines & Bishop, 2015).

Transparent Communication

Open dialogue about foresight processes enhanced legitimacy and stakeholder trust (Peters, Jandrić & Hayes, 2019).

These patterns affirm that anticipatory AI leadership is not just a conceptual aspiration but a practical governance strategy applicable across educational levels and cultural contexts (Fitzgerald & McCarthy, 2020; UNESCO, 2021).

5.5 Preparing for Challenges

Despite its promise, implementing anticipatory AI leadership faces obstacles. Time constraints, limited foresight expertise, and conflicting stakeholder values may hinder progress (Christensen, Horn & Johnson, 2011; Hodgkinson & Healey, 2011). Ethical evaluations can also slow procurement and policy decisions in fast-moving markets (European Commission, 2021; Carter & Bélanger, 2022).

Leaders can address these barriers through incremental institutionalization—starting with pilot foresight workshops, consulting external experts, and gradually embedding feedback mechanisms (Hines & Bishop, 2015; Facer, 2011). Such efforts yield long-term benefits by enhancing institutional resilience, stakeholder trust, and ethical consistency (Peters, Jandrić & Hayes, 2019; Fitzgerald & McCarthy, 2020).

In sum, these global and hypothetical cases collectively demonstrate that anticipatory AI leadership is both feasible and impactful. When foresight, ethics, and adaptability converge, education systems become better equipped to shape the future rather than react to it (UNESCO, 2021; European Commission, 2021).

6. DISCUSSION

The aforementioned experiences demonstrate that anticipatory AI leadership is not limited to a specific organizational type or national setting. Instead, it is a set of methods that may be used at many levels of the education system, such as horizon scanning, stakeholder engagement, scenario creation, ethical impact assessment, and adaptive strategy. This section talks about three main ideas that come up when you use the framework: corporate culture, the policy environment, and ethical stewardship.

Organizational Culture as a Facilitator of Anticipatory AI Leadership

Organizational culture serves as the invisible architecture that shapes how people think, behave, and interpret technological change. In the context of anticipatory AI leadership, culture determines whether artificial intelligence is perceived as a disruptive threat or a developmental ally. A learning-oriented and open culture cultivates the psychological safety and cognitive flexibility necessary for leaders and teams to engage with future-oriented practices such as scenario planning, ethical impact analysis, and strategic sensemaking. When culture supports curiosity and collaboration, AI-driven foresight becomes embedded in everyday decision-making rather than confined to isolated innovation projects.

A culture that promotes learning encourages continuous experimentation and reflective inquiry—essential elements of anticipatory governance. Instead of treating foresight as a compliance exercise, forward-thinking organizations institutionalize reflective practices through workshops, innovation labs, and cross-functional task forces. Leaders in such settings are not gatekeepers of knowledge but facilitators of shared intelligence. This collective intelligence allows institutions to detect weak signals of change—emerging technologies, policy shifts, or ethical dilemmas—and respond proactively rather than reactively (Peters, Jandrić & Hayes, 2019).

Moreover, anticipatory cultures challenge the "illusion of certainty" often prevalent in traditional organizations. By normalizing discussions about uncertainty, leaders enable their teams to consider multiple futures without fear of being wrong. This shift from a deterministic mindset to a pluralistic one nurtures adaptability. For instance, when faculty or administrators in educational institutions explore AI applications for personalized learning, predictive analytics, or administrative efficiency, an open culture encourages debate about both opportunities and risks. The emphasis shifts from "whether AI will replace jobs" to "how AI can augment human judgment and creativity." At the operational level, fostering an anticipatory culture involves structural enablers such as dedicated time for future-oriented work, knowledge-sharing platforms, and reward systems that value foresight contributions.

Organizations can institutionalize "future hours," where employees explore emerging trends or conduct ethical scenario simulations. Such practices prevent future thinking from being marginalized by short-term operational pressures. Recognition mechanisms—such as internal awards for innovative forecasting or cross-departmental foresight collaboration—signal that the organization values anticipatory behaviors. Equally critical is the role of communication. Open dialogue about uncertainty, ambiguity, and ethical concerns transforms foresight into a participatory activity When employees feel safe discussing potential threats or transformative opportunities, organizations can surface early indicators of change that might otherwise remain invisible. Psychological safety—defined by Edmondson (2019)—is therefore foundational. Leaders must model humility and vulnerability, acknowledging that they too are learning to navigate uncharted technological terrains. In higher education contexts, anticipatory AI leadership culture aligns closely with the idea of "learning universities" or "universities as living systems." Academic institutions must transcend bureaucratic inertia and cultivate distributed leadership structures where faculty, students, and administrators co-create the future. Embedding anticipatory practices in institutional culture can help universities transition from reactive digital adaptation to proactive AI stewardship. This includes nurturing academic curiosity toward AI ethics, fostering interdisciplinary research on digital transformation, and promoting lifelong learning as a strategic imperative.

Furthermore, anticipatory AI leadership requires the cultivation of what Senge calls a "learning organization"—one that is continually expanding its capacity to create its future (Senge; Bishop, Hines & Collins, 2007). Such organizations integrate systems thinking with foresight, emphasizing interconnections among technological, ethical, and social dimensions. Leaders champion dialogue rather than monologue, encouraging reflection on how AI-driven decisions influence inclusivity, equity, and sustainability (Peters, Jandrić & Hayes, 2019). For example, a culture that rewards responsible experimentation might allow a university department to pilot AI-assisted assessment tools while concurrently examining their bias implications through participatory ethics panels.

A strong ethical foundation also reinforces cultural readiness for anticipatory leadership.

When ethical reasoning becomes an integral part of organizational dialogue, AI adoption is guided by moral reflection rather than expediency. This requires embedding values such as transparency, accountability, and inclusivity into the fabric of everyday operations (Carter & Bélanger, 2022; European Commission, 2021). Employees must perceive ethics not as external regulation but as a shared cultural compass. Ethical foresight workshops, for example, can help teams visualize long-term consequences of AI policies on employment equity, academic integrity, or data privacy (UNESCO, 2021).

Cross-cultural collaboration further strengthens anticipatory capacity. In multinational or multi-campus institutions, cultural pluralism introduces diverse worldviews and moral frameworks, enriching foresight practices. Leaders who embrace cultural diversity as a strategic resource enable more comprehensive anticipation of AI's global social impacts. Thus, culture operates simultaneously as a learning mechanism, an ethical filter, and a strategic amplifier.

Finally, sustaining such a culture demands leadership commitment. Senior leaders must embody foresight through consistent behavior—engaging in horizon scanning (Hines & Bishop, 2015), participating in ethical scenario dialogues, and communicating long-term visions. Their visible engagement legitimizes anticipatory practices across organizational levels. Over time, these practices evolve from individual initiatives to institutional norms, ensuring resilience in the face of rapid technological evolution.

In essence, an anticipatory AI culture is not created through slogans or directives; it evolves through deliberate alignment of values, structures, and behaviors. It transforms organizations into adaptive ecosystems capable of learning from the future before it arrives. When curiosity replaces complacency and dialogue replaces denial, anticipatory AI leadership becomes self-reinforcing—a dynamic equilibrium between technological innovation and human wisdom.

7. CONCLUSION

Artificial intelligence will change education, including teacher training and school management. Educational leaders face bigger concerns than technology: strategy and ethics—how to thrive in a fast-paced, uncertain, and ever-changing future. This chapter argues that traditional leadership, while helpful for culture and stakeholder engagement, is unsuited for AI.

Anticipatory AI leadership requires a new attitude. The chapter used strategic foresight, scenario planning, ethical AI governance, and systems thinking literature to create a three-layer model. These three layers include change drivers, anticipatory leadership, and desired results.

Horizon scanning, stakeholder involvement, scenario planning, ethical analysis, and adaptive strategy can be used together to make an institution more flexible, reduce risks, and improve stakeholder trust (Carter & Bélanger, 2022; Christensen, Horn & Johnson, 2011; Schwartz, 1996; Carter & Bélanger, 2022; Bishop, Hines & Collins, 2007). Singapore, Finland, and a fictitious U.S. district showed that anticipatory AI leadership works in most circumstances (Facer, 2011; UNESCO, 2021; Bishop, Hines & Collins, 2007). Once foresight and ethics are established, institutions can transition to proactive governance. It means AI can help achieve long-term education and social goals.

The chapter also addresses resource shortages, stakeholder values, and short-term policy.

Leaders must be daring, facilitative, and advocates for national foresight laboratories and futures-literacy funding to solve problems (UNESCO, 2021; Fitzgerald & McCarthy, 2020).

Anticipatory AI leadership involves both technology administration and helping people thrive.

Everyday strategic planning and ethical thought can turn uncertainty into an opportunity for educational leaders. This will create digitally adaptable, equitable, innovative, and humanized education systems (Carter & Bélanger, 2022; Peters, Jandrić & Hayes, 2019).

Ultimately, anticipatory AI leadership is about more than managing technology; it is about shaping the conditions under which technology serves human flourishing. By embedding strategic foresight and ethical reflection into everyday practice, educational leaders can transform uncertainty from a threat into an opportunity, creating future-ready education systems that are innovative, equitable, and deeply human-centered in the digital age (Bishop, Hines & Collins, 2007; Hines & Bishop, 2015; Carter & Bélanger, 2022).

8. FUTURE RESEARCH DIRECTIONS

Future research on anticipatory AI leadership should advance beyond descriptive models toward integrative and empirical frameworks that explain how foresight, ethics, and adaptive strategy interact across institutional contexts. Conceptually, scholars may investigate the micro foundations of anticipatory culture, exploring how individual cognitive styles, learning agility, and digital literacy collectively shape an organization's readiness for AI-driven futures. Integrating psychological constructs such as curiosity, sensemaking, and moral imagination into leadership models could reveal how foresight becomes embedded as a behavioral competence rather than a procedural activity.

At the meso level, future studies can examine how organizational structures—particularly decentralization, cross-functional collaboration, and participatory governance—facilitate or hinder anticipatory practices. Comparative case studies across sectors like education, healthcare, and manufacturing may uncover contextual enablers of anticipatory capability, offering a more nuanced understanding of institutional adaptation to AI disruptions.

From a macro or policy perspective, longitudinal and cross-national analyses could assess how regulatory frameworks, national innovation systems, and ethical AI guidelines influence organizational foresight maturity (European Commission, 2021; UNESCO, 2021).

A promising research stream involves developing AI-readiness indices that incorporate ethical, cultural, and learning dimensions alongside technological and financial parameters.

Finally, future conceptual work should explore hybrid models that merge anticipatory governance with design thinking, systems dynamics, and digital ethics to construct multi-level leadership ecosystems (Facer, 2011; Peters, Jandrić & Hayes, 2019; Senge; Bishop, Hines & Collins, 2007). Such frameworks could inform capacity-building programs in higher education and public administration, emphasizing anticipatory thinking as a critical 21st-century leadership competency. By bridging foresight theory, organizational learning, and moral philosophy, forthcoming research can position anticipatory AI leadership as both a strategic and ethical paradigm for the future.

REFERENCES

Aggarwal, D., Rabby, F., Fahlevi, M., Muttaqin, A., & Bansal, R. (2024). Mapping the history, trajectory, and anatomy of slow and sustainable fashion: A bibliometric analysis. *Cogent Business & Management, 11*(1), 2423058.

Ajani, O. A., Gamede, B. T., & Bansal, R. (2024). Challenges and opportunities of integrating industry 5.0 and emerging technologies in higher education for enhancing employability skills. *Industry 5.0 and Emerging Technologies: Transformation Through. Technology and Innovation*, •••, 217–230.

Ao, L., Bansal, R., Pruthi, N., & Khaskheli, M. B. (2023). Impact of Social Media Influencers on Customer Engagement and Purchase Intention: A Meta-Analysis. *Sustainability, 15*(3), 2744.

Bansa, R., Bansal, T., & Pruthi, N. (2024). Demystifying the Benefits and Challenges of Virtual Learning for Differently Abled Students. In *Virtual Lifelong Learning: Educating Society with Modern Communication Technologies* (pp. 70-84). Bentham Science Publishers.

Bansal, R., Martinho, C., Pruthi, N., & Aggarwal, D. (2024). From virtual observations to business insights: A bibliometric review of netnography in business research. *Heliyon, 10*(1). PMID: 38163120

Bansal, R., Pruthi, N., Bansal, T., & Chaudhary, A. (2023). Diving Into the Consumer's Mind: Tools, Roles, and Ethical Concerns of Neuromarketing. In *Applications of Neuromarketing in the Metaverse* (pp. 206-222). IGI Global.

Bansal, R., Pruthi, N., & Singh, R. (2022). Developing Customer Engagement Through Artificial Intelligence Tools: Roles and Challenges. In *Developing Relationships, Personalization, and Data Herald in Marketing 5.0* (pp. 130-145). IGI Global.

Bansal, R., Saini, S., Ngah, A. H., & Durga Prasad, T. (2024). Proselytizing the potential of influencer marketing via artificial intelligence: Mapping the research trends through bibliometric analysis. *Cogent Business & Management, 11*(1), 2372889.

Bansal, R., Saini, S., Ngah, A. H., & Durga Prasad, T. (2024). Proselytizing the potential of influencer marketing via artificial intelligence: Mapping the research trends through bibliometric analysis. *Cogent Business & Management, 11*(1), 2372889.

Bansal, R., Shukla, G., Gupta, A., Singh, A., & Pruthi, N. (2023). Optimizing Augmented Reality and Virtual Reality for Customer Engagement. In *Promoting Consumer Engagement Through Emotional Branding and Sensory Marketing* (pp. 24–35). IGI Global.

Bishop, P., Hines, A., & Collins, T. (2007). The current state of scenario development: An overview of techniques. *Foresight*, *9*(1), 5–25. DOI: 10.1108/14636680710727516

Black, P., & Wiliam, D. (2018). Classroom assessment and AI: Emerging challenges. *Assessment in Education: Principles, Policy & Practice*, *25*(3), 299–314.

Brahmi, M., Hussain, Z., Majeed, M. U., Khan, A., Qureshi, M. A., & Bansal, R. (2025). Corporate Social Responsibility's Influence on Brand Image in the Automotive Sector: The Corporate Reputation and Product Quality Role. *Administrative Sciences*, *15*(4), 121.

Brynjolfsson, E., & McAfee, A. (2017). *Machine, platform, crowd: Harnessing our digital future*. W. W. Norton.

Bryson, J. M., & George, B. (2020). Strategic foresight and public value. *Public Administration Review*, *80*(4), 565–574.

Carter, L., & Bélanger, F. (2022). Ethical considerations for AI adoption in the public sector. *Government Information Quarterly*, *39*(3), 101664. DOI: 10.1016/j.giq.2022.101664

Christensen, C. M., Horn, M. B., & Johnson, C. W. (2011). *Disrupting class: How disruptive innovation will change the way the world learns*. McGraw-Hill.

Collins, A., & Halverson, R. (2018). *Rethinking education in the age of technology: The digital revolution and schooling in America* (2nd ed.). Teachers College Press.

. Das, S., Rao, N. V. J., Mishra, D., & Bansal, R. (2024). A Review of the Pre-and Post-COVID-19 Effects on the Tourism and Entertainment Industries: Innovative Methods and Predicted Challenges. *Utilizing Smart Technology and AI in Hybrid Tourism and Hospitality*, 98-117.

Dator, J. (2019). *Alternative futures at the Manoa School*. Springer.

Edwards, R., & Fenwick, T. (2016). Digital analytics and educational ethics. *Learning, Media and Technology*, *41*(2), 246–259.

Erstad, O., & Voogt, J. (2018). The twenty-first century curriculum: Issues in education and technology. *Journal of Educational Technology & Society*, *21*(1), 1–4.

European Commission. (2021). *Ethics guidelines for trustworthy AI*. https://digital-strategy.ec.europa.eu

Facer, K. (2011). *Learning futures: Education, technology and social change*. Routledge.

Fitzgerald, R., & McCarthy, J. (2020). Preparing school leaders for AI. *Journal of Educational Change*, *21*(2), 167–186.

Hines, A., & Bishop, P. (2015). *Thinking about the future: Guidelines for strategic foresight* (2nd ed.). Hinesight.

Hodgkinson, G. P., & Healey, M. P. (2011). Psychological foundations of dynamic capabilities. *Strategic Management Journal*, *32*(13), 1500–1516.

Kozma, R. B. (2011). Transforming education: Assessing and teaching 21st century skills. *Journal of Educational Technology & Society*, *14*(3), 1–3.

Kumar, A., Palta, P., Palta, A., Dhanka, S., Bansal, R., Fahlevi, M., Rabby, F., & Aljuaid, M. (2025). Dielectric characterization of sugar mill wastewater and its impact on soil properties in the khadar and bangar regions. *Scientific Reports*, *15*(1), 20802. PMID: 40595184

Luckin, R., Holmes, W., Griffiths, M., & Forcier, L. B. (2016). *Intelligence unleashed: An argument for AI in education*. Pearson.

Mahfouz, J., & Awad, T. (2021). Strategic foresight for school leaders. *Educational Management Administration & Leadership*, *49*(6), 885–905.

Mittal, G., & Bansal, R. (2023). Driving Force Behind Consumer Brand Engagement: The Metaverse. In *Cultural Marketing and Metaverse for Consumer Engagement* (pp. 164-181). IGI Global.

Mittal, G., Bansal, R., Fahlevi, M., & Aziz, A. L. (2025). Mapping the research patterns on fuzzy decision-making trial and evaluation laboratory technique in marketing: A bibliometric analysis. *Social Sciences & Humanities Open*, *12*, 101691.

. Murthy, Y. S. (2024). Mining Minds Sentiment Analysis of Public Perception. *Text Mining and Sentiment Analysis in Climate Change and Environmental Sustainability*, 61.

Murthy, Y. S., Bansal, R., Chodisetty, R. C. M., Chakravorty, C., & Sai, K. P. (2025). Transforming Minds AI and Machine Learning Applications in Cognitive Neuroscience. In *Transforming Neuropsychology and Cognitive Psychology With AI and Machine Learning* (pp. 107–128). IGI Global Scientific Publishing.

Murthy, Y. S., Rabby, F., Bansal, R., & Chakravorty, C. (2025). Building Resilient Brands: Harnessing Influencers, Evangelists, and Data-Driven Strategies. In *Data Analytics and Influencer Marketing for Cultivating Brand Evangelism and Affinity* (pp. 71-102). IGI Global Scientific Publishing.

OECD. (2022). *AI in education: Ethical and policy challenges*. OECD Publishing.

Painoli, A. K., Bansal, R., Singh, R., & Kukreti, A. (2021). Impact of Digital Marketing on the Buying Behavior of Youth With Special Reference to Uttarakhand State. In *Big Data Analytics for Improved Accuracy, Efficiency, and Decision Making in Digital Marketing* (pp. 162-182). IGI Global.

Peters, M. A., Jandrić, P., & Hayes, S. (2019). The digital university: A new model for the twenty-first century. *Educational Philosophy and Theory*, *51*(1), 1–7.

Rabby, F., Murthy, Y. S., & Bansal, R. (2025). Brand Evangelism in the Digital Era: The Impact of Data-Driven Influencer Marketing. *Journal of Open Innovation*, •••, 100552.

Rahman, K. T., Bansal, R., & Pruthi, N. (2023). Consumer adoption of technologies: A mindset-oriented approach. In Contemporary Studies of Risks in Emerging Technology, Part B (pp. 243-255). Emerald Publishing Limited.

Raja, M., Swamy, T. N. V. R. L., Das, S., Bansal, R., Fahlevi, M., & Aziz, A. L. (2025). Does human resource information system influence performance management? *Cogent Business & Management*, *12*(1), 2438862.

Raja, M., Swamy, T. N. V. R. L., Das, S., Bansal, R., Fahlevi, M., & Aziz, A. L. (2025). Does human resource information system influence performance management? *Cogent Business & Management*, *12*(1), 2438862.

Saini, S., & Bansal, R. (2025). Parasocial relationships and self-disclosure: Strengthening brand image through brand attitude in premium cosmetics. *Journal of Promotion Management*, *31*(2), 337–366.

Satar, M. S., Aggarwal, D., Bansal, R., & Alarifi, G. (2023). Mapping the Knowledge Structure and Unveiling the Research Trends in Social Entrepreneurship and Inclusive Development: A Bibliometric Analysis. *Sustainability*, *15*(7), 5626.

Schwartz, P. (1996). *The art of the long view: Planning for the future in an uncertain world.* Currency Doubleday.

Senge, P. (2018). *The fifth discipline: The art & practice of the learning organization* (rev. ed.). Doubleday.

Singh, R., Singh, V. P., Rabby, F., Bansal, R., & Gupta, N. K. (2025). The Road to Sustainable Tourism: Financial Mechanisms for Green Project Development. In *Regenerative Tourism for Social Development* (pp. 235-254). IGI Global Scientific Publishing.

. Thalpage, N., & Bansal, R. (2023). Exploring the Effectiveness of Coding Education Methods and Their Impact on the Data Science Job Market Requirements–a Systematic Review.

UNESCO. (2021). *Recommendation on the ethics of artificial intelligence*. UNESCO Publishing.

UNESCO. (2023). *Guidelines for AI and the futures of education*. UNESCO Publishing.

Venugopal, K., Das, S., Gopalakrishna, V., & Bansal, R. (2024). Customer Consciousness Towards Food Wastage in the Indian Hospitality Industry. In *Sustainable Disposal Methods of Food Wastes in Hospitality Operations* (pp. 38–56). IGI Global Scientific Publishing.

. Yamijala, S. M., Nimbrain, N., & Bansal, R. (2025). Enhancing remote workspaces: The role of virtual reality in shaping the virtual work environment. *Optimizing virtual reality and metaverse for remote work and virtual team collaboration*, 171-190.

Chapter 3

Augmented Creativity Uniting Human Intuition and Artificial Intelligence in Design

Subhankar Shome
https://orcid.org/0000-0002-1998-9512
Brainware University, India

Pritam Bhaumik
https://orcid.org/0009-0008-9673-3212
Brainware University, Kolkata, India

Suman Das
Brainware University, Kolkata, India

ABSTRACT

The process of design generation, its design and perception is undergoing transformation due to the coming together of artificial intelligence (AI) and the innovativeness in humans. An intelligent co-creation that transcends mere automation is a paradigm in which machine intelligence is collaborating with human intuition to enhance creative processes. This review examines the history and progression, theoretical foundation, applications, challenges and future developments of human-AI design collaboration. Since the dawn of computer-aided design, generative AI, and interactive co-creation sites, it provides a historical timeline chart of this development. To determine the useful models such as human-in-the-loop, AI-in-the-loop, and symbiotic co-creation, the article is able to synthesize numerous works of

DOI: 10.4018/979-8-3373-7153-5.ch003

literature. It then critically looks at the way these structures are applied in a range of disciplines, such as architecture, product design, visual communication, fashion and user experience (UX/UI) design.

1. INTRODUCTION

Figure 1. Conceptual Diagram of Human–AI Collaboration in Creative Processes

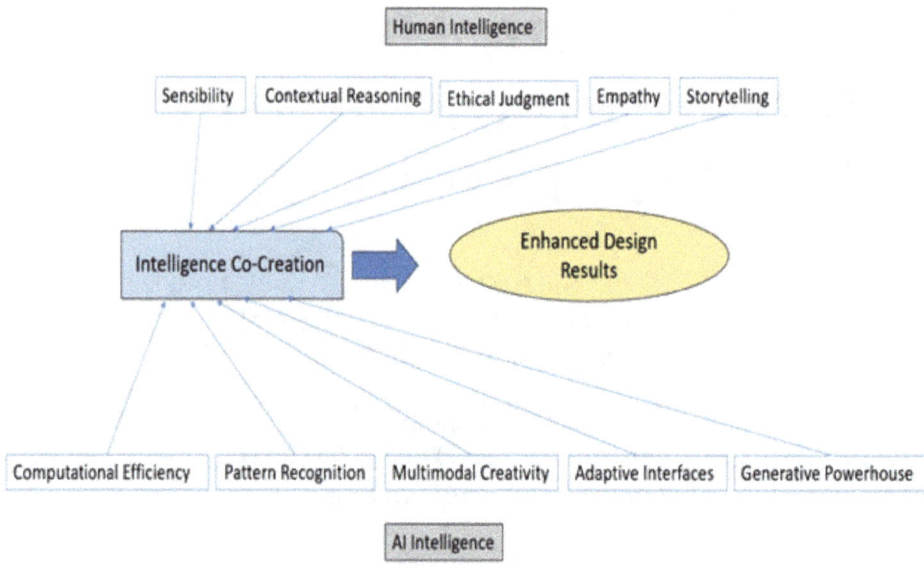

Human–AI collaboration has become an increasingly significant topic in discussions of creativity, design, and innovation in the digital era. Rapid developments in artificial intelligence, particularly in machine learning, deep learning, and generative models, have expanded the role of computational systems beyond automation and efficiency. AI systems are now capable of generating images, music, text, designs, and concepts that resemble human creative output, positioning AI not merely as a tool but as an active participant in creative processes. This shift challenges traditional assumptions about creativity as an exclusively human capability and opens new opportunities for collaborative intelligence between humans and machines.

In creative and design contexts, collaboration between humans and AI is increasingly framed as augmentation rather than replacement. Human creators provide goals, values, cultural context, and aesthetic judgment, while AI contributes computational power, pattern recognition, and generative diversity. This division of roles allows creative professionals to explore broader design spaces, test multiple alternatives rapidly, and overcome cognitive limitations such as fixation or limited exposure to unfamiliar ideas. As a result, creativity becomes a shared process, where human intention and machine intelligence are intertwined in producing innovative outcomes. The rise of generative AI technologies has significantly influenced how creative work is conceptualized and executed. Tools based on neural networks, such as generative adversarial networks (GANs), diffusion models, and large language models, can produce novel content by learning from vast datasets of existing works. These systems do not create in isolation but operate within parameters defined by human users, who curate inputs, refine prompts, and select outputs. This interaction highlights the importance of co-creation, where creativity emerges through continuous feedback loops between human judgment and algorithmic generation (Salma *et al.*, 2025).

Creative industries are among the sectors most affected by this transformation. In visual arts, AI systems assist artists in generating styles, compositions, and visual variations that inspire new directions. In architecture and industrial design, algorithmic tools support form-finding, optimization, and simulation, enabling designers to balance aesthetics, functionality, and sustainability. In media production and storytelling, AI-driven systems help generate scripts, characters, and interactive narratives, reducing production time while increasing personalization. These developments demonstrate that AI is reshaping not only creative outputs but also creative workflows and professional practices. Despite these opportunities, the integration of AI into creative processes raises fundamental questions about the nature of creativity itself. Traditional theories often associate creativity with human traits such as intention, emotion, and consciousness. AI systems, by contrast, operate through statistical learning and pattern generation without subjective experience. This contrast has led to debates about whether AI-generated content can truly be considered creative or whether creativity remains inherently human. In collaborative settings, however, creativity can be understood as a distributed process that emerges from interactions among humans, tools, and cultural systems, rather than residing in a single agent (Barrett *et al.*, 2021).

Human–AI collaboration also introduces complex ethical and legal challenges related to authorship and ownership. When creative works are produced through a combination of human input and algorithmic generation, determining who owns the resulting output becomes unclear. Questions arise regarding intellectual property rights, originality, and the reuse of training data derived from existing creative works. These issues are particularly relevant in commercial contexts, where creative outputs carry economic value and legal responsibility. Addressing these concerns requires new frameworks that recognize shared agency while protecting human creators' rights. Another critical concern is algorithmic bias in creative AI systems. Because AI models learn from historical data, they may reproduce dominant cultural norms, stereotypes, or exclusions present in their training datasets. In creative domains, this can lead to homogenization of styles, marginalization of minority perspectives, and reinforcement of existing power structures. Human oversight and intentional design are therefore essential to ensure that AI-supported creativity promotes diversity, inclusivity, and cultural sensitivity rather than limiting creative expression (Adamakis & Rachiotis, 2025).

The introduction of AI into creative labor markets has also sparked debates about displacement versus augmentation. While some fear that AI-generated content may reduce demand for human creators, others argue that AI primarily transforms creative roles rather than eliminating them. New professions are emerging, such as prompt designers, creative technologists, and AI-curators, who specialize in guiding and interpreting machine-generated outputs. In this context, creativity evolves into a hybrid skill that combines artistic sensibility with technical literacy and ethical awareness.

From a human-centered design perspective, the success of human–AI collaboration depends on maintaining human agency, control, and trust. Creative AI systems must be designed to support transparency, explainability, and user empowerment, allowing creators to understand how outputs are generated and to intervene meaningfully in the process. Human-in-the-loop approaches emphasize continuous human involvement, ensuring that AI remains aligned with human values and creative intentions rather than operating as an opaque or autonomous authority. Cultural perceptions of creativity are also shifting as AI becomes more visible in artistic and design practices. The identity of the "artist" or "designer" is no longer defined solely by manual skill or individual authorship but increasingly by the ability to orchestrate complex systems and collaborations. This transformation challenges long-standing cultural narratives about originality and genius, suggesting instead that creativity is relational, iterative, and socially constructed. Understanding these cultural implications is essential for developing responsible and meaningful human–AI creative ecosystems (Daly *et al.*, 2025).

Governance and policy frameworks play a crucial role in shaping the future of human–AI collaboration in creativity. Regulations related to data usage, copyright, transparency, and accountability directly affect how creative AI systems are developed and deployed. At the same time, overly restrictive policies may limit experimentation and innovation, while insufficient regulation may expose creators and audiences to ethical risks. Balanced governance approaches are therefore needed to foster innovation while safeguarding human rights and cultural values (Wong, 2020).

This chapter adopts a forward-looking perspective on human–AI collaboration in creativity, design, and innovation. Rather than focusing solely on technological capabilities, it emphasizes the importance of human-centered, ethical, and culturally informed approaches to AI-assisted creativity. By examining conceptual models, tools, and real-world applications, the chapter aims to provide a comprehensive understanding of how AI can enhance human creative potential without undermining authorship, authenticity, or agency. Ultimately, human–AI collaboration represents a new paradigm of creative practice in which intelligence is distributed across humans, machines, and socio-technical systems. When designed responsibly, AI can serve as a reflective and supportive partner that expands imagination, supports innovation, and enables new forms of expression. This chapter seeks to contribute to ongoing discussions by offering insights into how creative collaboration between humans and AI can be structured to benefit individuals, industries, and society as a whole.

2. CONCEPTUAL FRAMEWORK: HUMAN–AI COLLABORATION IN CREATIVITY, DESIGN, AND INNOVATION

2.1 Defining Human–AI Collaborative Creativity

Human–AI collaborative creativity refers to a creative process in which humans and artificial intelligence systems work together to generate, develop, and refine ideas, designs, or artistic outputs. In this context, AI is not positioned as a replacement for human creators but as a supportive collaborator that enhances human capabilities. Humans contribute intention, meaning, ethical judgment, and cultural understanding, while AI provides computational power, pattern recognition, and generative exploration. Creativity therefore emerges from interaction rather than from a single autonomous agent. This form of collaboration is enabled by advances in artificial intelligence technologies such as machine learning, deep neural networks, natural language processing, and multimodal generative models. These technologies allow AI systems to analyze large volumes of data, learn stylistic patterns, and produce novel combinations of visual, textual, or auditory elements. However, AI-generated outputs do not carry intrinsic meaning on their own. Their creative value depends on human interpretation, selection, and refinement, reinforcing the idea that AI functions as an enabler rather than an independent creator. Human–AI collaborative creativity also emphasizes an iterative and exploratory workflow. Instead of following a linear sequence from idea to final output, creators engage in continuous feedback loops where human input shapes AI generation, and AI output influences human thinking. Through this process, creators can rapidly test alternatives, explore unexpected possibilities, and overcome creative fixation. This iterative interaction expands the creative search space and supports innovation across design, art, and media practices. A key characteristic of collaborative creativity is the principle of human-in-the-loop interaction. Human creators remain actively involved at all stages of the creative process, including goal definition, constraint setting, evaluation, and final decision-making. AI systems respond to human feedback by adapting their outputs, creating a dynamic partnership that balances automation with human agency. This approach ensures that creative responsibility and authorship remain grounded in human control, even when AI contributes significantly to the creative outcome (Hutson, 2025).

From a cognitive perspective, human–AI collaborative creativity can be understood as a form of cognitive augmentation. AI systems extend human imaginative capacity by generating variations, visualizing abstract concepts, and revealing patterns that may not be immediately apparent to human designers. By reducing cognitive load and supporting divergent thinking, AI allows creators to focus more deeply on conceptual coherence, narrative meaning, and aesthetic quality, thereby enriching the overall creative process. In creative and design domains, this collaborative model shifts the definition of creativity from individual originality to relational and system-based innovation. Creativity is no longer seen solely as a personal talent but as a distributed capability emerging from interactions among humans, tools, and cultural contexts. Within this framework, AI becomes part of the creative ecosystem, influencing how ideas are generated, evaluated, and communicated. Understanding creativity in this way provides a more inclusive and realistic foundation for analyzing AI-supported creative practices (Rezwana & Maher, 2025).

Overall, defining human–AI collaborative creativity requires moving beyond technological novelty toward a human-centered understanding of collaboration. Effective creative collaboration depends on aligning AI capabilities with human values, intentions, and ethical considerations. By framing AI as a collaborative partner that augments rather than replaces human creativity, this conceptualization supports responsible innovation and sustainable creative practices in the age of intelligent systems (Henriksen *et al.*, 2024).

2.2 The Need for Human–AI Collaboration in Creative and Design Contexts

Creative and design practices today operate in environments characterized by increasing complexity, speed, and uncertainty. Designers, artists, and innovators are expected to produce original and high-quality outcomes while responding to rapidly changing user needs, market trends, and technological developments. At the same time, creative projects often involve large volumes of information, multiple constraints, and interdisciplinary collaboration. Under these conditions, purely human-centered creative processes may face limitations in terms of scalability, efficiency, and exploration of diverse design possibilities, highlighting the need for collaborative support from AI systems (Desolda *et al.*, 2025).

Human–AI collaboration addresses these challenges by combining human creativity with computational intelligence. AI systems can process large datasets, identify patterns, and generate multiple design alternatives within a short time frame. This capability allows creative professionals to explore broader idea spaces and consider options that may not emerge through human intuition alone. By delegating repetitive or computation-intensive tasks to AI, humans can focus more on conceptual thinking, storytelling, and aesthetic judgment, which remain central to meaningful creative work. In early stages of the creative process, such as ideation and concept development, AI supports divergent thinking by generating diverse and unconventional ideas. These AI-generated suggestions can act as creative stimuli, encouraging designers to question assumptions and move beyond familiar solutions. Rather than dictating outcomes, AI introduces variation and surprise, which are essential components of innovation. Human creators then evaluate, reinterpret, and refine these outputs based on contextual relevance and creative intent, maintaining control over the creative direction. During later stages of design and production, human–AI collaboration also supports convergent thinking and refinement. AI-driven tools can assist in optimizing designs based on functional, aesthetic, usability, or sustainability criteria. In architecture and product design, for example, AI systems help evaluate multiple design configurations against constraints such as material efficiency or environmental impact. This collaborative approach enables more informed decision-making while preserving the designer's role as the final authority over creative outcomes (Almaz *et al.*, 2024).

The need for human–AI collaboration is further amplified by the growing interdisciplinary nature of creative work. Modern creative projects often involve collaboration among designers, engineers, marketers, and stakeholders from diverse backgrounds. AI-powered platforms can serve as shared cognitive tools that facilitate communication, visualization, and alignment across teams. By providing common representations and rapid feedback, AI systems help bridge disciplinary boundaries and support collective creativity and innovation (Leon *et al.*, 2025).

From an economic and professional perspective, human–AI collaboration also responds to pressures for productivity and personalization in creative industries. Audiences increasingly expect customized and interactive experiences, while organizations seek to reduce production time and costs. AI-supported creativity enables scalable personalization without fully standardizing creative output, allowing creators to balance efficiency with originality. This capability reinforces the role of AI as an enabler of sustainable creative practice rather than a substitute for human labor (Gazi *et al.*, 2024).

In addition, the integration of AI into creative contexts supports learning and skill development among creators. By interacting with AI systems, designers and artists gain exposure to new styles, techniques, and perspectives embedded in training data. This interaction can function as a form of reflective practice, where AI acts as a mirror that reveals alternative approaches and inspires creative growth.

Such learning-oriented collaboration strengthens human creative capacity over time rather than diminishing it.

Overall, the need for human–AI collaboration in creativity and design arises from the limitations of isolated human or machine-centered approaches. Neither humans nor AI alone can fully address the demands of contemporary creative practice. By integrating human judgment, cultural understanding, and ethical responsibility with AI's generative and analytical strengths, collaborative systems offer a balanced and effective response to the challenges of modern creativity and innovation.

2.3 Models of Human–AI Co-Creation

Human–AI co-creation can be understood through several collaboration models that describe how creative agency, control, and responsibility are shared between humans and artificial intelligence systems. These models help clarify the different ways AI can participate in creative and design processes, ranging from supportive assistance to more autonomous generation. Understanding these models is important for designing collaborative systems that enhance creativity while preserving human agency and accountability.

The first and most common model positions AI as a creative assistant. In this configuration, AI supports specific creative tasks such as idea generation, style exploration, content variation, or rapid prototyping. Human creators define the goals, constraints, and evaluation criteria, while AI generates suggestions that serve as inspiration or starting points. The creative authority remains fully with the human, and AI functions as a productivity and exploration tool rather than an independent creator. A second model conceptualizes AI as a creative partner, where humans and AI engage in continuous interaction and mutual influence. In this collaborative arrangement, AI systems respond dynamically to human feedback, and creative outcomes evolve through iterative dialogue. Humans guide the overall direction and meaning of the work, while AI contributes alternative perspectives and unexpected combinations that may challenge human assumptions. Creativity in this model emerges from the interaction itself rather than from either agent alone. The third model frames AI as a semi-autonomous generator operating within boundaries established by human creators. Here, AI systems may generate substantial portions of creative content, such as design layouts, visual compositions, or narrative structures. However, humans remain responsible for framing the problem, setting ethical and aesthetic constraints, and selecting or modifying final outputs. This model is often used in large-scale or data-intensive creative applications, where AI efficiency is balanced by human oversight (Ziv & Nakash, 2025).

Across all co-creation models, the principle of human-in-the-loop creativity plays a central role. Human-in-the-loop approaches ensure that humans remain actively involved throughout the creative process, providing feedback, making decisions, and retaining creative responsibility. This principle helps prevent over-reliance on automated systems and supports transparency, trust, and ethical accountability in creative AI applications.

Another important dimension of human–AI co-creation models is the balance between divergent and convergent creativity. AI systems are particularly effective at supporting divergent exploration by generating numerous alternatives and variations. Humans, in turn, excel at convergent processes such as evaluation, contextual interpretation, and meaning-making. Effective co-creation models leverage these complementary strengths, allowing AI to expand the creative search space while humans shape coherence and relevance. These co-creation models also highlight that human–AI collaboration is not static but adaptive. As creators gain experience with AI tools, the nature of collaboration may shift over time, with humans learning to better guide AI and AI systems becoming more responsive to human preferences. Designing flexible collaboration models that can evolve with user expertise and creative goals is therefore essential for sustaining long-term creative innovation (Oham & Ejike, 2024).

Overall, models of human–AI co-creation provide a structured way to understand how creativity can be shared between humans and intelligent systems. By clearly defining roles, interaction mechanisms, and boundaries, these models support the development of creative AI systems that enhance human creativity rather than diminish it. They also offer a foundation for analyzing real-world applications and case studies of AI-assisted creativity in design and innovation contexts.

2.4 Theoretical Foundations of Human–AI Collaborative Creativity

Human–AI collaborative creativity draws from several foundational theories that explain how creativity emerges through interaction between humans, technologies, and socio-cultural contexts. Rather than treating creativity as an exclusively human trait, contemporary perspectives view it as a distributed and interactive process supported by tools, environments, and intelligent systems. Understanding these theoretical foundations provides a structured basis for analyzing how artificial intelligence (AI) can meaningfully augment human creativity without diminishing human agency. This study reviews relevant theories to explain the role of AI as a cognitive, interactive, and creative partner in collaborative creative processes, particularly in domains such as design, content creation, and artistic production.

1. Distributed Cognition Theory

Distributed Cognition Theory proposes that cognitive processes are not limited to the human mind but are distributed across individuals, artifacts, and external representations. In creative activities, tools such as sketches, digital platforms, and AI systems actively participate in shaping ideas and problem-solving processes. Within human–AI collaborative creativity, AI functions as an external cognitive component that supports ideation, pattern recognition, and iterative refinement. This allows creators to explore a wider creative space and manage complex creative tasks more effectively, transforming creativity into a shared cognitive process rather than an individual effort (Toumi *et al.*, 2021).

2. Extended Mind Theory

Extended Mind Theory argues that tools integrated into human activity can become part of the cognitive system itself. When creators rely on AI systems for inspiration, generation, or evaluation of creative outputs, these systems effectively extend human thinking and imagination. In creative collaboration, AI serves as a cognitive extension that enhances memory, exploration, and generative capacity. This perspective supports the view that AI does not replace creativity but amplifies human creative potential by expanding the functional boundaries of cognition through technology (Grilli & Pedota, 2024).

3. Co-Creativity Theory

Co-creativity theory emphasizes creativity as a collaborative process involving multiple agents who influence each other over time. In human–AI contexts, creativity emerges through continuous interaction, feedback, and shared control between humans and intelligent systems. AI-generated suggestions, variations, and recombinations shape human decisions, while human judgment, intention, and contextual understanding guide AI use. This reciprocal relationship positions AI as a creative partner rather than a passive tool, enabling the joint production of novel and meaningful creative outcomes (Creely & Blannin, 2025).

4. Human–Computer Interaction (HCI) Theory

Human–Computer Interaction theory provides essential insights into how AI systems should be designed to support creative collaboration. Effective human–AI creativity requires interfaces that promote transparency, usability, and user control. HCI principles emphasize interactive feedback, explainability, and adaptability, allowing creators to understand AI behavior and integrate it meaningfully into their creative workflow. Well-designed AI interfaces enhance exploration and experimentation, ensuring that humans remain active decision-makers throughout the creative process (Xu *et al.*, 2025).

In general, these theoretical foundations illustrate that human–AI collaborative creativity is not merely a technological advancement but a transformative process that reshapes how creativity is produced and experienced. AI enhances creativity by extending cognition, supporting collaboration, and enabling iterative exploration, while humans retain authorship, intention, and evaluative authority. This conceptual framework highlights that the true value of AI in creative collaboration lies in its ability to combine computational capability with human imagination, resulting in creative systems that are adaptive, inclusive, and human-centered.

2.5 Ethics, Authorship, and Creative Responsibility

The increasing integration of AI into creative processes raises important ethical questions related to authorship, responsibility, and creative ownership. As AI systems contribute to idea generation, content creation, and design execution, the boundaries between human creativity and machine assistance become increasingly blurred. This shift challenges traditional notions of creativity that have historically centered on individual human authorship, requiring new ethical frameworks to ensure that human agency and accountability remain central in AI-supported creative practices.

One of the primary ethical concerns in human–AI collaborative creativity is the issue of authorship and originality. AI-generated outputs are typically produced through models trained on large datasets that include existing creative works, raising questions about who should be recognized as the creator of the final output. In collaborative settings, authorship is best understood as shared or layered, where humans provide intent, direction, and evaluative judgment, while AI contributes generative variation and computational exploration. Ethical creative practice therefore requires transparent acknowledgment of AI involvement without diminishing the role of human creators (Das & Kundu, 2024).

Creative responsibility is another critical dimension of ethical human–AI collaboration. While AI systems can generate content autonomously, they do not possess moral awareness or contextual understanding. As a result, humans remain responsible for the ethical implications, cultural sensitivity, and societal impact of AI-assisted creative outputs. Designers, artists, and organizations must actively evaluate AI-generated content to prevent the reproduction of harmful stereotypes, misinformation, or culturally inappropriate representations. This reinforces the importance of human-in-the-loop frameworks where ethical judgment remains a human responsibility rather than an automated function (Chen *et al.*, 2023).

Bias and fairness also present significant ethical challenges in AI-supported creativity. Since AI systems learn from historical and cultural data, they may unintentionally reinforce dominant narratives while marginalizing underrepresented voices. In creative domains, such bias can influence aesthetic norms, storytelling perspectives, and design outcomes. Addressing this issue requires conscious dataset curation, inclusive design practices, and continuous human oversight to ensure that AI-enhanced creativity supports diversity, cultural plurality, and equitable representation rather than limiting creative expression (Zallio *et al.*, 2025).

Finally, ethical human–AI creative collaboration must be guided by principles of transparency, consent, and trust. Creators should understand how AI systems function, what data they rely on, and how outputs are generated. Audiences should also be informed when creative works involve AI assistance, fostering trust and authenticity in creative ecosystems. By embedding ethical considerations into the design and governance of creative AI systems, human–AI collaboration can evolve in a way that respects creative integrity while unlocking new forms of innovation and expression.

3. HUMAN–AI COLLABORATIVE CREATIVITY: THE FOUNDATION OF AUGMENTED DESIGN AND INNOVATION

Figure 2. Human–AI Collaborative Creativity Workflow in Augmented Design and Innovation

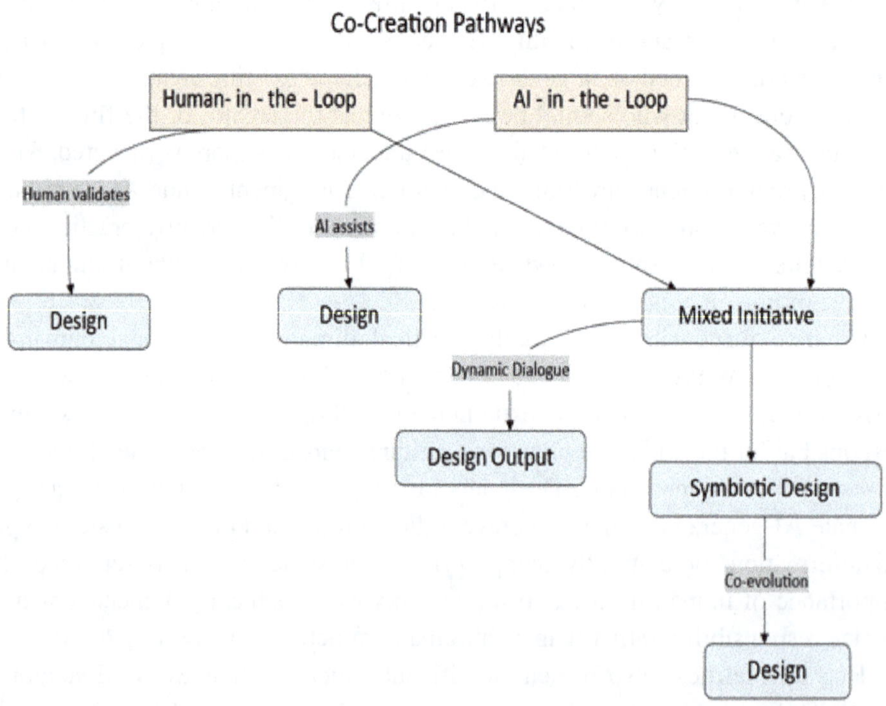

In the evolving landscape of creative industries and innovation-driven design, collaboration between humans and artificial intelligence has emerged as a transformative paradigm. Rather than functioning as autonomous creators, AI systems increasingly operate as collaborative agents that augment human imagination, accelerate experimentation, and expand creative possibilities. This shift reflects a broader transition from tool-based automation toward interactive, human-centered creative ecosystems, where meaning-making, judgment, and intent remain fundamentally human-driven while AI enhances executional capacity and exploration speed.

At the core of human–AI collaborative creativity lies the integration of generative models, machine learning algorithms, and adaptive systems into creative workflows. Technologies such as generative adversarial networks (GANs), diffusion models, and large language models enable AI to produce visual concepts, textual narratives, musical compositions, and design alternatives based on human input. Unlike traditional rule-based software, these systems learn from large-scale data and user interaction, allowing them to generate diverse outputs that inspire, challenge, and extend human creative thinking rather than merely replicating predefined patterns.

For designers, artists, and innovators, human–AI collaboration offers a strategic advantage in managing complexity and creative uncertainty. Creative tasks often involve ambiguous goals, open-ended exploration, and iterative refinement conditions under which AI excels at rapid variation and pattern discovery. For example, in product design, AI can generate hundreds of design variations based on functional constraints, while human designers evaluate aesthetic quality, usability, and cultural relevance. This division of creative labor enables creators to focus on higher-level conceptual decisions while delegating computational exploration to AI systems (Fügener *et al.*, 2022).

In creative industries, human–AI collaboration plays multiple complementary roles. AI supports ideation by proposing unexpected combinations, assists iteration by refining drafts and prototypes, and accelerates production through automation of repetitive creative tasks. Tools such as generative design platforms, AI-assisted image editors, and intelligent writing systems have become integral components of modern creative practice. These systems do not eliminate human creativity; instead, they reshape creative workflows into hybrid processes where authorship emerges through continuous interaction between human intention and machine-generated possibilities. The benefits of human–AI collaborative creativity extend beyond efficiency into strategic innovation. From a performance perspective, AI reduces time-to-concept, lowers production costs, and enables scalable personalization of creative outputs. From an experiential perspective, AI-enhanced creativity allows creators to experiment more freely, explore unconventional ideas, and push beyond cognitive limitations. Furthermore, each interaction with AI generates feedback data that can inform future creative decisions, leading to adaptive and evolving creative systems that learn alongside their human collaborators (Hughes *et al.*, 2021).

However, the integration of AI into creative processes is not without challenges. While AI systems excel at generating variations and recombining existing patterns, they often lack contextual awareness, emotional understanding, and ethical judgment. Creative outputs that rely too heavily on AI risk becoming aesthetically homogenized or culturally insensitive. As a result, human oversight remains essential to ensure that AI-generated content aligns with social values, artistic intent, and audience expectations. Effective collaboration therefore depends on maintaining humans in the loop as curators, critics, and ethical decision-makers. Another critical concern involves authorship and creative ownership. As AI contributes more substantially to creative outputs, questions arise regarding originality, intellectual property, and attribution. In collaborative creativity, authorship should be understood as shared yet asymmetrical: humans define goals, provide meaning, and assume responsibility, while AI functions as an enabling mechanism rather than an independent author. Transparent disclosure of AI involvement and clear governance structures are necessary to preserve trust within creative ecosystems and cultural institutions.

Data ethics and creative responsibility also play a crucial role in human–AI collaboration. AI systems are trained on large datasets that may reflect historical biases, dominant cultural narratives, or unequal representation. If left unchecked, these biases can influence creative outputs and marginalize alternative perspectives. Responsible creative AI therefore requires inclusive dataset curation, continuous evaluation, and ethical design practices that promote diversity, fairness, and cultural sensitivity in creative production. Despite these challenges, the potential of human–AI collaborative creativity continues to expand. Advances in multimodal AI, affective computing, and interactive interfaces are enabling more intuitive and responsive creative partnerships. Emerging systems are increasingly capable of adapting to individual creative styles, responding to emotional cues, and supporting reflective dialogue between humans and machines. These developments suggest a future where AI functions not merely as a generator, but as a reflective collaborator that enhances creative confidence and experimentation (Wei *et al.*, 2025).

From a strategic perspective, human–AI collaboration represents more than a technological innovation it signifies a conceptual shift in how creativity and innovation are understood. Creativity is no longer viewed solely as an individual act of genius, but as a distributed process supported by intelligent systems, social contexts, and digital infrastructures. Organizations and creators who embrace this paradigm position themselves at the forefront of innovation, leveraging AI not as a substitute for creativity, but as a catalyst for deeper, more inclusive, and more sustainable creative practices. Ultimately, the true value of human–AI collaborative creativity lies in its ability to integrate computational power with human imagination, ethical judgment, and cultural meaning. When designed responsibly, collaborative AI systems can expand creative horizons while preserving human authorship and identity. In this sense, human–AI collaboration becomes not merely a method of creation, but a foundation for the future of design, innovation, and creative expression in the digital age (Vinchon *et al.*, 2023).

4. HUMAN–AI CREATIVE ASSISTANTS: ENHANCING DESIGN, INNOVATION, AND CREATIVE PRODUCTIVITY

4.1 Overview

The rapid advancement of artificial intelligence (AI) has significantly transformed creative industries, reshaping how designers, artists, and innovators generate ideas, develop concepts, and produce creative outputs. One of the most influential developments in this transformation is the emergence of human–AI creative assistants AI-powered systems designed to support, augment, and collaborate with humans throughout creative and design processes. Unlike traditional software tools that execute predefined commands, creative AI assistants operate interactively, responding to human input, learning from creative preferences, and generating alternative possibilities in real time (Venkadesh *et al.*, 2024).

Human–AI creative assistants integrate advanced technologies such as generative models, machine learning, computer vision, and large language models to facilitate ideation, experimentation, and iteration. Tools such as Adobe Firefly, Midjourney, DALL·E, Runway, Figma AI, and AI-assisted writing platforms exemplify how AI has become embedded within everyday creative workflows. These systems assist users in producing visual designs, textual narratives, multimedia content, and conceptual prototypes with unprecedented speed and flexibility. In the context of design and innovation, human–AI collaboration shifts the creative process from a linear, labor-intensive activity into a dynamic and exploratory workflow. AI accelerates experimentation by generating multiple design alternatives, while human creators provide direction, judgment, and contextual understanding. This synergy enables individuals and organizations to manage creative complexity more effectively, explore broader design spaces, and respond rapidly to changing market and cultural demands. As creative work increasingly takes place in hybrid and digital environments, human–AI creative assistants play a critical role in sustaining productivity, originality, and collaborative innovation.

4.2 Core Functionalities of Human–AI Creative Assistants

The effectiveness of human–AI creative assistants lies in their diverse and interconnected functionalities that go beyond simple automation. These systems are designed not only to generate content, but also to support cognitive processes such as ideation, evaluation, and refinement. By combining computational intelligence with human intent, AI creative assistants function as collaborative partners within creative ecosystems (Rezwana & Maher, 2023).

Table 1. Core Functionalities and Benefits of Human–AI Creative Assistants

Functionality	Description	Example Tools	Key Benefits
Generative Ideation	Produces multiple creative alternatives based on prompts, constraints, or sketches.	Midjourney, DALL·E, Adobe Firefly	Expands creative exploration and inspiration.
Design Variation & Optimization	Automatically generates and refines design variations according to functional or aesthetic parameters.	Generative Design Tools, Figma AI	Reduces iteration time and supports complex decision-making.
AI-Assisted Prototyping	Transforms ideas into rapid visual, textual, or interactive prototypes.	Runway, Canva AI	Accelerates concept validation and experimentation.
Content Adaptation & Personalization	Adjusts creative outputs to different audiences, contexts, or platforms.	AI Writing Assistants, Branding Tools	Enables scalable and customized creative production.
Feedback & Refinement Support	Suggests improvements, edits, or enhancements based on patterns and user behavior.	Grammarly, Adobe Sensei	Improves quality while preserving human authorship.

These functionalities demonstrate how AI supports creativity not by replacing human imagination, but by extending it. AI systems handle computationally intensive tasks such as generating variations or analyzing patterns while humans retain control over meaning, intent, and aesthetic judgment. As a result, creative workflows become more adaptive, iterative, and collaborative.

4.3 Human–AI Collaboration in Creative Workflows

Human–AI creative assistants fundamentally reshape creative workflows by introducing continuous interaction between human intent and machine-generated possibilities. In traditional creative processes, ideation, production, and refinement often occur sequentially. In contrast, AI-enabled workflows are iterative and nonlinear, allowing creators to move fluidly between exploration, evaluation, and revision. For example, in product and industrial design, AI systems can rapidly generate hundreds of design configurations based on material constraints, ergonomics, or sustainability criteria. Designers then evaluate these outputs, selecting and refining those that align with brand identity, user experience, and cultural relevance. This collaborative division of labor allows humans to focus on strategic and conceptual decisions, while AI manages computational exploration. In digital media and storytelling, AI creative assistants support writers and content creators by generating drafts, alternative narratives, or stylistic variations. Rather than final outputs, these AI-generated materials function as creative stimuli, encouraging experimentation and reducing creative blocks. Human creators remain responsible for coherence, emotional depth, and ethical alignment, ensuring that final works reflect human values and intentions (Han *et al.*, 2022).

4.4 Benefits and Strategic Value

From a strategic perspective, human–AI creative assistants offer both operational and innovation-related benefits. Operationally, AI reduces time-to-concept, lowers production costs, and enables scalable creativity across multiple platforms and audiences. Creators can test ideas quickly, adapt designs efficiently, and respond to feedback in near real time. From an innovation standpoint, AI enhances creative confidence by allowing individuals to explore unconventional ideas without excessive risk or resource expenditure. The ability to visualize, prototype, and iterate rapidly encourages experimentation and supports more inclusive creative participation. Moreover, AI systems learn from repeated interactions, enabling adaptive creative environments that evolve alongside their users (Virvou, 2023).

4.5 Challenges, Ethics, and Responsible Use

Figure 3. Ethical AI Principles in Human–AI Creative Collaboration

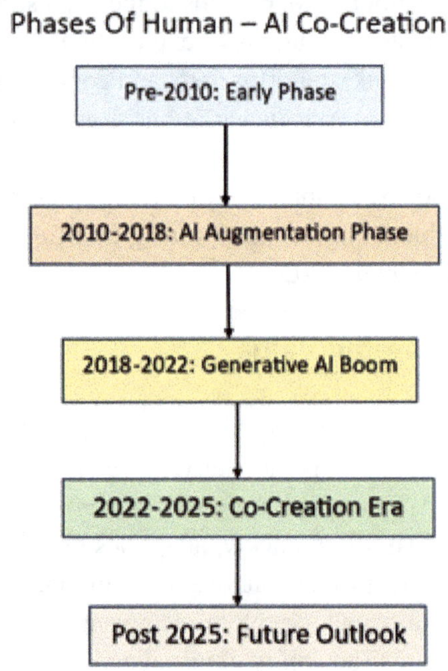

Despite their advantages, human–AI creative assistants introduce significant challenges related to authorship, originality, and ethical responsibility. AI-generated content may reflect biases present in training data, potentially reinforcing dominant cultural narratives or marginalizing underrepresented perspectives. Without careful oversight, creative outputs risk becoming homogenized or culturally insensitive. Maintaining human-in-the-loop oversight is therefore essential. Humans must act as curators, critics, and ethical decision-makers, ensuring that AI-generated content aligns with social values, artistic intent, and audience expectations. Transparent disclosure of AI involvement, responsible dataset curation, and clear governance structures are critical to preserving trust in creative ecosystems (George *et al.*, 2024).

Ultimately, the value of human–AI creative assistants depends on their design and use. When implemented responsibly, these systems function not as autonomous creators, but as augmentative collaborators that enhance human creativity, innovation, and cultural expression. In this sense, human–AI collaboration becomes a foundation for sustainable and human-centered creative practices in the digital age.

5. HUMAN–AI CREATIVE ASSISTANTS: ENHANCING DESIGN, INNOVATION, AND CULTURAL EXPRESSION

Figure 4. Human-Centered AI Framework for Ethical and Responsible Creative Collaboration

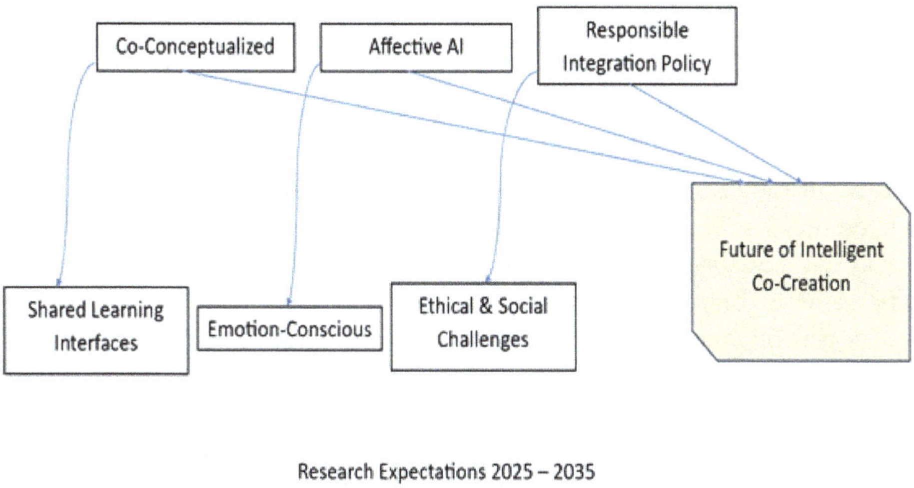

Creative processes have traditionally relied on human imagination, intuition, and experiential knowledge. However, the increasing complexity of design challenges and the demand for rapid innovation have pushed creative industries toward the integration of artificial intelligence as a collaborative partner. Human–AI creative assistants represent a new generation of AI systems designed not to replace human creativity, but to augment it by supporting ideation, experimentation, and iterative refinement. Tools such as generative design platforms, AI-assisted writing systems, and image generation models enable creators to explore a wider range of possibilities while maintaining human control over meaning, intent, and final decision-making. This shift reflects a broader transformation from isolated human creativity toward hybrid creative ecosystems where intelligence is distributed across human and machine actors (Peeters *et al.*, 2021).

At the core of human–AI creative assistants are advanced computational models, including generative adversarial networks (GANs), diffusion models, large language models, and multimodal learning systems. These technologies enable AI to generate visual concepts, textual narratives, design alternatives, and stylistic variations based on human prompts or constraints. Unlike traditional creative software that follows predefined rules, AI creative assistants learn from large-scale datasets and adapt to user interactions, allowing them to produce outputs that stimulate creative exploration rather than merely automate tasks. By rapidly generating multiple alternatives, AI reduces the cognitive and temporal burden associated with early-stage ideation, enabling creators to focus on conceptual depth, aesthetic judgment, and contextual relevance.

The practical applications of human–AI creative assistants are evident across various creative and innovation-driven domains. In product and industrial design, AI systems can generate hundreds of design configurations based on functional, material, and ergonomic constraints, while human designers evaluate feasibility, usability, and cultural fit. In visual arts and media production, AI assists artists by proposing compositions, color palettes, or stylistic transformations that inspire new creative directions. Similarly, in writing and content creation, AI-powered tools support drafting, editing, and idea expansion, helping creators overcome creative blocks and accelerate production cycles. In these contexts, AI functions as a creative catalyst that expands the search space of ideas rather than dictating final outcomes.

The benefits of integrating AI creative assistants extend beyond efficiency gains. From an innovation perspective, these systems enable rapid prototyping, experimentation with unconventional ideas, and scalable personalization of creative outputs. Organizations can reduce time-to-market while maintaining creative quality, and individual creators can explore concepts that may have been cognitively or technically inaccessible without computational support. Moreover, continuous interaction between humans and AI generates feedback loops that allow creative systems to evolve alongside user preferences and styles, fostering adaptive and learning-oriented creative environments (Ren, 2025).

Despite their advantages, human–AI creative assistants introduce significant challenges related to authorship, originality, and ethical responsibility. AI-generated content may reflect biases embedded in training data, potentially reinforcing dominant cultural narratives or marginalizing underrepresented perspectives. Overreliance on AI can also lead to aesthetic homogenization, where creative outputs converge toward familiar patterns. Consequently, maintaining human-in-the-loop oversight remains essential. Humans must act as curators, critics, and ethical decision-makers, ensuring that AI-generated content aligns with social values, artistic intent, and audience expectations. Transparent disclosure of AI involvement, responsible dataset curation, and clear governance mechanisms are critical to preserving trust in creative ecosystems (Dartanto, 2024).

6. INTEGRATION AND SYNERGY OF HUMAN–AI CREATIVE SYSTEMS

Figure 5. Integrated Framework of Human–AI Creative Systems in Design and Innovation

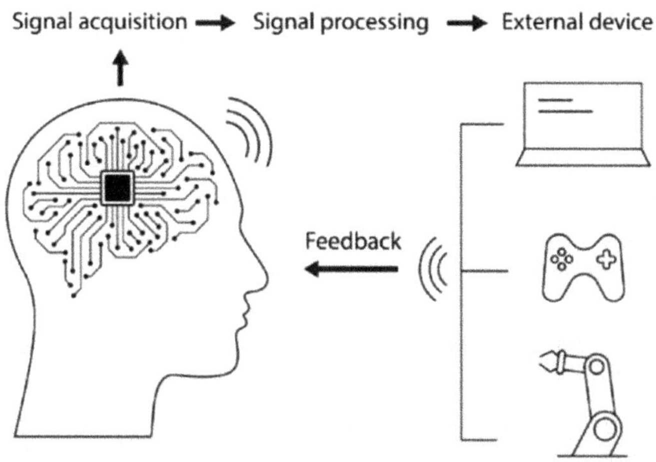

While generative design tools, AI assisted ideation platforms, and intelligent creative support systems each offer distinct contributions to creative practice, their full potential is realized when they are integrated into a cohesive human–AI creative ecosystem. Individually, these technologies address specific phases of the creative process: generative AI expands ideation through rapid variation, intelligent assistants support iteration and refinement, and adaptive systems personalize outputs based on user intent and contextual feedback. However, when deployed in combination, these tools create synergistic effects that enhance creative fluency, innovation capacity, and strategic decision-making in design and creative industries. Rather than operating as isolated applications, integrated human–AI systems transform creativity into an end-to-end, augmented workflow where exploration, evaluation, and execution are seamlessly connected.

In an integrated creative ecosystem, human–AI collaboration unfolds as a continuous loop rather than a linear process. For example, a designer may begin with an AI-powered ideation tool to generate a wide range of visual or conceptual alternatives based on functional constraints and aesthetic preferences. These outputs can then be refined using AI-assisted editing and prototyping systems that suggest improvements in structure, composition, or usability. When creative uncertainty arises, intelligent recommendation systems can introduce new inspirations drawn from diverse datasets, encouraging exploration beyond familiar patterns. Throughout this process, humans remain responsible for defining creative intent, evaluating cultural relevance, and making final design decisions, while AI accelerates exploration and reduces cognitive and operational burden (Shen *et al.*, 2025).

The integration of human–AI creative tools also enables unified feedback and learning mechanisms. Data generated across ideation, iteration, and production stages can be aggregated to provide insights into creative preferences, design performance, and audience reception. By analyzing patterns in human–AI interaction, creative teams can identify which design strategies are most effective, which concepts resonate with users, and where creative bottlenecks occur. These insights allow organizations to refine creative strategies, optimize workflows, and support evidence-informed innovation without constraining artistic freedom. In this way, integrated AI systems do not standardize creativity; instead, they support reflective and adaptive creative practice. From an organizational perspective, the synergy of human–AI creative systems supports scalability and agility in innovation-driven environments. Creative industries often face increasing demands for rapid prototyping, personalization, and cross-platform content production. Integrated AI systems enable teams to manage growing creative complexity without proportional increases in time or labor. Generative models can produce scalable variations of designs, while intelligent systems ensure consistency across formats and channels. This capability is particularly valuable for design studios, media companies, and innovation teams operating under tight deadlines and competitive pressure, allowing them to sustain creative quality while expanding output (Verganti *et al.*, 2020).

Importantly, the integration of creative AI systems reinforces a human-centered approach to innovation. Rather than displacing creative professionals, synergistic human–AI systems redistribute creative labor in ways that preserve human agency, authorship, and ethical responsibility. Humans focus on conceptual framing, emotional resonance, and cultural interpretation, while AI manages computational exploration, pattern recognition, and technical optimization. This balance ensures that creativity remains grounded in human values and social meaning, even as it is amplified by intelligent technologies. Integrated systems thus function as collaborative infrastructures that support, rather than overshadow, human creativity. At a broader level, the integration of human–AI creative tools signals a shift in how creativity and innovation are understood and organized. Creativity is no longer confined to individual tools or isolated moments of inspiration; it emerges from dynamic interactions between humans, intelligent systems, and sociotechnical contexts. Organizations that adopt integrated human–AI creative ecosystems position themselves to respond more effectively to uncertainty, diversity, and rapid change.

By connecting AI tools into a coherent creative workflow, they unlock new forms of innovation that are not only efficient, but also inclusive, reflective, and sustainable.

7. ETHICAL, PRIVACY, AND IMPLEMENTATION CONSIDERATIONS IN HUMAN–AI CREATIVE SYSTEMS

As human AI creative systems become increasingly embedded in design, innovation, and creative industries, organizations face growing responsibility to address ethical, privacy, and implementation-related challenges. These considerations extend beyond technical performance and creative efficiency to encompass legal compliance, social responsibility, trust, and organizational culture. Without appropriate governance, the integration of AI into creative workflows may lead to unintended consequences, such as biased creative outputs, unclear authorship, misuse of personal data, and diminished human agency. Addressing these dimensions is therefore essential for organizations seeking to adopt human–AI collaboration responsibly while maintaining long-term sustainability and creative integrity.

Human–AI creative systems frequently process sensitive data, including design drafts, user-generated content, creative prompts, interaction logs, and behavioral feedback. The collection and processing of such data require strict adherence to regulatory frameworks such as the General Data Protection Regulation (GDPR) and the California Consumer Privacy Act (CCPA). Beyond regulatory compliance, organizations are encouraged to adopt privacy-by-design principles, implement robust encryption mechanisms, anonymize personal and creative data where feasible, and ensure informed consent from users. Transparent disclosure regarding data usage, storage, and model training practices plays a critical role in fostering trust among designers, creators, and stakeholders. Regular audits, risk assessments, and incident response strategies are also necessary to protect creative assets and preserve system integrity. Despite their potential to enhance creativity, AI-driven creative systems may inadvertently reproduce or amplify biases embedded within training datasets. Generative models used in design, visual arts, and content creation may favor dominant cultural aesthetics, reinforce stereotypes, or marginalize underrepresented perspectives. Addressing algorithmic bias requires continuous evaluation of creative outputs, diversification of training data, and the integration of fairness-aware design principles. User feedback mechanisms that allow creators to flag biased or inappropriate outputs further support ethical oversight. Proactive bias mitigation not only upholds ethical standards but also ensures that human–AI creative systems remain inclusive, culturally sensitive, and socially responsible (Tariq *et al.*, 2025).

Successful implementation of human–AI creative systems also depends on organizational readiness and human capability development. Designers, artists, and innovators must be equipped with sufficient digital literacy to understand AI-assisted workflows, data governance practices, and system limitations. Seamless integration with existing creative tools and platforms is essential to avoid workflow fragmentation and loss of creative control. Clear ethical guidelines defining human–AI collaboration, authorship responsibility, and decision-making authority are necessary to ensure that AI augments rather than replaces human creativity. Change management strategies including training programs, stakeholder engagement, and continuous technical support play a crucial role in fostering acceptance and effective utilization of AI in creative environments (Patil *et al.*, 2024).

Beyond technical and organizational factors, human–AI creative systems raise broader ethical questions related to autonomy, transparency, and creative ownership. Organizations must consider how AI-generated suggestions influence creative decisions, originality, and the perceived value of human contribution. Ethical deployment requires clear disclosure of AI involvement in creative outputs, preservation of human control in critical design decisions, and responsible governance of creative data. These considerations are particularly important in global and cross-cultural contexts, where sensitivity to cultural values, diversity, and inclusivity directly affects creative legitimacy and public trust (Agbai *et al.*, 2024).

Sustainability and accountability further shape responsible adoption of human–AI creative systems. Organizations must continuously monitor AI performance, maintain transparency in AI-assisted creative decisions, and establish clear accountability for outcomes produced through human–AI collaboration. Iterative evaluation mechanisms enable stakeholders to assess both creative quality and social impact, ensuring alignment with organizational goals and ethical standards. Ethical foresight, supported by adaptive governance frameworks, helps mitigate long-term risks while strengthening trust, innovation capacity, and cultural value creation within evolving creative ecosystems (Perboli *et al.*, 2025).

8. FUTURE DIRECTIONS OF HUMAN–AI CREATIVE SYSTEMS IN DESIGN AND INNOVATION

The continued evolution of human–AI creative systems is expected to significantly transform design and innovation practices across industries. As artificial intelligence advances, creative AI tools will move beyond basic generative functions toward more context-aware, adaptive, and collaborative roles. Future systems are anticipated to support not only idea generation and design automation but also deeper cognitive, emotional, and cultural dimensions of creativity. This evolution positions AI not merely as a tool, but as an intelligent creative partner capable of augmenting human imagination, supporting complex decision-making, and fostering sustainable innovation ecosystems. One prominent future direction lies in the development of emotionally and contextually aware creative AI. Unlike current generative models that primarily rely on statistical patterns, next-generation systems are expected to integrate affective computing and contextual intelligence. By recognizing emotional cues, user intent, and creative frustration or uncertainty, AI systems can adapt their outputs to better support designers during ideation and refinement phases. Such emotionally responsive AI can enhance creative flow, reduce cognitive load, and improve user satisfaction, particularly in collaborative and iterative design environments (Wasosa, 2025).

Another important trend is the integration of human–AI creative systems with immersive technologies such as augmented reality (AR) and virtual reality (VR). These technologies will enable designers, artists, and innovators to collaborate with AI in shared virtual spaces, visualizing concepts in real time and manipulating design elements interactively. AI-driven assistants embedded within AR/VR environments can provide instant feedback, suggest design alternatives, and simulate outcomes before physical production. This convergence of immersive environments and AI-driven creativity has the potential to redefine co-creation by making design processes more intuitive, experiential, and globally collaborative (Gurel, 2025).

Multimodal creative intelligence represents another critical future pathway. Human–AI creative systems will increasingly combine text, image, audio, gesture, and spatial inputs to generate richer and more holistic creative outputs. By interpreting multiple modalities simultaneously, AI systems can better understand creative intent and context, enabling more nuanced and culturally sensitive designs. Multimodal creativity is particularly relevant in design innovation, where visual aesthetics, narrative elements, and user experience must be integrated seamlessly across diverse platforms and audiences (Song *et al.*, 2025).

Personalized and adaptive creative AI agents are also expected to become central to future design workflows. Through continuous learning from user interactions, these systems can adapt to individual creative styles, organizational norms, and project-specific constraints. Personalized AI assistants can anticipate designer needs, suggest contextually relevant inspirations, and proactively support decision-making throughout the creative lifecycle. This personalization enhances efficiency while preserving the uniqueness of human creativity, ensuring that AI supports rather than homogenizes creative expression (Garcia, 2025).

Beyond individual creativity, future human–AI creative systems will increasingly incorporate predictive and strategic intelligence. By analyzing trends, user feedback, and market dynamics, AI can help designers anticipate emerging needs, identify innovation opportunities, and assess the potential impact of creative decisions. Predictive creative analytics enables organizations to align design innovation with long-term strategic objectives, reducing uncertainty and enhancing the sustainability of creative outcomes. When combined with human judgment and ethical oversight, predictive AI becomes a powerful catalyst for responsible innovation (Buhmann & Fieseler, 2021).

9. CONCLUSION

This proposal has comprehensively explored the role of artificial intelligence as a collaborative partner in creative, design, and communication processes, emphasizing a shift from automation-oriented systems toward human-centered and augmentation-based AI frameworks. Rather than conceptualizing AI as an autonomous creator or decision-maker, this study positions AI as an enabling collaborator that supports human creativity, judgment, and strategic intent. Through an integrated discussion of conceptual foundations, theoretical perspectives, system functionalities, ethical considerations, and future trajectories, the proposal provides a structured understanding of how human–AI collaboration reshapes contemporary innovation ecosystems.

At a conceptual level, the proposal establishes that creativity and communication in the digital era are increasingly distributed across humans, intelligent systems, and organizational contexts. Human–AI collaborative creativity emerges not as a substitution of human agency, but as a hybrid process in which humans retain control over meaning, values, and responsibility, while AI contributes computational power, pattern recognition, and generative exploration. This reframing challenges traditional notions of authorship and creativity by highlighting interaction, iteration, and co-creation as defining characteristics of modern creative work.

The theoretical foundations discussed in this proposal further reinforce the view that AI functions as a cognitive and communicative extension of human capabilities. By drawing on perspectives related to cognitive augmentation, social presence, media richness, and collaborative intelligence, the study demonstrates that AI-enhanced systems can support deeper engagement, more adaptive collaboration, and improved decision-making. These theoretical lenses provide an analytical basis for understanding why AI-driven tools are not merely efficiency-enhancing technologies, but transformative infrastructures that reshape how humans communicate, collaborate, and innovate.

Through the examination of AI-powered creative assistants, automated communication systems, integrated AI frameworks, and synergistic tool ecosystems, this proposal illustrates how AI contributes across multiple stages of creative and communicative workflows. AI systems support ideation by generating diverse alternatives, facilitate iteration by refining drafts and prototypes, and enhance execution by automating repetitive tasks. When integrated into cohesive ecosystems, these tools move beyond isolated functionalities to form intelligent workflows that enable scalability, personalization, and global collaboration. Such integration allows organizations and creative practitioners to navigate complexity, manage uncertainty, and accelerate innovation without compromising human oversight.

However, the proposal also emphasizes that the benefits of human–AI collaboration cannot be fully realized without addressing critical ethical, privacy, and implementation challenges. AI communication and creative systems frequently process sensitive data and operate on large-scale datasets that may contain biases or unequal representation. Without appropriate governance, these systems risk reinforcing dominant cultural narratives, marginalizing alternative perspectives, or undermining trust among users. Therefore, the proposal highlights the importance of privacy-by-design principles, algorithmic fairness, transparency, and human-in-the-loop oversight as foundational requirements for responsible AI deployment.

Organizational readiness is identified as another crucial factor shaping the success of AI integration. Effective adoption requires not only technical infrastructure, but also digital literacy, ethical guidelines, and change management strategies that support human–AI collaboration. By clearly defining roles, accountability structures, and escalation mechanisms, organizations can ensure that AI augments rather than replaces human judgment. This alignment between technological capability and organizational culture is essential for sustaining long-term value creation and employee engagement.

Looking toward the future, the proposal outlines several promising directions for the evolution of human–AI collaborative systems. Advances in emotionally intelligent AI, multimodal interaction, immersive environments, and predictive analytics suggest that AI will increasingly support more intuitive, empathetic, and anticipatory forms of communication and creativity. These developments point to a future in which AI systems function not merely as tools, but as reflective collaborators that adapt to individual styles, contextual cues, and evolving creative goals. Such capabilities have the potential to redefine collaboration across industries, cultures, and geographic boundaries.

REFERENCES

Adamakis, M., & Rachiotis, T. (2025). Artificial Intelligence in Higher Education: A State-of-the-Art Overview of Pedagogical Integrity, Artificial Intelligence Literacy, and Policy Integration. *Encyclopedia*, *5*(4), 180. DOI: 10.3390/encyclopedia5040180

Agbai, E., Agbai, E., & Oko-Jaja, E. S. (2024). Bridging Culture, Nurturing Diversity: Cultural Exchange and Its Impact on Global Understanding. *Research Journal of Humanities and Cultural*, *10*(2), 42–58. DOI: 10.56201/rjhcs.v10.no2.2024.pg42.58

Almaz, A. F., El-Agouz, E. A. E. A., Abdelfatah, M. T., & Mohamed, I. R. (2024). The Future Role of Artificial Intelligence (AI) Design's Integration into Architectural and Interior Design Education is to Improve Efficiency, Sustainability, and Creativity. *Civil Engineering and Architecture*, *12*(3), 1749–1772. DOI: 10.13189/cea.2024.120336

Barrett, M. S., Creech, A., & Zhukov, K. (2021). Creative Collaboration and Collaborative Creativity: A Systematic Literature Review. *Frontiers in Psychology*, *12*(August), 1–15. DOI: 10.3389/fpsyg.2021.713445 PMID: 34434151

Buhmann, A., & Fieseler, C. (2021). Towards a deliberative framework for responsible innovation in artificial intelligence. *Technology in Society, 64*(December 2020), 101475. https://doi.org/DOI: 10.1016/j.techsoc.2020.101475

Chen, X., Wang, X., & Qu, Y. (2023). Constructing Ethical AI Based on the "Human-in-the-Loop" System. *Systems*, *11*(11). Advance online publication. DOI: 10.3390/systems11110548

Creely, E., & Blannin, J. (2025). Creative partnerships with generative AI. Possibilities for education and beyond. *Thinking Skills and Creativity, 56*(October 2023), 101727. https://doi.org/DOI: 10.1016/j.tsc.2024.101727

Daly, S. J., Hearn, G., & Papageorgiou, K. (2025). Sensemaking with AI: How trust influences Human-AI collaboration in health and creative industries. *Social Sciences and Humanities Open, 11*(October 2024), 101346. https://doi.org/DOI: 10.1016/j.ssaho.2025.101346

Dartanto, A. S. (2024). Transforming Curatorial Practices: The Role of AI and Blockchain in Shaping an Ethical Art-Science Paradigm for Public Policy. *International Journal of Creative and Arts Studies*, *11*(2), 140–164. DOI: 10.24821/ijcas.v11i2.14388

Das, S., & Kundu, R. (2024). The Ethics of Artificial Intelligence in Creative Arts: A Comprehensive Review. *Interdisciplinary International Journal of Advances in Social Sciences. Arts and Humanities, 01*(01), 27–34. DOI: 10.62674/iijassah.2024.v1i1.003

Desolda, G., Esposito, A., Lanzilotti, R., Piccinno, A., & Costabile, M. F. (2025). *From human-centered to symbiotic artificial intelligence: a focus on medical applications. Multimedia Tools and Applications* (Vol. 84). Springer US. https://doi.org/DOI: 10.1007/s11042-024-20414-5

Fügener, A., Grahl, J., Gupta, A., & Ketter, W. (2022). Cognitive Challenges in Human–Artificial Intelligence Collaboration: Investigating the Path Toward Productive Delegation. *Information Systems Research, 33*(2), 678–696. DOI: 10.1287/isre.2021.1079

Garcia, M. B. (2025). The Paradox of Artificial Creativity: Challenges and Opportunities of Generative AI Artistry. *Creativity Research Journal, 37*(4), 755–768. DOI: 10.1080/10400419.2024.2354622

Gazi, M. A. I., Rahman, M. K. H., Masud, A., Al, , & Amin, M. Bin, Chaity, N. S., Senathirajah, A. R. bin S., & Abdullah, M. (2024). AI Capability and Sustainable Performance: Unveiling the Mediating Effects of Organizational Creativity and Green Innovation with Knowledge Sharing Culture as a Moderator. *Sustainability (Switzerland), 16*(17). Advance online publication. DOI: 10.3390/su16177466

George, A. S., Baskar, T., & Pandey, D. (2024). Establishing Global AI Accountability : Training Data Transparency, Copyright, and Misinformation Partners Universal Innovative Research Publication (PUIRP) Establishing Global AI Accountability : Training Data Transparency, Copyright, and Misinform. *Partners Universal Innovative Research Publication, 2*(3), 75–91. DOI: 10.5281/zenodo.11659602

Grilli, L., & Pedota, M. (2024). Creativity and artificial intelligence: A multilevel perspective. *Creativity and Innovation Management, 33*(2), 234–247. DOI: 10.1111/caim.12580

Gurel, E. (2025). AI-driven experiences in cultural and creative industries: A review of literature and development of a multifaceted framework. *Service Industries Journal, 2069*, 1–40. DOI: 10.1080/02642069.2025.2542822

Han, S., Kelly, E., Nikou, S., & Svee, E. O. (2022). Aligning artificial intelligence with human values: Reflections from a phenomenological perspective. *AI & Society, 37*(4), 1383–1395. DOI: 10.1007/s00146-021-01247-4

Henriksen, D., Mishra, P., & Stern, R. (2024). Creative Learning for Sustainability in a World of AI : Action, . *Multidisciplinary Digital Publishing Institute*, 1–20. https://doi.org/DOI: 10.3390/ su16114451

Hughes, R. T., Zhu, L., & Bednarz, T. (2021). Generative Adversarial Networks–Enabled Human–Artificial Intelligence Collaborative Applications for Creative and Design Industries: A Systematic Review of Current Approaches and Trends. *Frontiers in Artificial Intelligence*, *4*(April), 1–17. DOI: 10.3389/frai.2021.604234 PMID: 33997773

Hutson, J. (2025). Human-AI Collaboration in Writing: A Multidimensional Framework for Creative and Intellectual Authorship. *International Journal of Changes in Education*. https://doi.org/DOI: 10.47852/bonviewijce52024908

Leon, C., Lipuma, J., & Oviedo-Torres, X. (2025). Artificial intelligence in STEM education: A transdisciplinary framework for engagement and innovation. *Frontiers in Education*, *10*(July), 1–18. DOI: 10.3389/feduc.2025.1619888

Oham, C., & Ejike, O. G. (2024). Creativity and collaboration in creative industries: Proposing a conceptual model for enhanced team dynamics. *Magna Scientia Advanced Research and Reviews*, *12*(1), 185–194. DOI: 10.30574/msarr.2024.12.1.0172

Patil, D., Rane, N. L., & Rane, J. (2024). Acceptance of ChatGPT and generative artificial intelligence in several business sectors: Key factors, challenges, and implementation strategies. *The Future Impact of ChatGPT on Several Business Sectors*, *5*(2), 50–70. DOI: 10.70593/978-81-981367-8-7_5

Peeters, M. M. M., van Diggelen, J., van den Bosch, K., Bronkhorst, A., Neerincx, M. A., Schraagen, J. M., & Raaijmakers, S. (2021). Hybrid collective intelligence in a human–AI society. *AI & Society*, *36*(1), 217–238. DOI: 10.1007/s00146-020-01005-y

Perboli, G., Simionato, N., & Pratali, S. (2025). Navigating the AI Regulatory Landscape: Balancing Innovation, Ethics, and Global Governance. Economic and Political Studies. (in press). *Economic and Political Studies*, *13*(4), 367–397. DOI: 10.1080/20954816.2025.2569584

Ren, X. (2025). The Impact of Generative AI-Driven Job Reshaping on Creativity Sustainability. *The Frontiers of Society. Science and Technology*, *7*(7), 5–21. DOI: 10.25236/FSST.2025.070703

Rezwana, J., & Maher, M. Lou. (2023). Designing Creative AI Partners with COFI: A Framework for Modeling Interaction in Human-AI Co-Creative Systems. *ACM Transactions on Computer-Human Interaction*, *30*(5). Advance online publication. DOI: 10.1145/3519026

Rezwana, J., & Maher, M. Lou. (2025). An Exploration of Mental Models of AI in Human-AI Co-Creativity: A Framework and Insights. *ACM Transactions on Interactive Intelligent Systems*, *15*(4). Advance online publication. DOI: 10.1145/3769072

Salma, Z., Hijón-Neira, R., & Pizarro, C. (2025). Designing Co-Creative Systems: Five Paradoxes in Human–AI Collaboration. *Information (Switzerland)*, *16*(10), 1–19. DOI: 10.3390/info16100909

Shen, Y., Kang, B., & Münch, F. (2025). Human-Centered AI in Design: Examining Educational Paradigms for Creativity and Responsibility. *Lecture Notes in Computer Science, 15799 LNCS*, 64–76. https://doi.org/DOI: 10.1007/978-3-031-93236-6_5

Song, Y., Zhou, H., Wei, J., & Qin, J. (2025). Research on the Application of Augmented Reality Technology in Museum Navigation System. [ACS]. *Journal OfArts and Cultural Studies*, *4*(1), 257–270. DOI: 10.5220/0013632200004671

Tariq, B., Ashraf, M. R., & Rashid, U. (2025). Ethical Imperatives in AI Design: A Comprehensive Framework for Risk Mitigation and Responsible Innovation. *Ubiquitous Technology Journal*, *1*(2), 61–73. DOI: 10.71346/utj.v1i2.23

Toumi, K., Girandola, F., & Bonnardel, N. (2021). Technologies for Supporting Creativity in Design: A View of Physical and Virtual Environments with Regard to Cognitive and Social Processes. *Creativity*, *8*(1), 189–212. DOI: 10.2478/ctra-2021-0012

Venkadesh, P., Divya, S. V., & Kumar, K. S. (2024). Unlocking AI Creativity: A Multi-Agent Approach with CrewAI. *Journal of Trends in Computer Science and Smart Technology*, *6*(4), 338–356. DOI: 10.36548/jtcsst.2024.4.002

Verganti, R., Vendraminelli, L., & Iansiti, M. (2020). Innovation and Design in the Age of Artificial Intelligence. *Journal of Product Innovation Management*, *37*(3), 212–227. DOI: 10.1111/jpim.12523

Vinchon, F., Lubart, T., Bartolotta, S., Gironnay, V., Botella, M., Bourgeois-Bougrine, S., & Gaggioli, A. (2023). Artificial Intelligence & Creativity: A Manifesto for Collaboration. *The Journal of Creative Behavior*, *57*(4), 472–484. DOI: 10.1002/jocb.597

Virvou, M. (2023). Artificial Intelligence and User Experience in reciprocity: Contributions and state of the art. *Intelligent Decision Technologies*, *17*(1), 73–125. DOI: 10.3233/IDT-230092

Wasosa, H. (2025). Influence of Psychological Well-Being and School Factors on Delinquency, During the Covid-19 Period Among Secondary School Students in Selected Schools in Nakuru County : Kenya. [IJRISS]. *International Journal of Research and Innovation in Social Science*, *VII*(2454), 1175–1189. DOI: 10.47772/IJRISS

Wei, X., Wang, L., Lee, L. K., & Liu, R. (2025). The effects of generative AI on collaborative problem-solving and team creativity performance in digital story creation: An experimental study. *International Journal of Educational Technology in Higher Education*, *22*(1). Advance online publication. DOI: 10.1186/s41239-025-00526-0

Wong, P. H. (2020). Cultural Differences as Excuses? Human Rights and Cultural Values in Global Ethics and Governance of AI. *Philosophy & Technology*, *33*(4), 705–715. DOI: 10.1007/s13347-020-00413-8

Xu, G., Murthy, S. V., & Jia, B. (2025). Enhancing Intuitive Decision-Making and Reliance Through Human–AI Collaboration: A Review. *Informatics (MDPI)*, *12*(4). Advance online publication. DOI: 10.3390/informatics12040135

Zallio, M., Ike, C. B., & Chivăran, C. (2025). Designing Artificial Intelligence : Exploring Inclusion, Emerging Technologies. *AI*, *6*(7), 25. DOI: 10.3390/ai6070143

Ziv, L., & Nakash, M. (2025). Behind the Algorithm: International Insights into Data-Driven AI Model Development. *Machine Learning and Knowledge Extraction*, *7*(4), 122. DOI: 10.3390/make7040122

Chapter 4
Empowering the Future Workforce:
Reskilling Strategies in the Age of Human–AI Augmentation

Lintang Tiaraningrum
https://orcid.org/0009-0000-4355-8168
Universitas Esa Unggul, Indonesia

Binastya Anggara Sekti
https://orcid.org/0000-0001-5489-4888
Universitas Esa Unggul, Indonesia

ABSTRACT

The convergence of artificial intelligence (AI) and human augmentation is redefining the global workforce, shifting the focus from automation toward collaboration and skill complementarity. This chapter explores how reskilling becomes a strategic imperative in preparing workers for an AI-augmented future. By examining theoretical models, cross-industry applications, and organizational strategies, it highlights the evolution from traditional to hybrid skills and the need for adaptive, inclusive learning cultures. The chapter further discusses ethical, educational, and policy implications while proposing a future research agenda to sustain human relevance and creativity in an AI-driven world. Ultimately, it argues that human–AI augmentation, when supported by strategic reskilling, can empower a more resilient, innovative, and equitable workforce.

DOI: 10.4018/979-8-3373-7153-5.ch004

1. INTRODUCTION

The rapid integration of artificial intelligence (AI) and human augmentation technologies has brought a transformative shift in how people work, learn, and collaborate. In today's evolving digital ecosystem, human capability is no longer defined solely by biological or cognitive limits. Instead, the line between human intelligence and machine intelligence is becoming increasingly blurred, creating what many scholars call the augmented workforce era. Within this context, individuals are no longer competing against machines, but rather learning to work with them to amplify efficiency, creativity, and decision-making.

The emergence of AI in the workplace represents not just a technological milestone but a fundamental cultural shift. It redefines how organizations operate, how leadership is exercised, and how skills are valued. According to Anghel, human–AI collaboration introduces new perspectives in leadership and recruitment, enabling decision-making that is more data-driven yet still rooted in human empathy. AI systems can process large amounts of information in seconds, while humans contribute emotional understanding and ethical judgment. This synergy creates a work environment that is both intelligent and humane one where technology extends human potential rather than replaces it (Anghel, 2023).

However, this transformation also brings an unavoidable consequence: the rise of skill obsolescence. As AI-driven systems automate routine tasks and redefine job roles, many existing competencies lose their relevance. Workers across industries face the pressing need to reskill to acquire new knowledge, adapt to emerging tools, and continuously reinvent themselves. The speed of technological advancement means that even highly skilled professionals must evolve to stay relevant. What was once considered advanced expertise a decade ago can now be performed by algorithms, making lifelong learning a professional necessity rather than a personal choice.

This phenomenon explains why reskilling has emerged as one of the most critical challenges in the era of human–AI augmentation. The issue is not merely about teaching technical skills such as programming, data literacy, or automation; it is also about nurturing adaptive intelligence the ability to think critically, solve new problems, and work collaboratively with intelligent systems. Reskilling thus becomes a multidimensional process, one that integrates technical, emotional, and ethical competencies. In this sense, the future of work is less about replacing human labor and more about redesigning human capability to align with augmented tools.

Another driving factor behind this urgency is the changing nature of work itself. Modern jobs demand a combination of creativity, analytical thinking, and technological adaptability. In augmented environments, humans are expected to interpret machine-generated insights, make contextual decisions, and maintain accountability for outcomes that algorithms alone cannot manage. This makes human oversight indispensable. Yet, such oversight requires continuous learning an ongoing cycle of reskilling to ensure that humans remain active contributors in AI-supported systems.

Organizations that fail to embrace reskilling risk creating a technological divide within their workforce between those who can collaborate effectively with AI and those left behind by automation. This divide is not only technical but also social, as it can lead to inequality in opportunities and job security. Therefore, companies must move beyond short-term training programs and develop long-term reskilling strategies that prepare employees for continuous change. Such strategies should combine personalized learning pathways, mentorship, and the use of AI itself as a learning facilitator.

At the same time, leadership plays a central role in shaping this transition. Leaders must guide their organizations through uncertainty, fostering cultures that value curiosity, collaboration, and adaptability. As noted by Anghel, the success of AI integration depends not only on technological infrastructure but also on how leaders align human values with digital transformation. Effective leaders in the age of augmentation must therefore serve as *translators* bridging the gap between human potential and algorithmic precision (Anghel, 2023).

The primary objective of this chapter is to explore how reskilling strategies can be effectively designed to prepare the future workforce for human–AI augmentation. It aims to identify approaches that balance human creativity and machine intelligence, ensuring that technological advancement contributes to collective empowerment rather than exclusion. In doing so, the chapter highlights that reskilling is not a reactive measure to automation but a proactive investment in human adaptability and resilience.

Ultimately, the age of human–AI augmentation demands more than technical readiness; it requires a redefinition of what it means to be skilled, adaptable, and human. Reskilling, in this light, becomes the bridge between potential and possibility between what workers can do today and what they must learn to do tomorrow. As the boundaries between human cognition and artificial intelligence continue to merge, cultivating this bridge will determine whether the workforce of the future becomes obsolete or truly augmented.

Figure 1. Conceptual Framework of Human–AI Augmentation and Reskilling

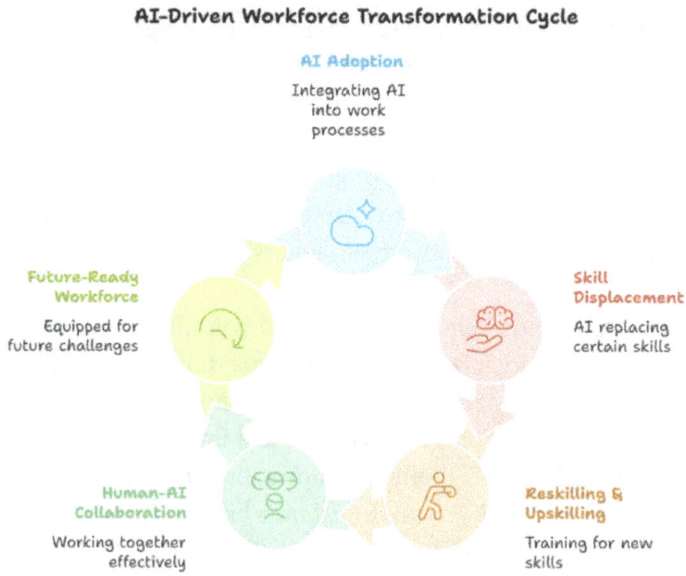

2. CONTEXT AND RATIONALE

The global labor landscape is undergoing one of the most profound transformations in modern history. The rise of artificial intelligence (AI), automation, and human augmentation technologies has blurred the traditional boundaries between human and machine roles. Unlike the automation era of the early 2000s where machines were primarily designed to replace repetitive tasks the current wave emphasizes augmentation, where AI amplifies rather than substitutes human capability. This shift introduces a new paradigm in how labor value is defined: instead of efficiency alone, the measure of productivity now increasingly depends on adaptability, creativity, and human–AI collaboration.

Technological acceleration, especially in machine learning, robotics, and cognitive computing, has created opportunities for industries to redesign work processes. Yet, this rapid transformation also disrupts existing labor structures, leaving millions of workers facing the threat of skill redundancy. Babashahi et al. emphasized that AI is not merely transforming *what* we do but *how* we learn and grow within our professions. Their systematic review of AI's role in workplace transformation reveals that tasks once considered highly specialized such as data analysis, logistics optimization, or quality inspection are now partially automated, requiring workers to shift toward more analytical, creative, and interpersonal competencies. The workforce of tomorrow, therefore, will not only be measured by what they know, but by how effectively they can adapt to intelligent systems (Babashahi et al., 2024).

This evolution marks a shift from the notion of automation machines taking over tasks to augmentation, where technology extends human cognitive and physical limits. As scholars such as Wang, Kim, Peng, and Wang argue, human–AI collaboration introduces a "co-creative" dimension into work processes. Rather than diminishing human input, AI becomes a creative partner that stimulates novel solutions and accelerates innovation cycles. This co-creation dynamic allows designers, engineers, and educators to engage in tasks that require high-level abstraction, emotional sensitivity, and contextual judgment qualities that AI, despite its computational prowess, cannot replicate autonomously (Wang et al., 2025).

The augmentation model also challenges traditional skill hierarchies. Workers are now expected to combine domain expertise with digital literacy, emotional intelligence, and the ability to interpret machine-generated insights. In manufacturing, for instance, Xu et al. note that the transition from skilled labor to *smart talent* is becoming the defining feature of Industry 5.0. Smart talent represents a hybrid capability: technical mastery infused with adaptability and creativity. This model acknowledges that while machines can optimize processes, it is human judgment and ethical discernment that ensure these optimizations align with broader social and organizational goals (Xu et al., 2025).

2.1 The Rise of the Augmentation Economy

The shift toward human–AI augmentation can be viewed as the emergence of a new economic order: the augmentation economy. This economy thrives on symbiotic interactions between humans and machines, creating new roles that did not exist a decade ago such as AI ethicists, human–machine interface designers, and digital twin analysts. Unlike previous industrial revolutions, where efficiency gains often came at the cost of human employment, the augmentation era aims to redefine human contribution rather than eliminate it.

Nevertheless, this transformation is not uniform across sectors or geographies. High-tech and creative industries, for example, adapt faster to augmentation than manufacturing or administrative sectors. This uneven pace has created what global organizations describe as the reskilling gap a mismatch between the skills workers possess and those demanded by AI-driven economies. Over 44% of workers' core skills are expected to change by 2027, and nearly 50% of all employees will require some form of reskilling or upskilling within the next three years. Despite this urgency, less than half of global companies have implemented structured reskilling programs capable of meeting future needs.

2.2 From Routine Tasks to Human-Value Work

As automation increasingly handles routine and repetitive tasks, human roles are shifting toward areas that require creative judgment, empathy, and critical thinking. In design and creative industries, AI tools such as generative models assist in brainstorming and prototyping, while humans provide the conceptual depth, narrative coherence, and ethical oversight that define originality (Wang et al., 2025). Similarly, in healthcare and education, AI supports professionals by streamlining diagnostics or personalized learning, but ultimate accountability remains a human responsibility.

This reorientation toward high-value, human-centered work demands new competencies what (Babashahi et al., 2024) refer to as *augmented intelligence skills*. These include not just digital fluency but also the ability to manage uncertainty, integrate feedback from algorithms, and maintain interpretability in AI-mediated decision processes. The future workforce must therefore embody a synthesis of technical and non-technical capacities, emphasizing resilience and ethical awareness alongside data proficiency.

2.3 The Skill Transformation Imperative

Despite widespread awareness, the transition to an augmented workforce exposes the limitations of traditional reskilling models. Conventional training frameworks often operate on static curricula, emphasizing domain-specific knowledge that quickly becomes obsolete. McKinsey Global Institute (2022) estimates that nearly one-third of the skill sets in today's job descriptions will evolve within the next five years, rendering traditional linear learning approaches inadequate.

Modern reskilling must adopt dynamic, ecosystem-based strategies that leverage AI itself as a learning partner. AI-driven adaptive learning systems can personalize training pathways, analyze skill gaps in real-time, and recommend targeted interventions for employees. Furthermore, organizations must integrate reskilling within strategic planning, treating it not as an auxiliary HR function but as a central pillar of innovation and competitiveness.

Another critical limitation lies in mindset transformation. Many workers perceive AI as a threat rather than a collaborator, leading to psychological resistance that undermines learning initiatives. (Xu et al., 2025) highlight that successful workforce transformation requires cultural adaptation shifting from a defensive stance against automation to an empowerment-oriented mindset. This shift ensures that workers view AI not as a rival but as an extension of their capability.

2.4 Rationale for a New Reskilling Paradigm

The rationale for developing new reskilling models in the age of augmentation lies in three interconnected needs: sustainability, inclusivity, and adaptability. First, reskilling programs must ensure sustainability by fostering continuous, lifelong learning ecosystems that evolve alongside technology. Second, they must promote inclusivity, ensuring that access to digital literacy and augmentation tools is equitable across socioeconomic and demographic boundaries. Third, they must prioritize adaptability, enabling workers to pivot across roles and industries as technologies evolve.

Traditional approaches characterized by classroom-based training or periodic workshops are no longer sufficient. The augmentation era demands immersive, experiential learning environments that replicate real-world human–AI collaboration. For example, simulation-based learning and virtual reality can train professionals to interact with AI in high-stakes scenarios, such as medical diagnostics or design innovation. These approaches not only enhance skill acquisition but also reinforce confidence in navigating augmented workspaces.

In this light, the reskilling imperative becomes both a moral and economic necessity. Organizations that invest in human development will not only enhance performance but also safeguard social stability. The augmentation age, therefore, challenges us to rethink workforce development as a shared responsibility between individuals, institutions, and intelligent systems.

The contextual analysis presented in this section underscores the urgency of developing adaptive, forward-looking reskilling strategies. The next section of this chapter will explore specific models and frameworks designed to operationalize reskilling in augmented environments balancing technological capability with human creativity and ethical responsibility.

3. KEY CONCEPTS AND FRAMEWORKS

The integration of artificial intelligence (AI) into the workforce has led to a paradigm shift from automation toward augmentation, where human and machine intelligence work in tandem to achieve higher efficiency, creativity, and adaptability. To navigate this transformation effectively, a clear understanding of the key conceptual pillars *human augmentation, AI augmentation, reskilling, upskilling, hybrid skills,* and *human-in-the-loop* systems is essential. These concepts form the intellectual foundation for designing new frameworks that prepare workers for the era of human–AI collaboration.

3.1 Defining Core Concepts

Human augmentation refers to the use of technology to enhance or extend human physical, cognitive, and emotional capacities. According to (Nguyen & Elbanna, 2025), augmentation represents a progressive continuum in which technology complements, rather than replaces, human intelligence. It can take multiple forms ranging from wearable devices that enhance perception, to AI-driven decision-support systems that amplify strategic reasoning. In workplace settings, human augmentation redefines the boundaries of performance by merging human intuition with computational precision.

Complementing this, AI augmentation focuses on how intelligent systems are designed to enhance human capabilities. Unlike automation where technology performs tasks independently AI augmentation emphasizes *symbiosis*: human input guides the system's reasoning, while AI provides analytical depth and speed beyond human capability. (Vaccaro et al., 2024) highlight that this synergy generates "cognitive leverage," enabling humans to operate at a higher level of abstraction. Rather than eliminating human roles, AI augmentation redistributes them, empowering workers to focus on creativity, empathy, and innovation.

Meanwhile, reskilling and upskilling represent two critical responses to technological transformation. *Reskilling* involves retraining individuals to perform entirely new roles or adapt to emerging occupations driven by AI disruption. *Upskilling*, in contrast, refers to deepening one's existing skill set to remain competitive in a changing environment. Both are essential to sustaining employability in an economy where human–AI collaboration continuously redefines job requirements. Together, they form the foundation of a lifelong learning mindset.

The concept of hybrid skills bridges technical proficiency and humanistic competence. As AI handles data-driven tasks, workers must cultivate skills that machines cannot emulate such as emotional intelligence, ethical reasoning, adaptability, and cross-disciplinary communication. These hybrid skills ensure that humans remain central to creative, interpretive, and ethical dimensions of work, reinforcing the complementary relationship between human and machine intelligence.

Finally, the notion of human-in-the-loop (HITL) systems formalizes this partnership. HITL frameworks position humans as active decision-makers who oversee, correct, and refine AI outputs. (Nguyen & Elbanna, 2025) argue that HITL mechanisms are vital for maintaining accountability, transparency, and trust in AI-driven environments. They embody the idea that augmentation should not only enhance efficiency but also safeguard human values and ethical considerations.

3.2 Theoretical Models of Human–AI Collaboration

To conceptualize how humans and machines interact in the modern workplace, researchers have proposed the substitution–complementarity framework. This model distinguishes between two opposing yet interrelated dynamics:

1) **Substitution**, where AI replaces human labor in routine or computationally intensive tasks.
2) **Complementarity**, where AI supports human judgment and creativity by handling complex data analysis, pattern recognition, or predictive modeling.

(Vaccaro et al., 2024) demonstrate through meta-analytic evidence that complementarity yields superior outcomes in productivity, decision accuracy, and employee satisfaction compared to substitution. In creative and knowledge-intensive sectors, the combination of human intuition and AI analytics results in "augmented intelligence" a state where both entities co-evolve through mutual feedback loops. For instance, in healthcare diagnostics or architectural design, AI can generate insights that humans refine through contextual interpretation, producing results unattainable by either agent alone.

Building on this model, (Nguyen & Elbanna, 2025) propose a human-centered augmentation framework that integrates three layers of collaboration:

- **Operational augmentation** (task-level): where AI enhances efficiency in repetitive processes;
- **Cognitive augmentation** (decision-level): where AI provides data-driven recommendations; and
- **Creative augmentation** (innovation-level): where AI acts as a partner in ideation and exploration.

This layered model underscores that effective augmentation depends not only on technological sophistication but also on human adaptability and learning culture. It reflects a shift from viewing AI as a tool to understanding it as an intelligent collaborator embedded in organizational ecosystems.

3.3 Dimensions of Reskilling in the Augmentation Era

Reskilling in the context of human–AI augmentation operates along several key dimensions. The first is the balance between technical and human skills. Technical competencies such as data analysis, machine learning literacy, and digital communication form the structural backbone of modern work. However, these must be complemented by human-centric abilities like creativity, empathy, and critical thinking. As (Vaccaro et al., 2024) note, AI can optimize processes but lacks the moral reasoning and imaginative insight that define human contribution.

The second dimension involves learning agility, or the ability to acquire, apply, and adapt knowledge rapidly. In augmented environments, tasks evolve faster than traditional training cycles can accommodate. Workers must therefore develop meta-learning capabilities: learning how to learn. This agility transforms reskilling from a one-time activity into a continuous process of self-reinvention. Organizations that embed learning agility into their culture are more resilient in facing technological disruption.

The third dimension centers on fostering a continuous learning culture. Rather than relying solely on structured training programs, the augmentation era promotes experiential and peer-based learning. Employees learn by doing interacting directly with AI systems, refining their understanding of machine outputs, and iteratively improving outcomes. (Nguyen & Elbanna, 2025) emphasize that such cultures rely heavily on feedback loops between humans and AI, where both entities adapt and co-evolve through shared learning.

Table 1. Comparison of Traditional Skills and AI-Augmented Skills

Skill Domain	Traditional Skills (Pre-AI)	AI-Augmented Skills (Post-AI)
Data Management	Manual data entry, spreadsheet use	Data interpretation, AI data validation
Creativity	Human-only ideation	Human–AI co-creation, prompt engineering
Communication	Face-to-face collaboration	Hybrid collaboration with AI tools
Decision-Making	Experience-based judgment	Data-driven, AI-assisted reasoning
Technical Skills	Basic digital literacy	Algorithmic literacy, adaptive tool use

3.4 Drivers and Barriers in Workforce Reskilling

The transition to augmented workforces is propelled by multiple drivers:

- Rapid technological advancement creating new job roles;
- Increased demand for adaptive and interdisciplinary skill sets;
- Policy initiatives supporting digital transformation; and
- Organizational recognition that human–AI synergy enhances innovation and performance.

However, several barriers hinder effective reskilling. Among them are:

- **Resistance to change**, where workers fear obsolescence rather than empowerment;
- **Unequal access to reskilling resources**, especially in low-income or rural regions;
- **Institutional inertia**, where organizational structures fail to prioritize learning; and
- **Ethical uncertainty**, as the integration of AI raises questions of accountability and transparency.

(Vaccaro et al., 2024) stress that overcoming these barriers requires shifting perceptions of AI from a competing entity to a collaborative augmentation partner. This psychological transformation is as crucial as technical upskilling. In essence, successful reskilling depends not only on acquiring new competencies but also on cultivating a growth-oriented mindset that embraces uncertainty as an opportunity for reinvention.

3.5 Synthesis

The theoretical and conceptual foundations discussed here establish reskilling as a multidimensional process within the augmentation era. It is not merely about equipping workers with digital tools but about reengineering how humans and machines co-create value. Reskilling represents the human side of technological evolution the mechanism through which individuals transform fear of automation into empowerment through augmentation.

Understanding these concepts and frameworks lays the groundwork for the next section, which explores practical reskilling strategies and implementation models for achieving sustainable workforce transformation in the human–AI age.

4. RESKILLING STRATEGIES AND MODELS

The rapid evolution of artificial intelligence (AI) has redefined how organizations perceive talent development and the future of work. In the age of human–AI augmentation, reskilling is no longer a technical retraining effort but a strategic transformation framework that enables organizations to cultivate adaptive, collaborative, and future-ready workforces (Atchley et al., 2024). This paradigm shift emphasizes humans as *partners* of AI rather than mere technology users.

4.1 Organizational Strategies in the Era of AI Augmentation

Modern organizations have moved beyond traditional training models and now focus on role remapping and individualized learning pathways. Instead of rigid hierarchies, they develop fluid skill ecosystems where employees can move across functions, developing *hybrid capabilities* that blend technical and human-centered competencies.

For instance, a data analyst is now expected not only to master statistical tools but also to understand ethics, communication, and user-experience design to collaborate effectively with AI systems. This shift demands AI-driven learning architectures that adapt to employees' learning needs. Through machine learning analytics, AI-based systems can assess an employee's strengths, weaknesses, and learning pace, recommending tailor-made educational content. This approach known as adaptive learning enables personalized, contextualized, and dynamic upskilling experiences.

Another increasingly adopted strategy is modular or micro-learning, which breaks down knowledge into short, digestible units. This model integrates seamlessly into daily workflows, making learning continuous rather than episodic (Blaurock et al., 2025). Micro-learning also supports just-in-time upskilling an essential feature in fast-paced, digitally augmented workplaces.

4.2 Implementation Models: Internal Mobility and Hybrid Roles

Organizational reskilling strategies often depend on internal flexibility. Internal mobility has emerged as a core mechanism for redistributing human capital, allowing employees to transition between departments or roles with minimal disruption. It helps organizations retain institutional knowledge and accelerate adaptation while reducing external hiring costs.

Closely related is talent redeployment, where employees are reassigned to new roles that align with their transferable skills but require new contextual understanding. For example, administrative staff can transition into *AI operations support* after receiving foundational training in data management and digital literacy. Such redeployment fosters workforce sustainability and mitigates unemployment risks due to automation.

Moreover, hybrid roles and learn-while-doing programs have proven to be highly effective in the augmentation era. In these models, employees acquire new skills through hands-on engagement with real projects, supported by intelligent mentoring systems. (Atchley et al., 2024) report that combining experiential learning with AI-guided tutoring improves knowledge retention and skill transfer efficiency by up to 50% compared to conventional training.

4.3 The Role of Technology and AI in Adaptive Learning

Technology plays a transformative role in enabling continuous reskilling. Traditional e-learning platforms have evolved into intelligent learning ecosystems integrating *AI tutors*, *learning analytics*, and *immersive simulations* using virtual or augmented reality. These systems continuously monitor progress, diagnose skill gaps, and recommend corrective pathways.

(Blaurock et al., 2025) emphasizes that collaborative intelligence systems frameworks designed for co-production between humans and AI are especially powerful. They not only teach technical competence but also cultivate creativity, empathy, and problem-solving skills that remain uniquely human. Through interactive simulations, these systems reinforce mutual adaptability between human cognition and AI reasoning.

Additionally, organizations increasingly use AI skill analytics dashboards to visualize capability distributions across teams. This enables HR managers to identify emerging skill clusters, forecast future needs, and design targeted learning interventions. By integrating AI-driven insights into strategic workforce planning, organizations can maintain a state of *continuous alignment* between technological change and human capability development.

4.4 Evaluating Reskilling Outcomes

Measuring the effectiveness of reskilling programs requires a combination of quantitative and qualitative metrics. Common Key Performance Indicators (KPIs) include:

1) **Skill acquisition rate** – how quickly employees master new competencies.
2) **Internal mobility index** – the frequency and success rate of role transitions.
3) **Productivity improvement** – performance gains attributable to reskilling.
4) **Engagement and satisfaction** – employee motivation toward continuous learning.

However, quantitative metrics alone are insufficient. Learning agility the ability to unlearn and relearn rapidly has become a critical qualitative indicator. Organizations that foster *learning agility* tend to demonstrate higher innovation and adaptability under technological disruption.

To operationalize this, organizations are adopting data-driven evaluation systems that link HR analytics with AI-generated learning data. For instance, performance reviews can be cross-referenced with AI tutor feedback to identify the most effective training modules. This approach supports evidence-based HR development, ensuring that reskilling initiatives contribute directly to strategic objectives.

(Atchley et al., 2024) further highlight that successful reskilling evaluation must also capture cultural transformation whether employees perceive learning as a lifelong journey rather than a temporary intervention. Embedding this mindset requires consistent leadership communication, recognition systems, and visible alignment between organizational goals and personal growth pathways.

4.5 Challenges and Pathways Forward

Despite the clear benefits, reskilling in the era of human–AI augmentation faces significant barriers. Common challenges include resistance to change, limited budgets, outdated corporate cultures, and the digital divide between high- and low-skilled workers (Atchley et al., 2024). Many employees view AI as a threat rather than a partner, creating psychological resistance that undermines learning adoption.

Leadership commitment is another decisive factor. Programs that are visibly supported by top management tend to receive greater legitimacy and sustained engagement. Organizations should establish AI Learning Governance Frameworks to align policy, funding, and evaluation across departments. Integrating adaptive AI monitoring also enhances accountability, ensuring learning remains responsive to workforce needs (Blaurock et al., 2025)

Ultimately, reskilling in an AI-augmented era represents not merely an educational intervention but a strategic reinvention of the social contract between employers and employees. It demands a shift from static training models to dynamic ecosystems of continuous capability renewal anchored in human adaptability, ethical awareness, and collaborative intelligence.

5. SECTORAL AND CROSS-INDUSTRY APPLICATIONS

The process of reskilling in the era of human–AI augmentation is not uniform across industries. Each sector faces unique challenges, skill demands, and contextual pressures that shape the nature of workforce transformation. While some industries experience AI as a driver of automation and efficiency, others leverage it as a co-creative tool that amplifies human judgment, creativity, and empathy. This section examines four key sectors creative industries, manufacturing, professional services, and healthcare to illustrate how reskilling initiatives are being designed, implemented, and adapted within distinct organizational contexts. These examples reveal that a *one-size-fits-all* approach to reskilling is ineffective; rather, sectoral nuances require tailored strategies that blend technical proficiency with enduring human capabilities.

5.1 Creative Industries: Human–AI Co-Creation and Hybrid Skillsets

The creative sector provides one of the most visible and complex arenas for human–AI collaboration. Far from replacing creative professionals, AI functions as a *co-creator* that extends human imagination and productivity. (Kirkby et al., 2025) conceptualize this relationship as a "human–AI brand colleague" framework, where AI assists in content generation, ideation, and audience analysis while humans contribute strategic thinking, cultural sensitivity, and emotional intelligence. For instance, in branding and digital marketing, generative AI tools such as DALL·E and ChatGPT have allowed designers and copywriters to prototype ideas rapidly, reducing production time while maintaining creative direction.

Reskilling in this sector therefore focuses on developing hybrid creative-technical skills such as prompt engineering, algorithmic literacy, and ethical curation of AI-generated media. Organizations have introduced internal "AI creativity bootcamps" to teach professionals how to effectively integrate AI tools without diminishing originality. According to the Resource-Based View (RBV), these initiatives strengthen the firm's intangible resources creativity, brand voice, and innovation culture by enhancing human capital with AI fluency. The outcome is not merely efficiency, but an expanded definition of creativity as a shared capability between humans and intelligent systems.

5.2 Manufacturing: Augmented Production and Continuous Technical Learning

In manufacturing, AI has transformed traditional workflows into cyber-physical ecosystems, where machines and humans operate in symbiotic feedback loops. Predictive maintenance systems, AI-driven quality control, and robotics have become central to modern factories, requiring workers to possess new technical literacies. Unlike the creative sector, where reskilling emphasizes soft and hybrid skills, manufacturing focuses on upskilling in automation technologies, including data interpretation, IoT integration, and human–machine interface operation.

Manufacturing firms are now establishing reskilling academies to support this transition. For example, global companies such as Siemens and Toyota have implemented in-house "AI Operator Programs," where assembly workers are trained to interpret AI diagnostic outputs and collaborate with autonomous robots.

However, reskilling in manufacturing also faces barriers. Many workers encounter technological anxiety, stemming from fears of displacement and limited digital literacy. Addressing these barriers requires not only training programs but also a cultural shift toward continuous learning and psychological safety. Firms that integrate mentorship and peer learning into their reskilling systems demonstrate higher retention rates and smoother adoption of AI-enabled production.

5.3 Professional Services: Cognitive Augmentation and Workforce Agility

In professional services such as finance, consulting, and law, AI is revolutionizing the cognitive core of work. Tools for data analytics, legal document automation, and intelligent customer interaction are redefining how expertise is delivered. Rather than substituting professionals, AI acts as a cognitive augmenter processing data at scale while humans apply contextual reasoning and ethical judgment.

(Rastogi & Pandita, 2025) highlight that the key success factor in this transformation is workforce agility, the ability of employees to adapt, learn, and innovate under continuous technological change. Professional service firms increasingly integrate *AI-assisted decision systems* into client advisory processes, which requires reskilling employees not only in data interpretation but also in *AI ethics, bias management, and human oversight*.

For instance, in finance, the adoption of AI risk assessment tools has led to reskilling programs that merge quantitative analytics with critical thinking. Similarly, in legal firms, AI document review has freed up lawyers to focus on negotiation and strategy areas requiring emotional intelligence and persuasive communication. As (Vaccaro et al., 2024) argue, the most effective human–AI combinations arise when machines handle structured, repetitive tasks while humans contribute interpretive and relational intelligence. Thus, reskilling in professional services aims to maintain this complementarity, cultivating professionals who can leverage AI outputs to provide deeper, more human-centered insights.

Figure 2. Sectoral Impact of AI-Augmentation on Workforce Skills

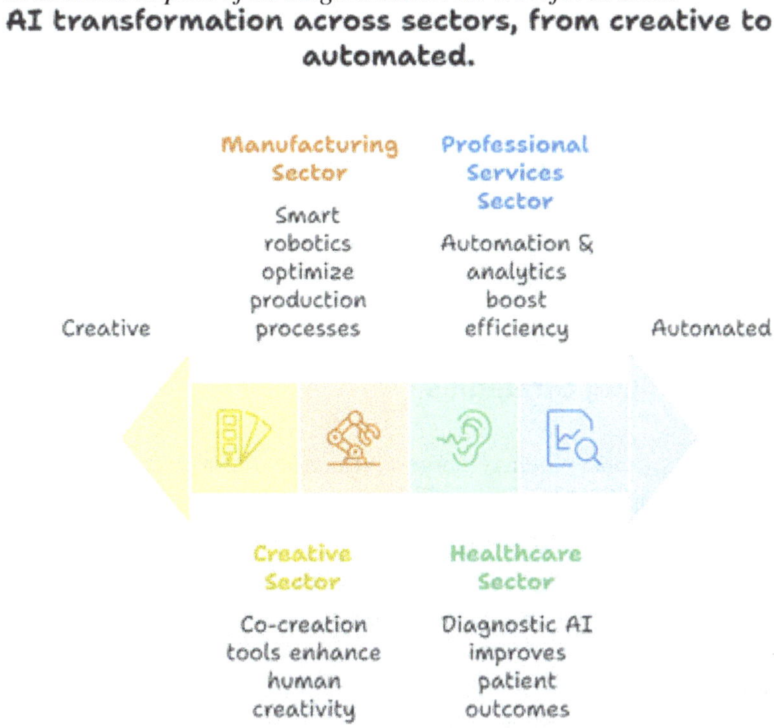

5.4 Healthcare: Empathy, Ethics, and Human-in-the-Loop Systems

The healthcare sector illustrates perhaps the most ethically sensitive and human-centric application of AI augmentation. From diagnostic imaging to patient triage systems, AI can enhance precision, speed, and scalability but only when embedded within human-in-the-loop frameworks. These models ensure that human clinicians retain decision authority, supported by AI's analytical power. As (Nguyen & Elbanna, 2025) note, this configuration epitomizes the "augmentation" paradigm: *AI as an enhancer of human capability rather than a replacement.*

Reskilling in healthcare, therefore, must balance technical fluency (understanding AI algorithms and medical data interpretation) with human skills such as empathy, patient communication, and ethical reasoning. Hospitals and medical universities have begun to include "AI literacy for clinicians" courses that teach practitioners how to evaluate algorithmic outputs critically. Meanwhile, reskilling initiatives for nurses focus on integrating data dashboards and remote monitoring tools into patient care workflows.

One striking example is the *AI-enabled radiology program* launched by Mayo Clinic, which pairs radiologists with machine-learning systems that detect anomalies in imaging scans. This partnership reduces diagnostic errors but also redefines the professional role from image interpreter to AI-assisted decision architect. The key challenge lies in maintaining trust and accountability, ensuring that reskilling programs equip medical staff not only to use AI tools effectively but to question and correct them when necessary.

5.5 Synthesis: The Need for Sector-Specific Reskilling Strategies

Across sectors, a clear pattern emerges: AI augmentation reconfigures the boundaries between human and machine capabilities, but the optimal reskilling strategy varies by context. Creative industries prioritize *hybrid creativity* and ethical design; manufacturing emphasizes *technical automation literacy*; professional services focus on *cognitive flexibility and ethical AI use*; and healthcare underscores *trust, empathy, and interpretive accountability*.

Therefore, a universal reskilling framework is insufficient. Each industry must craft its own "AI–human skill architecture" that aligns with its specific workflows, values, and social responsibilities. The success of reskilling in the augmentation era depends not only on acquiring new skills but also on cultivating adaptive learning cultures that embrace change as a permanent condition of work.

As AI technologies continue to evolve, the boundary between reskilling and continuous reinvention will blur demanding organizations to act not as trainers but as lifelong learning ecosystems. In this context, human augmentation becomes not just a technological upgrade, but a profound social transformation redefining what it means to work, learn, and create in partnership with intelligent systems.

6. POLICY, EDUCATION & ORGANIZATIONAL IMPLICATIONS

As human-AI augmentation reshapes the global workforce, the responsibility to ensure an equitable and adaptive transition extends beyond individual workers. Governments, educational institutions, and organizations must co-create systems that enable *continuous reskilling*, foster *human-AI complementarity*, and promote *sustainable employability*. This section examines policy directions, educational reform, and organizational strategies required to support a resilient workforce in the age of augmentation.

6.1 The Role of Governments and Regulation in Supporting Reskilling

Governments play a central role in building an enabling environment for workforce transformation. Traditional labor policies focused on job protection must evolve into policies that facilitate skill mobility and lifelong learning. Subsidies, learning funds, and fiscal incentives for corporate training programs are becoming crucial instruments to close the skills gap.

For instance, *national reskilling funds* can be allocated to sectors most affected by AI-driven automation, helping workers transition into augmented roles rather than being displaced. Moreover, policy frameworks should integrate *AI literacy* into national curricula and support *public-private partnerships* for digital upskilling initiatives.

(Hemmer et al., 2025) emphasize that governments should recognize *complementarity* rather than substitution between human and machine capabilities. This requires adaptive labor laws that promote collaboration between AI systems and human professionals while protecting worker rights, privacy, and data security.

In addition, governments can set ethical standards for AI use in employment, including transparency in algorithmic decision-making and fairness in AI-supported hiring or evaluation. Establishing *AI governance bodies* and *reskilling councils* at the national level ensures cross-sector coordination and evidence-based policymaking.

6.2 Education Systems and Lifelong Learning

Education systems form the foundation of societal resilience in an AI-augmented future. Universities and vocational institutions must move away from static curricula toward modular, interdisciplinary, and adaptive learning ecosystems. Instead of teaching isolated technical skills, educational institutions should integrate hybrid skill development combining coding, data analysis, and AI ethics with creativity, empathy, and critical thinking.

(Korzynski et al., 2024) argue that generative AI can act as a *cognitive amplifier* in education, transforming traditional learning processes into personalized and collaborative experiences. Integrating AI tutors, adaptive learning analytics, and simulation-based training can accelerate reskilling at scale. Massive Open Online Courses (MOOCs) and micro-credentialing platforms further democratize access to education, allowing workers from diverse backgrounds to update their competencies continuously.

Furthermore, lifelong learning should become a cultural norm, not a remedial measure. Governments and universities can collaborate to establish *national lifelong learning frameworks* that incentivize individuals to participate in continuous education through tax credits or learning accounts. The partnership between academia and industry is essential in aligning curricula with emerging skill demands, ensuring that educational outcomes remain relevant to the evolving nature of work.

6.3 Organizational Roles: HR, Learning & Development, and Leadership

Within organizations, the responsibility for workforce adaptation lies largely in Human Resources (HR) and Learning & Development (L&D) departments. However, traditional training programs are insufficient for the speed of AI-driven change. Instead, organizations must adopt agile learning architectures, where learning is embedded in daily work through digital platforms, mentoring, and experimentation.

(Korzynski et al., 2024) highlight that HR processes can be *bridged and enhanced through generative AI*, enabling personalized training recommendations, predictive talent analytics, and continuous feedback mechanisms. These innovations allow HR teams to identify emerging skill gaps early and respond proactively.

Leadership also plays a decisive role. Visionary leaders must cultivate an environment of *psychological safety* where employees feel encouraged to experiment, fail, and learn alongside AI systems. A leadership style grounded in empathy, openness, and innovation is key to fostering a culture of adaptive learning.

Organizations should institutionalize learning agility as a core competency, integrating it into performance metrics and promotion criteria. This shifts the organizational mindset from "training as an event" to "learning as a continuous cycle."

6.4 Multi-Stakeholder Collaboration Models

The complexity of reskilling in the age of AI augmentation necessitates a multi-stakeholder ecosystem that includes governments, industry leaders, educational institutions, and the workforce itself. Such collaboration can take several forms:

1) **Public–Private Partnerships (PPPs):** Governments can fund reskilling programs co-developed by technology companies and universities, ensuring that training aligns with real-world demands.
2) **Industry Alliances:** Multiple firms within a sector can pool resources to create *shared training hubs*, accelerating sector-wide adaptation.
3) **Workforce Councils:** Multi-sector councils can coordinate policies, forecast emerging job roles, and guide national skills agendas.

(Zirar et al., 2023) underscore the necessity of viewing AI and humans as *coexisting entities* within the workplace, where collective action determines the success of this coexistence. Collaborative models enable not just technical reskilling but also *social adaptation*, helping employees embrace AI tools as partners rather than threats.

In emerging economies, these collaborations are especially vital to mitigate inequalities in digital access and skill acquisition. By investing in *inclusive learning ecosystems*, stakeholders can prevent the polarization of labor markets between high-skill AI workers and low-skill displaced workers.

6.5 Building Adaptive Learning Cultures and Workforce Resilience

A critical implication for organizations is the cultivation of a continuous learning culture that supports experimentation, curiosity, and cross-functional collaboration. In this model, learning becomes self-directed and integrated into everyday workflows. Tools like *AI-powered knowledge assistants* can help employees access information, receive feedback, and practice new competencies in real time.

(Hemmer et al., 2023) describe *complementarity* as not only a technical alignment between human and machine but also a cultural alignment where employees trust AI systems and understand their boundaries. Organizational culture must therefore emphasize transparency and co-learning between humans and algorithms.

Building workforce resilience also requires rethinking career pathways. Instead of linear progressions, organizations should promote *lattice career models*, where employees can move horizontally across roles to gain hybrid experiences. This fluidity prepares them for rapid technological shifts and fosters adaptability.

Additionally, *resilience training programs* focusing on mental flexibility, emotional intelligence, and digital confidence are becoming essential in maintaining morale and engagement during AI transitions. Companies that embed these values into their culture report higher innovation and retention rates.

6.6 Toward a Coevolutionary Future

Ultimately, effective policy, education, and organizational strategies must recognize that human and artificial intelligences are coevolving. The success of this coevolution depends on aligning technological design, institutional frameworks, and human development.

Governments must act as *system architects*, building the infrastructure for equitable access to learning. Educational institutions must function as *knowledge accelerators*, continuously updating the talent pipeline. Organizations must serve as *learning ecosystems*, enabling individuals to thrive amid disruption.

As (Zirar et al., 2023) emphasize, the future of work will not be defined by machines replacing humans but by humans augmented through intelligent systems.

Therefore, investing in policies, education, and leadership that foster adaptability and learning agility is not merely a strategic choice it is an ethical imperative for a sustainable digital society.

7. ETHICAL, EQUITY & INCLUSION CONSIDERATIONS

As artificial intelligence and human augmentation redefine the dynamics of work, the question of *who benefits* and *who gets left behind* has emerged as one of the most pressing ethical concerns of the digital era. While AI-augmented work promises unprecedented productivity and creativity, it also risks deepening inequalities between those with access to reskilling opportunities and those without. Addressing these ethical, equity, and inclusion issues is therefore essential to ensure that technological progress translates into collective human advancement rather than social stratification.

7.1 Ethical Access to Reskilling Opportunities

The ethics of AI-driven reskilling revolve around access, agency, and autonomy. Not all workers begin this transition from the same starting point. Individuals with higher digital literacy, stronger educational backgrounds, or employment in technology-intensive sectors are more likely to benefit from AI augmentation and reskilling programs. In contrast, workers in manual or routine occupations face greater risks of technological displacement with fewer pathways to reentry.

(Furendal & Jebari, 2023) warn that human augmentation can lead to *"cognitive elitism"*, where only a subset of the workforce those already advantaged receives the training necessary to thrive alongside AI. This phenomenon threatens to create a two-tier workforce: the augmented elite and the digitally marginalized.

Ethical access requires that reskilling programs be universal and inclusive, supported by public funding, transparent eligibility criteria, and proactive outreach to underrepresented groups. Organizations should prioritize *needs-based access*, targeting workers most vulnerable to automation. AI systems themselves can help identify such groups by mapping workforce skill gaps and predicting future risks provided these algorithms are used responsibly and audited for bias.

Ensuring transparency in how training opportunities are allocated and how outcomes are measured is also key to avoiding structural inequities. Ethical AI reskilling thus demands not only technical fairness but also moral fairness: the commitment to ensuring that human dignity and potential are equally distributed across society.

7.2 Inclusion and the Vulnerable Workforce

A truly inclusive reskilling ecosystem must address the needs of low-skill workers, older employees, and individuals from marginalized socioeconomic backgrounds. These populations often lack the digital infrastructure, confidence, or support systems to engage effectively in AI-enhanced learning.

(Przegalinska et al., 2025) highlight that effective collaboration between humans and AI depends not only on technical compatibility through Resource-Based View (RBV) and Task-Technology Fit (TTF) but also on *psychological and social inclusivity*. Workers must feel empowered to participate in augmented environments, which requires addressing barriers related to access, design, and motivation.

For older workers, reskilling initiatives should integrate age-friendly design principles: intuitive user interfaces, peer mentoring, and flexible learning schedules. Likewise, for workers in rural or low-income areas, digital inclusion policies such as subsidized broadband, local training hubs, and mobile learning applications can bridge accessibility gaps.

Organizations must also address the *cultural dimension* of inclusion. In many workplaces, hierarchical structures or performance pressures discourage low-skill employees from admitting skill gaps. Creating psychologically safe learning spaces, where mistakes are treated as learning opportunities, is essential to enabling broad participation in reskilling programs.

Inclusion, therefore, is not merely a demographic metric but a structural principle an ongoing process of designing systems, technologies, and cultures that adapt to diverse human needs.

7.3 Psychosocial and Identity Implications of Human-AI Augmentation

Beyond access and opportunity, the rise of human-AI collaboration has profound social and psychological implications. Work has long been central to human identity, providing purpose, recognition, and community. When AI systems begin to share or even dominate core aspects of professional activity, many workers experience *identity dissonance* and *loss of agency*.

(Wu et al., 2025) found that while human–generative AI collaboration can significantly enhance task performance, it also undermines intrinsic motivation. Workers may feel that their creativity, expertise, or intuition is devalued when algorithms produce superior or faster outputs. Over time, this can erode self-efficacy and professional pride, particularly in creative and cognitive occupations.

The challenge, therefore, is not only to train workers *technically* but to support them *psychologically* through transitions. Organizations should implement well-being programs, counseling, and reflective learning sessions that help employees reinterpret their roles in AI-augmented contexts. Encouraging co-creation where humans guide AI outcomes rather than merely validate them can help preserve a sense of authorship and agency.

Ethical augmentation demands that humans remain at the center of meaning-making processes. Instead of viewing AI as a replacement, workers should be supported to see it as an extension of human capability, amplifying rather than diminishing their professional identity.

7.4 Fairness and Meaning in Human-AI Collaboration

A central ethical question in the age of augmentation is: *What remains distinctively human in work?* As AI assumes more cognitive functions, the danger is that human labor becomes relegated to oversight, correction, or "manual backup" roles. (Furendal & Jebari, 2023) describe this as the "stunting paradox" a condition where technology designed to enhance human potential inadvertently reduces human agency and creativity.

To avoid this, fairness in augmentation must go beyond distributive justice (who benefits) to existential justice (how humans find meaning in augmented work). The goal should be to design collaborative systems where humans and AI engage as partners in problem-solving, each contributing their unique strengths.

(Przegalinska et al., 2025) argue that in high-performing organizations, AI acts as a *complementary agent* enhancing rather than replacing human judgment. Ensuring such complementarity requires deliberate design of work processes, ethical governance frameworks, and leadership commitment to preserving human-centered values.

Organizations should also ensure transparency of augmentation boundaries clearly defining where AI decision-making begins and human oversight ends. This helps maintain accountability, ethical responsibility, and trust.

Moreover, AI systems must be explainable and auditable so that human workers can understand the rationale behind algorithmic outputs. This transparency reinforces a *sense of shared control*, which is essential to sustaining motivation and fairness in augmented environments.

7.5 Toward Ethical and Inclusive Augmentation

The future of work must be guided by a moral vision that places *human flourishing* at its core. Ethical reskilling and inclusive augmentation require a balance between innovation and justice, efficiency and empathy, performance and purpose.

Governments should legislate *fair access* to reskilling as a social right; educational institutions must design curricula that accommodate diverse learners; and organizations must ensure that augmentation enhances not diminishes human dignity.

Ultimately, the ethical question is not whether AI will take over human work, but whether humans will retain meaning, identity, and equity within the augmented future. If the next generation of workplaces can ensure that technology amplifies humanity rather than marginalizes it, then AI augmentation will not merely change how we work it will redefine *why* we work.

Figure 3. Ethical and Inclusive Reskilling Framework

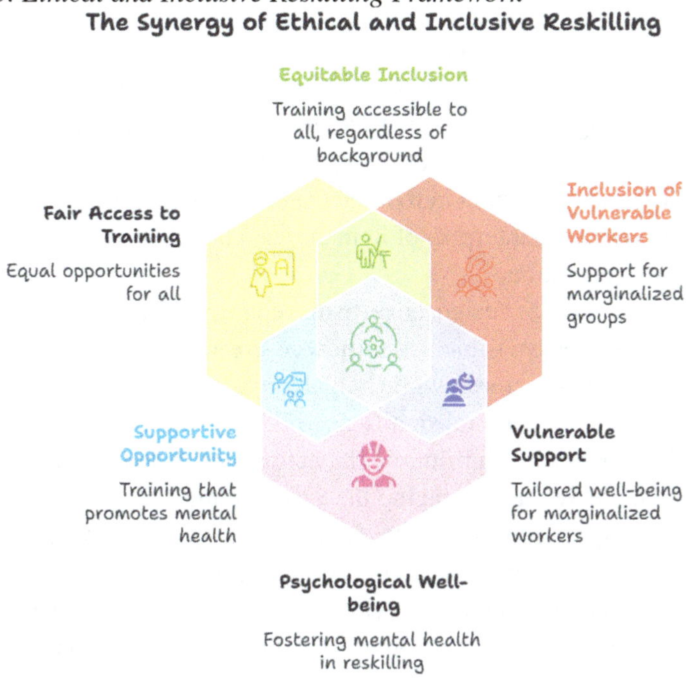

8. FUTURE OUTLOOK & RESEARCH AGENDA

The accelerating convergence between artificial intelligence (AI), human augmentation, and global creative industries signals the beginning of a new paradigm for work, creativity, and human development. As organizations, institutions, and individuals adapt to this new landscape, the future of reskilling will not simply be a matter of learning new tools it will represent a profound reconfiguration of what it means to be *skilled*, *creative*, and *human* in an increasingly digital and interconnected world.

This chapter concludes by outlining the emerging trends, open research questions, and future directions for policy, education, and creative industries within the context of AI-driven human augmentation.

8.1 Emerging Trends: Generative AI, Hyper-Automation, and Global Talent Fluidity

The next phase of AI integration is characterized by the rise of generative AI, hyper-automation, and global talent mobility. Generative AI represented by systems capable of producing high-quality creative outputs has shifted the boundaries between human and machine creativity. (Woolley, 2025) argues that the true potential of generative AI lies not in replacing individual expertise but in *cultivating collective intelligence*: the synergistic interplay of human imagination, contextual reasoning, and machine-scale generation.

In creative sectors such as design, advertising, entertainment, and digital media, this transformation is already visible. AI can now co-create visual concepts, compose music, or draft narrative structures, while humans curate, refine, and imbue outputs with emotional nuance and cultural significance. The challenge ahead will be integrating human judgment with algorithmic fluency, ensuring that creative industries remain human-centered while leveraging the vast potential of AI collaboration.

Simultaneously, hyper-automation the fusion of AI, robotics, and process automation will reshape production and service ecosystems. As repetitive or transactional work is increasingly automated, organizations will demand workers who can orchestrate, interpret, and creatively apply AI outputs. This transition underscores the urgency for meta-cognitive reskilling, including problem-solving, digital ethics, and cross-disciplinary adaptability.

Furthermore, global talent mobility will redefine how creative and technical expertise circulates. Remote and hybrid work models enable organizations to access worldwide talent pools, but they also demand new governance mechanisms to ensure equitable access, fair compensation, and cultural inclusivity. The next generation of workforce policies will thus need to address not only *how* people reskill, but *where* and *under what conditions* these reskilling opportunities are distributed.

8.2 Measuring the "Return on Reskilling"

One of the central research gaps in current workforce transformation studies is the absence of robust frameworks for evaluating the return on reskilling (RoR). While most organizations recognize the necessity of continuous learning, few possess systematic metrics to measure its long-term impact on performance, innovation, and employee well-being.

(Li, 2024) emphasizes that traditional training metrics such as course completion rates or short-term productivity improvements fail to capture the *dynamic and cumulative value* of reskilling in the context of Industry 4.0 and beyond. Future research should therefore focus on multi-dimensional performance indicators that link learning outcomes to innovation capability, organizational resilience, and sustainable employability.

Possible directions include:

- Developing **AI-assisted learning analytics** to measure skill progression across time and contexts.
- Investigating the **economic externalities** of reskilling, such as its contribution to national innovation indexes or regional productivity growth.
- Evaluating **career trajectory shifts** caused by human-AI augmentation how workers transition between creative, managerial, and technical roles as they integrate new digital skills.

A standardized RoR model would not only aid organizations in optimizing investments but also support policymakers in designing incentive systems for equitable workforce development.

8.3 Cross-National and Cultural Dimensions of Augmentation

Future studies should also address how cultural, economic, and regulatory differences shape the implementation and impact of AI-driven reskilling. In developed economies, the focus often lies on augmenting creativity and high-value innovation. In contrast, emerging economies face the dual challenge of technological adoption and inclusion ensuring that digital transformation does not exacerbate social inequality.

(Erzed et al., 2025) highlight that virtual and immersive environments such as the metaverse can serve as powerful platforms for *cross-border collaboration and social learning*. Within these environments, creative professionals from different countries can co-develop ideas, simulate real-world challenges, and exchange cultural insights in real time. However, this also raises questions of governance, data ownership, and cognitive sovereignty, as creative labor becomes distributed across digital ecosystems.

A research agenda for global reskilling must thus examine not only *how AI augments creativity* but also *whose creativity is represented, valued, and rewarded.* Issues of intellectual property, cultural appropriation, and algorithmic bias will become increasingly central to future debates on fairness in human-AI creative collaboration.

8.4 Implications for Creative Industries

Given that this book focuses on *Global Creative Sectors Through AI and Human Augmentation*, it is essential to consider how reskilling strategies can be specifically adapted to creative professions. Creative workers are uniquely positioned at the intersection of imagination and technology; they are both the drivers and subjects of AI transformation.

To remain relevant, creative industries must:

1) Foster **interdisciplinary learning ecosystems**, blending artistic creativity with computational literacy.
2) Encourage **AI-augmented design thinking**, where humans lead conceptual innovation and AI manages iteration and optimization.
3) Promote **ethical creativity frameworks**, ensuring transparency and authenticity in generative outputs.
4) Build **distributed creative networks**, collaborative environments where artists, technologists, and educators co-develop hybrid skills for the post-digital era.

These efforts will redefine creative reskilling as a *continuous dialogue* between human expression and machine intelligence. By positioning creativity as a strategic advantage rather than a vulnerable domain, industries can transform augmentation into a catalyst for cultural and economic renewal.

8.5 Toward a Research and Policy Agenda

In summary, the next decade of research must address three interrelated dimensions:

- **Measurement**: developing reliable methods to assess learning impact and augmentation outcomes.
- **Equity**: ensuring inclusive access to AI-driven upskilling and preventing digital marginalization.

- **Ethics and Governance**: crafting transparent, human-centered frameworks for augmented creativity and workforce transformation.

Scholars should explore longitudinal studies that capture the career evolution of augmented professionals, comparative analyses across industries and nations, and empirical models linking augmentation with innovation performance.

Policymakers, in turn, should view reskilling not as a reactive measure but as a strategic infrastructure investment a foundation for sustainable, inclusive, and creative economies. The integration of AI and human potential, if guided by ethical foresight and equitable access, can reshape the global workforce into one that is not only future-ready but *future-defining*.

Table 2. Future Research Directions in AI-Augmented Reskilling

Theme	Open Research Question	Potential Methodology
ROI of Reskilling	How to measure the long-term return on AI-related reskilling programs?	Longitudinal organizational studies
Global Talent Mobility	How does cross-border AI adoption affect workforce adaptability?	Comparative international analysis
Creative Sector Transformation	How can generative AI reshape creative skillsets sustainably?	Mixed-methods study (survey + case study)
AI Ethics in Training	How to balance automation benefits with human dignity in learning?	Normative ethical framework analysis

9. CONCLUSION

The era of human-AI augmentation marks a profound transformation in how work, creativity, and learning are defined. Throughout this chapter, we have explored how reskilling has become not merely a strategy but a fundamental necessity for sustaining employability and relevance in a rapidly evolving digital economy. As artificial intelligence continues to reshape both cognitive and creative labor, the ability to adapt through continual learning, collaboration, and redefinition of human value has emerged as the central differentiator between obsolescence and opportunity.

The key arguments developed in the previous sections converge on a single insight: reskilling is the bridge that ensures humans remain integral contributors in AI-augmented systems rather than passive observers of automation. Governments and policymakers must play a catalytic role by establishing supportive infrastructures such as subsidies, national learning funds, and lifelong learning policies. Educational institutions, in turn, should align curricula with emerging skill needs embedding AI literacy, digital ethics, and creative problem-solving as core competencies. Organizations must also take shared responsibility by nurturing learning cultures, enabling employees to experiment, fail, and grow in environments that value adaptability over static expertise.

Yet beyond structure and policy, reskilling embodies a humanistic dimension. It represents the resilience of identity amid disruption, the reaffirmation that technology should expand not limit human potential. Ethical and inclusionary considerations must remain central: workers of all skill levels, ages, and backgrounds deserve access to opportunities for reinvention. This democratization of learning ensures that augmentation becomes a force for equity, not division.

Looking ahead, the convergence of generative AI, hybrid work models, and global creative networks will further redefine what it means to be "skilled." Success in this context will depend not only on technical proficiency but also on emotional intelligence, creativity, and the capacity to co-create meaning alongside machines.

Ultimately, the transformation we face is not a threat but an invitation to evolve. Reskilling in the era of human-AI collaboration challenges us to envision a world where technology amplifies imagination, where work becomes more humane through augmentation, and where learning is both a lifelong right and a shared responsibility. If guided with foresight, inclusion, and courage, this evolution will not diminish humanity it will redefine its brilliance.

REFERENCES

Anghel, D. (2023). New Perspectives for Human and Artificial Intelligence Interactions for Leadership e-Recruitment. *Societies (Basel, Switzerland), 13*(3). Advance online publication. DOI: 10.3390/soc13030055

Atchley, P., Pannell, H., Wofford, K., Hopkins, M., & Atchley, R. A. (2024). Human and AI collaboration in the higher education environment: Opportunities and concerns. *Cognitive Research: Principles and Implications*, *9*(1). Advance online publication. DOI: 10.1186/s41235-024-00547-9 PMID: 38589710

Babashahi, L., Barbosa, C. E., Lima, Y., Lyra, A., Salazar, H., Argôlo, M., Almeida, M. A. D., & Souza, J. M. D. (2024). AI in the Workplace: A Systematic Review of Skill Transformation in the Industry. *Administrative Sciences*, *14*(6). Advance online publication. DOI: 10.3390/admsci14060127

Blaurock, M., Büttgen, M., & Schepers, J. (2025). Designing Collaborative Intelligence Systems for Employee-AI Service Co-Production. *Journal of Service Research*, *28*(4), 544–562. DOI: 10.1177/10946705241238751

Erzed, N., Laksana, R. P., Hasanudin, H., Yuhefizar, Y., Anwar, N., Gunawan, H., Sekti, B. A., & Ichwani, A. (2025). Exploring the metaverse: Foundations of social interaction and community building. In *Unveiling Social Dynamics and Community Interaction in the Metaverse* (pp. 1–25). https://doi.org/DOI: 10.4018/979-8-3693-8628-6.ch001

Furendal, M., & Jebari, K. (2023). The Future of Work: Augmentation or Stunting? *Philosophy & Technology*, *36*(2). Advance online publication. DOI: 10.1007/s13347-023-00631-w

Hemmer, P., Schemmer, M., Kühl, N., Vössing, M., & Satzger, G. (2025). Complementarity in human-AI collaboration: Concept, sources, and evidence. *European Journal of Information Systems.* Advance online publication. DOI: 10.1080/0960085X.2025.2475962

Hemmer, P., Westphal, M., Schemmer, M., Vetter, S., Vössing, M., & Satzger, G. (2023). Human-AI Collaboration: The Effect of AI Delegation on Human Task Performance and Task Satisfaction. *International Conference on Intelligent User Interfaces, Proceedings IUI*, 453–463. https://doi.org/DOI: 10.1145/3581641.3584052

Kirkby, A., Baumgarth, C., & Henseler, J. (2025). Welcome, new brand colleague! A conceptual framework for efficient and effective human–AI co-creation for creative brand voice. *Journal of Brand Management*, *32*(5), 385–399. DOI: 10.1057/s41262-025-00387-y

Korzynski, P., Kim, S., & Egan, T. (2024). Bridging human resource development processes through generative Artificial Intelligence. *Human Resource Development Quarterly*, *35*(3), 247–256. DOI: 10.1002/hrdq.21551

Li, L. (2024). Correction to: Reskilling and Upskilling the Future-ready Workforce for Industry 4.0 and Beyond (Information Systems Frontiers, (2024), 26, 5, (1697-1712),). *Information Systems Frontiers, 26*(5), 1713. https://doi.org/DOI: 10.1007/s10796-022-10308-y

Nguyen, T., & Elbanna, A. (2025). Understanding Human-AI Augmentation in the Workplace: A Review and a Future Research Agenda. *Information Systems Frontiers*. Advance online publication. DOI: 10.1007/s10796-025-10591-5

Przegalinska, A., Triantoro, T., Kovbasiuk, A., Ciechanowski, L., Freeman, R. B., & Sowa, K. (2025). Collaborative AI in the workplace: Enhancing organizational performance through resource-based and task-technology fit perspectives. *International Journal of Information Management*, *81*. Advance online publication. DOI: 10.1016/j.ijinfomgt.2024.102853

Rastogi, S., & Pandita, D. (2025). Driving entrepreneurial success: Navigating AI-driven transformation through workforce agility and sustainability. *Journal of Innovation and Entrepreneurship*, *14*(1). Advance online publication. DOI: 10.1186/s13731-025-00554-0

Vaccaro, M., Almaatouq, A., & Malone, T. (2024). When combinations of humans and AI are useful: A systematic review and meta-analysis. *Nature Human Behaviour*, *8*(12), 2293–2303. DOI: 10.1038/s41562-024-02024-1 PMID: 39468277

Wang, N., Kim, H., Peng, J., & Wang, J. (2025). Exploring creativity in human–AI co-creation: A comparative study across design experience. *Frontiers of Computer Science*, *7*. Advance online publication. DOI: 10.3389/fcomp.2025.1672735

Woolley, A. W. (2025). Generative AI and collaboration: opportunities for cultivating collective intelligence. *Journal of Organization Design*. https://doi.org/DOI: 10.1007/s41469-025-00199-z

Wu, S., Liu, Y., Ruan, M., Chen, S., & Xie, X.-Y. (2025). Human-generative AI collaboration enhances task performance but undermines human's intrinsic motivation. *Scientific Reports*, *15*(1). Advance online publication. DOI: 10.1038/s41598-025-98385-2 PMID: 40301425

Xu, X., Arshad, M. A., He, Y., Liu, H., Chen, Q., & Yang, J. (2025). From Skilled Workers to Smart Talent: AI-Driven Workforce Transformation in the Construction Industry. *Buildings (Basel, Switzerland)*, *15*(14). Advance online publication. DOI: 10.3390/buildings15142552

Zirar, A., Ali, S. I., & Islam, N. (2023). Worker and workplace Artificial Intelligence (AI) coexistence: Emerging themes and research agenda. *Technovation*, *124*. Advance online publication. DOI: 10.1016/j.technovation.2023.102747

Chapter 5
Ethics of Creativity in the Age of AI

Manya Wadhwa
https://orcid.org/0009-0007-8185-7637
Christ University, Delhi, India

Deeksha Gupta Ganguly
https://orcid.org/0000-0002-5502-8276
Christ University, Delhi, India

ABSTRACT

The accelerated development of generative artificial intelligence has challenged the principles of creative practice and has laid down them as the established assumptions about the originality, intentions, and cultural significance of humans. This chapter critically discusses the intersection of AI-generated creativity with psychological theories of the agency of humans, social and cultural structures of meaning-making and emerging ethical issues of authorship, ownership and cultural representation. With reference to past and present studies, empirical results and technological advances, the chapter aims to point out the two-sided character of AI as the accelerant of creative possibility and the de-disturbing factor in artistic, economic and cultural ecosystems. It assesses the most notable risks, such as bias, cultural homogenization, deepfakes, labour displacement, and environmental costs, besides acknowledging the opportunities to democratize, make it more accessible and allow human-machine collaboration.

DOI: 10.4018/979-8-3373-7153-5.ch005

1. INTRODUCTION

The concept of creativity has always been considered as one of the most unique and distinctive features of human thought that lie in their ability of creative thinking, willful articulation, and culturally-based meaning-making. Scholars have theorized creativity to be as follows over centuries the ability to create work not only new but also useful and valuable suiting to a particular situation, combining mental, emotional, and social cultural aspects of human life (Kaufman and Glaveanu, 2019). This highly human notion puts creativity in the crossroads of cognitively ingenious and humanly agentic, meaning that the creative act is that cannot be separated by human intention, a situation, and existential manifestation.

Nevertheless, at the beginning of the twenty-first century, technological innovations in artificial intelligence have been developed. This human-centric view has started to be challenged by intelligence (AI). creating artifacts which seem (at any rate, superficially) to reflect or even surpass them. The emergence of AIs that can be generatively created has led to the creation of generative systems, creating written work, pictures, music, and so forth that are similar. Human work has set in a new analysis of the meaning of creativity in an urgent way. Modern society and what codes of ethics are required to regulate its exegesis where intelligent machines are in control. In essence, the creativity phenomenon has been characterized by scholars both within and outside disciplines as something that brings forth something new and useful or meaningful in its sociocultural environment. Although the psychological definitions as others emphasize novelty and suitability of the task as the main criteria. The value of creativity is paid attention to in the theoretical models not only to the production. Original products but also in providing contributions towards the development of culture and problem-solving skills (Kaufman and Glaveanu, 2019).

This dual focuses on uniqueness and the topicality is central to learning the reason behind such a complex connection between creative and human agency. Creative behaviors are influenced by experience, purpose or intent and by cultural models that pervade meaning. The new abilities of generative AI challenge this anthropocentric model through the generation of outputs without necessarily having those qualities of novelty and appropriateness in it. Thus, consciously, out of personal intention or cultural subjectivity challenging what has always been presumed about the place and substance of creativity agency. The creativity technological world has experienced dramatic changes. Change over the last few years that has been spurred by the development of machine learning, neural network models, and big data processing. Generative transformer-based language models, generative adversarial networks, and diffusion models have shown impressive capabilities of doing. Create new text, images and other media based on acquired statistical trends of training data.

This is not generated by internal means of these systems. Subjective experience; instead, they get to know the patterns of coding through the gigantic corpus of inhuman content, which allows them to reassemble stylistic elements and generate outputs which in many situations can be seen as indistinguishable to humans work in form and quality. Although AI tools can improve as scholars point out, they might still be harmful human creativity through extending the collection of potential ideas and the provision of speed. They are also prototyping, and they also bring complicated issues of authorship, ownership and the ethical nature of machine-generated work (Ivcevic and Grandinetti, 2024).

The increasing complexities of these systems have heightened controversies between, on the one hand, the fact that such products are a creative work and, on the other hand, their meaning. Sense or the term creativity should be redefined within this new technological paradigm. AI has far-reaching ethical consequences of its use in production of creative work multifaceted. On the simplest stage, AI may be applied to the creative workflows that put current legal and intellectual property frameworks to the test, which have traditionally been constructed according to the idea of identifiable human authorship.

When machines perform new, recognizable, and work that is new of cultural influence, the question of rights of such work may arise, who owns it, whether credit is due, and whether there should be the means of current copyright laws to have a work accommodated by such phenomena. Additionally, systems based on generative AI tend to learn based on the datasets that are based on human work that exists today, it is concerned about the violation of human creativity and the possible threat to the undermining of the monetary worth of innovative effort. These problems become more complicated in case of bias or unrepresentative training data, which are capable of reproducing or enhancing social imbalances and cultural distortions in generative outputs. According to the scholars of ethics, there is the necessity to reform legal, moral and cultural systems to make sure that innovative AI systems are implemented conscientiously and in a manner that respects human autonomy and diversity (Flick & Worrall, 2022).

Besides legal and economic issues, there are the philosophical and existential concerns aspects of the creativity of AI-mediation must be scrutinized. Creativity has been long allied with subjective intentionality, the power to express humanity, emotionality, and individuality. Machine systems are deficient of the inner life which is the indication of the creative processes in humans, creating objects without having experienced them or intended interpretation. This disjunction poses a problem on the authenticity of works of creativity and whether cultural value is to be assigned differently to human versus machine outputs. As an illustration, the perceptions of the audience toward AI and human creativity has tended to show that machine-generated content can be valued because it is new or technologically advanced, it is often considered to be devoid of the emotional appeal and contextual richness of human creativity (Leong, 2025).

These differences highlight the moral significance of maintaining human values and willfulness in creative practices, despite the fact that AI becomes a greater co-creator with human agents. Generative AI is increasingly rapidly integrated into the creative industries, which also introduces to it. Light problems of economic and labour revolution. While some proponents say that AI will improve productivity and democratize access to creative, others warn, it can put human creative work that is done by humans at a loss, or devalue it artistic talents, which have never been taught in a few years. As AI systems assume activities as simple as early design and drafting as well as entirely. Independent content development, creative experts have to maneuver through the changing professional identity, value and skill paradigms. This transformation refers to wider debates in the sociology of work regarding automation and worker displacement, which insists on policies to safeguard creative labor and support markets and shift to hybrid forms of human-machine collaboration. Ethical discussion in this field tends to promote that provide fair payment, rewards, and possibility to mankind creators without disregarding the works of technological systems. Bearing these developments in mind, this chapter provides an in-depth analysis of the ethics of creativity in the era of artificial intelligence, organized to survey the theoretical basis as well as the implications of creative processes mediated by AI. It interacts with basic theories of creativity, critically examines the changing scene of creative production.Evaluates ethical dilemmas, incorporates the results of empirical studies and thinks of governance structures and directions. By synthesizing cognitive science, philosophy, law interdisciplinary perspectives. This analysis attempts to express a position regarding cultural studies, and technological research subtle manipulation of AI transforming creativity -and how society needs to modify its ethical, legal and cultural structures.

Placing AI-generated creativity in the wider context of historical and theoretical contexts, the chapter previews the main point that although AI systems can widen the creative perspectives of expression, they equally require a rediscovery of norms governing the creative agency, value, and

responsibility. This preface preconditions further passages, that explore the literature of creativity theory, empirical knowledge on AI and human ingenuity, and the moral systems which should inform the accountable involvement of AI into creative environments.

2. LITERATURE REVIEW

The history of creativity literature has developed throughout a century and was manifested in the literature changes in psychology, philosophy, sociology and cognitive science. Early theories defined creativity as an ability of thought based on divergent thinking, and with the historic speech of Guilford to the American Psychological. Association indicating the point of change by making creativity a subject of intellectual investigation instead of mystified art. He argued that creativity involved fluency, flexibility and originality which became central in further studies (Guilford, 1950). Later scholars expanded beyond cognitive aspects to take into consideration sociocultural factors, implicating creativity in the spheres of knowledge and social systems to evaluate and validate novelty.

Systems model of Csikszentmihalyi anticipated the interaction between individual ability, area knowledge, and those who ensure the validity, in refurbishing creativity as a relational as opposed to solitary activity (Csikszentmihalyi, 1997). This perspective proves that creativity has always been not just what production; it is contextual interpretation and meaning-making that is constituted by cultural norms. The importance of such theories is still present in the context of artificial intelligence questions the conceptualization of novelty, value and authorship in modern creative cultures. Another critical level is offered by the philosophical approaches to creativity and literature. Aesthetic genius is a concept that forms the creative thinking of Kant. Native and unlearned human power which can deliver work that is more than formal or codified technique. He says that creative works bear the mark of the inner sensibility of the maker, an idea afterwards and adopted by the Romantic philosophers who regarded creativity as an expression of emotional genuineness and personality (Kant, 1790 /2000). These philosophical standpoints strengthen the anthropocentric belief in that creativity is based on subjective experiencething which is naturally unattainable to machines.

Modern researchers develop these concepts by stating that creativity cannot be perceived as outputs only, but it must have intention, consciousness and depth of experience (Gaut, 2010). These organizational structure philosophies make the process of categorizing machine-generated difficult. The debates in AI creativity are innovative, as it puts forward founded not merely in the performance which serves its purpose but in more profound questions of purpose, intent, which is a meaning and a tradition of thought, centuries old. It was during the late twentieth that there was a growing scientific study of the creativity century having cognitive models of creativity as an interaction between problem solving, conceptual growth and associative processes. The impactful theory of Owen employs the approaches of combinational, exploratory and transformational creativity, which are a different mode of generating novelty (Boden, 2004). These groups assist in framing the discussion regarding.

Combinational and exploratory creativity can be artificial intelligence since they can be calculated algorithmically, but transformational creativity--the manipulation of the very rules of a field--is retained uniquely human. Neural and cognitive studies have also been investigated by researchers. Dynamics of creative thinking, the importance of executive network of control and associative processing during creation of new ideas (Runco).

& Acar, 2012). Through these insights creativity is a dynamic cognition phenomenon that implies the spontaneous and deliberate processes. When treated together with machine learning systems, which are based on statistical. Instead of cognitive processes, inference these models assert foundational still vary as much in the human and machine creative processes. Superficial resemblances of output become more and more believable. First artificial intelligence was brought to the creative literature.

The early computational models, which are modest, existed in the 1960s and 1970s. Systems similar to AARON, an art-generating program, the creation of which is autonomous and is run by Harold Cohen. Demonstrated that it was possible to simulate stylistic features of using rule-based algorithms human art. These early systems though revolutionary at the time were deficient in flexibility, situational sensitivity, and abilities to learn (McCorduck, 1991). The debate in philosophy was further escalated as Searle came up with the Chinese Room argument, an argument that asserts that machines are manipulating symbols without knowing, therefore without intentionality even though their outputs seem to be meaningful (Searle, 1980). This is the main point that is still important to modernity debates on AI creativity, which claims to achieve categorical difference between syntactic calculation and semantic understanding. As cognitive scientists and philosophers then proceeded to analyze computational creativity, they tended in general to conclude that machines were capable of simulating some formal formations of creativeness, they did not have the subjective consciousness and life experience that give human acts of creativity a sense.

These debates constituted the philosophical basis upon which current debates concerning exist generative AI rest. With the creation of AI, the modern age of creativity based on AI came machine learning frameworks that can be trained on the massive data with strata neural representations. Deep generative models were introduced, like generative adversarial networks, machines were allowed to generate highly realistic pictures by use of competitive training processes (Goodfellow et al., 2014). Transformer architecture The next development was the revolution of transformer architecture's natural language computing by permitting models to encode long-range dependencies, giving rise to unprecedented text (Vaswani et al., 2017).

Even finer models of diffusion were introduced generative capabilities, generating images of high resolution and style coherence. With these technological innovations, scholars decided to go back.

AI systems exhibited capabilities, and basic definitions of creativity were made which used to be considered as a prerogative of humans. It is claimed that such systems are ineffective as researchers believe that such systems fail to achieve their goals. The lack of creative understanding, they are computational in their creativity by means of their capability to produce novel patterns using learned distributions. (Colton & Wiggins, 2012). According to this school of thought, machine creativity can be viewed may form a separate type of study, independent of human useful creative but to the society. The literature on AI creativity has evolved at an accelerated rate in respect to ethics the implications of training data, authorship and the cultural issues impact of generative models. Research indicates that AI brought to learn on scraped internet contents often contain copyrighted information, cultural items and confidential information unwillingly, which casts serious ethical doubts concerning exploitation and intellectual property (Henderson et al., 2023). Scholars contend that due to this accrued knowledge, AI models are thus able to generate their capabilities.

Their outputs cannot be ethically disentangled with human knowledge authors the works of which constitute the training corpus. Others highlight fears of biasness in datasets, demonstrating that generative models frequently replicate racial, gender and cultural stereotypes found in the raw data (Buolamwini and Gebru, 2018). These results highlight the importance of the need to have strict datasets management and regulatory control, as innovative AI systems construct cultural discourses and shape the way societies perceive. Ethical concepts put forward by such organizations as UNESCO and the European Commission insist on transparency, fairness and accountability as fundamental. best practices in the creation of creative AI systems, which are stimulated mitigating risks and promoting responsible through technologists and policymakers innovation (UNESCO, 2021).On the whole, the literature proves that the meeting point of creativity and artificial intelligence is a place of deep theoretical, moral and practical complexity. Human creativity theories focus on intention technological developments, and sociocultural meaning, consciousness refute these intuitions by showing machine produced novelty. Computational understanding is also involved in philosophical discussions regarding the nature of understanding the empirical evidence on the cognitive processes, and there are ethical issues related to application of man-made data and cultural influence of AI-generated artifacts. This comprehension of scholarship underscores the necessity of caution theoretical and ethical reflection the more AI is incorporated into creative domains.

3. CREATIVITY IN THE AGE OF AI

This has changed the creativity landscape dramatically since it has become artificial intelligence systems are more and more enshrined in arts and literature, scientific, and commercial artistic practices. In the past, creativity used to be considered as a specifically human ability born out of individual will, emotional experience, and cultural meaning interpretation capability. With the generative artificial intelligence emergence, but at that point, the limits boundaries between machine and human creativity have become more porous. Creative production can no longer be a matter of individuals acting through. Conventional mental or artistic activities; rather, it has extended to embrace agentic algorithms that can generate new and aesthetically interesting outputs at scale. According to scholars, this technological turn is nothing but a development of tools of creativity, but a metamorphosis of the very ontology of creative practice, putting into question the belief that creativity has to have their origin in the conscious mental states or subjective human experience (Boden, 2004).

The introduction of AI into creative labor is a complete change the value of creativity is ascribed, and the conceptualization of authorship, and how new reality and meaning are perceived by the society (Gunkel, 2018). As these the technological systems are constantly developing, they challenge scholars and practitioners to rethink making something in a time when machines is capable of producing outputs that reflect or even exceed human handwork (Colton and Wiggins, 2012).

Artificial intelligence is a tool that is not similar to other traditional tools of creativity pattern generation with autonomy and massive combinatorical processing. Although, the old tools like the paintbrush, camera and musical instruments were used in the past amplified human intent, generative artificial intelligence systems roll out a novel paradigm where machines do not simply do what humans direct them to do, but add independent to the creative process. These systems are conditioned with huge volumes of data made up of human cultural production, allowing them to recognize patterns of style and re-combine features in a manner producing new artifacts and without the need to have a human operator to make every creative decision.

This shift is to say that creative products are not produced by humans alone but as a result of human prompting, algorithmic inference, and statistical pattern modeling. The scholars believe that such a dynamic of cooperation exists transforms the creativity as an individual process into a hybrid system in that are the machines involved as quasi-autonomous creative agents (Gervais, 2020). Even though AI systems lack subjective instincts, their competence to produce fluent, coherent and aesthetically competent productions makes the classical divisions of creator and tool complicated (Floridi, 2014). This novel form of shared innovation begs to be reevaluated as to how creativity agency is shared among sociotechnical networks and is blurred old traditional mental frontiers.

The other major aspect of the creative environment in flux is related to scale and speed. Creativity in human beings is a process that is traditionally iterative test and errors and the progressive improvement of skill. Generative AI systems, on the contrary, generate huge amounts of new content in seconds. The capacity to create hundreds of possible solutions, variations, or artistic ideas quickly change the creative processes allowing new ones escapes of bulk experimentation that had been limited to human cognitive and temporal weaknesses. Such acceleration can This acceleration can open up the scope of the creative exploration, yet it can bring risks of burdening human appraisal abilities and reducing the perceptions & price of separate creative works.

According to scholars, the spread of the artificial intelligence created content can lead to cultural saturation, where something new is desired. So prolific that its meaning is undermined (Manovich, 2020). Besides, the unparalleled magnitude of machine-generated creativity increases philosophical queries on whether novelty was generated by use of statistics recombination must be thought of as having the same value as novelty generated in human will and in experience (Gaut, 2010). As AI becomes faster, the society has to struggle with the implications of plenty on culture appreciation and meaning in art. Another important issue in the cultural homogenization is the cultural homogenization changing creative environment. The fact that generative AI models are trained on huge data makes them learn data sets frequently represent the prevailing cultural conventions and aesthetic patterns, their products are more likely to copy or support mainstream fashions as they do by ignoring artistic manifestations that are marginalized or underrepresented. Scholars have proven that training datasets are often overrepresented. Resulting in western, commercial, or popular cultural forms, the AI systems are create products that are biased in these aesthetics (Buolamwini and Gebru, 2018).

This brings ethical issues of erasure or co-optation of minority voices, especially as the AI-generated styles are perceived as global aesthetic standards. The machine learning effect poses a threat of homogenization the cultural diversity that is necessary in order to be innovative and in order to develop art, potentially reducing the scope of creative options in the modern society. This relationships demonstrates the need of deliberate dataset design and training techniques that are culturally inclusive, such that generative AI systems do not represent a single artistic tradition of humanity but its entire range strengthening the dominant discourses (UNESCO, 2021). Without such efforts, the inculcation of AI in creative sectors will propagate institutionalized injustices and reducing cultural plurality in worldwide creative-ecosystems.

Meanwhile, the developing creative environment also unveils the significant possibilities of human empowerment and enlarged artistic possibility. Generative AI solutions reduce the entry barrier, allowing individuals with low entry technical ability or preparation to engage in production of creativity. In contexts intuitive

AI systems are provided in such fields as music, visual art, and digital design user interfaces that enable non-expert users to make advanced outputs with low level of manual intervention. This creativity democratization is in line with greater cultural changes to participatory media and user-generated content, making more people creators and creativity in other forms is possible recognized. On behalf of people with disabilities or restricted access AI can serve as an enabling technology that can supplement traditional artistic device enables creativity that is not normally available. Scholars argue that this enlargement of the expressive possibility is a favourable and transformative. AI potential, enabling human prosperity through creating new ways exploratory creativity . This has been shown by these developments to indicate that AI has not only a disruptive role in creativity, it can be incredibly extensive human-centered ethical awareness deployed and empowering design. This is coupled with tensions that are associated with these opportunities originality of the artistic works in partnership with or wholly by AI. The concept of authenticity has always been considered as a foundation of art value, associated with the intent of the creator, expression of emotions and personal background. The produced artifacts in AI-generated works contradict this fact since they lack experience of man but able to call forth emotion in audiences. The aesthetics and art-theory research has indicated that visions of genuineness is a factor that determines the aesthetic value of artistic work by the audience. Artifacts created by humans are often viewed as being more important because of their relation to a subjective experience of the creator (Gunkel, 2018).

When AI generates similar products, the connection between authenticity and artistic value will be destabilized. Others say that authenticity ought to be redefined with respect to conceptual intent as opposed to origin, others warning that machine generated outputs should not be compared to human creativity at risk. Created a situation in which it reduces the cultural meaning of the human expression (Leong, 2025). These controversies highlight the importance of subtle ethical consideration as AI reinvents artistic categories of tradition.

The changing creative is also complicated by economic and labour dynamics landscape. The adoption of AI in various sectors like illustration, graphic design, writing, animation, and film production brings up job issues. dislocation and the demarcation of creative labour. AI systems can replicate traditional stylistic features which used to take years of artistic training to develop, diminished need of some types of human skills. Scholars warn that such disruptions can increase economic inequality and destabilize the.

sustainability of the creative professions (Hesmondhalgh, 2021). At the same time, new creative positions are emerging - AI art direction, computational curation, and timely engineering--that demand new expertise Combining aesthetic taste and technological expertise.

These hybrid professions depict that although the use of AI can revolutionize creative labour, it also enables the new creative identities and industries to emerge.

However, there has to be ethical governance in order to make sure that transitions in the creative economy do not take advantage of human creators and undermine the cultural and monetary worth of human artistic endeavor. When combined, the changing environment of creativity is an indicator of a complex interaction of human agency, machine possibility, cultural meaning and ethical responsibility. The change is neither gradual nor even; it is defined by possibilities to collaborate and empowerment as well as threats of homogenization, displacement and cultural distortion. Artificial intelligence has not only influenced the way the works of creativity are created but also the way the society perceives creativity. The developments require continuous critical thought, cross-disciplinary research, and sound ethical governance so that creativity should be an area that is in support of human living in the era of smart machines.

4. ETHICAL ASPECTS OF AI-GENERATED CREATIVITY

The ethical aspects of AI-created creativity are much broader than technological ability questions, right at the very heart of societal way of being know authorship, agency, accountability, as well as the cultural role of creative expression. The issue of authorship is central to these issues. Authorship has traditionally been associated with the existence of intentional, conscious human agency, one of the requirements that generative AI systems lack. While human creative works are influenced by purpose, practice and contextual interpretation AI systems produce outputs using algorithmic process and probabilistic modeling. This poses some issues in the field of law. and philosophical structures which suppose that the creator is a moral agent able to be responsible and have rights.

Researchers point out that AI-created writings disturb the established association between authorship and personhood, which has resulted in a reconsideration of the way in which societies attribute creative credit and defend the intellectual property in the age of automated creativity. (Samuelson, 2023). Also, AI systems are more expressive, as they are based on them capacities using the training data created by humans, there are questions as to whether the results of their production can never be really detached out of the creative labour embedded in that data . These overlapping problems show that AI does not only oppose legal frameworks but it also opposes grounding moral.

The other ethical issue of high importance is the bias in AI-generated content. Because they learn large collections of examples drawn out of human culture, using generative models always pass on the prejudices and stereotypes and power disparities that exist in those datasets. Such biases may be realized in creative products, which is possible strengthen negative cultural discourses or marginalize alternative identities. Scholars have demonstrated that AI-generated images, language and character representations usually reveal the presence of racial and gender stereotypes in the form of representations training corpora (Buolamwini and Gebru, 2018).

In the context of creative production, such that AI-generated stories, artworks or character are produced designs can continue to propagate discriminatory tropes as being neutral computation. According to the ethical scholars, the broad phenomenon is manifested through this phenomenon, sociotechnical problem of algorithmic bias, where apparently objective systems replicate structural injustices existing in society (Noble, 2018). To handle this prejudice, one has to pay keen attention to dataset maintenance, model disclosure enhancement, and constant testing to make sure that creative AI systems do not replicate discriminative images. Without such efforts, AI dangers of rooting bad cultural habits in the pretext of aestheticism. Innovation, Another important ethical aspect is transparency, which is related to the origin of creative works and creative work processes. As the outputs of AI are more and more realistic and hard to differentiate in man-made artifacts, revelation is a necessity to maintain trust in innovational and informational ecosystems. Creative presented to audiences will result in creative works, be it works of art, stories, or multimedia, and do not realize that they were created through AI, they might draw interpretations or judgment on the basis of it on false grounds of authorship. Scholars have proved that individuals tend to judge creative works in ways that they feel they were one that was made by a person compared to a machine, tend to give it the added emotional resonance or genuineness to human-created works (Chamberlain et al., 2021).

The difference in perception makes the ethical significance of this distinction evident openness, especially on issues like journalism, education and others political communication, in which the origin of information has a significant impact its meaning. Creators and other ethical guidelines are increasingly suggesting, that creators ought to behave ethically platforms reveal the presence of AI to prevent deception of viewers, uphold accountability, and maintain significant differences between human and machine expression. Ethical issues are also brought up by the loss of creative labour, especially in such industries as illustration, writing, design, animation and so on. The creative tasks can be replicated by the generative AI systems very rapidly speed and cheapness, alarming that the human inventors will be displaced or deprived of their work their skills devalued. According to the economic researchers it has been observed that automation is inclined to favor hard hit roles, which are frequently gateways, on the entry level and to cultivate the art of new artists (Hesmondhalgh, 2021).

This can restrict the opportunities of the would-be aspirants in creative industries experts and concentrating production creativity in organizations that will be able to invest in AI tools. Meanwhile, there are scholars who assert the same that AI can enhance and not substitute creative human work, and artists can work more effectively and develop new expressiveness (Runco and Jaeger, 2012). The ethical problem is in making sure the benefits of AI-assisted creativity are shared fairly and creators whose work makes a contribution. to training data get due reward and pay. In the absence of equal economic systems, the AI incorporation threatens to cement imbalances and compromising sustainable creative labour markets. Another fundamental ethical problem is accountability, especially when AI generated content is harmful or misleading. Creative works *can influence the opinion of the masses, mobilize, and affect political or cultural attitudes. In cases where AI systems produce harmful falsely, or deceptive matter, and who is to be held is made complex. According to scholars the responsibility should be left to the humans who design, deploy, and use AI systems, as machine systems are incapable of doing the same, have moral agency or be responsible about their actions (Floridi, 2014). To protect the end-users, developers are ethically required to put up measures, including usage guidelines or content filters, whereas the users have to use AI tools in a responsible and ethical and lawful manner. Without clearing the structures of accountability, AI-created creativity are going to be used as a transmission line of untraceable damage, undermining popular faith and disrupting the informational landscape. Cultural appropriation also makes the ethical landscape of AI a bit more complex creativity.

Most generative models are trained on datasets comprising of without artworks of a certain culture, conventional patterns, and stylistic motifs permission or context. When the AI replicates or copies these cultural words, it tends to deprive them of their historical and spiritual meanings, and degrading them into commodities that can be used commercially or not recreational use. Researchers have cautioned that such practices are some of the forms of digital colonialism, where such cultural heritage of Indigenous or marginalized communities is mined and used without permission or benefit (Lewis et al., 2020). To create ethical governance, it must have mechanisms prevent algorithmic abuse of cultural manifestation, make it consent-based data practices, and acknowledge the entitlement of communities to manage how their cultural materials are used.

Lastly, creative authenticity is redefined again as AI is transforming cultural demands and artistic standards. Artistic audiences have long treasured artistic works because of their relation to the human experience, emotion, and intention. The works produced by AIs break these expectations by generating affective or objectively, aesthetically complex products without experiencing. Ethically, this leaves one wondering whether individuals have emotional reactions to AI-generated. works are also lost or can artistic meaning be created by itself of creator intentionality. Philosophers believe that meaning is made through viewers and objects, which implies that artificial intelligence-created works can attain cultural value by interpreting them although they may not have been written by humans (Gunkel, 2018). The moral dilemma is on what to do to maintain the cultural values of human creativity and at the same time considering the interpretive richness created by viewers of machine-generated art. On the whole, the ethical aspects of AI creativeness disclose a complex terrain that necessitates cautious legal, philosophical and cultural navigation. Generative systems are more embedded in creativity as they become more ingrained practices, society has to evolve structures which safeguard human creators, maintain cultural diversity, accountability and ethical standards against the fast-changing technology.

5. HUMAN MEANING-MAKING, AUTHENTICITY, AND CULTURAL VALUES

Human Meaning-Making, Authenticity, and Cultural Values Human meaning making, probably, is a stage where humans begin to create and shape their personal identities through a system of meaningful theories and knowledge that informs their effectiveness in daily life. Human Meaning-Making, Authenticity and Cultural Values, Premiably, a human being stage in which human beings begin to create and shape their own identities through a paradigm of meaningful theories and knowledge, that informs their efficacy in the daily life. Historically, human creativity has been described as being based on the framework of meaning-making, the emotionality, and the deliberate expression of concepts based on individual and cultural contexts of life. Human creative acts are unlike the algorithmic processes in which they are formed based on contexts that have psychological, social, and historical meanings. Researchers repeatedly highlight the idea that the meaning is never directly imbued in creative artifacts but rather it is created as a result of interaction between producer, work and audience; that is in a trio relationship, which can not yet be reproduced by artificial intelligence (Gaut, 2010).

Human makers bring presence of experiences that are embodied, emotional, cultural, and interpretive nuances to their work, all elements of the latter add realistic value to the end product. Verisimilitude in artistic behavior hence cannot be divorced of existential and subjective aspects of human existence, of which generative AI, successful in its aesthetics modelling, is essentially deprived (Leong, 2025). This difference highlights the role of human will in locating the purpose and significance of creative objects that occur to inspire worries based on how artificial products created by AI might shift cultural conceptions of authenticity in artistic and communicative realms. Authenticity has long been associated with the existence of someone who creates the creative work with intentions that add a sense of direction and meaning to the work. The philosophical underpinnings of this idea go right back to the aesthetic theory, in which thinkers like Heidegger and then Danto postulated that the key to interpreting the meaning of a work was to know about the situation of the creator; their intentions, and their experience.

In this perspective, authenticity is not only a quality of the artifact but it is the connection between the lived experience, the life of the artist and the experience of the audience on the artifact (Danto, 1981). As generative AI is being introduced and creative artifacts lose their connections to intentional and subjective causes, this longstanding structure is challenged. In spite of the fact that the AI systems can reproduce some aspects of style with stunning precision, they are not able to give an original meaning as they are deprived of consciousness, emotional background, and historical context (Gunkel, 2018). The lack of intentionality, according to the arguments of scholars, does not exclude the meaningful interpretation of AI-generated works by viewers, but it radically changes the origin of such meaning, replacing it almost exclusively with the viewer (Chamberlain et al., 2021). The change causes serious inquiries on how society will draw the line between genuine and electrostatic creativity with the growth of machine-generated productions in artistic and cultural domains.The other relevant aspect of sense-making is in regard to how emotion can be applied in creative expression.

The creative acts of humans are often inspired by emotional experiences happiness, suffering, fear, wonder, nostalgia and, with the help of these feelings, it is possible to designate the process of creation as well as to influence the structure and the tone of the created artworks. Psychological research shows that the expressiveness of emotion is a feature of human performance art, which adds to the aesthetic depth, resonance, and interpretive richness (Ivcevic and Brackett, 2015). In contrast, AI systems are fake emotional contents generated by statistical trends acquired on training data; they are not emotional and do not change states of affect to creative output. This fact gives rise to suspicions that the products of AI-generated art, even with the high level of its imitation, will not be emotional as human creativity is seen. According to scholars, the danger here does not lie in the fact that AI may not trigger emotional responses in audiences but in the fact that audiences could start to mistake emotional simulation with emotional experience and undermine the cultural significance that they attach to emotional expression by a human being (Cuffari, 2022).

This brings ethical issues over the way the AI can redefine emotional norms in creative situations, and it can replace the role of a lived human experience in the production of art. There is also involvement of cultural values in AI-generated creativity issues wherein creative arts usually tend to act as archives of cultural memory, identity and tradition. The art of humans has often been produced in response to certain cultural context that assigns the piece of art a symbolic dimension, historical and communal scope. In the instances that AI systems produce creative outputs based on the patterns of globalization information, they can overturn or recreate such cultural settings to come up with outputs that seem aesthetically pleasing but without any cultural merit.

According to scholars, digital appropriation of some cultural materials extracted into the training dataset without a decent contextualization or consent might result in such types of cultural expressions losing their connection to the workforce that created them (Lewis et al., 2020). Indicatively, Indigenous motifs trained by AI as cultural irrelevance can be indifferent to erasing culture instead of preserving it. This problem highlights why the ethical data governance practice has to consider the cultural roots, spiritual implications and communal rights of creative heritage (UNESCO, 2021). The absence of these safeguards will mean that AI will disproportionately reduce the cultural differences to generalized aesthetical patterns, which are not pertinent and profound. Finding meaning is complicated further by the fact that the boundary between human content and machine content is continuing to be blurred. The more the AI systems are enhanced to generate outputs that can be similar to those created by humans, the more the audience may lose the ability to recognize the source industry of a creative work, thus, it may change the way meaning is attributed and perceived. It has been discovered that viewers tend to assign more depth, complexity, and authenticity to content they think is produced by humans than when the content is the same as that of works produced by AI (Chamberlain et al., 2021). This implies that the meaning we perceive about the creative artifacts is determined not simply by the content of the artifacts but also along the beliefs about the identity of the person who created the artifacts.

As such, once the delimitations between the human and machine creativity are fused, meaning making processes can change in a manner that removes the cultural importance of human created works. Experts warn that in the event that AI-generated creativity is perplexing everywhere, audiences may reset their standards on what creativity is all about and choose technical novelty over emotion or contextual cohesion (Gaut, 2010). This transition has become a cultural risk, since it may reduce the value attached to creative insight of truly human form.

Lastly, it seems that human meaning-making and machine-generated creativity are to be mixed, which complicates the issue of what culture will develop into in the future. Diversity of human creativity has traditionally shaped the cultural change by innovation, experimentation, and reinterpretation of shared symbols. In the instances where AI intrudes into this process as a cultural artifact producer, it can affect the development of cultures in ways determined by algorithmic tendencies, not intentionality on the part of humans. Researchers believe that AI can create new aesthetic possibilities that can broaden the cultural boundaries, whereas the opponents fear that algorithmic creativity will lead to homogeneity and a lack of diversity (Manovich, 2020). The issue is how to make AI to complement instead of to replace the human art of meaning-making upon which cultural liveliness should be based. In order to retain the richness and multi-faceted nature of the human creative expression, the ethical monitoring, culturally adaptable design, and policies that safeguard the human enterprise of cultural expression are crucial in an era of swift technological transformations.

6. ETHICAL USE CASES AND RISKS OF AI-GENERATED CREATIVITY

Due to the blistering development of generative artificial intelligence, it has been applied to a vast range of the creative sphere, encompassing both visual arts and the musical composition of music as well as in journalism, advertising, design, and the discovery of new facts in science. As much as these systems come with huge advantages of enhanced creative efficiency, affections, and creativity, they equally present a range of ethical threats that need critical analysis. Democratization of creativity is one of the glaring ethical opportunities. AI tools also allow people who might not be artists with the traditional background or have disabilities to create art, it reduces the level of barriers to engagement in cultural production.

In the case of text-to-image and text-to-video systems, users are given the power to create elegant images by merely describing them, which makes it sound, thus converting who is a legitimate consumer of creative expression (Manovich, 2020). Simultaneously, the systems assist professional creators in developing concepts quickly, doing experiments faster, and creating many new forms and materials to experiment with art . But this widening of access to creativity is accompanied by ethical issues of authorship, loss of skill, and the possibility of creative watering down with artificial values in case the machine-generated material becomes ubiquitous (Leong, 2025). The two-sidedness of the effects of AI on creative accessibility implies the necessity of sophisticated ethical guidelines that would recognize the empowering and destabilizing possibilities of AI.

Deepfakes and newly introduced synthetic media is one of the most commonly discussed and socially important threats to AI-assisted creativity. Deepfake technologies are based on generative models to produce a lot of very realistic and fabricated visual and audio images and audio that may be saying or doing things that did not take place. The technologies are potentially dangerous to not only the privacy and reputation of every single person but also to the political stability, citizens trust, and the democratic procedures. It has been revealed that deepfakes are applicable to the sharing of fake news and manipulation of the masses in opposition to various news media and institutions (Vaccari and Chadwick, 2020). Such dangers are magnified by the fact that the generative AI can create deceitful media at vast quantities, and the boundaries between real and fake are more challenging to view as audiences grow.

Researchers believe that the threat of deception of deepfakes extends beyond the field of deception; it jeopardizes the underlying epistemic models because it undermines the confidence in visual and auditory data that the societies of today use to determine what the truth is (Chesney and Citron, 2019). These threats make technical protection, regulatory controls, and informing the population inevitable to make sure that the generative AI tools are not used to control, deceive, or hurt people and society. Another risk factor that may lead to an ethical problem in AI systems is cultural appropriation, which may result when such systems are trained to work with culturally specific or sacred works of art. The online data collected by machine learning models may include many gigabits without regard to the cultural importance or copyright of the material contained in it. When these systems multiply or reuse Indigenous imagery, existing patterns, or culture-based stories, they can unwillingly become enrolled in the process of cultural heritage appropriation and commodification. Researchers claim that AI-based cultural appropriation is a type of digital colonialism whereby dominant technological infrastructure takes cultural worth without permission or even in exchange (Lewis et al., 2020). It works to destabilize the relational as well as communal contexts that attach cultural artifacts with a meaning to them, substituting them with decontextualized simulations, which are shallow and unauthentic.

Ethical governance should thus encompass ownership, consent and contextual integrity of cultural contents that AI training datasets include in addition to the right of a community to determine how their cultural attachments are used. The other ethical risk is that of the psychological and emotional effects of the AI-generated creative content. Generative systems are capable of generating very strong feelings (through generating art, music, or stories) that makes a viewer, listener or reader see something to which they can also connect emotionally, but they do so without feeling. This relationship begs concerns on whether emotional involvement is authentic when the source does not have subjective consciousness. Researchers have observed that users can anthropomorphize AI systems or give inputs emotional content to outputs that are actually computational simulation (Gunkel, 2018).

This may result in falsified emotional responses, inappropriate attachments or unrealistic expectations concerning the ability of technology. Furthermore, audiences may be manipulated by evocative artificial intelligence, by engaging in targeted advertising, or persuasive personal storytelling, or political-based messages, which makes them see the manipulation of psychological vulnerabilities. Emotionally driven AI content ethics is therefore crucial to safeguard people against unreasonable influence and safeguard the authenticity of emotional experience in the artistic setting.

The other less common risk of AI-created creativity is environmental sustainability, which is becoming relevant. The mathematical computations involved in training large-scale generative models are astronomical, and they use lots of energy, as well as, contributing to carbon emissions. Research has shown that carbon footprint of training one large neural network can be similar to a few vehicles in their total lives (Strubell et al., 2019). The overall environmental impact of using generative systems in creative industries is a burning ethical issue as more people in the industry will be engaging in routine use of such systems. Although improvements in effective model creation and the use of renewable energy can provide possible mitigation approaches, the ethical analysis should include whether the generation benefits of the creation of AI-based generators are worth the environmental cost and what the costs will be used in a responsible way. The sustainability aspect of the concept of AI creativity indicates that technological planning and responsibility across the industry need to be long-term. The application of creative AI systems also permeates the use of copyright and intellectual property risks. Since generative models are trained on large collections of already existing works, many of which have a copyright, the result of their run will introduce some style or structure of human-written output.

It brings up both ethical and legal issues concerning whether the AI-generated works fall under the category of derivatives or not, whether their training is a violation of copyright, or human creators whose work is used to create AI models are entitled to compensation or recognition. The past several years have seen AI firms exposed on how they use copyrighted content without permission in training sets, and it has been questioned whether current intellectual property systems can regulate the use of generative technologies (Samuelson, 2023). Ethical theorists believe that the current copyright law needs to be adapted in light of the distributed aspect of the creative contribution towards the AI systems to provide fairness to human creators, but be open to the distinctiveness of algorithmic generativity.

Lastly, AI created content is an extended cultural threat of homogenization and adverse creative overload. Since AI systems tend to reproduce the stylistic trends that prevail in the training materials, the ubiquity of the generative tools can contribute to a diminishing aesthetics diversity. When creative sectors start to value machine-generated output a great deal when it comes to efficiency or commercial sustainability, the human creativity will be replaced by algorithmic efficiency optimized designs. Lecturers are worried that this kind of homogenization diminishes cultural pluralism and leaves less opportunities to get original or disruptive creative viewpoints brought by human creators (Manovich, 2020). To mitigate this threat, there should be a deliberate curation of the training data, encouraging other voices of creativity, and building models that embrace human innovativeness as well as machine-made innovation.

Overall, the benefits and risks of AI-generated creativity ethical use cases provide a very intricate network of empowerment, destabilization, opportunity, and threat. Although generative AI is promising game-changing possibilities in enlarging creative expression and accessibility, it also has social, cultural, psychological, legal, economic and environmental risks. It requires strong ethical systems that can help manage these tensions and continue to develop AI and its application in creative professions in a responsible manner.

7. EMPIRICAL AND RESEARCHED FINDINGS ON AI-GENERATED CREATIVITY

Empirical studies about AI-generated creativity can offer the necessary insights into the ways in which individuals, industries, and societies toward machine-produced creative artifacts. Among the most notable results of the empirical literature, one of the key conclusions is that the impressions of creativeness hold a crucial role in the perceptions of the audience depending on the beliefs people have regarding the identity of a creator. Psychology experiments and human-computer interaction studies always show that subjects give different ratings of a creative work when informed that it was created by a human being in comparison to when informed that it was created by an artificial intelligence system. Although the content of the works can be the same, people tend to find greater expressive substances, cultural meaning, or aesthetic value in those works that are thought to have been made by humans as opposed to machines (Chamberlain et al., 2021).

This would mean that even the contribution of value that society imparts onto creative works is not purely based on the final product alone but on the perceived existence of human intent behind it (Gunkel, 2018). These results support the evidence that AI challenges are so culturally rooted in people's views about creativity that they make people question how the meaning and value will change when AI-generated content becomes more and more unclear about the originator (Leong, 2025). The experiments of public perception have also shown that trust, transparency, and AI-generated creativity acceptance have a complicated relationship.

Scholarly literature on the topic of survey research on various cultural groups suggests that people have a higher perception of AI-generated creative outputs when the generation method is transparent and when they are aware of the constraints of the related systems (Brynjolfsson & McAfee, 2019). On the other hand, the lack of transparency and ambiguity in the AI involvement can reduce the level of trust and make audiences feel uncomfortable and question the ethics and quality authenticity of the work. This is not isolated, as in the wider human-computer interaction literature, the general belief in transparency is presented as the foundational approach to responsible AI structure and design, especially when creative or informative content that originated with the source is directly used to draw conclusions about credibility, e.g., in the domains of journalism, education, or public communication . When generative AI systems become a part of cultural production, it will be of essence to keep the system transparent so that the population will not lose trust in it and that listeners and viewers are not deceived regarding the source of creative content they consume (Floridi, 2014).

The research at the industry level helps to understand additional ways in which creative industries are getting adjusted to the adoption of generative artificial intelligence. The concept of AI tools in these areas like animation, graphic design, illustration, marketing, journalism, and game development is becoming a daily type of workflow in many instances that do not supplant human creation. Research findings show that artificial intelligence saves creators considerably more time on ideation, prototyping and iteration and allows them to consider a larger range of options within a shorter time frame (Hesmondhalgh, 2021). To take just but a few examples, designers can apply AI to come up with hundreds of stylistic variations of a layout, whereas writers can use text-generation models to brainstorm plot or perfect narrative structures. Meanwhile, empirical evidence suggests that the incorporation of AI tends to alter work-related roles and demands, as innovators need to acquire new skills, including timely engineering, algorithmic proficiency, and multifunctional innovative-technical expertise (Sun and Medaglia, 2019). Such a change implies that the future of creative labour will rely on how efficiently the workers combine human intuition with the machine-inspired generativity through the collaboration with AI systems.

In spite of these advantages of AI, reports of its destabilizing impacts on creative labour markets also exist in studies of the industries. The lower-tier roles in creative industry- junior illustrators, copywriters, and storyboard artists are especially susceptible to automation since AI can potentially perform a lot of the menial work that was traditionally performed by these professionals in their initial years (Huang and Rust, 2021). The consequence of this displacement is being questioned as to the sustainability of creative career pipeline, since depriving the entry-level jobs deprives the conventional methods through which aspiring creative individuals gain knowledge and skill set and graduate their careers. In addition, empirical studies indicate that employees who depend more on manual forms of creativity also indicate that they feel anxious about losing their jobs when exposed to AI-generated material that threatens or surpasses their technical accuracy. These papers demonstrate the necessity of policies and systems that can assist creative professionals with the shifts in technology so that the implementation of AI does not contribute to inequality or loss of professional development opportunities.

Generative AI systems have been technologically assessed with positive results and significant shortcomings. Empirically, in terms of capability experts have shown that large-scale neural networks are superior at recognizing patterns, styling emulating, and multimedia generation, allowing them to create very realistic images, coherent text, and novel designs in accordance with the human creative norms (Goodfellow et al., 2014). Nonetheless, it has always been demonstrated that such systems are incapable of contextual awareness and their outputs tend to be factually incorrect, logically inconsistent, or even culturally unacceptable (Bender et al., 2021). An example of this can be seen with language models and fake information being hallucinated or the prompts being misunderstood, and with visual models having some distorted or impossible anatomiers. These restrictions are essential to highlight that, although AI is able to emulate the outward look of creativity, it lacks the cognitive and interpretative insight that drives creativity among humans. The value of human intervention and editorial judgment in such cases is justified, and it is especially needed in areas where accuracy, cultural sensitivity or moral subtlety is needed.

Other significant domains of empirical studies are the structure of AI training sets. Research indicates that a lot of the data utilized to train generative models is a copyrighted and culturally sensitive artifact, or a biased view of race, gender, and identity; most of this data is frequently scraped off the internet without obtaining informed consent. Due to this, the outputs of AI might unintentionally contain these biases or imitate styles of artists unwillingly, which not only raises ethical but also legal concerns. Empirical data show that datasets tend to promote the visual and linguistic norms of whites and western views more predominantly, thus resulting in no diversity of the generated output (Buolamwini and Gebru, 2018). These results are relevant to the fact that there is an imminent necessity of the clear results of the dataset management, ethical management and participation-based approaches, which would help to involve marginalized communities in the discourse concerning the utilization of their cultural products.

In the absence of these reforms, AI will still be used to reproduce and enhance the existing social inequities in creative settings. Lastly, there is contemporary scientific research use on the interaction of users with AI tools finding multidimensional psychological impacts. Users have also expressed greater creative confidence and expanded imagination as a result of working with computerized intelligent systems, and they cite AI as the factor triggering their creativity to overcome creative block or experiment with novel artistic forms (Sarkar and Cooper, 2022). Some are affected with low self-esteem, fear, or identity loss, especially when the results of the AI-generated output are seen to exceed their creative work.

This ambivalence is evidence of larger psychological controversies concerning automation, self-efficacy, and human-machine comparison relationships. The reviewed emotional reactions to AI cooperation illustrate the necessity of ethical designing behavior that contributes to human welfare, creates new realist expectations, and encourages empowerment instead of discouragement in the creative community. Altogether, existing empirical studies of creativity based on AI portray the image of radical change, which is both facilitating and disruptive. The results support the need to promote the use of interdisciplinary ethical frameworks, evidence-based policy-making and culturally sensitive governance to make sure that AI introduction in the creative industries improves instead of harms human prosperity.

8. GOVERNANCE, POLICY, AND BEST PRACTICES FOR ETHICAL AI CREATIVITY

The regulation of AI-generated creativity is one of the most urgent issues in the modern technological ethics since the current law, cultural and institutional frameworks are unable to keep up with the rapid development of generative systems. Conventional copyright, such as that, is based on the supposition that creative work is by identifiable human hands, that the moral and economic right of the creative work is vested in the author of the intellectual work. Generative AI systems essentially threaten this presupposition because they yield artifacts, which it is impossible to conceive as created due to the conscious agency, and they cast very important questions about the nature of ownership, responsibility, and the juridical status of machine-produced material.

Legal experts have claimed that the existing copyright legal frameworks should be made to handle AI creativity complexity given that they fail to create and acknowledge the contributory factor of datasets, they also fail to spare at least the absence of intentional authorship in AI works (Samuelson, 2023). Furthermore, legal courts and regulatory bodies all over the world have started to give conflicting decisions on whether AI-generated works should be considered a copyright-qualified work, but this clarifies that global systems should be harmonized to give a clear signal and to promote the ethical use of creative AI (Gervais, 2020). Arranged with no explicit governance frameworks, creators, companies, and consumers exist in the dark about their rights and obligations in the creative economy that is changing .

Another underlying issue that is necessary and urgent regulation is dataset governance. Giant AI models are trained on large collections of text, image, audio and video files, most of which are copyrighted, culturally sensitive, polygraphically gathered and more. Such datasets are the matter of AI creativity, as they give the patterns based on which new outputs are created. Empirical studies have demonstrated that training corpora frequently contain copyrighted works of art (and personal information and cultural artifacts) on which the creators have not granted a license to the use of machine learning). Consequently, copyrighted material can be adequately remixed or recreated following artistic styles by generative systems that are infringing intellectual property values. In this area, ethical administration should involve clear reporting of the sources of the data, ways to provide creators to consent or dissent, and suitable compensation structures, which will reflect the worth of the assistance provided by the artists. Quite a number of policymakers and scholars are now arguing in favor of dataset licensing frameworks wherein developers of AI make legally binding agreements with creators to grant access to their creations but still permit technological development (Crootof & Ard, 2022). These structures model a crucial move in the direction of making the advantages of generative AI come at a price other than misusing the creative human nature.

The systems of accountability are also at the heart of the AI-generated creativity management. The further the generative systems get in creation of complicated and self-directed outputs, the harder it is to fix accountability to harmful and misdirected content and even unethical content. In biases, developers can use the fact that machine learning models are unpredictable as an excuse to escape liability, whereas users can excuse themselves by stating that they gave prompts without incurring any harmful outcome. Such statements are refuted by ethical researchers who note that on the one hand, accountability should be kept squarely in human hands, both developers and users since machines are morally inactive and cannot be held responsible (Floridi, 2014). Governance structures should therefore consist of a clear division of responsibility, where the developers of the creative AI tools should set up protective measures like content filters, algorithm auditing, and safety measures protocols before such tools are released into the market. At the same time, it is important to inform the users of the ethical principles of using AI in creative practices, specifically in the professional world, such as journalism, education, political communication, and healthcare where the misuse of the generative content may cause considerable damage .

Responsible governance also centers on transparency as well as explainability. Considering the fact that AI-generated content is not always easy to identify as a piece of human-created work, transparency will help to prevent viewers and damage credibility. Transparency may exist in several different forms: a disclosure of the content created by AI, information on how the trained model was trained and how it was tested, as well as descriptions of the capabilities and shortcomings of the system itself. According to scholars, transparency is not only the key to preserving integrity of creative ecosystem but also to allowing the consideration of consumers when AI-generated content affects their decisions (Brynjolfsson, and McAfee, 2019). In the absence of precise disclosure, users can easily project human attributes on machine-generated texts or attribute unwarranted credence to emotional or informational levels of those texts. Transparency is one of the principles that regulatory bodies including UNESCO and the European Commission suggest as the basis of ethical

AI, particularly in those situations when generative content is applied in a public or other persuasive way (UNESCO, 2021). However, these international provisions form an essential basis even though they should be converted into policies that can be implemented to provide a real defense to both creators and receiver.

The economic policies also require consideration by the frameworks of governance since the AI generated creativity will alter the labour markets and break the traditional career movement in arts. Increased risk of occupational replacement is high in the areas of graphic design, animation, writing, and commercial illustration, where AI technology can do most tasks much faster than humans, who were supposedly talented (Hesmondhalgh, 2021). Policymakers should thus devise mechanisms of assisting creative employees in terms of technological changes. This can be portrayed through reskilling initiatives, tax subsidies on human-driven creative initiatives, and agreements on collective bargaining where the workers are not prone to exploitation. Also, the model of compensating artists who have their works in AI training datasets is a new field of policy development. Other researchers suggest that AIs also should pay licensing or royalties to the creators whose content is used to generate the activities of their models (Crootof and Ard, 2022). These policies would be used to reduce the economic injustices that occur when AI firms sell on human ingenuity without compensating the creative individuals involved.

The other critical aspect of AI ethics is cultural governance that is involved in ensuring security of minority and Indigenous cultural expressions. Since generative AI systems can unwillingly steal or distort cultural forms, communities ought to exercise some agency in the way their cultural materials are added into - or left out of - AI training systems. The Recommendation on the Ethics of AI by UNESCO focuses on preserving cultural diversity and sounds a warning against the technological practices that may result in the homogenization or erasure of cultures (UNESCO, 2021). The application of principles needs inclusivity principles of governance where cultural groups are actively engaged in weighing on decisions about datasets inclusion, representational limits, and ethical applications.

Through the lack of those safeguards, AI may lead to the increased cultural imbalance and the loss of the diversity of the creative traditions worldwide Ethical AI creativity best practices should thus be comprehensive enough to involve legal reform implementation, technology transparency, economic equality, cultural empathy, and civic education. Researchers point out that the implementation of ethical governance is not possible solely because of technical solutions but is characterized by interdisciplinary cooperation of technologists, jurists, artists, and policy-makers as well as cultural stakeholders (Floridi, 2014). Education among the masses is crucial especially because the societies should learn to be digital literate to guide people in an information world that is slowly becoming dominated by synthetic media. This educating the audiences on how to shop AI generated content, know the capabilities of AI, and the limits of AI enables a more resilient society against misinformation and makes the interactions with creative AI technologies more inform. Finally, the system of governance should be connected to preventing the use of AI as a method that would enhance human creativity instead of deter cultural integrity or social equality.

To conclude, the policy and regulation of AI-created creativity is a complicated and dynamic environment that should be further investigated by researchers, lawmakers, and ethics professionals. Since generative AI already changes the way societies create, consume and interpret the work of creative minds, quite sound governance ideologies that revolve around transparency, accountability, cultural sensitivity, and economic justice will be critical toward establishing an ethical creative future.

9. FUTURE SCOPE OF AI CREATIVITY AND ETHICAL HORIZONS

The future of creativity with artificial intelligence reflects a fast-changing environment where the innovations of technologies face the changing cultural, social, ethical demands. Generative models will further blur the divisions between human and machine imaginativeness as they get more advanced, and societies will start regarding the definition of authorship, worth, and artistic significance in a new light. The researchers believe that in the future, the creative ecosystems will not be typified by the deposition of human creativity, but rather by more intricate hybrid forms where humans and AI systems will exist in fluid and dynamic relationships (Odensen, 2004). This change might result in creative production models that favor direction, editing, and creative vision on the human creator, with the assistance of AI systems who can create, crossbreed, and enlarge artistic concepts. Some scholars say that this hybrid creativity can potentially expand the cognitive abilities of humankind because, by allowing creators to explore novel conceptual space and quickly test possible options, it can offer an alternative way of thinking (Gervais, 2020). Future, however, will also need ethical protection in order to keep the human agency at the center and to make sure that the role of technological means does not replace the irreplaceable levels of human meaning-making (Gaut, 2010).

Scientific breakthroughs in AI system design indicate that future generative systems can be more multimodal with the inclusion of visual, linguistic, auditory, and sensory input to generate generative products that are highly integrated.

These systems might facilitate immersive kinds of creativity within areas like virtual reality, game design, bio-art and mixed-media installation, as well as pushing the limits of artistic expression. Researchers are already looking at ways of integrating multimodal AI with human artists to work together in real-time and responded to gestures, voice cues, emotional cues, or environmental inputs to co-experience interactive experiences . These technologies can transform, not only the work of art, but also the way people think, leading to the possible changes in the way people to believe creativity, imagination, and the connection between the virtual and the real world (Manovich, 2020). These changes reveal the value of suggesting future AI systems that are explicitly based on augmenting but not diminishing of human creative agency.

These innovations notwithstanding, serious ethical issues are looming in the horizon. The ongoing creation of artificial intelligence-based content is one of the reasons to worry whether the issue of human uniqueness can be diminished in the cultural markets dominated by artificial objects. In case the future of the creative industries depends on algorithmic production more, human creators will find it harder to counter the efficiency and stylistic scalability of the generative systems. The experts caution that this phenomenon might lead to a cultural situation where innovation is created at such a scale that it eclipses the markers of artistic value (Hesmondhalgh, 2021). The danger is not merely the economic one but a philosophical one as well: with the spread of the machine-generated artifacts, the cultural concept of the creativity may simply shift to the way in which the creativity is humanized, and the optimization of the algorithms is encouraged. Cultural and policy intercessions will have to be undertaken in order to ensure future societies still appreciate the subjective, experiential and intentional aspects of human creativity (Leong, 2025).

The policy frameworks and future governance policies will be particular in their role in determining the manner through which AI creativity will be influenced ethically. With the increasing autonomy and incorporation of generative models in the daily production of media, legal institutions will be forced to tighten the legal definition of authorship, ownership, and intellectual property. The researchers claim that new models of licensing, data consent systems, and attribution will constitute the fundamental elements of ethical AI ecosystems (Crootof and Ard, 2022). Additionally, due to the international character of the generative technologies, cross-international collaboration is required to avoid the aspect of inequality in the enforcing regulations resulting in the use of ethical exploitation or cultural abuse. UNESCO and other agencies insist on the idea that the new model of governance should focus more on cultural diversity, human dignity, and equal rights to technological benefits (UNESCO, 2021).

These principles will require operationalization into tangible policies that would guarantee innovation and security in creative spheres.

Future AI creativity will also involve frameworks of ethics to deal with psychological and emotional effects of creative work handy and collaboration with machines. The more responsive, interactive, emotionally expressive AI systems are in their results, the more the user is likely to anthropomorphize them or become psychologically connected to co-creative systems. Empirical studies permit one to conclude that when people already perceive intentionality and emotional expressiveness in AI-generated art, they are conscious of the fact that the system is not conscious (Chamberlain et al., 2021). The possibility of over-attributing influence could also become more significant in the context of the future situation when creativity and AI lose their ways of interacting, so the dependence on AI can change self-perception, emotional experiences, and artistic identity formation. The ethical principles of design should, therefore, make sure that AI systems are designed in a manner that aids and not manipulates the psychological well-being of a human being.

Also, the continuum of creativity of AI needs to be expanded in response to the ongoing dilemma of cultural representation. The danger of cultural homogenization grows with the rise of generative systems, and this indicates that, unless the training data are changed,emphasizing major cultural narratives over that of the marginalized voices, it probably will continue doing so. The next-generation growth of AI should focus on more inclusive and representative data, informed by a culturally minded reviewing process, community consultation, as well as ethical data custodianship (Buolamwini and Gebru, 2018). These strategies will be useful in deter new generative systems to repeat the cultural imbalance, and so, AI can be used to preserve, but not to erase, cultural diversity. Theorists propose the creation of culturally pluralistic AI, which will recognize and honor the diversity of artistic traditions in the world (Lewis et al., 2020). When put to work, such models might help to broaden the boundaries of creativity and strengthen cultural dignity and heritage.

In the future, the issue of AI creativity and its ecological impact will also require more and more attention. Large generative models are costly in terms of their environmental impact and, with the increasing demand of creative AI applications, so will its environmental impact. Future studies are needed to cover the sustainable strategies in AI development, including energy-efficient model designs, carbon-neutral training procedures, and industry-wide standards of environmental responsibility (Strubell et al., 2019). Ethical future of creativity through AI cannot be untangled regarding larger global issues and long-term sustainability by incorporating sustainability into technological innovation will be vital to guaranteeing sustainability.

Finally, the future of AI creativity is pegged on the unity of humankind to strike a balance between innovation and responsibility. As the generation systems change further, they will have more influence on human creativity, cultural ecosystem and social organization. It will be necessary to develop a future where AI opens up more opportunities to creative expression without compromising the cultural, ethical, and psychological foundations upon which creativity is a uniquely human activity. This future presupposes the interdisciplinary approach to collaboration, effective work of education of the population, the involvement of all people in the policy-making process, and a long-term investment in ethics-centered reasoning (Floridi, 2014).

It is only in these combined efforts that societies will be able to guarantee that AI will be used in a thriving creative environment and preserve the values, identities and cultural histories that have so far made human creativity so eternally important.

Fashion industry transformation is a significant trend as the sustainability issue becomes a burning global concern, and the use of AI-based recommender systems gives an effective roadmap to more responsible consumption. This chapter has demonstrated that artificial intelligence can be used to reduce waste, enhance transparency, customer decision-making, and enhance sustainable business processes. Meanwhile, the fashion industry is under tremendous pressure because of the use of resources, pollution, and waste of textile that is more important than ever before. Scientists continuously emphasize that AI can resolve numerous age-old issues within the fashion industry by enhancing predicting, aiding circling, and making consumers more aware of sustainability-related facts (Rathore, 2023). The results in the literature and in real-life cases prove that AI-based recommender systems are not merely technological instruments but also decision tools that help to make a positive change.

One theme which stands out in the context of this chapter is the need to have trustworthy and transparent sustainability information. The quality of information that the AI-driven sustainable recommender system is provided with is crucial. Even the most advanced AI tool cannot be able to bring reliable recommendations on a lack of precise information on materials, supply chains, emissions, certifications, and product durability. The fact that there are no uniform sustainability criteria, which remain a source of confusion to consumers and nuisance to system developers, is a theme of many researchers (EEA, 2022). This issue needs cooperation between brands, policymakers, certification agencies, and technology creators to address it. The development of the sustainable fashion industry in the future will rely on the development of a single reporting framework and data-sharing schemes where AI systems can receive verified information.

The other key finding is that AI can minimise attitude-behaviour gap by making sustainable decisions easy to consumers. People usually say that they want to shop responsibly but have difficulties in making a sustainable choice in the real-life circumstances as they do not have time, they have no knowledge, or they are not sure about the claims concerning sustainability. The barriers described can be overcome through AI recommender systems that offer sustainable alternatives with explanations and paring the results with personal preferences. Studies indicate that the shopping experience should be user-friendly so that sustainability can be instilled into the shopping experience as the consumers will always be ready to make greener decisions (Kimiagari and Asadi Malafe, 2021). This means that properly built AI systems can assist behavioural change, and thus sustainable consumption will be a possibility among the regular shopper.

At the same time, this chapter also highlights that AI will not be able to address sustainability issues without considering the ethical issue. Trust and objectivity, transparency, privacy as well as fairness should be embedded in the system. Assuming that AI models are trained on biased information, they can be used to support unsustainable consumption and preferences towards bigger fast-fashion brands. According to researchers, AI has the potential to inadvertently boost malicious trends unless it is designed with adequate responsibility in mind (Dhiwar, 2024).

10. REFERENCES

Bender, E. M., Gebru, T., McMillan-Major, A., & Shmitchell, S. (2021). On the dangers of stochastic parrots: Can language models be too big? *Proceedings of the 2021 ACM Conference on Fairness, Accountability, and Transparency*, 610–623. https://doi.org/DOI: 10.1145/3442188.3445922

Boden, M. A. (2004). *The creative mind: Myths and mechanisms* (2nd ed.). Routledge., DOI: 10.4324/9780203508527

Brynjolfsson, E., & McAfee, A. (2019). *The second machine age: Work, progress, and prosperity in a time of brilliant technologies*. W. W. Norton.

Buolamwini, J., & Gebru, T. (2018). Gender shades: Intersectional accuracy disparities in commercial gender classification. Proceedings of Machine Learning Research, 81, 1–15. https://proceedings.mlr.press/v81/buolamwini18a.html

Chamberlain, R., Mullin, J., Scheerlinck, E., & Wiggins, G. A. (2021). Perceptions of creativity in human versus AI-generated art. *Psychology of Aesthetics, Creativity, and the Arts*. Advance online publication. DOI: 10.1037/aca0000435

Chesney, R., & Citron, D. K. (2019). Deep fakes: A looming challenge for privacy, democracy, and national security. *California Law Review*, *107*(6), 1753–1819. https://www.californialawreview.org/print/deep-fakes-a-looming-challenge-for-privacy-democracy-and-national-security

Colton, S., & Wiggins, G. A. (2012). Computational creativity: The final frontier? *Proceedings of the European Conference on Artificial Intelligence*, 21, 21–26. https://doi.org/DOI: 10.3233/978-1-61499-098-7-21

Crootof, R., & Ard, B. (2022). The data we breathe: Reconsidering "publicly available" data and AI. *Washington Law Review (Seattle, Wash.)*, *97*(1), 167–222.

Csikszentmihalyi, M. (1997). *Creativity: Flow and the psychology of discovery and invention*. HarperCollins.

Danto, A. C. (1981). *The transfiguration of the commonplace: A philosophy of art*. Harvard University Press.

Flick, C., & Worrall, K. (2022). The ethics of creative AI. In *The language of creative AI: Practices, aesthetics and structures* (pp. 73–91). Springer International Publishing.

Floridi, L. (2014). *The ethics of information*. Oxford University Press., DOI: 10.1093/acprof:oso/9780199641321.001.0001

Gaut, B. (2010). The philosophy of creativity. *Philosophy Compass*, *5*(12), 1034–1046. DOI: 10.1111/j.1747-9991.2010.00351.x

Gervais, D. (2020). The machine as author. *Iowa Law Review*, *105*(5), 2053–2106. https://papers.ssrn.com/sol3/papers.cfm?abstract_id=3359524

Goodfellow, I., Pouget-Abadie, J., Mirza, M., Xu, B., Warde-Farley, D., Ozair, S., Courville, A., & Bengio, Y. (2014).

Guilford, J. P. (1950). Creativity. *The American Psychologist*, *5*(9), 444–454. DOI: 10.1037/h0063487 PMID: 14771441

Gunkel, D. J. (2018). *The machine question: Critical perspectives on AI, robots, and ethics*. MIT Press., DOI: 10.7551/mitpress/8975.001.0001

Hesmondhalgh, D. (2021). *The cultural industries* (4th ed.). SAGE Publications.

Huang, M.-H., & Rust, R. T. (2021). https://uk.sagepub.com/en-gb/eur/the-cultural-industries/book250830

Ivcevic, Z., & Brackett, M. (2015). Emotional creativity: The generation and experience of novel emotional responses. *Creativity Research Journal*, *27*(1), 1–8. DOI: 10.1080/10400419.2015.992676

Kant, I. (2000). *Critique of the power of judgment* (Guyer, P., Ed.). Cambridge University Press. (Original work published 1790), DOI: 10.1017/CBO9780511804656

Kaufman, J. C., & Glăveanu, V. P. (2019). A review of creativity theories: What questions are we trying to answer?.

Leong, W. Y. (2025). Ethical and philosophical perspectives on artificial intelligence-generated art. *International Journal of Social Sciences and Artistic Innovations*, *5*(2), 7–20. DOI: 10.35745/ijssai2025v05.02.0007

Runco, M. A., & Jaeger, G. J. (2012). The standard definition of creativity. *Creativity Research Journal*, *24*(1), 92–96. DOI: 10.1080/10400419.2012.650092

Samuelson, P. (2023). Generative AI and copyright: A brief introduction. *Communications of the ACM*, *66*(7), 23–25. DOI: 10.1145/3609380

Sarkar, S., & Cooper, A. (2022). Creativity in the age of artificial intelligence: User perceptions of human–AI collaboration. *The Journal of Creative Behavior*. Advance online publication. DOI: 10.1002/jocb.632

Searle, J. R. (1980). Minds, brains, and programs. *Behavioral and Brain Sciences*, *3*(3), 417–457. DOI: 10.1017/S0140525X00005756

Strubell, E., Ganesh, A., & McCallum, A. (2019). Energy and policy considerations for deep learning in NLP. *Proceedings of the 57th Annual Meeting of the Association for Computational Linguistics*, 3645–3650. https://doi.org/DOI: 10.48550/arXiv.1906.02243

Sun, T. Q., & Medaglia, R. (2019). Mapping the challenges of artificial intelligence in the public sector: Evidence from public health. *Government Information Quarterly*, *36*(2), 273–282. DOI: 10.1016/j.giq.2018.09.008

UNESCO. (2021). Recommendation on the Ethics of Artificial Intelligence. United Nations Educational, Scientific and Cultural Organization. https://www.unesco.org/en/articles/recommendation-ethics-artificial-intelligence

Vaccari, C., & Chadwick, A. (2020). Deepfakes and disinformation: Exploring the impact on trust in news and democracy. *Social Media + Society*, *6*(1), 1–13. DOI: 10.1177/2056305120903408

Vaswani, A., Shazeer, N., Parmar, N., Uszkoreit, J., Jones, L., Gomez, A. N., Kaiser, Ł., & Polosukhin, I. (2017). Attention is all you need. *Advances in Neural Information Processing Systems*, *30*. Advance online publication. DOI: 10.48550/arXiv.1706.03762

Chapter 6
Future of Work in Creative Industries

Avya Singh Chirana
https://orcid.org/0009-0000-6775-9853
Christ University, Delhi, India

Pratibha Giri
Christ University, Bengaluru, India

ABSTRACT

Digital technologies, platform-based labour and AI are causing a significant transformation in the future of work in creative industries. This chapter looks at how the changes are transforming creative professions, work models and career expectations. In the digital transition, numerous cultural barriers to entry have been eliminated and individuals can tap into international markets without institutional intermediaries. With creative employees becoming more freelance and web based entrepreneurs, artists have to manage an increased pressure to balance between creativity and commercial and technological concerns. Lastly, it also gives future research and policy implications such as the need to provide structural systems that safeguard mental health, equitable pay and inclusiveness to opportunities. This chapter contends that creators, platforms, educators and policymakers must work together in order to achieve a healthy and equitable creative economy and sustainable creative futures.

1. INTRODUCTION

One of the most significant directions of the world economy is turning out to be creative industries. Such sectors are film, music, design, advertising, animation,

DOI: 10.4018/979-8-3373-7153-5.ch006

game, fashion, digital content development and other types of artistic and cultural production. Not only do they produce entertainment, they also produce innovation, identity, social meaning and economic growth. Numerous nations are also accepting the advantage that creativity is currently a propellant of economic development and even plays the capacity to designate national competitiveness in the digital era (Howkins, 2001). Meanwhile, technology and digital space are transforming the world of work in the most creative industries at a rapid pace. Talent and training are no longer the sole bases as to the future of work in this sector. It has now turned to be dependent on the relationship workers have with the digital techniques, online audiences, and new ways of labour arrangements (UNCTAD, 2022). This is why it is necessary to research in relation to the evolving state of creative working and what is to expect and be aware of the challenges and opportunities.

Previously the creative careers were organized in terms of massive organizations where film studios, broadcast houses, publishing houses and advertising agencies were involved. These organisations had control over access to resources and dictated who would become a successful professional creator. Demand to have good social networks, cultural capital or high degrees of formal training to get a job in these areas of industry (Bourdieu, 1993). There were few individuals who could get in and establish steady jobs. The development of digital technology, and the internet, however, enabled creative work to be opened-up. Today the creators are not necessarily required to seek permission at institutions. They are able to publish, distribute and sell their work online themselves and reach audiences that are located in different parts of the world (Cunningham and Craig, 2019). This revolution has made it more democratic and participatory regarding creativity.

Even though digital technology eliminated some barriers, it came with new pressures. Previously, the institutions offered secure positions, stable income and definite career lines. After all, currently numerous creative employees are freelance employees or independent creators without a stable flow of money. They must seek employment everywhere, stay online and concentrate and compete with numerous people in busy online platforms (Hesmondhalgh and Baker, 2011). The creative worker of modern times has to take care of not only his art but also marketing, branding, finance and digital performance analytics. The skill is not the only requirement, as the creation of an audience, active work online, and knowledge of the trends in platforms are also needed to be successful (Abidin, 2018). This is inspirational and simultaneously overwhelming to creative work.

The other significant transformation, which defines the future work in any creative industry, is the relationship between personal identity and professional role. A lot of digital creators nowadays make money by posting their personality, lifestyle and values and their creative output. This is frequented by influencers, YouTubers, streamers, online teachers and digital artists. Their financial potential will be tied to the degree of emotional attachment of audiences to them (Duffy and Wissinger, 2017). Consequently, there is the amalgamation between personal life and professional life. This emotional labour is what is involved in the business, creators have to remain active and relatable at all times on the Internet. This puts psychological strain and heightens the chances of burnout even to the most successful creators (Berryman and Kavka, 2017).

Creative work is also being transformed by technology, in particular, the idea of artificial intelligence (AI). It is now possible to use AI to assist in or even produce music, images, videos, scripts, animation and other forms of creative work. Initially, a good deal of people terrified themselves with the idea that AI is going to eliminate human creativity entirely. Nonetheless, it is also proposed that AI does not eliminate human creativity but alters the work division but does not eliminate the need for human creativity. Using AI is helpful in repetitive or time-consuming work, which leaves creators with more time to concentrate on ideas, feelings, narratives, novelty and significance (Shneiderman, 2020). This implies that human creativity will still be valued but the skills required to perform well will change. Innovative employees should also be trained to embrace technology and not to struggle against new technology.

Despite these possibilities there are still numerous inequalities when creative work is concerned. Although digital platforms can make it appear that anyone has the same opportunity to become a success, control resources, geography, language, education and internet have been shown to impact those who gain the most (UNCTAD, 2022). Artists in a richer part of the place or a big city usually access more professional gear and a high-speed internet, sponsorship agreements and connections. The individuals in disadvantaged regions are disadvantaged despite having similar talent and devotion (Comunian et al., 2014). Thus, the online creative economy is not necessarily equal and fair. Opportunities are increasing although not all groups have an equal chance.

It is also necessary to note that digital creativity as a factor of the economy relies on algorithms significantly. Social media including YouTube, Instagram, Tik Tok and Spotify have algorithms that dictate the visibility of the content. Such algorithms can help the career of a creator to be boosted overnight, or cut down their reach without any warning. One shift in platform rules/trends can make a difference on the income and prospects. It implies that creative labour has been transformed through platforms that appear to be less secure, and in which visibility is the primary commodity, with the creator having very little behind the scenes influence on how their work is found and consumed by audiences (Cunningham and Craig, 2019). As much as platforms cause empowerment, they cause dependency.

Meanwhile, creative work does not only affect the economy, but also society and culture. Creative material influences the way individuals think, feeling and identitatively. Movies, music, fashion patterns, visual arts, literary work and digital artifacts may challenge beliefs, motivate people and shape social movements (Howkins, 2001). Thus, the future of work in the creative industries is not only a question of economics, but also a question of culture and emotions. The future narrative and messages consumed by the society will all depend on how the creative workers are treated, enabled and appreciated.

Due to all this, the future of work in creative industries should be studied in various aspects such as economic, technological, psychological, social and cultural. This chapter aims at discussing how creative work has seen its transformation to be instigated by institution-based employment into being digital and platform-based labour, the forces that are shaping the future of occupations operating in creativity, and what problems need to be addressed in achieving sustainable and justifiable occupations of the creative (Hesmondhalgh and Baker, 2011). The chapter puts emphasis on the downsides and pros of digital transformation, such as creating independence and expression possibilities and the creations of new precariousness, emotional stress and disparity (Cunningham and Craig, 2019). It further recognises those areas where future research is required, policy and education to develop creative ecosystems to sustain artistic freedom, equitable payments and psychological health (UNCTAD, 2022).

In general, creativity is moving towards the core of economic and cultural life. Nevertheless, creativity work should not be tied solely to technology and digital markets in the future. It also needs to take into account the human makers of the cultural production. One of the key measures to ensure the future of creativity will be supporting sustainable careers, equitable working environments and healthy working. All these supports are missing, and the creative economy may resort to using passion instead of untapping it (Duffy and Wissinger, 2017). Working in creative industries is not only a change in business model, however, it is a total change in the way the society perceives imagination, identity and emotional labour.

2. LITERATURE REVIEW

2.1. Survey of the Studies of Creative Industries

The study of creative industries also developed when the scholars started perceiving culture and creativity not only as the soft social factors but as the major aspects of contemporary economies. Early theorists of the creative economy maintained that the ideas, symbols and intellectual capital was assuming the position of the primary source of value in the post-industrial societies, and was replacing traditional manufacturing as the primary source of economic evolution (Howkins,

2001). Subsequently reports on security policy in the international organisations indicated that cultural industries and creative industries are significant contributors to the GDP, employment and exports, particularly in cities and regions oriented toward innovation and creative clusters (UNCTAD, 2022). Meanwhile, critical cultural studies made us aware that a creative work is never simply economical, but it equally constitutes identities, definitions and dominant relationships in society, in other words, that creative industries should be perceived as an economic system as well as a cultural sector (Hesmondhalgh & Baker, 2013).

2.2. Institutional Control and Half-closed Economies in Traditional Creative Economies

Much of the early studies on cultural production were concerned with the way in which large institutions mediated the access to creative professions. The hierarchies in cultural fields including literature, art and media were demonstrated by sociologists such as Pierre Bourdieu as cultural field gatekeepers determine apparently which works should be published, shown or on TV (Bourdieu, 1993). These institutions were based on specific types of cultural capital, including education, style and taste, which tend to be more reachable by advantaged social components of society to cement preexisting inequalities in access to creative jobs (Hesmondhalgh & Baker, 2013). Broadcasting, film, music and publishing studies in the twentieth century discovered that the majority of workers were relying on full-time employment in big organisations, and commonly there exist a clear distinction between professional creators and amateurs (McRobbie, 2009). The future of creative work in this paradigm seemed to be related to gaining employment and organizational acknowledgement although entry competition was still strong.

2.3. The Renovation of the Digital Disruption and the Increase of Creative Participation

The trend of the internet and computer technologies shook most of these previous trends. With digital systems of production becoming less expensive and online platforms allowing direct publication, the distinction between professional and amateur creators started disappearing (Cunningham and Craig, 2019). User-generated content and participatory culture studies revealed that fans and the common people could now create and share videos, music, fan fiction, memes and other types of creative in a mass-like way and this did not require any approval of traditional media firms (Jenkins, 2006). According to scholars, this seemed to democratize creative participation since individuals in various locations and backgrounds could share their work on the internet and possibly reach the international markets (Abidin, 2018).

Simultaneously, subsequent research noted that most of them could take part but a marginal percentage also received much exposure and even monetary compensation, resulting in a winner-takes-most phenomenon where a limited number of creators received the majority of attention and earnings (Duffy & Wissinger, 2017).

2.4. Freelancing, Project work and Portfolio Careers

Since digital technologies transformed the way content was generated and shared, they transformed creative job opportunities. Studies on cultural labour have reported a change of long term, full time jobs to freelance work, project and contract work, particularly in the film, TV, design, music and advertising industry (Gill and Pratt 2008). Creative workers tend to spend their time moving in and out of projects, clients and teams, assembling a livelihood out of various temporary projects (Hesmondhalgh and Baker, 2011). According to the scholars it is referred to as the emergence of what they call portfolio careers, where people choose to take many jobs together, designer, teacher, consultant and content creator, creating sufficient income throughout the year (Mould et al., 2020). Such an arrangement provides some flexibility and variety to workers, but it is also associated with instability, as workers do not have a stable pay, and they have to find another job all the time.

2.5. Individualisation, Image and Aspirational Labour

One of the major current lines of research is the way in which creative workers should market themselves as brands. Influencer, vloggers/digital creator research indicates that they have to maintain a recognisable and attractive image of themselves to achieve followers, sponsors and collaboration prospects (Duffy and Hund, 2015). This was termed by the scholars as aspirational labour and in this context, individuals spend time and resources creating content and managing their online identity hoping later benefits would come regardless of the income levels or uncertainty at present (Duffy and Wissinger, 2017). Studies about social media cultures also indicate that people tend to expect the creators to tell their personal stories, feelings and daily activities, which transfers the personal experience into the core of the professional activity (Abidin, 2018). This is the fact that creative labour is emotionally charged since lack of availability or criticism will be perceived as an attack on an individual rather than a product per se (Berryman and Kavka, 2017).

2.6. Dependency on Platforms Dependable algorithms Visible algorithms

Algorithms and control over the platform is a more recent subject of literature attention. The digital platforms and YouTube, Instagram, Tik Tok and Spotify not only host the creative content but also structure the algorithm of its promotion, ranking and monetisation. According to scholars, creators rely on the tools to get discovered by viewers, yet they learn very little about how such systems operate and why certain content is favored over others (Cunningham and Craig, 2019). This state of affairs is termed as algorithmic precarity, as a single tweak in the masks of the platform, monetisation or ranking priorities can abruptly increase or decrease the exposure of a creator and the revenue (Duffy and Wissinger, 2017). Studies indicate that this has prompted the reaction of numerous creators to constantly check the analytics and change posting schedules, pursue trends and make changes to their creative decisions, creating the false impression that it is the algorithms and not the artists controlling the culture manufacturing (Abidin, 2018).

2.7. Stress and burnout, Emotional Well-Being

The emotional and psychological implications of modern creative work are the subject of a particular scientific literature that is becoming increasingly diverse. Passion, self-expression and identity have always been connected to cultural labour, making it be very rewarding and, at the same time, potentially risky to certain individuals (Hesmondhalgh and Baker, 2011).

With the platform environment, creators are constantly under pressure due to their constant publicity, spectators, and expectations to be always visible on the internet (Berryman & Kavka, 2017). Influencers, YouTubers and streamers report having experienced exhaustion, anxiety and burnout because of the pressure and stress posed by the obligation to post multiple times per week, unpredictable reactions as well as continuous comparisons with others (Duffy and Wissinger, 2017). As researchers say, what on the one hand looks like a cool, Free style of life can include plenty of working hours, disrupted sleep habits, and the inability to create a clear separation between work and life (Abidin, 2018).

2.8. Access to Resources, Inequality and Geography

Despite the general consensus that digital platforms are open and inclusive, studies have indicated that the creative economy will continue to have inequalities regarding its beneficiaries. Research of creative clusters indicates that cities that have well-developed cultural facilities like arts support, educational establishments and networking environments have the capability to attract and retain more successful creative employees (Comunian et al., 2014). Reports on the international communities also state that creators in more affluent areas tend to be more connected to high-speed internet connections, modern technology, training, and collaborations with brands than in lower-income areas (UNCTAD, 2022). The language differences also define the opportunities because creators with English as the mother tongue can have easier access to the global markets, whereas others might confine to smaller local target markets (Cunningham & Craig, 2019). This means that digital participation has widened, although structural disparities in education, geography and wealth persist in determining who is able to develop sustainable careers in the creative sector.

2.9. Artificial Intelligence, Creative Tool and Authorship.

The emergence of artificial intelligence in production of works of art has created a new field of scholarly controversy. Artificial intelligence now has the capability of creating paintings, music, stories, and designs that look similar to those created by humans and this has made some people fearful of the future of this occupation where artists, designers and writers will be unemployed (Elgammal et al., 2017). Most researchers argue, however, that AI can be seen to be a device that can complement human creativity, such as accelerating routine processes, proposing novel combinations or permitting experimentation, which would otherwise be challenging to execute by hand (Shneiderman, 2020). According to the legal and economic specialists, another controversial aspect of AI deals with authorship and copyright, in particular, in case training data includes millions of already existing works of art or texts that are made by humans via machine learning (Kretschmer and Towse, 2020). This has prompted the demands of new policy frameworks that define the ownership of AI-assisted works, as well as the attribution or payment of creators in the case of their work being used as a training aid (Elgammal et al., 2017).

2.10. Creative Clusters, City Development and Culture Policy.

The other noteworthy theme in the literature is that of relationship between creative industries, cities and public policy. According to researchers working on the topic of urban development, creative employees are likely to be agglomerated in specific neighbourhoods or districts where they can afford their workspaces as well as cultural facilities and networks (Comunian et al., 2014). Such creative clusters can also draw tourism, investment and symbolic prestige and over time, local governments are increasingly encouraging the idea of cultural quarters, festivals and creativity centres as a part of economic policy (UNCTAD, 2022). Nevertheless, researchers also caution about such threats of gentrification because as a result of the success of creative districts, the same artists and communities that initially made such areas appealing start to get displaced with soaring property prices (Hesmondhalgh & Baker, 2013). This proves that although the creative industries can enrich the urbanization, when not properly designed, they might also promote the emergence of unprecedented social and geographical inequalities.

2.11. Unofficial Learning, Talents and the purpose of Schooling

Recent studies also address the acquisition of skills by creative workers in changing digital environment. Although formal training in art schools, media programmes and design courses still play a crucial role, informal training based on online schooling, community, and experimentation is also significant to many creators (Comunian et al., 2014). Research on YouTubers, indie game designers and digital artists demonstrates that they also tend to teach themselves which tools and techniques by observing other creators, gathering on forums on the internet, and working on small projects together, instead of in a classroom (Cunningham & Craig, 2019). Meanwhile, there is a burgeoning discussion on whether contemporary education systems are sufficiently training students to be prepared to face the reality of the freelance, platform-based work, which involves the need to have business literacy, as well as skills in self-management and digital marketing skills in addition to artistic practice (Gill & Pratt, 2008). This has prompted the scholars to propose curriculum changes that incorporate creative, technical and entrepreneurial learning.

2.12. Diversity, Representation and Cultural Power

Another last line of literature is perceiving who is represented in creative industries and whose narration is presented. Although new space is created by the digital platforms so that the marginalized voices find a voice, research indicates that structural issues around race, gender, disability and class are still contributing to creative opportunities and outputs (Hesmondhalgh & Baker, 2013). Film, television, music and digital media studies demonstrate that some groups continue to be under-represented both on-screen and behind-the-scenes, and how stereotypes have the power to perpetuate when decision-making continues to be dominated by like social groups (UNCTAD, 2022). Meanwhile, researchers record the use of digital tools by independent creators, most of whom are part of marginalised communities, to contest the mainstream discourse and make alternative media space and supportive audiences around the basis of common identities and farmers (Abidin, 2018). This piece of work makes us remember that the discussion of the future of creative labour concerns not just jobs and income but also cultural power, visibility and social justice.

2.13. International Shocks, Crisis and Sustainability of Creative Labor

Another question that has also been touched and discussed in the literature is impact that global crises, like the COVID-19 pandemic, have on creative industries as well as on the professional lives of artists and cultural workers. As the creative workers with physical spaces like theatres, cinemas, galleries and concert halls shut down, a lot of them were forcibly deprived of the primary source of income almost overnight, making the business models grounded on in-person events rather fragile (UNCTAD, 2022). Concurrently, researchers noted that a radical transformation towards digital products, such as live-stream performances, online exhibitions and virtual festivals enabled certain creators to entertain more people but in most cases resulted in much less income than offline ticket sales (Comunian et al., 2014). These articles indicate that although creative employees are quite versatile and robust, the industry itself is susceptible to the impacts of economic and health crises, particularly, when it is not supported by solid safety nets and government funding and targeted policy insurance (Hesmondhalgh and Baker, 2011).

2.14. Literary Gaps in the Existing Literature

Despite the rapid increase in research on creative industries, there are still many gaps in the study which are relevant in informing the future of work in the arena. Most research concentrates on the concrete industries or popular case studies, and less visible forms of everyday creative labour are under-researched, e.g. micro-influencers, small scale artisans or local cultural labourers that do not fall into high profile domains (Mould et al., 2020). More comparative and longitudinal studies that trace creative careers across time and different nations should also be required instead of looking primarily at the instant images of specific cities in the Global North (Comunian et al., 2014). Lastly, researchers also mention that the issue of mental health, care work, disability and the ageing creative labour is only now starting to get some long-term attention, despite it being at the heart of the development of equitable, inclusive creative futures (Hesmondhalgh and Baker, 2011).

3. PARADIGM SHIFT IN WORK MODELS

3.1. Change of Paradigm in Work Models

3.1.1. The Stable Employment and To Flexible, Independent Work

A shift in creative labour has been to move to flexible and independent work, which was the largest alteration. Even prior to modernization, the goal of majority of the creative workers was to obtain full-time employment in big institutions like film studios, publishing firms, television companies, advertisement agencies or design firms. These positions provided stable salaries, medical cover and definite career development and thus long term planning is unproblematic (Hesmondhalgh and Baker, 2011). At present however a large number of creative workers are in the form of freelancers, gig workers or independent entrepreneurs as opposed to employees. Digitalisation, globalisation and reshaping of organisations have brought about this shift of organisations being able to employ workers on a project basis rather than have permanent teams (Gill and Pratt, 2008). Although the thing provides creators with more artistic freedom and flexibility, it also puts more individual responsibility on income, mastering the skill and securing future without governmental assistance (Mould et al., 2020).

3.2. The Emerging Project-Based Production

The trend in the world has seen a shift in creative work to project-based production in most fields. A movie is filmed on a temporary basis. The development cycle is composed of artists, programmers and musicians assembled in a video-game studio. The designers, writers and videographers are united in a digital marketing campaign in a short period of time. After the project has been terminated, the team members break up and each team member tries to find the next workplace (Gill and Pratt, 2008). Project based systems enable organisations to hire large numbers of staff within a short span of time, cut down the labour expenses in the long-term and recruit professional talent to do special work. Project-based labour may be thrilling and active to creative workers due to the fact that every project is a chance to meet new challenges and work together. But this form of work also leaves gaps between work, unpredictable revenues and permanent stress in order to keep business contacts to guarantee future opportunities (Hesmondhalgh and Baker, 2011). Autonomy and insecurity are thus involved in project work.

3.3. Multi-disciplinary Identities and Portfolio Careers

Due to the lack of predictable income to support it, most creative professionals today are developing a so-called portfolio career, engaging in multiple occupations and roles at the same time. As an example, a graphic designer can work in an agency part time, online courses, selling online templates and run freelance assignments. An artist may have income on concerts, streaming online, brand deals and music film production. The researchers refer to it as the movement in the direction of multi-disciplinary creative identities, where the successfulness of specific work relies on the ability to combine a range of different skills instead of focusing on one role only (Mould et al., 2020). The trend has got even more prevalent in the case of digital creators and production of content on several platforms to ensure that they have various sources of revenues. Although portfolio careers are beneficial in terms of income security and creative variety, they also make the work-rest boundaries misconstrued, motivating creators to sell themselves all the time to sustain their visibility and various sources of income (Duffy & Hund, 2015).

3.4. In the foot of Creative Production to Creative Entrepreneurship

Creative employees no longer exist as artists, writers, musicians or designers as they are supposed to be entrepreneurs. Digital platforms give creators an opportunity to make money on their own, but they also demand creators to do branding, marketing, negotiating and planning finances and artistic work simultaneously (Abidin, 2018). This has compelled creators to be more enterprising upon themselves by where they have to treat oneself like microbusiness. Numerous creators currently produce merchandise, negotiation of sponsorships, analytics analysis, formation of partnerships and maintenance of a public image. The notion of doing what you love turns into the business success, and the market turns into a daily part of every creativity (Duffy and Wissinger, 2017). Despite the opportunities of the entrepreneurial type of creativity to extend a sense of independence, it is a type of creativity that adds both emotional and cognitive burden, because a creator must always consider the commercial effectiveness in performing artistic decisions (Cunningham and Craig, 2019).

3.5. Remote and Hybrid collaboration as a New Paradigm

Working at a distance is a standard of creative sectors. Remote teamwork that cut across geographic regions and time zones was facilitated with the use of digital tools even before the pandemic. Filmmakers were allowed to edit on-line, musicians were able to record by remote, designers were able to work in cloud-computers and advertisers were able to lead campaigns online. Nowadays, most creative teams are completely remote or hybrid in their organization, and organizations are ready to hire talent at the global, rather than the local, level (Comunian et al., 2014). Remote work gives creators in non-urban settings more options such that they can work on international projects without having to move. Nevertheless, scholars have observed that remote working also raises the level of competition since producers at the global scale are currently competing with each other regarding employment, potentially driving prices and the bargaining power down (Cunningham and Craig, 2019). The flexibility in remote work hence establishes access in the world coupled with raising labour competition.

3.6. Immersive and Interactive Production Cycles

The other notable change in work models is the change in one-way creative product production into interactive and feedback-based production. In the traditional mode, artists created to passively entertain. On the digital platform, viewers on the platform react instantly by liking, commenting, sharing and drop-off ratings. Such reactions subsequently affect the following development of the creative work. Producers modify their content, tone, style and timing according to the performance metrics and user engagement data, building an endless production cycle under the influence of constant feedback. Such immediate reaction at the audience has the potential to facilitate innovation and enhance reach, yet at the same time it may push creators to focus on what is trending and not necessarily relevant in personal terms. Studies indicate that the creators tend to modify their creations in response to platforms and the audience instead of their creative instincts (Duffy and Wissinger, 2017). Therefore, online communication not only fundamentally alters the way the creators work, but it transforms the things that they make.

3.7. DIA and Production 24/7 Creative Cycles

Digital labour works to an expedited time scale. Formerly, creative work on such products as films, paintings or albums might take months or years. Digital spaces promote unceasing publishing today, as the engagement rate declines rapidly in the event that their creators go dormant. The pressure on lots of independent creators is to create content on a daily or weekly basis to continue reaching the algorithm (Abidin, 2018). This has pushed creators to work at a rapid rate and acquire new tools on a routine basis, and take on more than one role at a time. It also eliminates any distinct division between working time and leisure since creators stay in mind to performance statistics, audience reception and future ideas of content (Berryman & Kavka, 2017). The rate of modern creative production then encourages more productiveness but has risks of burnout and fatigue.

3.8. Flattened Hierarchies and in the form of Networking Collaboration

The old creative organisations were highly hierarchical: director, producer, editor, junior designer etc. Conversely, the creative work of the present day tends to take place within the flat networks where creators work as peers and not based on any strict forms of authority (Comunian et al., 2014). The music production and the production of graphics and content, leadership in the filmmaking sector more often than not changes based on expertise, not position. The greater egalitarian and innovative cultures can be achieved through network-based collaboration, however, it deprives staff of clear responsibility in professional development and well being since no long-term responsibility of workers exists, as it is not within a single institution (Gill and Pratt, 2008). In the absence of formal support structures, workers have to depend on self-education and individual stamina.

3.9. The Personal and Professional Life Blending

A creative work today unlike in the traditional jobs where hours are set is heavily connected with personal life. Content creators combine personal experiences with their work, revealing behind-the-scene content, routine and feel-good shots as part of their brand (Duffy & Hund, 2015). Such a lack of boundaries renders creative labour an affective experience, since it becomes difficult to distinguish the self and the product. Since trying to express myself via criticism or low response is perceived as an attack on me, many creators feel vulnerable (Berryman and Kavka, 2017). Loss of self and work also make it difficult to rest and relax since we are able to have potential content creation and online presence is needed everywhere to keep us visible (Abidin, 2018). This leaves work very fulfilling, as well as, psychologically exhausting.

The creative industries have experienced a shift in the work model of the industrial stable employment, to flexible, project-based, entrepreneurial and mediated labour through platforms (Hesmondhalgh and Baker, 2011). Creative employees are currently creating a career by integrating various sources of income, becoming multidisciplinary, or keeping public personalities and operating on international online markets (Cunningham and Craig, 2019). These innovative models provide freedom and independence in their creativity, but they also cause more insecurity, work, emotional pressure (Duffy and Wissinger, 2017). Creative work will demand striking a balance amidst flexibility and protection, innovation and well-being, independence and fair labour conditions in the future.

4. TECHNOLOGICAL AND DIGITAL TRANSFORMATION

4.1. Introduction: Technology as the Platform of the New Creative Economy

Technology has emerged as the primary driver of the creative work production, distribution and commercialisation. Previously, creativity needed physical space in terms of recording studios, film sets, printing presses and design facilities. A large portion of that work is now able to be completed at home using a laptop, smartphone or tablet. The digital production environments, software applications and online platforms have enabled even the small creators to create work of professional quality and access global audiences. Consequently, technology has not solely transformed the creativity tools, but the work organization, the work skills and work demands and expectations on creative workers (Tryon, 2013). This has been a fast-paced and constant transformation that affects all the entities in the creative ecosystem such as independent artists to giant media organisations (Yoo et al., 2010).

4.2. Physical Tools to Digital Software Ecosystems

There is replacement of many older production systems using digital creative tools. As an example, artists do not need to go to a full-scale recording studio in order to record anymore, as digital audio workstations enable recording, mixing and mastering to be done at a home studio. Graphic design, photo editing, animation and film making can be done on the available computer software at the comfort of the personal computers. The move has made the barriers to entry less significant and allowed creators to experiment more cheaply. Such tools have also homogenised worldwide processes through introducing shared data formats, cloud storage and shared editing solutions, which has simplified the collaboration of creative teams that are not at a single location (Tryon, 2013). Nevertheless, such greater accessibility does not necessarily ensure equal results. Designers who have access to expensive technology and education usually have more benefits than those who have little access to professional resources (Yoo et al., 2010).

4.3. Mechanization and Speeding up of Creative Industry

Automation is one of the key elements of digital transformation. Lightroom Software is becoming more and more automated in tasks like colour adjustment, audio levels, 3D rendering, subtitle generation and video transitions. Automation helps to shorten the production time and allows small teams to produce high quality work within a short period. Nonetheless, this pace has transformed the expectations. Moviemakers and campaigners are no longer supposed to take months to create a movie or a campaign and expect it to go viral; now they are supposed to create content at all times to appeal to the digital audiences and algorithms of platforms. According to scholars, the use of automated tools boosts productivity and heightens the need to keep up with rapid trends and the 24/7 digital cycles (Tryon, 2013). It makes creative work less episodic and more continuous thus there is less opportunity to take long breaks and reflect on something (Yoo et al., 2010).

4.4. Artificial Intelligence and Human-Machine Cooperation

The application of artificial intelligence has brought about a new level of transformation. Now AI can produce voice over, logos, scripts, music, visual art and animation. This has first brought fright that AI will drive out artists and designers (Elgammal et al., 2017). Nevertheless, studies are starting to propose that AI is most effective when implemented to complement as opposed to overthrow human imagination. AI has the opportunity to automate repetitive or technical processes, suggest alternative styles, or create a first draft that humans may improve, but creators retain emotional content, narrative voice and aesthetic judgment (Shneiderman, 2020). Scholars say that AI is changing the role of the creative worker to transform it towards directing, curating and personalising instead of manually performing all the details (Kretschmer and Towse, 2020). Therefore, rather than abolishing creative labour, AI is altering the most valuable skills.

4.5. Artificial Intelligence Ethical and Ownership Problems in AI-Generative Creativity

Although AI can provide new creative opportunities, it also has significant intellectual property and ethical issues. The vast majority of AI models are trained on the massive amount of creative output that is already created by humans. The issue of AI systems being trained on the work of many artists without their consent raises concerns among many artists, and the worth of AI-generated content could lower their market value (Elgammal et al., 2017). Copyright laws are meant to be written by humans and not machines, and it is not clear who owns the final product when it is created by both the creator and AI (Kretschmer and Towse, 2020). Researchers highlight the importance of legal changes that would make creativity safe and the creators compensated and acknowledged in case their ideas affect the content generated by AI (Shneiderman, 2020). In the absence of these safeguards, AI may enhance inequality rather than the empowerment of artists.

4.6. Immersive Media: VR, AR and Spatial Creativity

VR (or virtual reality), AR (or augmented reality) and XR (or mixed reality) are transforming the way creative content is experienced by the audience. In the immersive media, unlike the traditional media where people sit back and passively listen to the content, they are encouraged to enter into online environments and engage with the media. As a case in point, VR storytelling is putting the audience within a narrative space, whereas AR superimposes digital imagery on the physical environment (Liestol, 2021). The novel forms enable designers to experience emotions and sensations that transcend the traditional film or game design. Nevertheless, to develop the immersive content, one will need to learn about 3D modelling, spatial audio, interaction design and programming. Researchers observed that immersive media broadens the horizons of creativity but requires new hybrid skills of creators wishing to compete in this new place. With the increased use of immersive technology in the market, education, entertainment, tourism and advertising industries are increasingly using interactive storytelling in their practice (Jenkins, 2006).

4.7. Analytical Storytelling and Content Generation

Digital transformation has altered the process of making creative decisions. In the traditional creative industry, there was no prediction of success and much relied on intuition and artistic taste. Nowadays, social media can monitor the duration of the video viewing, the emotional reaction, and frequency of the content distribution and the storytelling style that is more effective. This data is examined by the creators and organisations in order to improve their content. As an example, musicians can increase and decrease the length of their songs accordingly to the streaming trends, filmmakers can modify the pace to correspond to the retention rates and influencers can change the timing to align with the hours of maximum activity. Analytical creativity can make creators get to know their audience more, yet academics have cautioned that overreliance on analytics can make creators less risky in their creative work and create more formulaic material to simply score highly in measurements (Couldry and Mejias, 2019). The difficulty of creators is to strike a balance of creativity and data instead of allowing analytics to determine the artistic direction.

4.8. Digital Cooperation and Production Globalisation

The collaboration has also been reorganised in creative teams through technology. Creative workers do not always sit in the same place or studio but work around the world via remote computing, cloud computing and collaboration in shared online spaces. Video editors, musicians, sound designers and animators will be able to work on the same project across countries, and do not have to physically relocate (Comunian et al., 2014). The short-term effect of this is that international opportunities become more accessible, whereas competition also rises, as an organisation can now hire anybody and may choose the worker with the lowest price or quickest turnaround (Cunningham and Craig, 2019). Although global collaboration enhances cultural diversity and innovation, globalisation is also likely to undermine wages and bargaining power of specific creators who do not have labour protection (Gill & Pratt, 2008). Digital technology, thus, broadens but also grows the economic competition among the creative workforce.

4.9. The Reconfiguring Time and Significance of Creative Employment

Technology not only altered the activities of the creative workers but also the knowledge of creativity itself. Creativity, to a great number of creators nowadays is not about inspiration and artistic identity only. It entails constant optimisation, speed, platform application and emotional execution. Online spaces embrace timely reactions, instant contact and being always accessible (Berryman & Kavka, 2017). Although technology offers unbelievable freedom to experiment, lots of creators have a tendency to follow trends, to please algorithms and impress viewers. As research indicates, the creators occasionally lessen the depth or novelty of their thoughts because they want to continue their rapid generation schedules and algorithmic reach (Duffy & Wissinger, 2017). In this way, creativity is made technologically enabled and commercially limited.

4.10. Eyes on the Prize: Technology as Collaborator, Not Competitor

In spite of the fact that creative technology is still evolving at high rates, the essential position of human creativity is still maintained. Emotional meaning, cultural awareness as well as lived experience are unique to human creativity and cannot be imitated by machines (Shneiderman, 2020). The use of AI, VR, automation and data tools may influence the ways of the work process but still make human imagination and empathy essential. The future of creative industries will rely on the capacity of creators to implement digital tools efficiently and not lose their creative spirit or on the ability of policy and education to accommodate new conditions without having to turn a blind eye to human feelings (Couldry and Mejias, 2019). The next level of creative work will be determined by technology, but individuals will still determine the purpose and values of creativity.

5. THE CREATOR AND PLATFORM ECONOMY

5.1. Creative Work being Reformed on Platforms

The rise of online platform technologies e.g. YouTube, Instagram, TikTok, Spotify, Twitch and Patreon has radically transformed the practising and monetising of creative labour. Historically, the content creators had to be granted the mass audiences by institutional gatekeepers. At present, online sources enable users to share their work directly with the audience followers and listeners all over the globe (Cunningham & Craig, 2019). This has changed the situation where the creators were either employees or contractors of the major media outlets into self-directed workers creating careers through online exposure and participation of the audience (Abidin, 2018). Consequently, platforms not only accommodate creative work, but also form the form, speed and content of creative work. The better phrasing is the creator and platform economy, which is one of the most significant systems of labour in the twenty-first century (Duffy and Wissanger, 2017).

5.2. Democratisation and the Equal Opportunity Delusion

The conception of anyone being a creator stands as one of the most glorified traits of the platform economy. Having a smartphone and internet connection, individuals are able to post videos, music, tutorials, artwork, stories or performances without any agencies, studios or publishers (Cunningham & Craig, 2019). This has decreased most traditional barriers to entry, and increased creativity with access by diverse creators with diverse backgrounds to express themselves and reach out to others (Abidin, 2018). Nonetheless, studies indicate that platforms have the power to make participation democratised, but not success. The vast majority of creators have even less than a small percentage of the attention and the revenue since algorithm recognition ranking and followers concentration habits (Duffy and Wissinger, 2017). In this way, the prospect of open participation is combined with the grossly unequal effects.

5.3. An Argument about Creative Visibility and the CVC of Audience Engagement

Visibility as a currency of the platform economy. Cultural producers need to develop and sustain an audience to be economically significant, which cannot be achieved without constant interaction. The likes, comments, shares, watch and subscriber figures have a direct impact on the algorithm ranking and a recommendation of a creatorship. This is influential on creative behaviour, since creators are always thinking of what will sell them an audience to continue watching. Creators track the analytics dashboards and optimize the content to achieve a higher performance than concentrating on the artistic expression. This requirement of continual involvement also implies that the creative process does not entirely stop, which is what adds stress and overworking even to the most successful creators (Duffy and Wissinger, 2017). It is thus that the audiences not only are made into a consumer but also participants whose reactions influence the creative decisions.

5.4. Personal Branding, Identity and Authenticity

Contrary to the old model jobs designed to work in areas where the creative worker was no longer attached to the work, platform based creators tend to use personality and identity as the core elements of their brand. It has been found that seemingly authenticity appeals to the audiences, stimulating the creators towards sharing personal tales, truly feeling and daily routines (Duffy and Hund, 2015). The personal and professional self are mixed over time, since personal aspects of life are included in the image of the creator and his economic policy (Abidin, 2018). The assumption of endless transparency may be an emotionally heavy burden, which creators are under the pressure to stay positive and receptive even when addressing stress or facing personal issues (Berryman, and Kavka, 2017). In this way, identity performance turns out to be a labour demand, but not an individual choice in the platform economy.

5.5. Platform Dependency and Algorithmic Labour

Even though creators seem autonomous, they rely on the algorithms of the platforms to have a presence and earn money. The algorithms determine what the users see on their feeds and recommended lists, and thus they remain unnoticed as the cultural production managers. The algorithmic rankings are beyond the control of creators, and the fluctuations of reach may go unexplained and sudden because of the fluctuations of the platform or shifting consumer behavior (Cunningham and Craig, 2019). This addiction results in what researchers refer to as algorithmic precarity wherein employment security gives way to a state of unwavering predictability and anxiety to meticulously follow the requirements of the ever-changing platforms (Duffy and Wissinger, 2017). Not just talent and creativity determines the livelihood of the creator, but also, the capacity of the creator to change according to the automated system that one cannot completely understand and presence agreement.

5.6. Digital Creativity: Monetisation Models and Economics

Multiple revenue opportunities exist on platforms, such as advertising income, creator funds, brand sponsorship, affiliate marketing, product placement, fan contributions and subscription income. These alternatives enable creators to earn money beyond the conventional jobs and own their own enterprises (Cunningham & Craig, 2019). The monetisation, however, needs a long-term visibility which is volatile. The revenue of advertising is subject to change, corporate sponsorship is contingent on brand movements, and fan revenue is always subject to constant emotional motivation and bonding (Abidin, 2018). A lot of creators refer to the earning pattern as irregular since an income may fluctuate significantly between one month to the other. Although successful creators tend to have numerous sources of income to get by, they are forced to multitask and keep trying new things, all the time (Duffy and Hund, 2015). The platform economy thus does not promise a lot but hardly secures.

5.7. Parasocial Relationship and Relational Labour

Creators and audiences tend to form parasocial relationships one-way emotional relations in which the viewer is personally attached and the creator has no knowledge of them. (Berryman and Kavka, 2017). Such relationship may boost faithfulness and have a larger monetisation influence since fans are encouraged to invest in creators, scale turnouts to occasions, get merchandise or join fan clubs (Duffy and Hund, 2015). This is however accompanied with emotional labour in order to sustain a parasocial bond. To maintain contact, creators have to act on the remarks, show appreciation, make an impression of friendliness and open up to be in a vulnerable position (Abidin, 2018). Other creators have concerns about being too emotionally intimate with the followers yet they are afraid to isolate them as they will be less engaged. In this way, the relationship performance is another aspect of labour in the platform economy.

5.8. Unhealthy Criticism, Bullying and Personal expenses

As much as the online exposure may bring fame, the creators may also face harassment, hate speech, and unsolicited online criticism. It has been found that female inventors, minority creators and LGBTQ+ creators face particularly elevated levels of gender-based or identity-based bullying (Berryman and Kavka, 2017). Exposing the creators to continual public commentaries, positive, and negative adds immeasurable emotional pressure, which may result in feelings of anxiety, depression, and burnout (Duffy and Wissinger, 2017). Lots of creators do not want to take a break since less posting usually results in a decrease in the reach, i.e. rest has an economic cost (Abidin, 2018).

5.9. Inequality and Aggregation of Fortune

Despite the seeming openness of the platform economy, it has been revealed that the dominant attention and income concentrate in the hands of a small group of creators. This trend is found in previous creative industries, in which gatekeepers were institutional primarily tending to favour a select few (Hesmondhalgh & Baker, 2013). Suicide is frequently successful in platforms, which demand early start, investment in quality of production, access to professional networks and a significant rate of posting - not necessarily available to everyone (UNCTAD, 2022). The algorithms of platform sometimes logically strengthen inequality since creators with high engagement are rewarded, and it is more challenging to advance new creators (Cunningham and Craig, 2019). In this way the creator economy is full of democratic and unequal features which are juxtaposed to each other.

5.10. Commodified Time, Commodified Emotion and Commodified Social Energy

Everything becomes a part of the creative process in the platform economy, time and emotions, relations and even personal life. According to scholars, it is the commodification of everyday life when the time that used to be a part of personal life is transformed into the monetisable content (Duffy and Hund, 2015). Vacations are turned into vlogs, celebrations are turned into brand partnerships and hobbies are turned into performance opportunities. To the mind of most creators, surviving becomes challenging without considering whether one is living content-worthy lives. Such a form of hyper awareness limits time to rest and self-care and can cause one to feel isolated as even friendship relations and family life become subsumed within the professional branding economy (Berryman and Kavka, 2017). One of the strongest forces of contemporary creative labour is the emotional pressure of transforming personal identity into a commercial product (Abidin, 2018).

5.11. Creator Economy as Cultural System

The creator economy that is produced on the platform also has significant effects on culture and society beyond the economic one. The creators assist in forming popular discourse, young identity, ideal beauty, political beliefs, consumer behavior and lifestyle dream (Cunningham and Craig, 2019). They often have an influence that is equal to publicity of typical celebrities and is sometimes even more influential compared to journalists or other figures in the society. Since the creators belong to various groups and resonate directly with audiences, they will be able to break the mainstream media discourse and give voices to certain groups that were historically marginalized (Abidin, 2018). Nevertheless, platform logic but not cultural institutions influences the cultural impact of creators. It implies that algorithmic trends can be more likely to elevate something culturally dominant than artistic or socially beneficial. Measurements, participation and exposure to the platform, influence culture.

The creator and platform economy has altered what kind of people can become a creator, how this creative work can be monetised, and what skills can be the keys to success. Global visibility and autonomy is enabled through platforms, which bring insecurity within economies, emotional strain and reliance on algorithms (Duffy and Wissinger, 2017). Professional value is then integrated with personal identity, and relationships with the audience prove to be the most important to revenue (Abidin, 2018). Creator economy opens the new possibilities of self-expression and cultural engagement, but it recreates inequality and creates new types of precarity (Cunningham and Craig, 2019). This platform ecosystem thus can be seen as empowerment and vulnerability of the creative workers and hence sustainability and well being are vital to the discussion in the future.

6. CHANGING WORKFORCE COMPETENCIES AND ORGANIZATIONAL STRUCTURES

6.1. New Landscape of Skills in Creative Work

The innovative technologies and business models in the creative industries are not the only character defining the future of work but also new demands in terms of skills and professional behaviour. Previously, creative professionals only had to be talented in artistry and technically at ease with whatever they were doing. Nowadays, the ability to be digitally literate, possess marketing skills and have collaboration skills, emotional intelligence and self-management is the determinant of success. The transformation is an indication of the increased complexity of creative labour as employees have to become artists and entrepreneurs (Cunningham & Craig, 2019).

Due to this, the skills environment of the creative sectors is growing larger, and employees are continually being forced to change in response to emerging tools and demands in order to remain competitive (Gill & Pratt, 2008). In creative professions today, transferential learning, perennial mental resilience and strategic professions identity development are thus designed by constant learning (Duffy and Hund, 2015).

6.2. Skill Sets and Multidisciplinary Competence

Innovative employees nowadays are supposed to integrate various kinds of skills instead of acting using one kind of skills. To illustrate, a videographer must in many cases also know the social media, branding, visual trends, audio editing, and analytics of viewers. On the same note, a designer can also require appreciation of design software, retailing skills and marketing techniques to prosper on the internet (Gill & Pratt, 2008). This is the emergence of the so called hybrid professional who combines the creative, technical and managerial abilities in his or her daily work. The rapid growth of the digital tools has broadened the scope of hybrid skill requirements due to the ability of the creators to manage entire production procedures without many people involved (Cunningham & Craig, 2019). Although hybrid competence enhances autonomy and flexibility, it putting a significant stress on creative employees who have to continuously reshape their skills to remain relevant in rapidly evolving markets (Mould et al., 2020).

6.3. Emotional Intelligence and Soft Skills as the Prerequisites of a Professional

Creative careers have been dominated by soft skills that were once regarded to be optional. Communication, conflict resolution and empathy, as well as emotional intelligence have become critical components of cooperative creative setting and engagement with online audience (Berryman and Kavka, 2017). The creative employees tend to work with different people including programmers, marketers, clients and fans globally. This takes cultural sensitivity and inter-personal patience. Also, users operating within digital environments have to overcome criticism, spectators demands and unceasing criticism in a manner that safeguards their self-worth and emotional health (Duffy and Wissinger, 2017). Consequently, emotional intelligence is becoming increasingly a professional ability, not a personality characteristic since the success of creative initiatives is not based solely on the technical performance, but there is also emotional labour (Abidin, 2018).

6.4. Continuous Learning and Continuous Self-Development as a Permanent Labour

The velocity of the changes in technology has rendered lifelong learning to be a professional advantage rather than a professional need. The creative tools, visual trends, platform algorithms and preferences of users are in continuous change, which means creative workers always have to learn new software, change the workflow and experiment with types of content. Nowadays unlike in the past when formal education enabled people to be in long-term careers, creative training is very informal and self-directed and ongoing. Most of the creators study, not in a conventional educational environment, but via online sights of instruction, along with peer networks and online communities (Cunningham and Craig, 2019). This has transformed the role of professional development as it was formerly the responsibility of institutions to individual responsibility. Creative workers are required to use their time and money to learn with no career rewards (Gill and Pratt 2008). It is a continuous self-development, which brings empowerment and pressure.

6.5. Self- Management, Time Discipline and Entrepreneurial thinking

With the shift in employment models to freelancing and platform work, the creative professionals will have to build on self-management skills. They are expected to schedule production cycles, work with expenditures, negotiate contracts, satisfy the deadlines and sell their work independently (Mould et al., 2020). Discipline in time is a significant issue since the schedules of work based on digital and platform are not definite. According to many creators, it is challenging to manage time, disengage the mind at work and separate personal space since digital presence is a round-the-clock factor (Berryman and Kavka, 2017). In addition, creative industries, where employees are now expected to think as entrepreneurs and not employees, have become subject to entrepreneurial thinking, even in a situation when the person did not make a purposeful decision to become an entrepreneur (Duffy & Hund, 2015). The capacity to plan income, collaboration and interactions with the audience is a main strength within the new labour environment (Abidin, 2018).

6.6. Organization Structures: The Networking of Organizations

Creative industries are changing their organizational forms through the rigid hierarchies to flexible and collaborative networks. Previously, creative projects had to be based on fixed teams with well-specified job descriptions. Now, multidisciplinary freelancers are being assembled on a temporary basis through projects, where teams are disbanded as soon as the project finishes (Mould et al., 2020). The flexible nature of these structures enables quicker response to shifts in the market and minimise real labour costs to the companies (Gill & Pratt, 2008). Simultaneously, creative employees have to continuously establish and sustain relationships since jobs in the future usually rely on personal contacts at the expense of organisational devotion (Hesmondhalgh and Baker, 2011). As a result, networking is transformed into a continual process and a kind of invisible work that is a necessary survival to a career (Abidin, 2018).

6.7. Working at a distance and becoming global is transforming patterns of collaboration

Remote work has emerged as one of the central characteristics of creative labour and has allowed cooperation between employees in various locations and time zones. File sharing services, remote meeting services, cloud editing services and project management services contribute to distributed team work (Tryon, 2013). Remote collaboration gives access to the world market and multi-national projects without geographical mobility, extending possibilities of innovative workers that are not part of creative cities (Comunian et al., 2014). Nevertheless, remote working is also making competition more intense because the company is able to employ employees wherever they are, with the company frequently choosing based on the price and not based on the geographical area (Cunningham & Craig, 2019). This labour globalisation is creating more diversity and opportunity, and the wage pressure and economic inequalities, especially to those creators in high cost areas (Gill & Pratt, 2008). Telecommuting requires close communication, discipline among self and personal problem solving.

6.8. Changing Leadership models in Innovative workplaces

Leadership model is shifting in the creative industries as structures continue to change in an organization. Traditional leadership was characterized by top-down leadership where managers dictated creative workers with minimal or no possibility of negotiating with them. It has become the accepted wisdom of many creative organisations today that innovation is born out of teamwork, interest and emotional security (Hesmondhalgh and Baker, 2011). Innovative environments where creative industries are led by capable leaders empower independence, exploration and openness instead of rigid hierarchies (Berryman & Kavka, 2017). Managers must support both creativity and well-being through providing positive feedback, securing the work-life balance, and harnessing emotional labour as a component of creative work (Duffy & Wissinger, 2017). Nevertheless, even creative workplaces are often unprotected (formally and mentally) and lack mental health resources, thus reforming leadership remains a major challenge to the sustainability requirements in the future (Abidin, 2018).

6.9. Mental Health and Well Being as Workforce Concerns

Emotional investment in working is of high level in creative workers since creativity is an expression of personal meaning and identity. The burden to deliver in front of the camera and remain visible on the internet platforms leads to anxiety and burnout (Duffy and Wissinger, 2017). According to the scholars, mental health issues increase due to the lack of stability in creators incomes, anxiety about being out of relevancy or/and the belief of being compared with people in competitive markets (Berryman & Kavka, 2017). Nevertheless, these problems do not mean that most creative organisations have statutory policies that promote mental health, and that freelancers are not insured by conventional employee rights (Hesmondhalgh and Baker, 2011). Thus, the responsibility on mental health support should no longer be the individuality prerogative but the structural responsibility such as the platform responsibility, policy intervention and educational support (Comunian et al., 2014). The creative professional longevity depends on the lack of well-being frameworks.

6.10. Online Professional Identity and Reputation Management

One more competence to have in contemporary creative labour is the skill to control a professional online identity. The nature of collaborations, sponsorships and audience trust depend on the online presence of a creator, such as branding style, tone, portfolio and professional message (Duffy and Hund, 2015). At the same time, creators have to be consistent in their messages delivered through various platforms and be able to adjust their tone to suit various audiences without being untrue to themselves (Abidin, 2018). Digital identity is a reputation resource that has long-term value and has to be minded because any negative review, internet scandals or mismatch with anticipated brand behavior may influence employment prospects (Berryman and Kavka, 2017). Reputation management is hence a strategic labour and not an incidental result.

6.11. The Increasing necessity of the Collective Support and Labor Protection

With the shift in production and labour towards the so-called freelance and platform-based creative industries, the traditional forms of labour protection: stable payments, health cover, sick leave and retirement provisions become harder to achieve (Gill & Pratt, 2008). This growing precarity has brought fresh demands to unions, co-operatives and laws to secure the creative workers (Hesmondhalgh and Baker, 2011). Portable benefits, minimum platform pay, creator universal basic income, or collective bargaining negotiated in response to the freelance and digital labour, are some of the policies suggested by scholars (UNCTAD, 2022). In the absence of structural support, the burden of well-being and sustainability of career is entirely left on individuals, resulting in high dropout rates and burnout even in cases of talented workers (Duffy and Wissinger, 2017).

There is significant change in competency expectations and organisational structures in the creative industries. A hybrid skillset, emotional intelligence, business skills, lifelong learning and digital identity management are needed in the creative work (Cunningham and Craig, 2019). Organisational designs are moving to flexible, remote and networked ones, which provide freedom but enhance the level of insecurity (Gill and Pratt, 2008). Creative employees need to be more emotionally and financially responsible than ever as audience engagement, platforms, remote working and self-management roles start playing greater roles in the work process (Duffy and Wissinger, 2017). The challenge of securing sustainable creative futures will involve more powerful individual capacities as well as legislative changes in the leadership and labour policy, psychological care and professional education (Hesmondhalgh and Baker, 2011).

7. SOCIOECONOMIC, LEGAL, AND ETHICAL CHALLENGES

7.1. The Darker Side of Digital Creativity

Due to digital transformation, a significant opportunity opened in the job of creative workers, however, this transformation has also created a lot of socioeconomical, legal and ethical problems. The creative economy is being established through freelance labour, algorithmic regimes and emotionally-driven social interaction with the public, rendering creative labour empowering and unstable. The multitude of creators is now available to audiences worldwide and they have to work without obvious protection of labour, guaranteed income or assurance of psychological safety (Hesmondhalgh and Baker, 2011). Internet has altered the value of creative work, the creators and the ones that gain or the ones that lose. Such pitfalls allow concluding that future processes of creative working will have to find solutions to structural fragilities and cannot be based on personal resistance (Duffy and Wissinger, 2017). To develop equitable and sustainable creative careers, it is important to understand those issues.

7.2. Creative Labour Economic Insecurity and Irregular Income

Among the most widespread problems of the creative professions is economic insecurity. A recent situation is that most creative employees are no longer on full-time staff but instead rely on temporary positions, freelance work or platform-based income as opposed to an unchanging paycheck that arrives at the end of a month (Gill & Pratt, 2008). Although there are creators making huge incomes, the majority of them encounter volatile incomes that fluctuate monthly depending on the demand, the exposure of the platform or project revolve (Hesmondhalgh and Baker, 2011). A lot of creators do not have stable earnings when their business is pegged on audience engagements (views, views per 30-second ad, and so on) or even dealings with sponsors or auto-recommendation solutions. Long-term financial planning is not so easy in the absence of stable wages, and a lot of creative employees do not have money in their wallets, insurance, and retirement security. This economic uncertainty scares away the talented people who may be perfect in the creative fields despite their great abilities and interest (Cunningham & Craig, 2019). Creativity could make industries to get high monetary profits but in most cases, the economic risk is taken by the individuals that create it.

7.3. Time Wasting and Working More in the Name of being Visible

In numerous creative professions today there is a lack of time. It is not enough that creators produce their work but promote them and have relationships with audiences and administrative duties including contracts and finances (Duffy and Hund, 2015). The greater the need to frequent their accounts constantly, interact with users and monitor platform statistics without pauses because it is easy to lose online presence if a person does not post something at least every two hours. Inspiration When makers are not engaged in work, they have ideas that are mentally linked, platforms and expectations of the audience (Berryman & Kavka, 2017). Creative work on the internet thus does away with definite working and leisure time. Weekends, holidays, and intimate time can soon become content possibilities and rest seems to be a waste of time instead of a rejuvenating journey. The outcome is a tendency towards overwork that turns into an order of things, where creators feel guilty of halting the work due to the fact that the only condition of visibility is constant production (Abidin, 2018). Time poverty is an organisational problem as opposed to a personal output question.

7.4. Psychological Pressure, Burnout and Emotional Labour

Since creative activity usually integrates the approach to personal identity, the creators develop a personal attachment to the work. Every day, digital creators share their personalities and feelings with their audiences and can only be positive and entertained to retain a connection with the followers (Duffy and Wissinger, 2017). It is an emotional labour that is highly self-regulated and may result in stress, anxiety and burnout. Studies indicate that creators often feel the fear of irrelevancy, disappointment due to the adverse response and low numbers with which the creators interact (Berryman and Kavka, 2017). It is draining as you have the pressure to look happy and confident even in times when you are dealing with personal or emotional issues and the income you earn will be determined by how you perform before the people. Digital creative work requires constant emotional control as a component of the labour process in contrast to traditional work, when emotional states may be rather secret (Abidin, 2018). Not only is burnout a personal danger, but it is a systemic impact of the contemporary creative labor.

7.5. Digital Harassment, Hate Speech and Identity-Based Abuse

High visibility is equated to high vulnerability. Most creators have been harassed, bullied and subjected to hate speech on the internet, in particular women, LGBTQ+ creators and creators of marginalised communities (Berryman & Kavka, 2017). The commentaries, messages, as well as such information on Facebook, offer creators a direct contact with the critics, who may at times comment on how they appear, live, or identify with culture, or on personal connections or relationships. This continued self-exposure to societal scrutiny destroys self-esteem and feelings of emotional state and may deter creators to express themselves (Abidin, 2018). Plateforms are not always able to regulate the abusive actions, and creators tend to handle harassment themselves, struggling to apply their mental well-being and protect their professionalism (Duffy and Wissinger, 2017). As much as internet popularity can be flattering, it also introduces enmity to creators, and mental security is a very essential but in most cases overlooked labour concern.

7.6. Imbalances in Advantage and Performance in the Creative Economy

Structural inequalities have a very clear impact on beneficiaries of the creative economy although digital platforms appear to offer equal opportunities. The artists in high-income regions usually have more access to high-speed internet, devices, funds, and professional connections which provide them with competitive advantages

(UNCTAD, 2022). Large cities that are well equipped in terms of creativity attract talent and investments and creators in countryside or poor areas find it hard to be noticed and funded. Opportunities are also defined by language and culture where English speaking creators can get access to global audiences more effortlessly than their English speaking counterparts (Cunningham and Craig, 2019). Such inequalities ensure success is unequal even in cases whereby participation will increase. The platform creator economy hence reflects instead of eradicating economic inequality (Comunian et al., 2014). The online creative field will continue to strengthen the social divides, and without special assistance, this issue is likely to escalate.

7.7. The Digital Age of Intellectual Property and Ownership

The legal landscape of creative work has been made complex by the digital technology. When creative work is put online, it may be copied, reused or modified with ease without authorization thus copyright protection is hard with independent creators not having legal means (Kretschmer & Towse, 2020). Meanwhile, user-generated content can frequently work to the advantage of the creative platform since user generated content pumps up the engagement and advertising income whilst individual creators do not have much bargaining power to sell the rights to their output. The emergence of the generative AI exacerbates these issues. A large number of AI systems are trained in and based on existing artworks, music or writing with no express permission of anyone, and one can wonder who will own what and who will be paid (Elgammal et al., 2017). The existing copyright regulations have not completely addressed the question of whether AI-generated material should be considered the property of the developer of the AI, the user of the human or neither (Shneiderman, 2020). Due to a lack of renewed intellectual property policy, digital innovation is a threat to mishandle creators instead of making them enabled.

7.8. Algorithms and Non-Transparency

Algorithms used on digital platforms shape the visibility of creators and the amount of income they get. Yet, creators are unaware of the decision-making process of these algorithms and why they have more coverage and less coverage. A simple shift on rules of the platform can drastically shift the participation, incomes and professional sustainability. Since the algorithms focus on popular content, they make creators, who do not have many followers, develop, which strengthens inequality. Lots of makers spend their time on researching platform analytics, changing their posting styles and creating trend-based material to meet the demands of the algorithm (Cunningham & Craig, 2019). Through such a process algorithmic systems are creative labour managers with impunity. This is because creators run a risk of being fired without warning (so-called invisible dismissal), and they cannot appeal to the established cause or work negotiation channels (Duffy and Wissinger, 2017). This uncertainty and fear generate and make the income unpredictable.

7.9. The Rights to Labour and the Lack of Customary Guarantees

Creative labour is among those who are now carried out beyond the conventional working relationships. The majority of creators fall under the category of freelancers, independent contractors or self-employed persons and not employees (Gill & Pratt, 2008). This grouping would enable the businesses and platforms to escape offering benefits like health insurance, paid leaves, minimum wage assurances or even retirement saving. Even very successful workers do not feel safe as they cannot get any stable incentives due to their legal situation (Hesmondhalgh and Baker, 2011). Platform-based work is decentralised and competitive and collective actions are challenging because some creators have tried to form unions, collectives or cooperatives to assert their rights, yet few have found success (UNCTAD, 2022). In the absence of labour protection, financial risk and survival of individual creators are entirely in their own hands, making them more unstable in the long term.

7.10. Competition and Wage Pairs in Digital Markets in Creative Economies

The technology also allows creative workers to deliver to global clients or audiences with resultant global labour competition also reducing revenue. Most employers and brands are not finding local talent because they are after the lowest possible costs, thus, disadvantaged creators in expensive areas (Cunningham & Craig, 2019). The markets of creative professionals are prone to become the race-to-the-bottom markets where masses of workers do their best to secure the available chances with references to the prices but not to the knowledge and experience (Gill and Pratt, 2008). This force will cause wage compression throughout the sector and can deter long-term investment in skill development by creators who experience that they cannot earn rates sustainable to them. Globalization further raises both the opportunity and competition simultaneously, resulting in an imbalance of labour performance between countries and between people with different incomes (Comunian et al., 2014).

7.11. Diversity, Representation and Power Ethical Questions

The creative industries largely control the formulation of cultural discourses. Nevertheless, cultural representation can be affected more by digital values than social relevance when the decision of what voice should be made visible is made by platform algorithms. It has been revealed that creators of marginalised groups have lower chances, and are more prone to online harassment, which hinders their success despite digital accessibility (Berryman & Kavka, 2017). Although digital services offer communities of different kinds, they may be strengthening prejudices too, in the situation when the algorithms promote mainstream aesthetics, Western ideals of beauty or stereotypical content (Abidin, 2018). The ethical dilemmas of creative labour are thus related to more general problem of cultural power, as well as social justice. Fairness of inclusion cannot be ensured by simply access to platforms, but involves cultural and structural transformation.

7.12. The Tension of being creative and commercialized

The emotional, social and cultural worth of creative expression has not been eliminated in the platform media but is measured more by indicators like views, clicks and shares. Most creators testify to changing their vision of creativity since the platforms give rewards to some kinds of content - trends, entertainment quickly and without critical thought, deepest or slow forms of creativity are monetized badly in theory (Duffy and Wissinger, 2017). This struggle leads to an ethical dilemma, but in choosing to remain true or rather visible. Other creators believe that their artistic principles are violated when they focus on getting more likes or trending topics to remain afloat on a financial basis (Abidin, 2018). The danger is that the innovation in the cultural sphere can be substituted by the algorithms of repetitions, that make creative expression in the society less diverse (Cunningham and Craig, 2019). The debate on creative work ethics should therefore concern the implications that commercial interests have on artistic freedom.

The digital creative economy offers new working opportunities, identities, and targeting but it has proven to present serious socioeconomic, legal and ethical issues. Creative workers are overburdened by economic insecurity, emotional labour, algorithmic control and no labour protection (Hesmondhalgh and Baker, 2011). Platform-based work introduction widens involvement yet strengthens inequality and bullying and does not help individuals to enjoy psychological or financial security (Duffy and Wissinger, 2017). The laws on intellectual property and labour have not adapted to AI and digitalisation, which means that creators are prone to abuse and insecurity (Kretschmer and Towse, 2020). It will demand more than personal expertise or strength to support sustainable creative futures, it will demand structural support, policy innovation and ethical responsibility at all levels, on a governmental, industrial and platform level (UNCTAD, 2022).

8. RESEARCH AND FUTURE SCOPE

8.1. The Question of Future Research

With the fast-growing transformations in creative industries under the impact of digital technology, platform labour, and artificial intelligence, it is necessary to conduct further research to comprehend the issues and opportunities that the future will entail. Numerous existing studies explain the transformation of creative work, but less studies reflect on the impact of the specified changes on the sustainability of careers in the long-run, economic stability, and psychological welfare (Hesmondhalgh and Baker, 2011). Besides, technological innovation can be very rapid in its rapidly distributing aspect, so in many cases, academic research finds itself falling behind the real-life scenario. To successful creative workers, research should be futuristic, not merely examining existing trends but how they expect future labour structures, technologies and policies to define creative practices in the future (Cunningham and Craig, 2019). This is meant to serve as a guide in upholding innovation in the future without reducing fairness, dignity and human well-being (Duffy and Wissinger, 2017).

8.2. The Dynamics of Creative Industry Long-Term Career Sustainability

The creative professions are hardly stable or linear. A majority of the workers start off with passion and zeal and end up being faced by financial crisis, exhaustion or lack of opportunities. Nevertheless, studies tend to overlook these long-term experience due to the fact that most of the research looks at a short duration of time or particular industry or sector (Hesmondhalgh and Baker, 2011). Longitudinal studies that monitor creative laborers over decades are needed in order to know how their careers advance, their income changes, how their skills develop and come to a retirement age. Such evidence may assist teachers, policy makers and labour unions to establish more effective support systems to creative employees. The absence of long-term research continues to imprint the societal notions of creative careers with only a handful of high-profile success stories and not what the majority of them go through on a daily basis (Gill & Pratt, 2008). Hopeful creative practices must extend into the way individuals construct, in fact, creative lives.

8.3. The Mental Health and Emotional Well-Being research

The more pressing issue of creators has become the psychological well being. Even though creative work may lead to happiness and pleasure, it is also a possible cause of depression, anxiety and burnout because of stresses and the exposure to social disapproval and unreliable earnings (Berryman and Kavka, 2017). Online artists tend to think they do not have the right to take a break in lieu of being forgotten, which means being poorer. Although there are studies which record this challenge, there is a lot more research on the subject.

Additional studies are also required to assess possible mental-health solutions digital well-being application, community of creator peer-supporters, counselling, and platform-specific safety features (Abidin, 2018). The issue of well-being should be considered by research since the future innovation should not be at the cost of the psychological safety.

8.4. Discovering Skill Development and Competing Educational Needs

Creative employees are currently required to have a blended body of skills that can incorporate artistic, technical as well as entrepreneurial skills. Nevertheless, classical learning and media education mostly emphasize on craft and theory leaving the students ill equipped with real working conditions in the world (Gill & Pratt, 2008). It should be investigated how the education system can be changed to incorporate the training of digital platforms, brand management, communicating with clients, financial literacy, time management, and emotional coping strategies. The literature must also examine informal learning platforms such as online tutorials, communities of creators and mentorships networks that have turned into the main actors in skill development in digital creative workplaces (Cunningham and Craig, 2019). Identifying what creators get and do not get in their learning processes will enable teachers to formulate a curriculum that equips the students not only to generate creativity, but also to make a career out of creativity throughout their lives (Comunian et al., 2014).

8.5. The necessity of a research on the subject of labour rights and the platform governance

With creative workers no longer occupied on a full-time basis but moving to freelance and platform based work, much of the labour protections are dissolved. Whether the status of workers can be identified should creators create economic value to the platforms but in the absence of employment contracts is increasingly being debatable (Gill & Pratt, 2008). Further studies are required to study the ways in which labour regulations, tax and benefits policies would have to be modified to accommodate freelance workers and platform-based workers. Researchers also need to examine the links between the platform governance models such as policies on monetisation, content moderation and algorithmic transparency and the earnings of creators and their career sustainability. The effectiveness of future policies in terms of protecting the lives of creators will not be proactive but reactive unless an empirical study that will provide strong evidence in this context is conducted. Governments, platforms and educational systems, and research ought to have the common duty to ensure fair creative labour conditions, and the mechanisms should be established through research on the optimal ways to do so (UNCTAD, 2022).

The study of Intellectual Property and AI-based Creativity.

Creative economy has become a domain of artificial intelligence and thus has raised certain new ethical and legal concerns. It is possible that AI systems create music, images, videos and writing with training data that contains millions of works created by humans, without their express permission (Elgammal et al., 2017). It has left ambiguity as to the proprietors of AI-generated content and whether or not original human creators have the right to profit when they help to train machine learning models (Kretschmer and Towse, 2020). The studies need to investigate legal provisions capable of favouring technological advancement as well as safeguard human genius. Researchers should also examine the models of human-AI collaboration hybrids in order to know when AI boosts creativity and when it suppresses creative identity (Shneiderman, 2020). There should be clear legal and ethical provisions in order to make sure that artistic labour does not suffer and artistic labour is supported by future creative technology.

Getting to know Inequality and Inclusion in Creative Futures.

Despite the increasing participation of creativity that is conveyed by digital platforms, not every social group gains equally. It has always been demonstrated through research that there exist disparities in opportunities and earnings depending on the gender, race, language, disability, education, and location (UNCTAD, 2022). As the example of creators in rich cities can demonstrate, creators atwealthy may have an advantage due to the availability of superior resources, professional contacts and brands owned, whereas creators in the resource-deprivate regions may face difficulties with basic exposure (Comunian et al., 2014). People of colour and creators of marginalised communities have also been proven to experience more online abuse, less sponsorship, and increased pressure to be able to sustain ideal personal images (Berryman and Kavka, 2017). Future research ought to focus on making the creative systems more open to different groups of people as well as explore how alignment of creative systems may serve minority groups better than perpetuating past societal disparities (Cunningham & Craig, 2019). The futures of the creative methods must not only be technologically sound, but also, socially just.

Future studies in Community and Support Systems and Collective Action.

People tend to regard creative work as a solitary process, whereas in reality, a great number of creators use the community to collaborate, learn, get emotional support and solve certain issues. Nonetheless, there is also scant study about the group dimensions of creativity activity. Further research is required on how peer networks, unions, creator cooperatives and communal spaces can help with resilience and lessen precarity (Hesmondhalgh and Baker, 2011). Research must also be on the ways in which platforms can help in the construction of communities by facilitating the positive interaction, shielding creators against harassment, and allowing back avenue of resolution of disputes. With the growth of the creator economy, it may become critical to recognize what sort of collective forms digital, legal or social assist creative workers in feeling connected and not isolated (Duffy and Wissinger, 2017). Creative careers will rely on collective support systems, which will be necessary in both economic and emotional sustainability.

Assessing Policy Interventions and Public Model Funding.

The policy of the state will largely influence the future of the creative work force. There are numerous funding schemes in many countries that finance cultural projects, but there are only a few schemes that offer schemes of financial safety nets and long term security measures to the individual creators. Studies should be conducted on the most efficient models of the programs of the public that contribute to the activities of creative workers in case of fluctuations in income, change of occupation, and crisis periods (UNCTAD, 2022). Comparison over the various nations would help in shedding light on how cultural support models vary that is; between countries that value commercial creative industries and those that value cultural production as a societal good (Comunian et al., 2014). It is also necessary to research the effectiveness of policy interventions addressing the marginalised creators or perpetuating the existing hierarchies. Economic development in creative industries will not result in equity among creative employees without effective evidence-based policymaking (Cunningham & Craig, 2019).

2021 Future Vision: Sustainable Creative Ecosystems.

Sustainable creative futures will require more than just a technological innovation to be able to go forward. In order to make creativity look and to be a healthy and prospective career choice, stakeholders in the industry are required to establish systems that are sensitive to both economic and emotional realities. As a number of studies begin to indicate, autonomy is not the only aspect of creativity that affects creativity in a positive way: safety, empathy and community also have their share (Hesmondhalgh and Baker, 2011). Further innovation will have to strike a balance between flexibility and steadiness - allowing creators to operate and work on their own but allowing fair terms of work, clear policies of the platform, and mental health safety (Duffy and Wissinger, 2017). The collaboration between education, policy, labour rights, platform accountability and mental-health support should ensure the world creates the future in which creators are allowed to achieve success without losing their health (UNCTAD, 2022). Creative industry is a just and sustainable environment that is not just beneficial to the individual worker but also culture and the entire society.

Summary of Section

Future scope and research on creative labour allows stating a necessity to abandon description and to find structural solutions. Researchers need to explore the long-term creative career sustainability, psychological wellbeing issues, cross-skilling, labour-rights, intellectual property and embedded inequalities of the digital creative systems (Cunningham & Craig, 2019). Although technological innovation is valuable, it should not take priority among the needs of human beings. Creative work will only be secured in the future by being able to come up with systems where creativity is not employed and overworked but rather supported and rewarded (Hesmondhalgh and Baker, 2011). Knowing both the emotional and economic and legal aspects of creative labour, the future research will be helpful to develop a creative economy that is not only productive - but humane, fair and sustainable (Duffy and Wissinger, 2017).

9. CONCLUSION

The second wave swamping new technology is redefining the future of work in the creative business by creating new opportunities through digital mediums and demands on the creative practitioners. People are now able to access audiences around the world without any intermediaries and creativity is becoming a viable economic activity with various global sectors of people contributing through the media, design, music, game and digital content creation. The movement has increased involvement and promoted new cultural expression. Nevertheless, the turning point poses huge challenges which should be overcome to provide sustainable creative careers.

One of the themes that comes out is the tension that is pitting freedom and insecurity. The makers possess more control over their content and professional image than ever before, but have to deal with unpredictable revenues, feeling a place in an algorithm, and the need to keep audiences glued to them. The necessity to always share and have a social image outweighs the delimiting the personal and professional space that can seriously influence the state of mental health and emotional stability. Consequently, creative employees are exposed to a different type of stressors, which used to be less evident in the conventional working environments.

Artificial intelligence and automation are some of the technological developments that present both opportunities and concerns. The AI has the capacity to assist creativity by decreasing monotonous work and allowing innovative arts to be experimented, yet the issue is who can own, be rewarded by copyright or fairness. The digital inequality also makes the situation even more complex as who is given an opportunity to succeed remains to be dictated by access to resources, educational and professional networks, even though the online platform itself seems to have been open.

To continue in the future, creative work will be sustainable with shared responsibility. Governments, schools, digital platforms and industry organisations should collaborate to ensure better labour regulations, to encourage transparent platform policies, to help foster mental health, and encourage more people to achieve training and funding. Likewise, education should also change to equip the future creative laborer not only with artistic and technical competences, but also with self management, communication and entrepreneurial thought.

Innovativeness is a useful social resource that adds cultural, identity and human relations. The creative economy needs to appreciate and safeguard the individuals that make it go in order to realize all its potential. When innovativeness and well-being are cultivated in unison, the future of creative work can not only be very economically motivating but also traditionally fulfilling.

10. REFERENCES

Abidin, C. (2018). *Internet celebrity: Understanding fame online*. Emerald Publishing., DOI: 10.1108/9781787560765

Berryman, R., & Kavka, M. (2017). Crying on YouTube: Vlogs, self-exposure and the performance of emotional labour. *Journal of Gender Studies*, *26*(3), 278–292. DOI: 10.1177/1354856517736981

Comunian, R., Taylor, C., & Smith, D. (2014). The role of universities in the creative economy: Comparative perspectives from the UK and the US. *Creative Industries Journal*, *7*(2), 117–135. DOI: 10.1080/09654313.2013.790589

Couldry, N., & Mejias, U. A. (2019). *The costs of connection: How data is colonizing human life and appropriating it for capitalism*. Stanford University Press., DOI: 10.1515/9781503609754

Cunningham, S., & Craig, D. (2019). Social media entertainment: The new intersection of Hollywood and Silicon Valley. NYU Press. https://nyupress.org/9781479846894/

Duffy, B., & Wissinger, E. (2017). Mythologies of Creative Work in the Social Media Age: Fun, Free, and "Just Being Me". *International Journal of Communication*, *11*, 4652–4671.

Duffy, B. E., & Hund, E. (2015). "Having it all" on social media: Entrepreneurial femininity and self-branding among fashion bloggers. *Social Media + Society*, *1*(2), 1–11. DOI: 10.1177/2056305115604337

Elgammal, A., Liu, B., Elhoseiny, M., & Mazzone, M. (2017). CAN: Creative adversarial networks — Generating "art" by learning about styles and deviating from style norms. *Proceedings of the 8th International Conference on Computational Creativity (ICCC)*, 97–104. https://doi.org/DOI: 10.48550/arXiv.1706.07068

Gill, R., & Pratt, A. (2008). In the social factory? Immaterial labour, precariousness and cultural work. *Theory, Culture & Society*, *25*(7–8), 1–30. DOI: 10.1177/0263276408097794

Hesmondhalgh, D., & Baker, S. (2011). 'A very complicated version of freedom': Conditions and experiences of creative labour in three cultural industries. Variant: cross currents in culture, 41, 34-38.

Hesmondhalgh, D., & Baker, S. (2013). *Creative labour: Media work in three cultural industries*. Routledge.

Howkins, J. (2002). The creative economy: How people make money from ideas. Penguin UK.

Jenkins, H. (2006). Convergence Culture: Where Old and New Media Collide. NYU Press. https://www.jstor.org/stable/j.ctt9qffwr

Liestøl, G. (2021). Situated simulations and augmented reality: Design principles and empirical studies. *Digital Creativity*, *32*(4), 227–244. DOI: 10.1007/978-1-4614-0064-6_14

Mould, O., Vorley, T., & Liu, Y. (2020). Rethinking creative clusters: Towards new typologies of geographic assemblages. Environment and Planning A: Economy and Space, 52(2), 305–326.https://www.taylorfrancis.com/chapters/edit/10.4324/9781315712598-9/freelancers-freelancing-creative-economy?context=ubx

Shneiderman, B. (2020). Human-centered artificial intelligence: Reliable, safe & trustworthy. *International Journal of Human-Computer Interaction*, *36*(6), 495–504. DOI: 10.1080/10447318.2020.1741118

Tryon, C. (2013). *On-demand culture: Digital delivery and the future of movies*. Rutgers University Press., https://www.jstor.org/stable/j.ctt5hjcmk

UNCTAD. (2022). Creative economy outlook 2022: Trends in international trade in creative industries. United Nations Conference on Trade and Development. https://unctad.org/publication/creative-economy-outlook-2022

Yoo, Y., Henfridsson, O., & Lyytinen, K. (2010). The new organizing logic of digital innovation: An agenda for information systems research. *Information Systems Research*, *21*(4), 724–735. DOI: 10.1287/isre.1100.0322

Chapter 7
Human Augmentation and Enhanced Creativity

Ved Srivastava
https://orcid.org/0009-0006-6278-7840
Department of Management, FMS, India

Yusuf Kamal
https://orcid.org/0000-0002-1557-8775
University of Lucknow, India

Raj Kumar Mishra
https://orcid.org/0000-0002-6912-6694
IMS, University of Lucknow, India

ABSTRACT

This chapter delves into how human augmentation reshapes creativity, drawing from Garry Kasparov's 1997 chess defeat by Deep Blue as a pivotal moment. He realized true strength arises when skilled minds pair with smart machines. Creativity, once viewed as a lone intuitive flame started blooming through partnership. Humans offer emotion, ethics, and purpose while AI started delivering speed, enormous memory, and pattern spotting. Bounded rationality confines us, as Simon and Kahneman noted, yet augmentation stretches those edges without deleting our gut instincts. Dispersed creativity shatters the introverted genius myth, fostering flow by facilitating frictions in "Ideation" and "Refinement". The chapter examines the Asian contexts.

DOI: 10.4018/979-8-3373-7153-5.ch007

1. INTRODUCTION

When Garry Kasparov lost his historic chess match to IBM's Deep Blue (1997), the world interpreted it as the victory of "Machine Intelligence" over "Human Ingenuity". Yet Kasparov himself later reframed that moment, arguing that true power emerged when a skilled human worked with a capable computer (Kasparov, 2021). This comprehension marked the beginning of what we now call "Human Augmentation", the merger of "Human Cognition" with "Intelligent Systems" to achieve creative results that neither could have produced alone.

In the twenty-first century, this phenomenon has moved far beyond the chessboard. It has penetrated the very heart of the creative economy,encompassing design, music, architecture, film, advertising, and even academic research. So, we must accept that "*What once appeared as the domain of intuition and emotion is now shared terrain between humans and machines*". Simultaneously, Richard Florida's theory of the Creative Class (Florida, 2002) supported the statement "Creativity has become an economic engine". But today, this engine runs not only on talent and culture, but it also runs on algorithms, sensors, and data-enhanced imagination.

Traditionally, creativity is seen as a deeply human trait. In Asian philosophies acknowledges "Creativity has long been linked to balance, intuition, and spiritual insight rather than analytical process" (Nisbett, 2013). In Indian artistic thought, the notion of "Rasa", the aesthetic essence or emotional flavour of an artwork, signifies creativity as a lived, emotive experience (Sarma, 2018). Machines, being unemotional, seemed powerless of grasping that spirit. However, recent advances in machine learning and cognitive computing have begun to challenge this hypothesis. Generative AI models can now compose music, write poetry, or produce intricate visual art. Yet what these outputs reveal is not machine originality but machine collaboration i.e. systems amplifying human intention through computation (Shneiderman, 2022).

In my view, creativity in the AI era is less about the disappearance of human genius and more about its expansion. Tools have always shaped creative expression. The printing press, the camera, and the synthesizer each redefined what was possible in their time. AI and augmentation technologies merely continue that trajectorybut with a deeper form of integration. They extend not only the artist's hand but also the mind itself. Cognitive scientists like Herbert Simon (1983) long argued that humans operate under bounded rationality, meaning our decisions are shaped by limited information and time. Augmentation stretches those limits by amplifying perception, memory, and analysis.

This is not entirely new. Kahneman's dual-system model of thinking, where "System 1" represents fast intuition and "System 2" slower reasoning, shows that human cognition constantly toggles between instinct and reflection (Kahneman et al., 2011). Creative work, from composing a melody to designing a marketing campaign, relies on this interplay. Machine augmentation can strengthen both systems: it can accelerate intuition by offering rapid pattern recognition and deepen reflection through complex data visualization. But the essential spark of purpose, wherein one decides why something matters, remains human.

Jack Welch, during his years at General Electric, often reminded managers that no data can substitute for a leader's gut instinct. The same holds true for artists and innovators. Even in data-rich creative industries, intuition decides which insights to follow. Hence, the task ahead is not "replacing intuition with information," but combining them and letting human sensitivity work alongside machine precision.

Moreover, there are examples to show that augmentation in creativity is not a Western import, but a global evolution shaped by local culture.Already, creative sectors across Asia illustrate this blend vividly. In India's fashion and textile clusters, small firms use AI-based colour prediction tools to forecast market preferences while preserving handloom traditions. In South Korea's entertainment industry, virtual K-pop idols are co-created by human choreographers and AI-driven facial animation. Japanese architects, meanwhile, employ augmented reality (AR) systems to simulate Zen-inspired spatial experiences before construction begins.

Of course, this partnership raises questions. Does machine assistance dilute originality or heighten it? Some critics argue that excessive automation could lead to "derivative creativity," where originality gives way to algorithmic predictability (Boden, 2016). Yet research by Runco,M. A., & Acar, S. (2024) suggests otherwise that augmentation can enhance divergent thinking by exposing creators to broader idea sets. It depends, however, on how consciously it is used. If technology becomes a crutch, it can dull human curiosity. But when used as a catalyst, it frees time and cognitive energy for exploration. The key lies in intention and awareness.

We can say, then, that creativity in the age of human augmentation is no longer about isolated genius but about orchestrated synthesis. The creator becomes part designer, part curator i.e. someone who navigates between human experience and machine-generated possibilities. Machines may provide the range, but humans still provide the reason. A marketing manager might analyse emotional data to shape a brand story but deciding which emotion to evoke still demands empathy and cultural insight. That combinationof scale and sensibilityis the real frontier of augmented creativity.

This transformation is also reshaping skills and education. In the past, creative training emphasized mastery of technique. Today, it emphasizes adaptability and interdisciplinary thinking. Designers must now understand code, musicians must experiment with generative software filmmakers should collaborate with visual AI tools. Some business schools in India and abroad already include modules on co-creation with AI, where students critique and refine machine-generated ideas. The aim, as educators like Mitra et al (2024) note, is not to replace human imagination but to teach students how to think alongside machines.

Still, equity remains a major concern. Large firms and studios can afford advanced creative AI platforms, while independent creators rely on open tools that may lack sophistication. Without deliberate support, this could deepen what scholars call the augmentation divide (Zuboff, 2019)a new form of inequality where cognitive tools themselves become barriers. For developing economies, the policy challenge is to democratize accessthrough open data, affordable creative infrastructure, and inclusive digital literacy programs. Otherwise, augmentation may reinforce global hierarchies rather than disassemble them.

2. TYPES OF HUMAN AUGMENTATION

Human augmentation manifests in multiple forms, but within creative domains, four categories are particularly relevant: cognitive, sensory, creative, and collaborative augmentation. Together, they represent the continuum from individual enhancement to collective intelligence.

2.1 Cognitive Augmentation

Cognitive augmentation involves using technologies to enhance core mental functions such as perception, memory, problem-solving, and decision-makingas elaborated in Table 1. These tools support humans in transcending the limits of bounded rationality (Simon, 1972). AI systems can analyse vast data sets, suggest alternatives, and reveal hidden patterns which is something human cognition struggles with due to limited working memory and processing speed.

For instance, in film editing, AI-assisted software can automatically identify emotional beats within a narrative by analysing tone and expression, allowing editors to make more informed creative decisions. Similarly, financial analysts use augmented dashboards to visualize risk factors beyond what the human brain could synthesize manually. In creative fields, the most significant outcome of cognitive augmentation is not faster work but wider vision. It gives creators the ability to explore “adjacent possibilities”, new ideas lying just outside the current mental reach. Yet the human remains in control as judgment, context, and emotional depth cannot be delegated to an algorithm.

Table 1. Examples of Cognitive Augmentation in Practice

Function	Technology Type	Application Example
Enhanced Memory	Knowledge management AI	Design history recall tools
Pattern Recognition	Machine learning algorithms	Creative trend forecasting
Decision Support	Predictive analytics	Marketing campaign simulations
Concept Expansion	Generative language models	Ideation in advertising copywriting

Attribution: Conceptually synthesized from Davenport & Kirby (2016).

2.2 Sensory Augmentation

Sensory augmentation refers to expanding the perceptual boundaries of human senses like sight, sound, and touchthrough immersive or responsive technologies. It's where AR, VR, and haptic systems play a central role. For example, an architect can now "walk" through a digital building before it is constructed, or a dancer can choreograph performances in virtual environments that respond dynamically to body movement.

AR and VR have become powerful tools for embodied creativity idea that imagination is not only in the head but also in the body's interaction with its environment (Gallagher, 2011). Artists equipped with haptic gloves can sculpt in virtual space, feeling texture through simulated touch. Similarly, visual designers use augmented vision systems to enhance colour precision or to perceive visual composition in new dimensions. One fascinating example from India is the rise of ARdriven craft preservation. Designers collaborate with rural artisans, using AR visualization to recreate ancient embroidery patterns digitally. These augmented systems bridge traditional tactile craft with digital immersion, preserving heritage while introducing innovation (Figure 1).

Figure 1. Expanding Human Senses with Technology

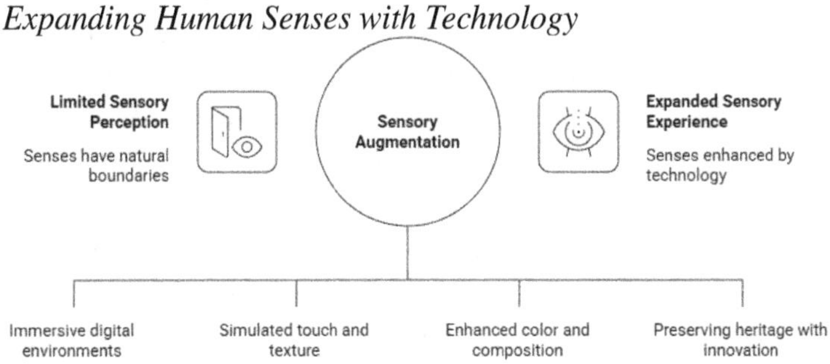

Source: Authors

2.3 Creative Augmentation

Creative augmentation focuses directly on expanding human imagination using AIdriven tools and computational creativity systems. Generative models like DALL·E, Midjourney, or Runway ML allow artists to prototype ideas, test composition, or simulate entire environments as explained in Table 2. However, the output is not creativity but a mirror through which humans can view new possibilities.

Here, the tension between bounded rationality and augmented potential becomes clear. AI offers nearunlimited combinatorial power, but without human intention or emotional framing, it remains a tool. When a filmmaker uses generative AI to conceptualize different lighting moods for a scene, the technology performs the exploration, while the filmmaker performs selection and meaning making. Anecdotally, we can see this in Indian advertising, where AI tools now generate rough layouts or headline variants, which creative directors refine with cultural nuance and humour. This dual process shortens the iteration cycle while preserving authenticity.

Table 2. Levels of Creative Augmentation

Level	Description	Example
Assistive	AI provides reference or inspiration	Idea prompts for logo design
Generative	AI creates variations or prototypes	Image synthesis for concept art
Curatorial	Human selects from AI outputs	Editorial use in publishing
Symbiotic	Continuous human–AI feedback loop	Music composition with generative partners

Attribution: Adapted and extended from Dellermann et al. (2021).

2.4 Collaborative Augmentation

Creativity rarely happens alone. Collaborative augmentation extends teamwork through technology that mediates, enhances, or even participates in creative exchange. Shared virtual workspaces, co-design platforms, and intelligent brainstorming systems enable distributed creativity, merging human diversity with machine-scale insight.

In this collective cognition, humans supply emotion, empathy, and contextual sense, while machines manage complexity and memory. For instance, a group of architects across different cities may co-develop a 3D model in a shared augmented reality interface, with AI suggesting structural improvements in real time. This convergence of human and machine teamwork reflects what Dellermann et al. (2021) call hybrid intelligence, a dynamic interplay between human insight and algorithmic support.Collective augmentation signifies perhaps the most social face of human–AI partnership. It aligns with what Kasparov once observed and strongly advocated.

3. BOUNDED RATIONALITY INDUCED NEED FOR AUGMENTATION

Insightof bounded rationality remains fundamental to understand"Why augmentation matters?" (Simon, 1957). The contest is "Integration". If augmentation simply adds data without supervisory attention or significance, it may overwhelm rather than sanction. Human decision-making is not only based on information but also on intuition and emotion (Kahneman et al., 2011). Therefore, successful augmentation must respect human cognitive architecture, not override it. Table 3 elucidates the point further.

Table 3. Human Cognitive Limits and How Augmentation Extends Them

Cognitive Function	Human Limitation	Augmentation Mechanism	Creative Impact
Memory	Limited recall, information decay	AI-based knowledge retrieval systems	Broader contextual thinking
Attention	Narrow focus, distraction	Smart filtering and visualization tools	Enhanced pattern recognition
Decision-Making	Heuristics, emotional bias	Predictive analytics, simulation models	Betterinformed creative choice
Imagination	Limited by prior experience	Generative AI models	Discovery of novel visual and conceptual patterns

Attribution: Conceptually synthesized from Simon (1957), Kahneman (2011)

3.1 The Rational–Intuitive Dichotomy

In management, design and creative thinking, we often operate under two different modes of decision-making: the rational and the intuitive. These have been explored by scholars such as Herbert A. Simon (bounded rationality) and Daniel Kahneman (System 1/System 2), while business leaders like Jack Welch emphasised intuition ("gut feel") in strategy and innovation.

Simon argued that humans, despite being rational up to a point, face cognitive limits in processing information, time and alternatives. His concept of bounded rationality emphasises that decisionmakers settle for "good enough" rather than optimal because of these constraints. Kahneman built on this by showing that our minds work with two systems: System 1 (fast, intuitive, automatic) and System 2 (slow, analytical, effortful). Welch, in contrast, raised the flag for intuition as he believed that in uncertain, fast-moving business environments a leader's gut instinct which is anchored in experiencematters more than pure data.

In creative sectors, this dichotomy plays out all the time. An art director might feel "this layout just works" (intuition) even before any metrics come in. At the same time, a design firm might run analytics about user interaction (rational) to support creative choices. The interplay is crucial and relying only on data can stifle innovation, while relying only on instinct may ignore broader patterns or emerging trends, as is nicely brought forth in Table 4. Thus, in my view, the challenge for creative professionals is to build workflows where data and instinct are not adversaries but collaborators. That means the machine supplies insights and the human filters those insights through cultural sense, emotional intelligence and aesthetic judgment.

Table 4. Characteristics of Systems and their Implication

Mode	Characteristics	Implication in Creative Work
Rational (System 2)	Deliberate, slow, analytical, datadriven	Provides structure and evidence for creative decisions
Intuitive (System 1)	Fast, automatic, often emotional, patternbased	Offers insight, originality, aesthetic feel
Hybrid	Data feeds intuition and intuition interprets data	Enables both innovation and informed decisionmaking

Attribution: Conceptually synthesized from Kahneman (2011), Simon (1957) and management practitioner insights.

3.2 Bridging Rational and Intuitive modes

Human augmentation with technologies that extend our cognitive or sensory capacitiesusher in new ways to bridge rational and intuitive modes. For instance, digital note-systems allow designers to capture fleeting ideas (intuition) while linking them to data dashboards showing user behaviour (rational). Visual search engines convert large image databases into patterns, freeing the mind for more creative leaps. Ideation bots propose variations, allowing the human to choose, refine and imbue meaning.

In essence the data feeds intuition and intuition guides data interpretation. Augmentation makes this loop more efficient, deeper, and iterative. Whereas in a pre-digital era a creative director may rely purely on experience and manual sketching, now they may sketch, consult generative AI, review analytics, then refine. This layered process exploits the best of both systems.

Consider a marketing team in Bengaluru working on a campaign. They use sentimentanalysis AI to detect consumer mood polarity ("optimistic", "value-seeking", "eco-aware"). The machine delivers numbers but the team then uses that emotional insight to craft an intuitive storyline that feels culturally resonant in the Indian context.

4. MYTH OF SOLITARY GENIUS AND FLOW AUGMENTATION

Creativity today is becoming less of a lonely spark and more of a shared process. We talk about it now as a conversation between people, between people and tools, and often between groups of people mediated by digital systems. This move away from the solitary genius myth is important. It helps us see creativity as something distributed, situated, and social. In plain terms the creativity often lives in the relationship between the human plus the tool rather than inside a single mind (Figure 2).

Figure 2. The Synergy of Human and Tool in Creativity

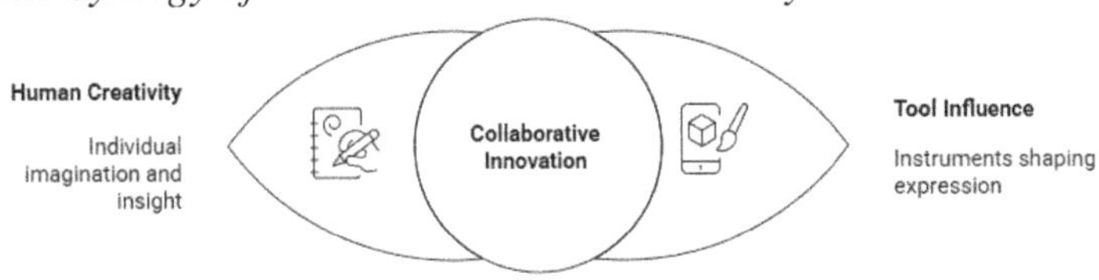

Source: Authors

4.1 Distributed Creativity

The idea of distributed creativity says that creative work often emerges from interactions among people, systems, artifacts, and environments (Glăveanu, 2014; Hutchins, 1995). It draws on the broader notion of the extended mind (Clark & Chalmers, 1998) which says our cognitive processes sometimes extend into external tools and social contexts. So, when a designer sketches on a tablet, stores references in a cloud board, runs a generative prompt, and then meets with colleagues to pick the best idea, the creativity is not only "in" the designer. It's distributed across the sketch, the cloud memory, the generative model, and the team, as is obvious from Table 5.

Why does this matter? Two reasons. First, it frees us from the pressure of single-person originality. We can accept that good ideas often arise from iterated dialogue between human sensibility and tool suggestion. Second, it changes how we structure creative work. If creativity is distributed, then tools, workflows, and team practices matter as much as individual talent.

This distributed view fits well with local traditions of collaborative making. Think of a textile cluster in Panipat or Surat where artisans, dyers, designers, and traders work together andknowledge is shared across hands and tools. Today, when a small textile design house combines artisan sketches, digital colour simulation, and AI-driven market forecasts, the creative outcome is genuinely distributed and often more resilient and culturally rooted.

Table 5. Components of Distributed Creativity

Component	Role in creative process	Example (creative sector)
Human insight	Provides intent, emotion, cultural sense	Art director choosing theme for campaign
External memory	Stores and indexes past ideas	Cloud mood boards used by design teams
Generative tools	Propose variants, expand idea space	AI image generators for concept art
Social exchange	Negotiation, curation, critique	Team workshops refining final concept
Environment / artifacts	Physical/digital objects that shape thought	Prototype models or AR simulations

Attribution: Conceptually inspired by Clark & Chalmers (1998) and Glăveanu (2014); author synthesis for creative sectors.

4.2 Flow Augmentation

Csikszentmihalyi described flow as that absorbing experience where skill matches challenge and time seems to fade (Csikszentmihalyi, 1997). Flow matters for creativity because it lets people dive deep into a problem without being pulled away by small distractions. The good news is that augmentation can help more people enter and sustain flow if done carefully.

How? By reducing friction. By friction I mean anything that interrupts a creative rhythm like searching for a reference for thirty minutes, redoing repetitive edits, hunting for a forgotten colour swatch. Assistive systems can remove those frictions. Externalised memory like notebooks, digital mood boards, etc. reduce the cognitive load of remembering and organising, so the mind can focus on making connections. One-click prototyping and rapid rendering is utilized in architecture or film, when an idea can be instantly visualised in VR, the creator can test and refine without breaking the flow to translate a concept into a physical mock-up.

Systems can well defer non-urgent notifications when they detect sustained concentration via keyboard patterns and help preserve attention.

Also the Generative scaffolds and other tools that produce rough alternatives, let the human focus on judgment and refinement rather than the tedium of initial exploration. Importantly, augmentation does not create flow by itself. It makes flow more likely by removing small obstacles as it clears the desk so the mind can sit down and work. In many of my classes, students say they hit flow when their creative tools become invisible and not when they are flashy. So, usability and subtle assistance matter. Digital note and linking systems e.g., thematic databases, linked cards externalize connections across ideas so creators can follow threads without mental bookkeeping. Instead of scrolling thousands of images, a designer can find visually similar items instantly, preserving momentum through Visual search and reference engines. Adaptive UIs are the interfaces that change complexity based on user expertise The novices get guided flows, and the experts get minimalist canvases to stay immersed. Ambient assistive AI offer quiet suggestions and not intrusive pop-ups e.g., offering alternate colour palettes in a corner rather than disturbing the workspace. These tools must be designed to fit innovative workflow rhythms. The wrong tool can be poorer than none. An overbearing assistant that repetitively suggests changes will explode flow rather than sustenance.

5. EVOLUTION OF TOOLS AS THINKING PARTNERS

Creative tools aided mainly as devices of efficiency. A camera made painting faster and a computer made editing smoother. We are now entering a phase where tools themselves become thinking partners. This transformationfrom instrumental to "Cognitive Partnership" is the describingswing of our time.

5.1 Implication of Tools for Attention, Flow, and Cognitive Load

If the Cognitive load is too high, then, being a "Working memory space" it can inhibit creativity. Augmentation helps in multiple ways with varied advantages for improving upon the cognitive load and, henceattention with better flow states (Figure 3).

Figure 3. Cognitive Augmentation

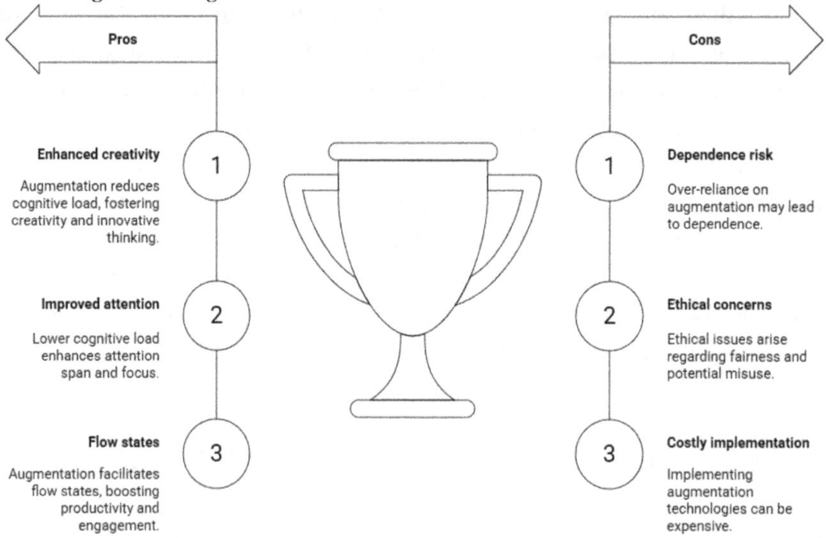

Source: Authors

Digital note systems and memory supports like Evernote, Notion, and idea-mapping apps capture ideas, tag them, and link them. The creator no longer needs to keep everything in mind (Table 6). With the help of visual search engines and patternrecognition assistants, the creative experts can input a mood board image and receive visually similar designs or palette suggestions. This condenses the time and intellectual effort of exploring thousands of possibilities manually (Figure 3). This augmented process supports flow by reducing interruptions, simplifying logistics, and letting the creator stay immersed.

We live in a rapidly evolving creative ecosystem where machines are no longer just tools but cognitive partners. The rational–intuitive dichotomy that Simon and Kahneman explained is increasingly bridged by augmentationwhere data feeds intuition, and intuition guides data interpretation. Creative professionals who understand and apply this interplay will enjoy enhanced flow, reduced cognitive load, richer emotional output and deeper human-machine synergy.

In my view, the future of creative work belongs to those who can think with machines, not just use them, and feel with humans, not just design for them. Because at the heart of art, design and media is not efficiency but expression. And if we let machines support our expression rather than supplant it, we enter a new era of creative possibility.

Table 6. Sensory-Emotional Augmentation Technologies

Technology	Creative Domain	Enhancement Type
Neuromarketing (EEG, eye-tracking)	Advertising, film trailers	Emotion-driven content optimisation
BCIs (neural headsets)	Immersive art, live performance	Direct mind-to-machine generative interface
Emotion AI (face/speech analysis)	Music, interactive media, gaming	Real-time emotional adaptation of creative output

Attribution: Conceptually synthesized from Plassmann et al. (2015), Li et al. (2023) and design-tech industry reports.

6. AUGMENTATION ACROSS CREATIVE GROUPS

6.1 Advertising and Branding

In the changing world of advertising, human creativity and AI augmentation are blending in a way that few could have imagined even a decade ago. Advertising used to be an industry built purely on intuition, on a copywriter's ear for rhythm or a designer's feel for colour. But now, AI tools can track consumer sentiment in real time and create draft campaigns in seconds. Yet, it is the human insight that gives these raw patterns meaning.

For instance, at Ogilvy, creative teams now use AI copy generators that test multiple slogan variants while human editors refine the emotional tone. The result is what we might call emotion editing (Figure 4), the ability to adjust campaign messaging instantly based on empathy and social context. Coca-Cola's "Create Real Magic" project in 2023 reflected this synergy wherein the campaign invited people worldwide to use generative AI tools to remix Coca-Cola imagery, while professional designers ensured that the brand message remained consistent and culturally relevant.

Figure 4. AI and Human Collaborations in Creative Campaigns

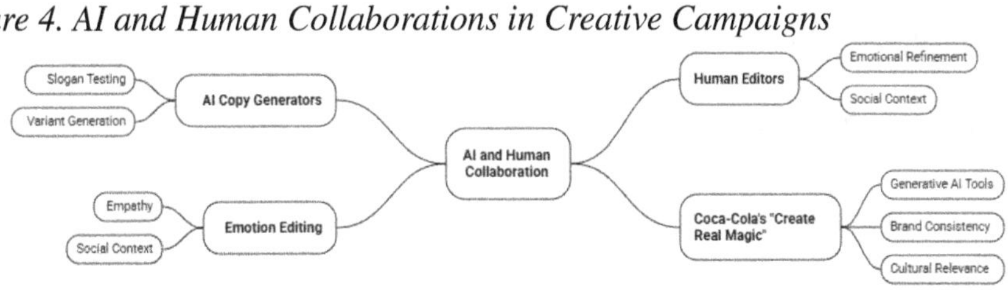

Source: Authors

The potential of augmentation here lies not in trading the copywriter but in intensifying their mental horizon. AI enables what Herbert Simon might call a widening of bounded rationality (Simon, 1971). Advertising strategistsnow speak of "co-creative campaigns," where the digital mechanism provides a canvas of billions of insights, and the creative director paints the story.

The real power of this association is evident in personalized marketing. AI-driven analytics platforms like Persado or Jasper can simulate audience reactions before the campaign even launches. Advertising augmentation is therefore not about speed alone. The agencies that will thrive are those that use AI as a cultural microscope rather than just a productivity tool.

6.2 Film, Music, and Entertainment

Entertainment industries have long been early adopters of technology. But AI and human augmentation are now redefining both how stories are made and how audiences experience them. AI tools like AIVA and Jukebox can compose music in any style, yet musicians use them mostly for scaffolding, for creating rhythm or harmonic structures that they later personalize. This keeps the emotional core human while letting the system handle the technical volume of ideas (Bryan-Kinns, 2024).

Similarly, in film production, editors now rely on augmented tools for smart editing with systems that can detect continuity errors, colour balance, or even emotional pacing in scenes. Yet, creative directors still decide what "feels right." The fusion of Netflix's data analytics with screenwriting is a prime example. Netflix algorithms can indicate what genres or plot arcs are trending in specific regions, but it is the human writer who decides how to turn that insight into a living story (Napoli, 2019).

Production houses experiment with AI-driven pre-visualization tools that create 3D storyboards, allowing directors to explore camera angles and lighting virtually before shooting begins. This not only saves cost but also gives creative flexibility. One Indian cinematographer recently observed that "AI helps me see the story from ten lenses, but my eyes still choose the one that matters."This remark captures the philosophical heart of augmented entertainment where the plurality of perception is combined with singular human meaning.

6.3 Fashion and Design

Fashion, perhaps more than any other creative industry, thrives at the intersection of imagination, intuition, and material experimentation. Human augmentation has started to influence this domain in subtle yet significant ways.Generative design algorithms, powered by artificial intelligence, now help designers ideate faster and visualize patterns that might have remained unseen through conventional sketching.

Tools such as Midjourney, Runway ML, and DALL-E 3 offer creative scaffolds rather than replacements, producing thousands of possible iterations of form, colour, or fabric drape that designers later refine with human taste and contextual knowledge (Lee & Kim, 2025).

In practical terms, augmented systems compress the time to ideation. For example, Adidas's automated design labs combine predictive analytics with sensory data from athletes to create customized footwear patterns. Meanwhile, Zara's data-driven design units in Spain and India use generative style forecasting which is trained on cultural and seasonal datato decide silhouettes and palettes, but final decisions rest on human teams who understand nuanced cultural cues, especially in diverse markets like Asia.

The interplay between machine pattern recognition and human cultural aesthetics underlines the hybrid intelligence model. While algorithms detect market shifts and fabric behavior, human designers inject emotional resonance, storytelling, and ethical sensibility which are the values that machines cannot intuit. This fusion represents not an erosion of artistry but a widening of its cognitive canvas.

At a metaphysical level, this dynamic reflects Simon's (1957) principle of bounded rationality. Designers face cognitive restrictions when imagining possibilities under time or informational boundaries. Augmented systems effectively extend these limits, providing the scaffolding for bounded creativity.

6.4 Education and Learning Design

Education, particularly in the creative disciplines, is undergoing its own renaissance through augmentation. Education design has shifted from static instruction toward dynamic, co-creative experiences where students engage with digital companions. This shift is not about outsourcing cognition but enhancing exploration and reflection (Dron, J., & Anderson, T., 2014).

In management and design institutions, experimental "AI studios" now integrate platforms like ChatGPT, Miro, or Notion AI to support students in brainstorming, prototyping, and revising projects (Figure 5).

Figure 5. AI- powered Learning

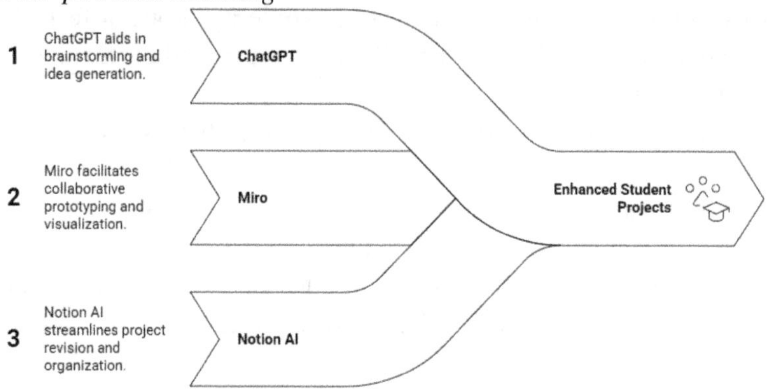

Source: Authors

In design schools, augmented learning ecosystems now use AR/VR environments where students visualize spatial concepts and manipulate materials virtually before physical construction. The hybrid system amplifies flow (Csikszentmihalyi, 1997) by minimizing interruptions and providing instant feedback. Moreover, emotionally aware AI tutorsadapt tone and challenge level based on student affective signals, creating more personalized learning rhythms (Huang, Y., & Wang, H., 2025).

However, ethical stewardship remains crucial. Faculty must ensure that students learn to co-create rather than delegate their creative effort. The idea is to build "critical digital literacy," where learners understand both the affordances and limitations of augmentation (Selwyn, N., 2023). Balanced augmentation cultivates creative humility, a recognition that intelligence, whether human or artificial, is always partial and evolving.

7. THE CHALLENGE OF DATASET BIAS AND LOSS OF CULTURAL DIVERSITY

The biggest structural challenge in Asian augmented creativity is dataset bias. Most global AI models are built on Westerndominant visual and linguistic corpora, leading to distortions when representing Asian cultural elements. Scholars have shown how generative systems misinterpret Indian temple geometry, confuse Korean hanbok with unrelated historical garments, or reproduce Japanese calligraphy strokes without understanding their spiritual and aesthetic lineage (Liu, Z., 2023).

These distortions are more than surfacelevel inaccuracies. They dilute cultural authenticity and create what some researchers call algorithmic flattening. Asia's resource limitations have encouraged frugal and flexible invention, pushing inventers to adapt augmentation tools in inventive ways rather than depending on expensive exclusive systems. This ongoing strain underscores the need for localized datasets and policy frameworks that defend cultural authenticity in augmented inventiveness as is aptly illustrated in Figure 6. For animation and game design, bias leads to incorrect body proportions, hybridized motifs, and weakened narrative symbolism. In advertising or design, the misrepresentation can inadvertently stereotype cultural elements.

Dataset bias also affects emotional interpretation. Emotional data derived from Western contexts may fail to capture the subtler nonverbal cues prevalent in Japanese or Korean expressive cultures, or the emotionally layered storytelling of India (Rao, 2023).

Figure 6. Balancing Cultural Authenticity in Augmented Creativity

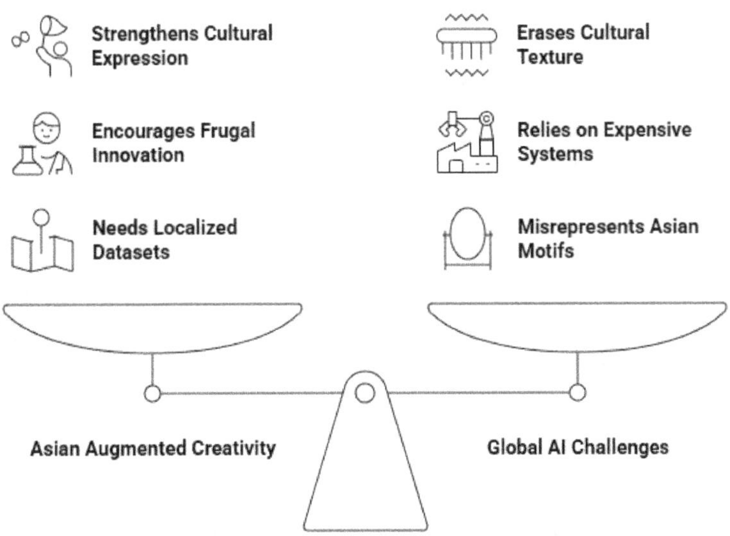

Source: Authors (Based on Rilliard et al (2025); Han et al., (2024)

7.1 Building Local Creative Datasets and Inclusive Innovation Frameworks

To counter cultural distortion, several Asian regions have begun developing localized creative datasets. India's Bhashini initiative expands linguistic corpora across major and minor languages. Japan's Culture-AI Consortium works on digital preservation of traditional crafts, performance arts, and museum archives. South

Korea's AI-Hangeul Lab focuses on typography, semantic nuance, and emotional expression embedded in the Korean language.

Such initiatives emphasize not only representation but also cultural stewardship. Asian researchers argue that communities should retain agency over how their creative heritage is sampled, digitized, and reproduced (Liu, Z., 2023).This implies policy interventions in areas such as IP protection, ethical digitization, and revenue-sharing frameworks. It also calls for academic–industry collaboration through design labs, interdisciplinary studios, and creative incubators that train the next generation in culturally informed augmented creativity.

Cross-border creative hubs in ASEAN, India–Japan digital art residencies, and Korean–Southeast Asian game exchanges further strengthen regional synergy (Rilliard et.al., 2025). These collaborations, as elucidated in Table 7, create a distributed ecosystem where tools, datasets, and creative practices circulate in culturally respectful ways.

Table 7. Categories of Support Needed for Inclusive Asian Creative Augmentation

Area	Description	Regional Examples	Intended Benefit
Dataset Development	Digitization of arts, crafts, languages, archives	Bhashini, Culture-AI	Reduction of cultural distortion
Ethical Governance	Rights, IP, consent, cultural stewardship	National AI frameworks	Responsible use of augmentation
Creative Education	Co-creation studios, interdisciplinary labs	IIT Bombay IDC, KAIST, NTU	Culturally grounded skills
Regional Collaboration	Hubs, residencies, cross-border R&D	ASEAN creative networks	Shared learning and innovation

Attribution: Adapted and extended from Liu, Z., (2023), and Rilliard, A., et.al. (2025)

7.2Augmentation in Resource constrained and Frugal environments

Asian creatorswork within infrastructural constraints. Rather than halting innovation, these constraints nurture a culture of inventiveness that aligns with frugal innovation principles (Figure 7) (Radjou et al., 2012). Indian animators, for instance, frequently rely on open-source AI plug-ins, cloud-based rendering farms, and mobile-friendly motion-capture kits that can be assembled in small studios. Korean indie game designers use modular augmentation tools allowing rapid prototyping without heavy licensing costs.

Figure 7. The Power of Constraints

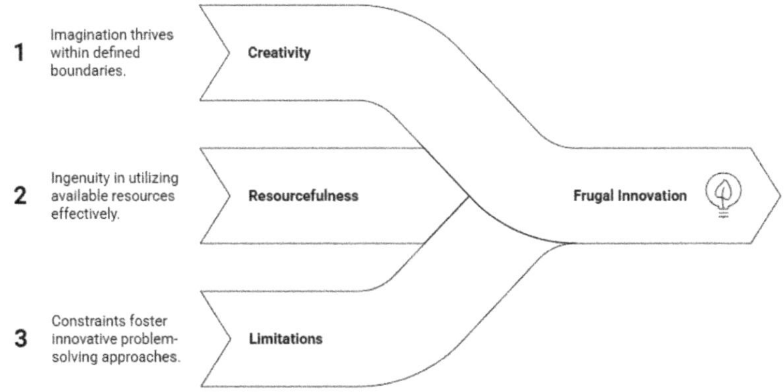

Source: Authors (Based on Radjou et al., 2012)

This frugal adaptive approach reflects community-based learning. Creators often exchange toolkits informally through shared labs, workshops, and online collectives. Southeast Asian digital craft societies frequently use AI-assisted pattern creators or fabric-layout tools while retaining manual refinement grounded in cultural symbolism.

8. AUGMENTATION AND EMOTIONAL WARMTH

A central concern in debates on augmented creativity lies in emotional authenticity. While AI tools can produce prose, melody, colour palettes, and stylistic variations at unprecedented speed and scale, critics argue that these outputs may lack the human intentionality and experiential grounding that give artistic works their emotional deepness (Colton & Wiggins, 2012) (Figure 8). This becomes more distinct when augmented systems imitate human affect by generating poems of loss, songs of longing, or visual art referencing cultural memorywithout ever experiencing these situations.

Figure 8. Emotional Authenticity in AI-Generated Art

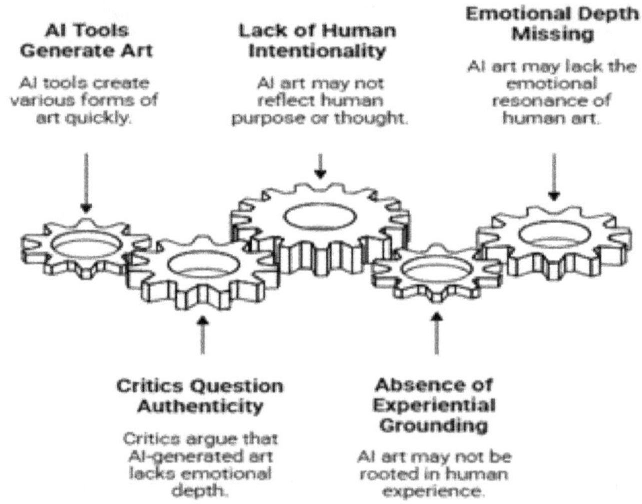

Source: Authors (Based on Colton & Wiggins, 2012)

9. MANAGERIAL AND EDUCATIONAL IMPLICATIONS IN AN AUGMENTED CREATIVE ERA

The shift toward human–AI augmentation is bringing a quiet but deep change in how creative managers lead teams and how educators prepare future professionals. In many Asian settings, one can already notice that leadership discussions in advertising agencies, media houses, animation studios, and design labs now include questions about how far AI should help, when it should step back, and how human intuition can stay at the center. This combination of practical concerns and cultural expectations makes the managerial and educational implications quite layered. As some scholars note, digital augmentation does not simply add speed; it reshapes authority, learning, and the meaning of creativity itself (Shneiderman, 2022; Amabile, 2020). What follows is a detailed look at how managerial roles shift from control to curation and how educators must redesign creative learning toward co-creation, ethical grounding, and cultural sensitivity.

9.1 Dictator to Curator: Changing role of Managers

In traditional creative industries, the manager was often seen as the central decision-maker. This position came partly from the manager's experience, partly from the structure of creative industries that valued hierarchy, and partly from the belief that coordination required a single guiding voice. However, once AI tools enter the daily workflow, this structure begins to stretch. A machine can generate hundreds of design drafts or slogan ideas in minutes. It can analyse audience sentiment at a scale that no team can process manually. Such speed and depth make old commandandcontrol approaches feel slow and sometimes unnecessary.

In this augmented environment, managerial authority shifts into something more like curation. A curator does not produce everything by hand, and does not impose a uniform answer. Instead, the curator navigates between options, filters possibilities, interprets meanings, and shapes direction by weaving human sense-making with available tools. This resembles what Nonaka and Takeuchi (1996) describe as leadership based on knowledge flow rather than hierarchical decisions.

One often hears this shift in creative agencies where team leads say things like "let the system throw ten rough cuts, and we will feel which one carries the right mood". This is a different managerial mindset. It is less about control and more about sensing, guiding, and assembling. The manager becomes a sense-maker who notices cultural nuance, emotional tone, and stakeholder expectations that AI cannot fully grasp (Kahneman et al., 2011). By working as a custodian, the manager shapes how human instinct and machine exploration blend profoundly (Table 8).

The managerial mind-set also moves toward cooperation literacy. A creative manager must comprehend how to prompt systems, how to interpret machine patterns, and how to guide teams in using intensification responsibly. Many managers mention that lower management employees often feel speechless by the volume of machine-generated material. Without thoughtful supervision, this leads to artistic fatigue rather than empowerment. The manager's role becomes one of emotional grounding. They remind crews that machine diversity is not a demand but achance, and that the final creative meaning still depends on human choice.

Management education must cultivate leaders who can handle uncertainty. They should be comfortable accommodating that neither humans nor machines have full control. Creative leaders will have to bargain between rapid AI-generated substitutes and the slower, reflective process of human storytelling. They will need to guide teams through emotional challenges, encourage ethical reasoning, and ensure that cultural wisdom stays visible even as workflows modernize.

Table 8. Shifting Managerial Roles in Augmented Creative Workplaces

Traditional Role	Augmented Role	Key Implication
Directive decision-maker	Curator of possibilities	Managers evaluate and interpret AI-generated options
Authority based on hierarchy	Authority based on sense-making	Leadership depends on judgment, narrative understanding, ethics
Workflow controller	Creative facilitator	Managers support mixed human–machine ideation
Producer of answers	Designer of creative ecosystems	Focus on orchestrating people, tools, and datasets

Attribution: Conceptually inspired by Nonaka and Takeuchi (1996); Amabile, 2020; and Shneiderman (2022).

9.2 Human Values as Anchors in Decision-Making

Even though AI can do extraordinary work, managers quickly realize that the heart of creativity still lies in narrative, empathy, ethics, and cultural thoughtfulness. Machines can identify sentiment through large datasets but cannot comprehend what grief in one culture or humor in another truly denotes. Thus, human values become the anchor points around which augmented creativity revolves (Figure 9).

Figure 9. Bridging the Gap

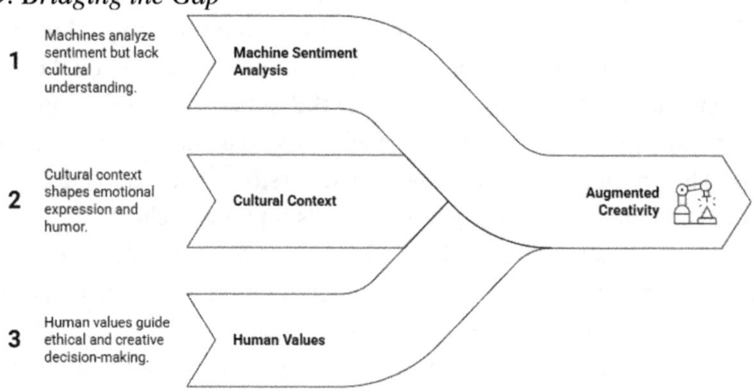

Source: Authors

Empathy helps teams choose not only what is catchy, but what is meaningful as well. Ethics guide decisions around bias, fairness, and demonstration. In Asia, where cultural landscapes are multilayered and multilingual, narrative sensitivity is especially important. A system trained mostly on Western data may miss subtle cues that matter in Indian advertising or Korean character design. Managers,therefore, step into arevealing role, ensuring that augmented creativity does not dilute cultural canvas.

Some scholars call this value-based monitoring, where machines augment technical capabilities while humans preserve moral and cultural integrity (Floridi, 2019). This blend is especially vigorous in sectors like branding, entertainment, and design.

9.3 Creative Education and Changing Expectations from Educators

As business landscapes shift, educators cannot remain with older models of teaching creativity that focus primarily on brainstorming, design thinking, or case-based learning. Students now need training in questioning AI outputs, not simply accepting them. They must learn to ask as to why the system produced some result. What data patterns might influence this direction? Is there any ethnic bias involved in it? What emotional tone is absent in it?

When students learn to "Question Outputs", they treat AI as a partner, not an authority. Researchers like Luckin (2018) argue that education must expand meta-cognitive skills so that learners guide machines rather than letting apparatuses guide them. This is even more important in creative education because intuition, aesthetic sense, and narrative judgment still describe"Human Uniqueness".

For managers of creative units and for educators training the next generation of creative professionals, the implications are clear. Training must integrate both intuition and data literacy. The students must be taught to interpret AI outputs and when to override them with human insight. The tools should be used for generation or search, but human review, reflection and iteration should be incorporated. To encourage experiential immersion BCIs, VR and emotional AI should be used in labs to help students experience the sensory emotional side of creativity (Figure 10). Ethics and authenticity must be core pillars and discussions must include data-privacy stakes, ownership of co-created art, cultural bias in AI models. Smaller studios or start-ups must gain access to augmentation tools early or risk being left behind.

Figure 10. Synergy for Creative Learning

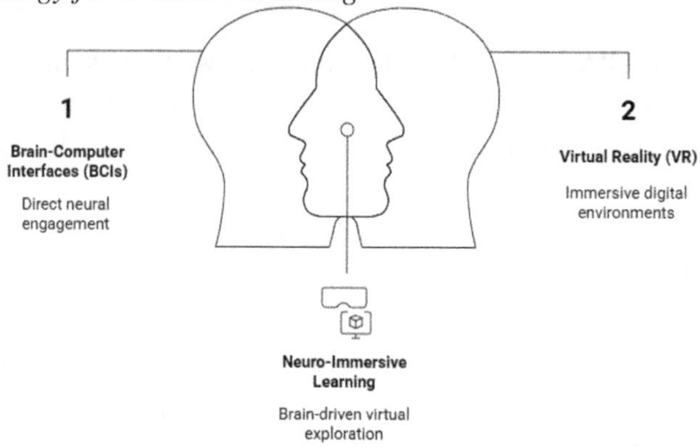

Source: Authors

The future of creative businesses will demand hybrid competencies. Graduates must be content engaging with algorithms, but also knowledgeable about stories, social meaning, and human behavior. Educators, therefore, need to redesign courses with blended competencies (Table 9). Scholars argue that creative advantage will shift toward those who can manage complication across cognitive, social, and technological domains. Management schools therefore, need to adopt a configuration where learning involves real-world creative labs, collaborative software, and reflective sessions that address the psychological aspects of machine partnership.

Ethical education must also expand. Learners need to realize how data bias, cultural misrepresentation, and automation risks affect society. For Asian contexts, this includes sensitivity to linguistic nuances, regional identities, and traditional art forms that may not be represented in global datasets. Scholars should develop a sense of augmentation equity, safeguarding creative tools uplift rather than distribute.

A conceptual table clarifies how educational priorities evolve.

Table 9. Changing Educational Focus in Creative Management Programs

Old Emphasis	New Emphasis in Augmented Era	Reason
Individual idea generation	Collaborative human–AI ideation	Creativity becomes networked
Aesthetic critique	Data-informed + intuition-guided critique	AI expands options but humans refine meaning
Skill-based learning	Meta-skill learning (judgment, ethics, curiosity)	Machines automate skills, humans keep higher cognition
Tool literacy	System literacy (ecosystems, datasets, workflows)	Tools evolve fast but ecosystem logic · remains stable

Attribution: Adapted and extended from Luckin (2018).

10. THE FUTURE OF HUMAN-AUGMENTATION

The future of creativity is moving toward a world where humans and intelligent machines co-evolve, co-learn, and co-create in increasingly intertwined ways. Rather than operational as separate sources of intellect, humans and AI systems are beginning to form synergetic creative units, blending human intuition, emotional depth, and contextual judgment with machine precision, speed, and computational diversity. Engelbart (1962) and Licklider (2008) foresaw this route decades ago, arguing that the maximum form of digital augmentation would not swap human intelligence but enlarge its boundaries. As generative systems, multimodal AI, neuro-interfaces, and immersive computing mature, this vision is quickly materializing, laying the foundation for human–AI creative ecologies far more fluid, shared, and distributed than current models.

10.1 Evolution Toward Human–Centred AI

Symbiotic intelligence denotes to systems in which humans and machines advance by learning from each other's outputs, amendments, and contextual refinements. Modern generative models already support iterative co-learning loops. According to Shneiderman (2022), these interactive feedback cycles form the basis of "Human–Centred AI," where the goal is not sovereignty but strengthening. Symbiotic intelligence will thus not be a static capability but a dynamic ecosystem, evolving as each node.

The table 10,below conceptualizes how symbiotic intelligence will shape different layers of creative activity.

Table 10. Layers of Symbiotic Intelligence in Future Creative Work

Layer	Human Strength	Machine Strength	Symbiotic Outcome
Interpretive	Context, culture, values	Pattern detection, semantic clustering	Richer meaning and relevance
Generative	Emotional intentionality	High-volume content exploration	Expanded creative range
Evaluative	Judgment, ethics, narrative coherence	Multidimensional comparison and scoring	Higher creative quality and alignment
Meta-Learning	Adaptive creative growth	Continuous model fine-tuning	Evolving joint intelligence

Attribution: Conceptually synthesized from Engelbart (1962), Licklider (2008), and Shneiderman (2022).

10.2 Neural and Immersive Augmentations

One of the most transformative developments in future creative practice lies in neural and immersive augmentations. Recent innovations in non-invasive BCIs enable the detention of neural signals associated to attention, mental imagery, or emotional stimulation (Nijboer 2015). When combined with generative AI, these systems could permit brain-linked ideation, where raw cognitive impulses are translated into sketches, soundscapes, or spatial forms.

Similarly, immersive technologies such as XR/VR will advance from imagining platforms to real-time creative ecosystems, where users sculpt ideas in 3D space, collaborate with virtual creative agents, or receive emotion-tracking feedback based on physiological signals. Emotion-aware generative locomotives could adjust colour palettes, musical tensions, or textual tones in response to the creator's affective state.

To intellectualize this, the following table 11 illustrates how forthcoming neural–immersive augmentations may restructure creative workflows.

Table 11. Neural and Immersive Augmentations in Future Creativity

Augmentation Type	Creative Function	Potential Impact
Brain–Computer Interfaces	Ideation capture, emotional mapping	Reduce friction between thought and creation
Immersive XR Studios	Spatial prototyping, multisensory blending	Expand creative modalities beyond 2D/3D tools
Emotion-Aware Generators	Real-time creative modulation	Enhance emotional resonance and immersion
Cognitive Load Assistants	Distraction filtering, flow optimization	Support sustained creative focus

Attribution: Adapted and extended from Nijboer (2015) and contemporary XR research.

11. CONCLUSION

The trail of human–machine augmentation ultimately leads back to anuntruthfull-ytruth. Machinerygains its prominence only through human intent and interpretation. As creative industries, educational institutions, and managerial systems integrate increasingly intelligent augmentation tools, the central cross-examination ceases to be whether machineries can think or create. The ultimateimage of augmented creativity is less about technological supremacy and more about human prospect.

Across the entire debate of cognitive processes, sectoral applications, emotional considerations, and embryonic workflows, one constant insight has emerged,as "Augmentation is not a story of substitution but of synergy" (Figure 11).

Figure 11. Augmentation: Synergy, Not Substitution

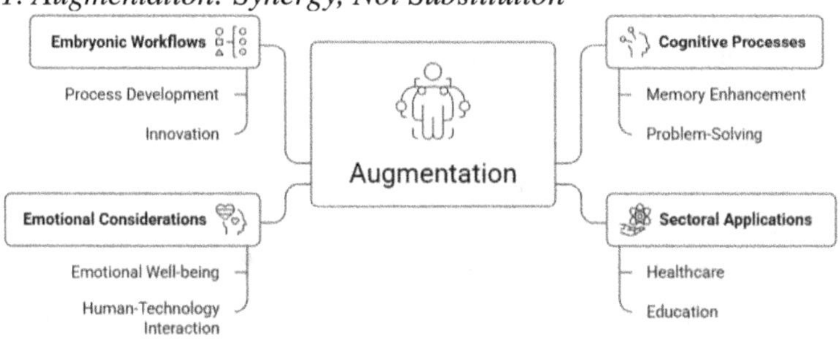

Source: Authors

The rise of generative models, multimodal neural networks, adaptive learning systems, and emotion-responsive interfaces has added new layers to this chronicle. These tools intensify human agency by compressing time, extending memory, generating alternatives at scale, and depressing the cost of exploration. When ideation aides draft multiple variations, designers can focus on nuance. When analytical systems detect subtle audience patterns, marketers can construct more empathetic narratives; when educational systems offer adaptive framework, learners can reach higher levels of investigation. In each instance, the device plays the role of an amplifier, but meaningmaking remains distinctlywith human.

This perspective also recasts the fear of automation, which often clouds discussions of AI and creativity. Empirical studies increasingly show that technology rarely eliminates entire creative professions; instead, it reshapes job architectures by shifting emphasis toward higher-order, human-centred capabilities such as judgment, ethical reasoning, emotional interpretation, and narrative coherence (Brynjolfsson & McAfee, 2017). This reframing aligns with the managerial implications we explored earlier: leaders of the future must become orchestrators of hybrid workflows, cultivators of human-machine fluency, and guardians of ethical and aesthetic values. Rather than enforcing rigid systems, they will curate processes that blend algorithmic strengths with the intuitiveness and emotional resonance only humans possess.

Educational systems, likewise, will need to cultivate co-creative habits of mind rather than treat AI literacy as a purely technical skill. As argued by scholars in learning sciences, true digital fluency emerges when learners not only operate tools but question them—interrogating their biases, limitations, and assumptions (Selwyn, 2023). Teaching students to ask, "Why did the AI suggest this?", "Whose data shaped this recommendation?", and "What human meaning do I want this output to carry?" become essential for nurturing reflective creators.

Ethics is not a fringe concern in augmentation, but it is the structural backbone. Issues of data ownership, representation, and algorithmic fairness shape not only the technical legitimacy but also the cultural legitimacy of augmented creativity. Without sensible design, global AI systems risk strengthening metropolitan or Western-centric aesthetics while underscoring regional textures, indigenous sensibilities, and minority voices. This is particularly critical in diverse ecosystems such as Asia and Africa

As the ecology evolves toward more immersive and neural forms of augmentation, the stakes with real-time visualization, emotion-responsive feedback loops, and BCI-enabled ideationrise. These systems promise exceptional creative flow like"Imagine Sketching" with thought-level control or composing music shaped by moment-to-moment emotional changes, or designing environments that deliver spatial concepts. However, these advancements demand new frameworks for consent, privacy, and psychological safety.

Eventually, the path ahead reflects a deeper rational transition. Creativity is shifting from an individual-centric model to a distributed, networked, relational process. Concepts will increasingly emerge from webs of human–machine interactionsand dynamic cross-cultural exchanges (Figure 12). Yet this does not reduce the role of the individual. Augmentation gives the individual creator more reach, more power, more perspective.

REFERENCES

Amabile, T. M. (2020). Creativity, artificial intelligence, and a world of surprises. *Academy of Management Discoveries*, *6*(3), 351–354.

Boden, M. A. (2016). *AI: Its nature and future*. Oxford University Press.

Bryan-Kinns, N. (2024). Reflections on explainable AI for the arts (XAIxArts). *Interaction*, *31*(1), 43–47.

Brynjolfsson, E., & Mcafee, A. N. D. R. E. W. (2017). The business of artificial intelligence. *Harvard Business Review*, *7*(1), 1–2.

Clark, A., & Chalmers, D. (1998). The extended mind. *analysis, 58*(1), 7-19.

Colton, S., & Wiggins, G. A. (2012). Computational creativity: The final frontier. In *ECAI 2012* (pp. 21–26). IOS Press.

Csikszentmihalyi, M. (1997). Flow and the psychology of discovery and invention. *HarperPerennial, New York*, *39*, 1–16.

Davenport, T. H., & Kirby, J. (2016). Just how smart are smart machines? *MIT Sloan Management Review*, *57*(3), 21.

Dellermann, D., Calma, A., Lipusch, N., Weber, T., Weigel, S., & Ebel, P. (2021). The future of human-AI collaboration: a taxonomy of design knowledge for hybrid intelligence systems. *arXiv preprint arXiv:2105.03354*.

Dron, J., & Anderson, T. (2014). Learning and teaching with social media. In *Ubiquitous learning environments and technologies* (pp. 15–29). Springer Berlin Heidelberg.

Engelbart, D. C. (1962). Program on human effectiveness. *Reprint in: Nyce, James M./Kahn, Paul (1991)(Hg.)(1962)*, 237-244.

Florida, R. (2002). The economic geography of talent. *Annals of the Association of American Geographers*, *92*(4), 743–755.

Floridi, L. (2019). Translating principles into practices of digital ethics: Five risks of being unethical. *Philosophy & Technology*, *32*(2), 185–193.

Gallagher, S. (Ed.). (2011). *The Oxford handbook of the self.* Oxford Handbooks Online.

Glăveanu, V. P. (2014). Distributed creativity: what is it? In *Distributed creativity: Thinking outside the box of the creative individual* (pp. 1–13). Springer International Publishing.

Han, H., Liu, Z., Li, J., & Zeng, Z. (2024). Challenges in remote sensing based climate and crop monitoring: Navigating the complexities using AI. *Journal of Cloud Computing (Heidelberg, Germany), 13*(1), 1–14.

Huang, Y., & Wang, H. (2025). Chinese engineering students' perceived emotional experiences in AI-mediated education: An expectancy-value theory (EVT) perspective. *Learning and Motivation, 92*, 102180.

Hutchins, E. (1995). *Cognition in the Wild.* MIT press.

Kahneman, D., Lovallo, D., & Sibony, O. (2011). Before you make that big decision. *Harvard Business Review, 89*(6), 50–60. PMID: 21714386

Kasparov, G. (2021). *How life imitates chess.* Random House.

Lee, J., Kim, J., & Lee, H. (2025). Diffusedesigner: Sketch-based controllable clothing image generation. *Fashion and Textiles, 12*(1), 26.

Li, C., Wang, J., Zhang, Y., Zhu, K., Hou, W., Lian, J., . . . Xie, X. (2023). Large language models understand and can be enhanced by emotional stimuli. *arXiv preprint arXiv:2307.11760.*

Licklider, J. C. (2008). Man-computer symbiosis. *IRE transactions on human factors in electronics*, (1), 4-11.

Liu, Z. (2023). Cultural bias in large language models: A comprehensive analysis and mitigation strategies. *Journal of Transcultural Communication, 3*(2), 224–244.

Luckin, R. (2018). *Machine Learning and Human Intelligence. The future of education for the 21st century.* UCL institute of education press.

Mitra, A., Seetharaman, A., & Maddulety, K. (2024). Adoption of Artificial Intelligence Enabling Value Creation in Business. In *2024 4th International Conference on Robotics, Automation and Artificial Intelligence (RAAI)* (pp. 213-220). IEEE.

Napoli, P. M. (2019). *Social media and the public interest: Media regulation in the disinformation age.* Columbia university press.

Nijboer, F. (2015). Technology transfer of brain-computer interfaces as assistive technology: Barriers and opportunities. *Annals of Physical and Rehabilitation Medicine, 58*(1), 35–38. PMID: 25595535

Nisbett, R. E., & Masuda, T. (2013). Culture and point of view. In *Biological and cultural bases of human inference* (pp. 49–70). Psychology Press.

Nonaka, L., Takeuchi, H., & Umemoto, K. (1996). A theory of organizational knowledge creation. *International Journal of Technology Management*, *11*(7-8), 833–845.

Plassmann, H., Venkatraman, V., Huettel, S., & Yoon, C. (2015). Consumer neuroscience: Applications, challenges, and possible solutions. *JMR, Journal of Marketing Research*, *52*(4), 427–435.

Radjou, N., Prabhu, J., & Ahuja, S. (2012). *Jugaad innovation: Think frugal, be flexible, generate breakthrough growth.* John Wiley & Sons.

Rilliard, A., De Moraes, J. A., Erickson, D., Guerry, M., Hönemann, A., Lee, T., & Shochi, T. (2025). Cross-cultural dimensions organizing prosodic attitudes reception. *Journal of Speech Sciences*, *14*, e025012.

Runco, M. A., & Acar, S. (2024). Assessing divergent thinking: recent advances. *Handbook of Creativity Assessment*, 128-147.

Sarma, M., Ghahremani, P., Povey, D., Goel, N. K., Sarma, K. K., & Dehak, N. (2018, September). Emotion Identification from Raw Speech Signals Using DNNs. In *Interspeech* (pp. 3097-3101).

Selwyn, N. (2023). The critique of digital education: Time for a (post) critical turn. In *Rethinking sociological critique in contemporary education* (pp. 48-62). Routledge.

Shneiderman, B. (2022). *Human-centered AI.* Oxford University Press.

Simon, H. A. (1972). Theories of bounded rationality. *Decision and organization, 1*(1), 161-176.

Simon, H. A. (1983). Why should machines learn? In *Machine learning* (pp. 25–37). Morgan Kaufmann.

Zuboff, S. (2019). *The age of surveillance capitalism: The fight for a human future at the new frontier of power, edn.* PublicAffairs.

Chapter 8
Human-AI Collaboration in Creativity and Leadership:
Redefining Innovation in the Future of Work

Hemadribahen Ishvarlal Tikawala
https://orcid.org/0009-0004-5017-767X
Prof. V.B. Shah Institute of Management, R.V. Patel and V.L. Shah College of Commerce, Amroli, India

ABSTRACT

The convergence of artificial intelligence (AI) and human creativity is reshaping how ideas form, teams collaborate, and leaders drive innovation. As organizations rely more on intelligent systems, leadership must integrate ethics, culture, and imagination into human–AI synergy. This chapter applies a three-phase model—Human-in-the-Loop (HITL), Human-on-the-Loop (HOTL), and Human-out-of-the-Loop (HOOTL) - to examine cases from Microsoft, Adobe, Unilever, and Spotify. Findings show that effective collaboration depends on ethical oversight, cultural awareness, and adaptive leadership. The framework introduces a human-centered paradigm where moral imagination anchors creative governance, concluding that the future of leadership lies in uniting intelligence, ethics, and empathy for sustainable innovation.

INTRODUCTION

Over the past decade, *cognitive technologies* have evolved from niche research endeavours into transformative catalysts that now shape the operational pulse of

DOI: 10.4018/979-8-3373-7153-5.ch008

modern organizations and industries worldwide.What once began as a quest for computational efficiency has evolved into a profound redefinition of creativity, collaboration, and leadership. Today's enterprises operate in an ecosystem where intelligent systems do not merely automate processes—they participate in ideation, problem-solving, and strategic foresight. According to recent analyses by the World Economic Forum (2023) and Deloitte (2022), the hallmark of organizational resilience lies in the capacity to integrate AI ethically and intelligently into human workflows. As a result, leadership is being reimagined: influence is no longer measured solely by vision or charisma but by the ability to harmonize human ingenuity with algorithmic precision, fostering innovation that remains deeply anchored in human values.

Creativity has long been considered a uniquely human faculty grounded in imagination, emotion, and contextual awareness. Yet the emergence of generative AI, capable of composing music, designing visual art, and producing text, challenges the assumption that creativity belongs solely to human cognition. Instead, creativity is becoming a distributed process in which human and algorithmic intelligence co-evolve. Organizations such as Adobe, Google, and Microsoft demonstrate this shift vividly. Adobe Firefly transforms verbal prompts into sophisticated designs, Google's Gemini suite supports ideation through pattern recognition, and Microsoft Copilot enhances collaborative problem solving by summarizing and re-framing complex information. These examples illustrate that technology now functions less as an instrument and more as a thinking partner in the creative process.

For leaders, this transformation implies a new form of literacy. They must learn to interpret machine reasoning, translate data insights into human understanding, and balance algorithmic speed with ethical sensitivity. Leadership is no longer restricted to managing people or capital; it now involves cultivating environments where humans and machines learn from one another. The capacity to build such environments defines the new frontier of creative leadership in the future of work.

From Automation To Collaboration: Redefining The Human Role

Early organizational uses of AI focused on automation—delegating repetitive, data-heavy tasks to algorithms to reduce human error and cost. Automation achieved efficiency but often displaced creative engagement. As technologies matured, attention shifted toward augmentation, emphasizing how AI could expand human capability rather than replace it. Recent scholarship on augmented intelligence (Davenport & Bean, 2022; Shrestha et al., 2019) highlights that the most productive systems are those in which human judgment and algorithmic precision complement each other. This marks the emergence of **human–AI collaboration (HAC)** as a defining paradigm of twenty-first-century work.

In HAC settings, creativity results from a dialogic process: humans generate intent and context, while AI supplies associative diversity, data-driven insights, and rapid prototyping. The human retains interpretive authority, deciding which outcomes hold meaning or ethical legitimacy. Leadership thus evolves from directing people to curating relationships among humans, technologies, and information ecosystems. A creative leader becomes a sense-maker who frames the purpose of collaboration, ensures fairness in algorithmic processes, and nurtures trust across digital boundaries.

This progression fundamentally redefines professional identity. Whereas automation sought to make the human invisible, collaboration restores the human as the ethical and imaginative anchor of technological systems. Organizations embracing this philosophy treat AI as a cognitive partner—an amplifier of curiosity rather than a substitute for judgment. Such a perspective calls for leaders capable of empathy toward both human and algorithmic agents, recognizing that each possesses different but complementary strengths.

The Research Gap: The Missing Human Dimension In AI Discourse

Despite the vast literature on AI adoption, most studies remain technologically centered, concentrating on performance metrics, data accuracy, or automation efficiency. The human dimensioncreativity, emotion, and moral reasoning—often receives peripheral attention. As Amabile and Pratt (2016) argue, creativity flourishes within social systems that allow psychological safety and intrinsic motivation. When AI enters these systems, it alters feedback dynamics and sense of agency, yet few empirical models capture this shift.

Existing leadership research similarly privileges structural efficiency over relational intelligence. Traditional frameworks such as transformational or transactional leadership rarely account for algorithmic collaboration. They emphasize charisma, vision, and reward mechanisms but not the ability to manage hybrid teams of humans and machines. Recent exploratory work (Wilson & Daugherty, 2023) suggests that leaders who treat AI as a teammate—rather than a subordinate tool—achieve higher innovation outcomes, but theoretical consolidation remains limited.

A noticeable gap also exists within the cultural dimension of human–AI collaboration. Leadership practices and creative values vary significantly across societies, shaping how humans interpret and engage with intelligent systems. In collectivist settings—common across many Asian and African regions—leadership often emphasizes mutual dependence, relational balance, and shared achievement. Conversely, in more individualist environments such as Europe and North America, autonomy, originality, and personal accountability dominate organizational life. Yet, little is known about how these cultural orientations influence levels of trust, ethical expectation, and emotional comfort toward algorithmic decision-making. This question is vital, as perceptions of fairness, bias, and transparency are inherently embedded in cultural narratives (Floridi et al., 2018). Without comparative understanding, global discourses on ethical AI leadership may unconsciously privilege certain cultural logics while overlooking others, resulting in frameworks that are inclusive in language but limited in worldview.

Rationale and Aims

The core intention is to illuminate how human–AI collaboration redefines creativity, innovation, and leadership in the evolving world of work. Drawing on interdisciplinary perspectives from organizational behaviour, cognitive psychology, and technology management, the discussion emphasizes that the greatest value of AI lies not in automation but in augmentation—the mutual enhancement of human imagination and machine intelligence.

Specifically, the chapter pursues four objectives:

1. To conceptualize human–AI collaboration as a progressive journey of trust and capability across distinct stages of technological maturity.
2. To analyse cross-industry experiences—from technology and consumer goods to digital-creative sectors—showing how AI transforms leadership practice and creative output.
3. To introduce a theoretical model encompassing the phases of "Active Human Oversight (HITL)," "Supervisory Human Oversight," and "Autonomous AI Operation (HOOTL)," each representing the evolving balance between human control and AI autonomy.
4. To discuss the ethical, cultural, and organizational implications of these transitions, highlighting governance mechanisms that preserve accountability and human dignity.

Through these objectives, the chapter contributes to bridging a persistent divide between technological innovation and humanistic leadership. It argues that genuine progress in AI integration requires leaders who combine analytical competence with moral imagination.

Overview of Conceptual Framework: the "HITL–HOTL–HOOTL" Maturity Model

To structure this inquiry, the chapter adopts the "**HITL–HOTL–HOOTL**" maturity model, which captures the progressive deepening of human–AI synergy, driven by expanding trust and enhanced technical robustness. The framework captures three overlapping stages rather than discrete steps, emphasizing adaptation and ethical recalibration at each level.

In the **Human-in-the-Loop** phase, humans retain tight control. AI provides recommendations or assists in data synthesis, but final decisions rest with human experts. Leaders operate as evaluators who supervise algorithmic outputs, ensuring alignment with strategic intent and ethical norms. Most current creative applications—such as design assistance, content suggestion, or predictive editing—belong to this stage.

The **Human-on-the-Loop** phase denotes shared control. AI executes semi-autonomous tasks while humans oversee performance metrics and intervene selectively. Leadership responsibility shifts from micromanagement to systemic supervision. Unilever's AI-enabled recruitment and sustainability initiatives exemplify this arrangement: algorithms screen data, but human managers verify cultural fit and fairness. Here, creativity stems from iterative dialogue between human context and machine learning.

Finally, in the **Human-out-of-the-Loop** phase, AI systems act with considerable autonomy in bounded domains such as music curation, logistics optimization, or digital personalization. Humans set ethical boundaries and strategic objectives but do not supervise every operation. Spotify's AI DJ is a prominent case—it designs user experiences based on contextual and emotional cues derived from data analytics. For leaders, this phase requires building organizational cultures that trust algorithmic partners while maintaining transparent governance and accountability.

The framework thus portrays human–AI collaboration as a continuum rather than a replacement trajectory. It demonstrates that leadership must evolve from control to coordination, and finally to curation—guiding systems that learn, adapt, and create alongside humans. Each stage demands distinct competencies: critical evaluation, boundary setting, and ethical foresight.

The Structure of the Chapter

Following this introduction, the chapter proceeds through six interrelated sections. The Literature Review and Theoretical Foundations section synthesizes existing scholarship on creativity, leadership, and AI ethics, identifying conceptual convergences and research gaps. The Research Framework and Methodology section describes the design logic of the HITL–HOTL–HOOTL model and outlines the comparative, cross-industry approach used to derive insights. Subsequently, the Case Studies and Industry Insights section analyses implementations across sectors including technology, consumer goods, and digital media. The Discussion and Analysis section interprets these observations through theoretical lenses, linking them to the broader discourse on ethical and sustainable innovation.

The Implications and Future Directions section distills actionable recommendations for leaders and policymakers seeking to embed human-centered AI governance. Finally, the Conclusion synthesizes the central findings, reaffirming that the future of creative leadership depends on cultivating synergy—not competition—between human wisdom and artificial intelligence.

The acceleration of AI technologies compels organizations to re-evaluate what it means to be creative, ethical, and human. The core challenge is not technological capability but responsible integration: aligning machine efficiency with human purpose. When designed and led ethically, AI can expand rather than diminish human potential, enabling leaders to focus on imagination, empathy, and strategic foresight. As Brynjolfsson and McAfee (2022) observe, the next productivity frontier arises from "machine intelligence that complements human ingenuity rather than competes with it." This perspective reframes leadership as the art of partnership—guiding systems that think differently but share common goals.

Accordingly, this chapter positions human–AI collaboration as a transformative lens for understanding the evolution of creativity and leadership in the digital age. By examining how trust, ethics, and innovation intertwine across the HITL–HOTL–HOOTL continuum, the discussion aims to offer scholars and practitioners a roadmap for designing organizations that are not only intelligent but humane. In this way, the collaboration between humans and machines becomes both a technological necessity and a moral imperative for the sustainable future of work.

LITERATURE REVIEW AND THEORETICAL FOUNDATIONS

Foundations of Creativity and Leadership

Creativity can be understood as the capacity to develop solutions and approaches that are both original and meaningful within the contexts in which they operate. Seminal psychological research describes creativity as a process that integrates expertise, intrinsic motivation, and the ability to reframe problems (Amabile, 1996). Subsequent studies have reinforced that creative output arises not solely from individual talent but also from environments that support experimentation, trust, and cross-disciplinary dialogue (Mumford et al., 2019). Within organizations, these environmental factors are strongly influenced by leadership styles, communication patterns, and reward systems. Transformational and participative leadership models, in particular, have been associated with fostering creativity because they emphasize vision sharing, empowerment, and tolerance of ambiguity (Northouse, 2021).

Leadership thought has evolved over timefrom early trait-oriented approaches to behavioral and contingency modelshighlighting that successful leaders adapt their style and strategies in response to specific situations and the maturity levels of their followers. In the innovation-driven economy, leadership extends beyond coordination to creative facilitationguiding collective sense-making amid technological disruption. Scholars note that creative leaders differ from traditional managers in their comfort with uncertainty and their ability to integrate knowledge across diverse domains (Puccio et al., 2018). They act as catalysts, aligning organizational structures with psychological safety and cognitive diversity, both of which are essential prerequisites for innovation.

A recurring theme in leadership scholarship is the tension between control and autonomy. While structure provides direction, excessive control suppresses experimentation. The contemporary shift toward digital and networked work amplifies this tension. Remote collaboration, cross-functional teams, and algorithmic systems demand leaders who can balance procedural clarity with creative freedom (Dinh et al., 2014). This balance becomes even more intricate when artificial intelligence enters the creative process, introducing a non-human actor capable of contributing ideas or evaluating options. Thus, understanding creativity in leadership now requires re-examining how authority, trust, and decision rights are distributed between human and machine agents.

Evolution of Intelligent Systems In Creative And Organizational Domains

The adoption of Intelligent systems within organizational processes has progressed through recognizable phases. Early applications emphasized automationmachines executing repetitive or data-intensive tasks once performed by humans. The underlying rationale was efficiency and cost reduction rather than cognitive partnership. However, with advances in machine learning and generative algorithms, AI systems began to perform functions traditionally associated with human judgment, such as content generation, forecasting, and design iteration. This evolution prompted a conceptual transition from automation to augmentation.

Augmented intelligence, as distinguished from artificial intelligence, emphasizes complementarity: machines expand human capacity by handling scale and pattern complexity, while humans contribute contextual interpretation and ethical oversight (Davenport & Bean, 2022). Empirical studies indicate that organizations adopting augmentation strategies achieve higher innovation returns than those focusing solely on automation (Shrestha et al., 2019). By freeing employees from routine analysis, AI allows cognitive resources to be redirected toward ideation and strategic reasoning.

Creative industries illustrate this transformation vividly. In design, platforms such as Adobe Firefly and DALL-E assist artists in generating prototypes that accelerate conceptual exploration. In marketing, generative algorithms produce multiple narrative variants that teams refine into emotionally resonant campaigns. In journalism, AI summarizes data trends, allowing reporters to focus on interpretation and storytelling. These examples demonstrate a feedback relationship between human imagination and machine capability. Creativity becomes iterative humans provide prompts, algorithms produce variations, and humans again evaluate and refine.

Within leadership contexts, AI adoption introduces both opportunities and anxieties. Decision-support systems improve forecasting accuracy, yet their recommendations can appear opaque, challenging leaders' accountability. Scholars warn against "automation bias," the human tendency to over-trust algorithmic outputs (Parasuraman &Manzey, 2010). Conversely, skepticism toward AI may lead to under-utilization. Effective leaders therefore require algorithmic literacy—an understanding of how models learn, where they err, and how their outputs should be ethically integrated into collective decision making.

Recent studies on digital transformation leadership suggest that success depends less on technical proficiency and more on a leader's ability to articulate purpose, manage change, and cultivate trust across human-machine boundaries (Westerman et al., 2021). This aligns with the notion of "digital ambidexterity," the capacity to exploit existing efficiencies while exploring emerging technologies. The leader's role shifts from directing workflows to designing ecosystems that enable human-AI co-creation.

Human–AI Collaboration And Augmented Leadership

Human–AI collaboration (HAC) represents a socio-technical system in which human cognition and machine computation jointly contribute to creative and strategic outcomes. Scholars describe HAC as a continuum of shared agency rather than a hierarchical relationship (Wilson & Daugherty, 2023). The human provides contextual framing, ethical intent, and domain knowledge, while the AI system contributes computational power, pattern recognition, and associative diversity. Effective collaboration arises when both agents learn from feedback loops, gradually building mutual predictability and trust.

Leadership research has begun to interpret this collaboration through the lens of augmented leadership. Augmented leaders use AI to amplify—not replace—their cognitive and emotional intelligence. They rely on data-driven insights to inform empathy, inclusion, and vision articulation. For instance, sentiment-analysis tools can help leaders gauge team morale in real time, while predictive analytics can forecast skill gaps and inform personalized development. Yet, the ultimate responsibility for judgment and fairness remains human.

A theoretical foundation for augmented leadership can be found in sociotechnical systems theory, which posits that organizational effectiveness depends on the joint optimization of social and technical subsystems (Trist & Bamforth, 1951). Applying this principle to AI, success emerges when algorithms are designed to serve collective human goals rather than narrow performance metrics. This approach contrasts with techno-centric views that prioritize efficiency over ethics.

Scholars also highlight the cognitive dimension of HAC. Research on distributed cognition suggests that intelligence resides not within individual minds but across networks of humans and artifacts (Hollan et al., 2000). Under this view, AI functions as an external cognitive node that extends memory, computation, and associative reasoning. Leaders operating within such systems act as coordinators of distributed cognition, ensuring that human and artificial contributions remain aligned with organizational values.

However, literature still lacks comprehensive models linking augmented leadership behaviours to measurable creative outcomes. Most empirical studies remain exploratory, focusing on case anecdotes rather than systematic theory testing. This absence underscores the need for integrative frameworks that describe how human oversight, machine autonomy, and ethical governance evolve together—a gap addressed by the HITL–HOTL–HOOTL model introduced later in this chapter.

The Interplay of Ethics, Culture, and Artificial Intelligence in Creative Endeavours

Ethical and cultural considerations take on a central role as artificial intelligence becomes increasingly integrated into leadership and creative processes. The ability of algorithms to learn from biased data, produce persuasive content, and operate autonomously raises concerns about accountability and fairness. Ethical AI frameworks emphasize principles of transparency, explainability, and human oversight (Floridi et al., 2018). However, operationalizing these principles in creative contexts remains complex. Creativity thrives on surprise and experimentation—qualities that can sometimes conflict with algorithmic predictability. Leaders must, therefore, carefully navigate the boundary between responsible governance and creative freedom.

Trust emerges as a critical mediator of human–AI collaboration. Studies on technology acceptance identify perceived transparency and perceived control as key determinants of trust (McKnight et al., 2021). When users understand how AI systems produce outcomes and retain the ability to intervene, they are more likely to collaborate effectively. Effective leadership critically influences how these perceptions are formed. By clearly articulating both the potentials and boundaries of AI, leaders can ease anxieties around job displacement and cultivate a collective sense of direction.

Cultural values further shape ethical judgments about AI. In collectivist societies, decisions often emphasize harmony and social benefit, leading to higher tolerance for algorithmic mediation if perceived as community-enhancing. In contrast, individualist cultures prioritize autonomy, sometimes resisting AI interventions that appear to constrain personal creativity (Hofstede et al., 2010). These variations affect how leaders design and implement AI systems across global teams. Cross-cultural sensitivity thus becomes integral to ethical AI governance.

Contemporary policy dialogues are increasingly framing AI ethics through the lens of sustainability and planetary responsibility. Growing attention is being directed toward the substantial energy demands of large-scale artificial intelligence systems and their role in exacerbating global digital divides—issues now firmly on the leadership agenda (UNESCO, 2023). In this context, ethical leadership entails a commitment to the triple bottom line: advancing economic value while safeguarding social equity and ecological integrity. Responsible integration of AI into creative processes thus demands more than technical ambition; it calls for deliberate stewardship of both human potential and environmental resources.

Scholars propose multi-layered governance approaches combining technical audits, participatory design, and ethical training. Leaders who embed these mechanisms signal that AI serves human creativity rather than commodifies it. This ethical stance reinforces trust and ensures that technological advancement remains aligned with societal progress.

Conceptual Synthesis And Theoretical Gap

The reviewed literature reveals substantial advances but also notable fragmentation. Research on creativity and leadership provides rich psychological and managerial insights yet seldom accounts for algorithmic collaboration. Conversely, technological studies of AI emphasize efficiency and predictive power while under-theorizing the human, ethical, and cultural dimensions. Bridging these domains requires an integrative framework that recognizes creativity as a relational phenomenonarising from interaction among humans, machines, and organizational contexts.

Three theoretical insights emerge from this synthesis. First, creativity and leadership are inherently co-adaptive processes: leaders shape environments that influence creative behaviour, and creative outcomes reshape leadership demands. Second, AI introduces a **new** layer of cognition that extends but also challenges human capabilities, requiring leaders to cultivate humility and learning orientation. Third, sustainable innovation depends on ethical equilibriummaintaining transparency, fairness, and inclusivity as technological autonomy expands.

Existing models address fragments of this triad. The Componential Theory of Creativity explains individual and environmental factors but excludes machine agency. Transformational leadership theory accounts for inspiration and vision but not for algorithmic partners. Sociotechnical systems theory stresses joint optimization but lacks explicit stages describing how human control transitions to shared or autonomous AI decision making. Hence, there is a conceptual void in understanding how leadership adapts across increasing levels of AI maturity.

The "HITL–HOTL–HOOTL" maturity framework proposed in this chapter responds to this void. It integrates insights from creativity research, leadership theory, and AI ethics into a coherent progression. The model portrays collaboration as evolving through three interdependent modessupervised, shared, and strategic autonomyeach requiring distinct leadership competencies and ethical safeguards. Unlike linear adoption models, it emphasizes continuous calibration: even as AI autonomy grows, human values remain the anchoring force.

By situating human–AI collaboration within this structured continuum, the framework offers both theoretical and practical contributions. Theoretically, it unifies dispersed literatures under a relational paradigm of creativity and leadership. Practically, it guides managers and policymakers in assessing readiness for AI integration while preserving cultural and ethical integrity.

In summary, the literature highlights that creativity, leadership, and AI are increasingly converging domains that require integrative thinking. Although considerable research has advanced understanding within each field individually, few studies have explored how these areas intersect to influence organizational creativity and ethical governance. The following section builds on these theoretical foundations to present the research framework and methodology underpinning this chapter's analysis. It illustrates how the "HITL–HOTL–HOOTL" model operationalizes human–AI collaboration across industries and cultural contexts, providing a foundation for the subsequent case studies and comparative insights.

RESEARCH FRAMEWORK AND METHODOLOGY

Conceptual Framework Development

The conceptual foundation of this chapter rests on the premise that creativity, leadership, and artificial intelligence constitute a mutually reinforcing triad that defines the contemporary innovation ecosystem. Insights from the preceding literature review suggest that although numerous models explain creative behaviour and technological diffusion, few articulate how human and artificial agents co-evolve within leadership systems. The framework of *Active Co-Creation*, *Supervised Autonomy*, and *System-Led Execution*—representing direct human involvement, conditional oversight, and full AI independence, respectively—has been developed as an integrative lens to capture the progressive evolution of collaboration, trust, and ethical maturity in human–AI partnerships.

Key Improvements

The logic of derivation

The framework emerged through inductive synthesis rather than statistical modeling. Patterns identified in studies of augmented intelligence, transformational leadership, and sociotechnical design were compared to real-world practices observed in global corporations. Recurrent ideas—human oversight, shared agency, and autonomous governance—were abstracted into three relational modes representing increasing technological independence and evolving leadership roles. Each mode signifies not a rigid hierarchy but a flexible configuration responsive to organizational culture, ethical regulation, and task complexity.

Stage 1: "Human-in-the-Loop/Direct Oversight" (HITL)

The first stage depicts contexts where humans retain direct control of algorithmic operations. AI acts as a decision support instrument that amplifies analytical reach but remains subordinate to human judgment. Leaders function as interpreters who validate outputs, ensuring that creative integrity and ethical boundaries are maintained. Examples include Microsoft Copilot facilitating team ideation or design tools suggesting variations under human supervision. The primary leadership competency at this level is ethical supervision the ability to detect bias, contextualize data, and translate algorithmic suggestions into humanly meaningful actions. Creativity remains anthropocentric, but AI accelerates exploration by expanding informational diversity.

Stage 2: "Human-on-the-Loop/ Supervisory Oversight" (HOTL)

The second stage represents a transition toward shared autonomy. Here AI performs semi-independent tasks while humans monitor system performance and intervene selectively. Leaders shift from operators to strategic collaborators, setting rules, validating boundary conditions, and interpreting anomalies. The creative process becomes dialogic: algorithms propose, humans critique, and iterative refinement produces hybrid originality. Unilever's AI-enabled sustainability campaigns or content-curation engines in digital media illustrate this mode. The leadership challenge is cultivating trust calibration—knowing when to rely on algorithmic output and when to re-assert human reasoning. Ethical responsibility broadens from error prevention to maintaining transparency and explainability.

Stage 3: "Human-out-of-the-Loop/Autonomous Operation" (HOOTL)

In this advanced stage, artificial intelligence operates with a high degree of independence, guided by predefined ethical parameters and strategic objectives. Human involvement transitions from direct supervision to the creation of governance frameworks that oversee and calibrate system behaviour. Leadership assumes the role of curatorial stewardship a responsibility focused on ensuring that autonomous technologies continue to serve organizational missions and uphold social values. Platforms such as Spotify's AI DJ and other generative design systems illustrate the early realization of this paradigm. The focus thus moves beyond operational control toward meta-governance, requiring leaders to harmonize technological accountability, intercultural ethics, and continuous learning within a cohesive oversight structure.

Integrative Relationships Among Stages

Although the three stages appear sequential, in practice they coexist dynamically across organizational units. A single enterprise may operate customer analytics at the HOTL level while maintaining HITL controls in product design and aspirational HOOTL prototypes in predictive maintenance. Movement across stages is iterative, driven by improvements in model reliability, regulatory context, and cultural acceptance. The framework thus depicts a maturity continuum in which leadership competencies evolve from supervisory vigilance to strategic orchestration and finally to ethical governance.

Theoretical Alignment

Conceptually, the model synthesizes three disciplinary perspectives:

1. Componential Theory of Creativity (Amabile, 1996) → explains the motivational and environmental conditions that foster creative performance; HITL governance safeguards those conditions.
2. Transformational and Shared Leadership Theories (Northouse, 2021) → emphasize vision, empowerment, and collective learning; HOTL collaboration operationalizes these behaviours in human-machine teams.

3. Sociotechnical Systems Theory (Trist & Bamforth, 1951) emphasizes the balanced integration of human and technological components within organizations. The HOOTL governance model embodies this balance by achieving harmony between social dynamics and technical efficiency at an organizational level.

By weaving these theories together, the HITL–HOTL–HOOTL continuum provides a multi-level framework for understanding how creativity and leadership adapt as AI capabilities mature. It recognizes that technological progress alters not only operational processes but also moral architecture—the way responsibility, authorship, and trust are distributed across human and machine agents.

Conceptual Significance

The significance of the proposed framework lies in its reconceptualization of intelligent system adoption as a relational and co-evolutionary process rather than a transactional or purely technical shift. Leadership in the contemporary landscape of intelligent systems is thus characterized not by the delegation of cognitive authority to machines but by the establishment of ethical and structural mechanisms that harmonize human creativity with algorithmic intelligence. This reframing advances the discourse from efficiency-driven implementation toward intentional and value-oriented collaboration, aligning with the broader paradigm of human-centered innovation emphasized in current academic and policy debates. The subsequent sections elaborate on how this conceptual framework guided the methodological orientation, selection of case illustrations, and analytical reasoning underlying the chapter.

Research Design And Interpretive Approach

This chapter adopts a qualitative, interpretivist research orientation grounded in conceptual synthesis and cross-case comparison. The interpretivist perspective is suitable because the study seeks to understand meanings and relationships rather than to measure variables. Human–AI collaboration is inherently contextual: it evolves through social interpretation, organizational culture, and technological design. A positivist approach—seeking numerical generalization—would obscure the subtle negotiation of trust, creativity, and ethics that defines these interactions. Therefore, the analytical logic employed here emphasizes understanding, pattern recognition, and theoretical integration rather than statistical inference.

This study relies exclusively on secondary and documentary sources, reflecting an intentionally conceptual-theoretical rather than empirical approach. Its aim is to integrate insights from diverse disciplines into a cohesive framework that explores leadership and creativity in the context of human–AI collaboration. The absence of primary data is therefore not a limitation but a deliberate methodological choice, suited to the development of the framework and the articulation of underlying theoretical principles.

Philosophical Orientation

The philosophical foundation rests on constructivist epistemology: knowledge about AI collaboration is co-constructed by human observers, organizational participants, and the technologies themselves. This view aligns with social-constructionist scholarship that interprets leadership as a relational process rather than a fixed trait (Uhl-Bien, 2006). In this paradigm, reality is not independent of interpretation; it is produced through interaction between people, tools, and contexts. The interpretive approach recognizes that AI systems mediate perception and decision-making—meaning that the study of leadership must include the *technological actor* as part of the social field.

Consequently, the methodology privileges thick description and reflective reasoning. It treats case materials, corporate documents, and prior empirical findings as textual evidence from which conceptual patterns can be distilled. The aim is not to claim causal generality but to articulate a framework capable of guiding subsequent empirical testing and practical adoption.

Research Logic And Design Type

Methodologically, the chapter follows a multi-case interpretive design. This design allows examination of diverse manifestations of human–AI collaboration across industries and cultural settings. Multiple-case logic enhances theoretical robustness by enabling replication and contrast: patterns observed in one context can be compared with others to reveal both universal and context-specific elements (Yin, 2018). The cases—drawn from technology, consumer goods, and creative sectors—serve as *illustrative exemplars* that illuminate different stages of the HITL–HOTL–HOOTL continuum.

Because the investigation relies primarily on secondary and documentary sources—annual reports, organizational white papers, peer-reviewed case studies, and media analyses—the research design is conceptual-comparative rather than field-survey based. This approach aligns with established expectations for conceptual and theoretical research that synthesizes cross-disciplinary knowledge for emerging phenomena such as AI leadership. It also ensures methodological transparency: every analytical inference is traceable to publicly verifiable sources.

Scope of Analysis and Conceptual Boundaries

The core analytical focus of this framework lies in examining the interactive moments where human leadership converges with AI systems within organizational decision-making and creative processes. Each episodesuch as Unilever's AI-assisted hiring or Adobe's generative design workflowrepresents a microcosm in which human intention and algorithmic capability intersect. By analysing these episodes across multiple organizations, the study captures variations in trust calibration, creative augmentation, and ethical governance.

Boundary conditions are explicitly acknowledged. The analysis focuses on organizations that have publicly documented AI implementations; purely speculative or experimental systems are excluded. Furthermore, the study considers AI collaboration in the context of knowledge-intensive and creative work rather than manufacturing automation. This delimitation maintains conceptual coherence with the chapter's focus on creativity and leadership.

Nature and Sources of Data

Secondary data for this study were drawn from authoritative academic databases, verified corporate disclosures, and well-established industry publications spanning the years 2018 to 2024. These materials included peer-reviewed research on AI in management, corporate reports on sustainability initiatives, and documented cases of innovation practice. To minimize single-source bias and enhance interpretive credibility, data were triangulated across scholarly and professional perspectives. For example, Unilever's sustainability initiatives were examined by juxtaposing academic discussions of green marketing with the company's official communications, ensuring a balanced and contextually grounded interpretation. This approach follows the logic of methodological triangulation, emphasizing the validation of meaning and insight rather than numerical measurement.

The data set was treated as textual discourse. Each document was read iteratively to identify recurring concepts: human oversight, creative augmentation, trust, ethics, and autonomy. These concepts were coded into thematic categories corresponding to the three framework stages. Coding followed an open-to-axial progression—first noting descriptive ideas, then relating them to theoretical constructs such as transformational leadership or sociotechnical alignment. The resulting pattern map provided the empirical grounding for articulating how leadership competencies evolve across the HITL–HOTL–HOOTL continuum.

Analytical orientation

Interpretation employed a cross-case synthesis method. After coding, each case was summarized in terms of context, AI function, leadership response, and creative outcome. Comparative reading revealed repeating cycles: initial skepticism replaced by trust as transparency improved; efficiency gains accompanied by new ethical dilemmas; creative acceleration moderated by human sense-making. These cycles were then aligned with the three framework stages to verify conceptual fit. The process generated a narrative matrix linking theoretical propositions to observable organizational practices.

The interpretive stance ensures that meaning is derived through *abduction*—reasoning from observed phenomena to plausible explanation. Rather than testing a predefined hypothesis, the study constructs theoretical coherence by iteratively matching literature-based expectations with real-world manifestations. This approach resonates with grounded-theory logic but remains conceptual, as the aim is to refine theory rather than generate it from raw field data.

Reliability and Credibility

Because interpretive research relies on judgment, ensuring credibility is essential. Several strategies strengthen reliability. Source triangulation balances academic and practitioner perspectives. Temporal triangulation compares developments across time (pre- and post-2020 AI adoption waves). Peer debriefing, achieved through informal consultation of published expert commentaries, provides external perspective on the interpretation of patterns. Finally, theoretical saturation was monitored: when additional sources ceased to add new conceptual insights, categories were considered stable. These measures collectively enhance trustworthiness, aligning with quality criteria commonly used in qualitative research (Lincoln & Guba, 1985).

Justification of Methodology

The chosen interpretive, multi-case design emphasizes methodological clarity and conceptual innovation. It balances analytical rigor with practical relevance by integrating cross-disciplinary literature and real-world organizational insights. This design allows theoretical reflection to coexist with empirical illustration, producing findings that are both academically grounded and applicable to managerial practice. Moreover, the framework's three-stage structure provides a replicable analytical tool for subsequent empirical research, offering theoretical scaffolding to a still-developing field of inquiry.

This methodological architecture establishes the foundation for exploring how human–AI collaboration manifests across distinct organizational environments. The following section, **Case Selection and Context**, describes the rationale for choosing representative industries and the way contextual factors—technological maturity, cultural orientation, and creative domain—shape progression along the HITL–HOTL–HOOTL continuum.

CASE STUDIES AND INDUSTRY INSIGHTS

Introduction to the Case Analysis

The progressive maturity of human–AI collaboration described in the HITL–HOTL–HOOTL framework finds tangible expression in several industry examples where creativity and leadership converge with intelligent systems. Case-based analysis provides a bridge between conceptual reasoning and practical evidence: it illustrates how abstract principles of ethical supervision, collaborative trust, and autonomous governance unfold within real organizational environments. Each case examined here—Microsoft Copilot, Adobe Firefly, Unilever's AI-driven sustainability and HR programs, and Spotify's AI DJ—represents a distinctive stage along the collaboration continuum and reflects the cultural and strategic choices that shape AI adoption.

The purpose of analysing these cases is not to celebrate corporate success stories but to trace behavioral and leadership patterns that define responsible creativity in the digital era. By situating these examples across technology, creative design, consumer goods, and entertainment industries, the analysis captures how sectoral logics influence the design of AI interaction. Technology companies emphasize cognitive augmentation and productivity; creative firms focus on originality and authorship; consumer-goods corporations integrate ethical branding and sustainability; and media platforms experiment with personalization at cultural scale. These contrasting orientations offer fertile ground for observing how human oversight diminishes or transforms as algorithmic capability increases.

Each case narrative begins with contextual background and proceeds to interpret the interaction through the lens of the framework. The emphasis lies on leadership adaptationhow managers and creative directors redefine authority, empathy, and decision-making when intelligence becomes distributed between human and machine. Patterns of trust calibration, ethical reflexivity, and creative acceleration are examined not as isolated phenomena but as markers of organizational learning. Through this interpretive comparison, the section seeks to demonstrate that the path toward autonomous creativity is neither uniform nor linear; it is mediated by culture, governance, and the moral imagination of leadership.

Case 1: Microsoft Copilot — Human-in-the-Loop Collaboration in Knowledge Work

Microsoft's launch of *Copilot* in 2023 marked a pivotal moment in the integration of generative intelligence system within mainstream productivity software. Embedded across applications such as Word, Excel, PowerPoint, and Teams, Copilot enables users to generate content, summarize meetings, and visualize data through natural-language prompts. Rather than creating a stand-alone AI system, Microsoft deliberately positioned Copilot as an assistant within the loop—a design choice that keeps human cognition at the center of creative and managerial tasks. This positioning corresponds closely with the Human-in-the-Loop (HITL) stage of the collaboration continuum, where algorithmic suggestion operates under human supervision and evaluation.

From an organizational perspective, the introduction of Copilot coincided with the global transition toward remote and hybrid work arrangements, which amplified the strategic demand for digitally mediated coordination and collaborative efficiency (Microsoft, 2023). During this period, knowledge workers were increasingly burdened by information overload, virtual meeting fatigue, and the pressure to make rapid yet accurate decisions. Microsoft's strategic response was to design an intelligent interface that augmented human capability without compromising autonomy or accountability. The company positioned Copilot not as a replacement for human expertise but as a collaborative ally—intended to reduce repetitive tasks and empower employees to focus on the creative, analytical, and relational dimensions of their work.

Application of the HITL Framework

Within the HITL logic, Copilot exemplifies a co-dependent workflow where human prompts guide machine generation, and human judgment validates outputs. The system's architecture reinforces cyclical feedback: users issue instructions, Copilot produces drafts or analyses, and humans refine results based on contextual knowledge. This iterative pattern operationalizes what Amabile's componential theory of creativity identifies as task motivation and domain expertiseelements that remain exclusively human even when assisted by AI. The tool's design ensures that creativity remains supervised and ethically bounded; no action is executed without explicit user consent. Leadership at this stage revolves around establishing protocols for responsible use and cultivating trust in algorithmic suggestions without succumbing to over-reliance.

Leadership Transformation

Introducing Copilot required new forms of digital leadership within Microsoft and its client organizations. Managers were compelled to redefine productivity metrics, shifting from output quantity to *insight quality*. Leaders also had to nurture psychological safety so that employees felt comfortable experimenting with AI assistance. Trust calibration became a recurrent theme: users initially exhibited skepticism, questioning data privacy and output reliability; over time, guided workshops and transparent governance frameworks mitigated these concerns. This process mirrors the ethical supervision capacity highlighted in the HITL model—leaders acting as guardians of fairness, data security, and interpretive accuracy.

Another important transformation involved distributed leadership. In virtual collaboration platforms like Teams, Copilot mediates interactions by summarizing discussions or suggesting task priorities. Decision-making authority thus becomes diffused between human participants and the AI facilitator. Leaders must interpret AI-generated insights without abdicating accountability, maintaining what scholars call *algorithmic stewardship*—a balance between delegation and oversight. In this sense, Copilot functions as both a cognitive amplifier and a test of managerial integrity: it reveals whether leaders can integrate technological intelligence while preserving human values.

Creativity and Cognitive Augmentation

Copilot also redefines creative workflows. In Word or PowerPoint, it generates preliminary drafts, storylines, or visual layouts that spark further ideation. This accelerates the divergent phase of creativity, idea generation, while leaving the convergent phase of judgment and refinement to humans. The resulting human-machine symbiosis increases both speed and quality: employees can explore multiple conceptual directions before committing to one. Nevertheless, leadership must monitor ethical implications such as unintentional plagiarism or over-standardization of expression. Creative authenticity depends on humans exercising discernment rather than accepting AI outputs uncritically.

Ethical and Governance Considerations

Microsoft established explicit guidelines for responsible AI use, emphasizing transparency, explainability, and human control. Copilot logs interactions and provides disclosure prompts that remind users when content has been AI-generated. This transparency mechanism sustains the ethical perimeter of HITL operations. Leaders adopting Copilot in other organizations must translate these technical safeguards into cultural norms—encouraging reflective use, ongoing learning, and open dialogue about bias and accountability. The leadership role thus expands beyond supervision to include ethical sense-making within teams.

Lessons From The Case

The Microsoft Copilot case demonstrates that human-AI collaboration at the HITL stage thrives when three conditions coincide:

1. Transparent system design that visibly retains human agency.
2. Leadership education that reframes AI from threat to tool.
3. Ethical reinforcement through organizational policy and peer discussion.

These elements create an environment where creative confidence and technological trust develop simultaneously. The case also reveals the tension between efficiency and originality: as AI accelerates task completion, there is a risk that humans may conflate *speed* with *insight*. Effective leadership must counter this by championing depth, reflection, and contextual intelligence.

Microsoft's experience embodies the opening phase of the HITL–HOTL–HOOTL continuum. Human supervision dominates, yet collaboration already begins to reshape cognitive and ethical norms within organizations. The lessons derived from Copilot provide the baseline for understanding more advanced phases of partnership, where autonomy and co-creation expand beyond supervision. The following case, Adobe Firefly, illustrates this next stage—Human-on-the-Loop (HOTL) collaborationwhere creativity becomes a shared endeavour between designer and algorithm rather than a strictly guided interaction.

Case 2: Adobe Firefly — Co-creation and Creative Empowerment

Adobe's introduction of Firefly, a generative-AI model integrated into its Creative Cloud ecosystem, marked a decisive moment in the democratization of creative design. Unlike experimental art generators that often bypass authorship ethics, Firefly was developed from licensed and openly available data, reflecting Adobe's longstanding commitment to intellectual-property transparency. The model enables users to create images, stylized text effects, and digital artwork through natural-language prompts, directly inside tools such as Photoshop, Illustrator, and Express. Its purpose is not to replace artists but to empower creators with augmented ideation, situating humans *on the loop*—a level where collaboration becomes reciprocal rather than supervisory.

In the years following its 2023 public beta, Firefly became emblematic of a new design philosophy in which creative professionals and algorithms share authorship. Adobe emphasized the idea of "content authenticity," embedding metadata that identifies AI-assisted content to ensure traceability. This innovation positions Firefly at the "Human-on-the-Loop (HOTL)" stage of the framework, where autonomy is balanced with ongoing human validation and where creativity evolves through *dialogue* between intuition and computation.

Application of the HOTL Framework

Within the HOTL model, the human role transitions from controller to strategic collaborator. Designers provide conceptual prompts, evaluate outputs, and iterate jointly with the system, using algorithmic variation as a springboard for originality. Firefly's interface facilitates rapid experimentation: one textual prompt can yield multiple visual interpretations, enabling users to navigate a spectrum of creative possibilities before choosing a final direction. This interplay operationalizes the "co-creation loop"—a cyclical process of suggestion, reflection, and selection that epitomizes mid-level autonomy.

From a leadership perspective, this stage challenges traditional hierarchies within creative organizations. Creative directors now orchestrate interactions between human imagination and machine generation, guiding teams to interpret algorithmic suggestions rather than dictate outcomes. The leader's expertise lies in curating creative diversity—recognizing valuable serendipity without compromising project coherence. By reframing leadership as facilitation rather than command, Firefly accelerates the move from individual genius to collective intelligence.

Leadership and Organizational Transformation

Adopting Firefly demanded both cultural and procedural shifts inside Adobe and among its professional community. Internally, Adobe redefined leadership metrics: the value of design was measured not only by output aesthetics but by collaborative fluency—the ability to integrate AI feedback into human workflows. Leaders encouraged open dialogue about the system's limitations, fostering psychological safety around experimentation. By legitimizing failure as part of exploration, they reinforced an innovation minds*e*t consistent with agile-leadership principles.

Externally, creative-industry leaders who adopted Firefly faced new responsibilities: ensuring that AI-assisted works respected originality, client confidentiality, and cultural symbolism. Leadership in this context meant ethical arbitration—deciding how far to delegate aesthetic decisions to algorithms while maintaining artistic integrity. Some agencies established internal review committees to monitor AI-generated material, demonstrating that effective HOTL collaboration depends as much on institutional norms as on technical capacity.

Creativity, Authorship, And Emotional Resonance

Firefly expands the traditional notion of creativity from solitary mastery to interactive emergence. The system's generative capabilities encourage divergent thinking, allowing users to explore visual metaphors they might never have imagined manually. Yet emotional authenticity remains rooted in human judgment: the artist chooses which image "feels right," a decision inseparable from lived experience and cultural awareness. This dynamic illustrates what scholars term *augmented authenticity*—a synthesis where technological novelty gains emotional depth through human sensibility.

Moreover, Firefly democratizes creativity by lowering technical barriers. Non-designers can produce professional-quality visuals, thereby broadening participation in the creative economy. Leadership must therefore adapt inclusively, guiding diverse contributors to use these tools responsibly. Training initiatives that pair artistic literacy with AI literacy become vital; they equip creators to engage with technology critically rather than passively.

Ethical and Governance Dimensions

Ethical governance sits at the core of Firefly's strategy. Adobe's "Content Authenticity Initiative" sets explicit standards for attribution and data provenance, helping address global concerns about intellectual-property violations in generative AI. By embedding metadata tags that reveal when content has been AI-assisted, Adobe establishes a culture of disclosure. This transparency not only protects creators but also reinforces public trust in AI-enabled media.

For leaders, such governance frameworks provide both guidance and moral precedent. Ethical oversight moves from reactive policing to proactive design: systems are built with transparency rather than retrofitted with disclaimers. This proactive approach aligns with the HOTL principle of embedded ethics, where moral reasoning becomes integral to the creative process itself.

Lessons from the Case

The Firefly experience demonstrates that sustainable AI-driven creativity requires four intertwined competencies:

1. Collaborative literacy—understanding the language of prompts and algorithmic suggestion.
2. Ethical sensitivity—recognizing authorship and fairness obligations.
3. Adaptive leadership—facilitating experimentation while maintaining coherence.
4. Cultural empathy—translating algorithmic possibilities into designs that resonate globally.

These competencies transform creative leadership from an aesthetic role into a cultural-technological mediationfunction. The success of Firefly suggests that organizations thrive when they treat AI not as a creative competitor but as a partner in expanding human imagination.

Bridging insight, Adobe Firefly captures the essence of the HOTL phase: creativity and leadership operate in partnership with autonomous systems, guided by ethical awareness and inclusive collaboration. Where Microsoft Copilot showed the discipline of supervision, Firefly reveals the freedom of dialogue. The next case, Unilever, advances this trajectory further—demonstrating how AI collaboration extends beyond creativity into governance, sustainability, and large-scale ethical decision-making, illustrating the transition toward Human-out-of-the-Loop (HOOTL) maturity.

Case 3: Unilever — Ethical and Sustainable AI Leadership

Unilever, one of the world's largest fast-moving consumer goods (FMCG) corporations, has positioned artificial intelligence at the heart of its sustainability and human resources transformation. Operating in over 190 countries, the company faces immense complexity in supply chains, consumer behaviour, and environmental accountability. To navigate these challenges, Unilever integrates AI across marketing, production, and recruitment systems. The goal is not merely operational efficiency but *ethical sustainability*—ensuring that technological adoption supports social responsibility and planetary well-being.

Over the past decade, Unilever's "Sustainable Living Plan" and its subsequent "Compass Strategy" have provided the corporate scaffolding for embedding AI within ethical governance frameworks. AI-driven tools are used to optimize water consumption, reduce packaging waste, and personalize marketing aligned with sustainability values. In human resources, AI platforms assist in recruitment by screening candidates through gamified psychometric tests that measure cognitive and emotional traits. The company collaborates with technology partners such as Pymetrics and HireVue, emphasizing fairness, inclusivity, and transparency in algorithmic decision-making. These initiatives exemplify the Human-out-of-the-

Loop (HOOTL) transition, where AI systems act autonomously within predefined ethical boundaries while humans focus on strategic oversight and cultural guidance.

The HOOTL Framework In Practice

At the HOOTL level, human leadership recedes from continuous supervision and instead establishes governance architecture that defines acceptable behaviour for autonomous systems. In Unilever's sustainability programs, AI algorithms autonomously adjust manufacturing parameters to reduce energy consumption based on real-time sensor data. Similarly, in talent acquisition, machine learning models independently evaluate applicant suitability using pattern recognition, while human managers review outcomes for fairness and compliance. These applications demonstrate a shift from procedural control to policy-driven delegation: human leaders design the moral and operational perimeter within which AI operates.

This evolution demands a new kind of leadershipone grounded in ethical governance and systemic foresight. Executives no longer intervene in each decision but are responsible for designing the moral compass of algorithmic behaviour. The HOOTL mode reflects the maturity of organizational trust: humans trust machines to act ethically because the governance framework itself embodies shared values. Leadership thus becomes curatorial rather than supervisory—overseeing principles rather than actions.

Leadership Transformation

The Unilever case illustrates how leadership evolves from operational management to value orchestration. The company's senior leadership, under the guidance of its Chief Digital and Technology Officer, advocates what it terms "responsible digital transformation." This philosophy regards technology not as a neutral instrument but as a moral agent that must embody the organization's overarching purpose: "making sustainable living commonplace."

To achieve this, Unilever established cross-functional *digital ethics boards* comprising legal, technical, and social-impact experts. These boards review AI models before deployment, assessing them for bias, data provenance, and environmental impact. This practice institutionalizes the principle of *human accountability for non-human actions*—a hallmark of the HOOTL stage. It signifies an evolution from reactive oversight to proactive moral design, ensuring that autonomy does not erode responsibility.

Leaders within Unilever have also redefined employee engagement. Through internal education initiatives such as *"Intelligent Leadership"* and *"Digital Readiness,"* the company fosters awareness of ethical and responsible use of intelligent systems across managerial levels. This decentralization of technological literacy enables employees to engage critically with algorithmic outputs rather than defer unreflectively to machine judgment. In this way, ethical literacy becomes a shared organizational competence, reinforcing mutual trust and collective accountability.

Creativity, Sustainability, And Stakeholder Trust

While Unilever's AI integration primarily serves operational and ethical goals, it also fuels *creative innovation*. Marketing teams use predictive analytics to identify sustainable product trends and co-create campaigns that resonate with eco-conscious consumers. For example, AI-driven sentiment analysis informed Unilever's campaigns for Dove and Ben & Jerry's, ensuring cultural sensitivity while amplifying authenticity. Creativity here extends beyond artistic expression—it encompasses strategic imagination: envisioning future markets, lifestyles, and social norms shaped by sustainability.

By coupling creativity with conscience, Unilever redefines innovation as a moral pursuit. AI's role in this configuration is not to produce novelty for its own sake but to translate ethical intention into measurable impact. This alignment generates stakeholder trust, which is central to brand loyalty and legitimacy in a socially aware marketplace. Thus, the company's AI initiatives illustrate how the HOOTL paradigm can reconcile technological autonomy with human-centered purpose.

Ethical and Cultural Implications

The Unilever case also exposes the *paradoxes of delegation*. While autonomy enhances efficiency, it also raises questions about accountability in cases of error or bias. Unilever addresses this by implementing algorithmic audit trails that record decision logic for later review, preserving transparency and traceability. Additionally, its multicultural workforce requires that ethical AI standards accommodate diverse norms of fairness and privacy. Leadership must therefore interpret global ethical principles in culturally sensitive ways—acknowledging that values such as transparency, inclusivity, and sustainability manifest differently across societies. This adaptive governance represents a pragmatic balance between global uniformity and local responsiveness.

Another challenge lies in maintaining human empathy in automated systems. For instance, AI-based recruitment could risk depersonalizing the candidate experience. Unilever mitigates this by blending digital efficiency with human feedback loops—candidates receive personalized insights from the AI assessment, but final hiring decisions involve human evaluators. This *hybrid empathy* ensures that technological fairness coexists with humane interaction.

Lessons from the Case

The Unilever experience provides a mature illustration of the HOOTL phase. Three leadership lessons emerge:

1. Design ethics into systems rather than applying them retrospectively.
2. Institutionalize cross-functional governance to maintain transparency and accountability.
3. Educate for ethical literacy, enabling every employee to act as a moral agent within an automated environment.

These principles reflect the culmination of the human–AI collaboration journey: when systems operate autonomously, leadership responsibility shifts from control to conscience. The case confirms that autonomy without moral infrastructure leads to alienation, but autonomy guided by shared purpose produces sustainable innovation.

Bridging insight, Unilever demonstrates that the future of leadership lies not in micromanaging algorithms but in *governing the values* they embody. By embedding ethical design, cross-cultural inclusivity, and sustainability into AI operations, the company achieves a rare synthesis of autonomy and accountability. This case thus represents the upper threshold of the collaboration continuum—a prelude to how creative autonomy unfolds at the cultural scale, as illustrated in the next example, Spotify AI DJ, where algorithmic creativity interacts directly with human emotion and identity across global audiences.

Case 4: Spotify AI DJ — Autonomous Creativity and Cultural Personalization

Spotify's 2023 launch of its AI DJ feature marked a milestone in consumer-oriented algorithmic creativity. Powered by large language models integrated with adaptive recommendation engines, the system curates personalized playlists and delivers spoken commentary through a synthetic voice modeled after human presenters. For listeners, the experience blurs the line between human curation and computational authorship—the DJ engages in conversational interaction, anticipates mood shifts, and dynamically tailors music selections in real time. This innovation exemplifies theAutonomous Intelligence Phaseof the collaboration continuum, wherein intelligent systems exercise creative agency within predefined ethical and cultural boundaries, while humans serve as designers, auditors, and narrative stewards of governance rather than direct operators.

Spotify developed this capability through its internal AI systems and emotional speech synthesis technology from Sonantic (acquired in 2022), drawing on billions of listening interactions to construct a dynamic, affect-responsive user interface. The system's objective is not only to recommend tracks but to shape affective journeys through sound. It therefore functions as an emotional-intelligence interface, translating behavioural data into cultural expression. The scale and intimacy of this relationship raise new questions about authorship, taste formation, and the ethics of personalization—questions that define the frontier of autonomous creativity.

HOOTL Framework In Application

In the HOOTL paradigm, autonomy is structured through ethical architecture. The AI DJ operates independently of real-time human supervision, yet its design reflects a set of governing principles—fair representation of artists, avoidance of explicit or harmful content, and respect for listener privacy. Human oversight enters only at the policy and system-design stages. Once deployed, the DJ continuously refines its recommendations through feedback loops derived from user engagement metrics such as skip rate and dwell time. Creativity here emerges algorithmically: combinations of songs and commentary create narratives unique to each listener, producing what scholars describe as algorithmic culture—a form of cultural production mediated by code rather than by curators.

Leadership in this environment moves beyond organizational boundaries. Spotify's executives and product managers embody meta-leadership, orchestrating alignment among data scientists, ethicists, artists, and policymakers. They do not script playlists but craft *rules for creativity*: fairness in artist exposure, diversity in genre representation, and safeguards against echo-chamber reinforcement. This leadership of principles rather than processes epitomizes the HOOTL ethos—governance through design rather than continuous intervention.

Leadership Transformation And Ethical Governance

The autonomy of the AI DJ necessitated a new layer of algorithmic accountability. Spotify established internal review boards to audit model training data and to ensure diversity across cultural and linguistic spectra. Transparency measures include public explanations of recommendation logic and opt-out controls that empower users to limit data usage. These measures convert ethical aspiration into operational practice, reaffirming that leadership at scale involves shaping *institutional conscience*.

Furthermore, the company adopted an approach of participatory ethics by engaging artists and listeners in feedback dialogues. Users can rate DJ sessions or flag content that feels repetitive or culturally insensitive; these signals feed directly into model retraining cycles. This distributed oversight system extends the notion of leadership to the community level, reflecting a democratization of governance consistent with global digital-ethics frameworks. Through such participatory loops, the AI DJ becomes both autonomous and socially responsive.

Creativity, Emotion, And Cultural Identity

The Spotify DJ exemplifies how AI can generate affective creativity—the orchestration of mood through data-driven storytelling. By sequencing tracks to match circadian rhythms or contextual cues, the system simulates an empathetic presence. Listeners report a sense of companionship and discovery that surpasses static playlists. This interaction transforms the consumption of music into a co-creative ritual: algorithms learn emotional preferences, while humans reinterpret those outputs as expressions of identity.

However, this intimacy introduces ethical tensions. When algorithms infer mood or identity, they enter the realm of psychological influence. Leaders must ensure that personalization does not cross into manipulation—particularly in cultures where music serves therapeutic or communal functions. Spotify addresses this through content-policy firewalls that restrict exploitative targeting and by collaborating with cultural researchers to validate emotional-model accuracy. Such interdisciplinary engagement reinforces the company's role as a *cultural steward* rather than merely a platform provider.

Cross-Cultural Implications

Operating in more than 180 markets, Spotify's AI DJ must interpret cultural meaning with nuance. Musical preference embodies linguistic, regional, and generational codes; an algorithm trained predominantly on Western data could inadvertently marginalize local expressions. To counter this, Spotify localizes models through regional data enclaves and partnerships with domestic artists, ensuring representation of vernacular sounds. This strategy illustrates how autonomous systems can sustain cultural diversity when guided by inclusive leadership frameworks.

From the HITL–HOTL–HOOTL perspective, the AI DJ demonstrates the endpoint of distributed creativity: humans design the moral and cultural infrastructure, while AI performs within it—adapting fluidly to audience feedback without direct command. The leadership challenge shifts from supervising tasks to orchestrating ecosystems that balance global reach with local authenticity.

Lessons from the Case

The Spotify AI DJ offers several insights for understanding autonomy in creative collaboration:

1. **Ethical design precedes autonomy.** Governance embedded in system architecture prevents misuse once oversight diminishes.
2. **Emotion is the new frontier of creativity.** Algorithms capable of affective reasoning require empathetic leadership to avoid manipulation.
3. **Cultural pluralism ensures resilience.** Localization of data and artistry transforms global AI into a mosaic of regional identities.
4. **Community participation strengthens legitimacy.** Inviting user feedback institutionalizes collective moral responsibility.

These lessons affirm that sustainable creative autonomy depends on *ethical ecosystems*, not on isolated technological achievements.

Bridging insight, The Spotify case completes the arc of human–AI collaboration: from the supervised intelligence of Microsoft Copilot to the dialogic creativity of Adobe Firefly and the governance-driven autonomy of Unilever. Spotify extends this evolution into the cultural domain, where algorithms not only execute tasks but also *curate emotions*. Leadership at this stage transcends organizational management to become a custodianship of culture, ensuring that technological autonomy enriches rather than erodes the human experience. As societies increasingly inhabit algorithmic environments, the capacity to design and govern such systems ethically will define the next era of creative leadership.

Cross-Case Synthesis and Sectoral Insights

The four cases—Microsoft Copilot, Adobe Firefly, Unilever, and Spotify AI DJ—together trace a progressive continuum of human–AI collaboration, illustrating how leadership, creativity, and ethics co-evolve across technological maturity stages. Viewed collectively, they demonstrate that the relationship between humans and intelligent systems is not linear but *dialectical*: each advance in autonomy generates a new demand for ethical reflection, cultural adaptation, and imaginative leadership.

Comparative Patterns Across Sectors

Across the technology, creative, consumer-goods, and entertainment sectors, three patterns emerge.

First, leadership evolution follows a clear trajectory from supervision to orchestration. In Microsoft's HITL environment, leaders act as ethical gatekeepers who validate and contextualize AI outputs. At Adobe's HOTL stage, leadership becomes facilitative—encouraging experimentation and dialogue between human and machine creativity. Unilever's HOOTL practices elevate leadership to moral governance, embedding ethics within system architecture. Spotify extends this evolution into the cultural sphere, where leaders operate as custodians of affect and identity, guiding autonomous systems to reflect collective values. Across these phases, leadership shifts from control over processes to care for principles.

Second, the role of creativity transforms from problem-solving to meaning-making. Copilot accelerates ideation, Firefly democratizes artistry, Unilever translates ethical commitment into creative strategy, and Spotify curates emotional experiences. The common thread is *augmentation rather than replacement*: AI amplifies human imagination by removing functional constraints, while humans provide narrative and moral coherence. The creative process thus becomes distributed, iterative, and socially embedded.

Third, ethical governance matures from procedural transparency to embedded conscience. Early systems rely on disclosure and human review; later systems institutionalize ethics through design and community participation. This progression mirrors the broader shift from compliance-oriented regulation to value-based governance, where integrity is engineered into both technology and organizational culture.

Cross-Cultural and Global Dimensions

The comparative analysis also reveals how cultural context shapes AI collaboration. Western technology firms such as Microsoft and Adobe emphasize innovation and intellectual property, reflecting individualist traditions that value autonomy and authorship. In contrast, Unilever's multinational operations and Spotify's global audience highlight collectivist sensibilitiestrust, inclusion, and cultural resonance. These variations confirm that ethical AI is *context-dependent*: governance models must harmonize universal principles with local moral grammars. Effective leadership, therefore, entails cross-cultural empathy and the ability to mediate between algorithmic universality and human diversity.

Strategic Insights and Implications

The synthesis suggests several strategic imperatives for organizations pursuing AI-enabled creativity:

1. **Institutionalize ethical design early.** Governance mechanisms should precede technological autonomy, not follow it.
2. **Invest in creative and ethical literacy.** Training should cultivate dual fluency—technical competence and moral reasoning.
3. **Adopt ecosystem leadership.** Future leaders must govern networks of humans and intelligent agents rather than hierarchical teams.

4. **Foster participatory governance.** Transparency and user inclusion increase trust and reduce algorithmic alienation.

These imperatives reposition leadership as a systemic capacity rather than an individual attribute. The ability to design trustworthy, culturally aware AI ecosystems will become a central criterion of institutional legitimacy in the digital era.

Concluding Synthesis

Together, the cases affirm the robustness of the HITL–HOTL–HOOTL framework as an analytical lens for understanding AI maturity and leadership transformation. They reveal a unifying pattern: as automation deepens, *humanity becomes the differentiator*. Ethical imagination, cultural intelligence, and empathy emerge as the true sources of competitive advantage. The subsequent section of this chapter builds upon these empirical insights to articulate a broader theoretical discussion on how human–AI collaboration redefines creativity, leadership, and innovation in the future of work.

DISCUSSION AND THEORETICAL IMPLICATIONS

Integrative Interpretation of Findings

The evidence drawn from the four cases collectively affirms that human–AI collaboration evolves along a continuum of maturity—beginning with supervised augmentation, progressing through dialogic co-creation, and culminating in autonomous governance. This trajectory reflects not a technological chronology but an organizational learning **curve**, where leadership consciousness expands in parallel with algorithmic capability. The findings demonstrate that as autonomy increases, human intervention becomes less procedural and more philosophical: leaders move from *doing things right* to *defining what is right*.

Across industries, creativity has shifted from being a skill owned by individuals to a relational capability shared between human and artificial agents. In Microsoft's case, creativity was accelerated by algorithmic suggestion under human supervision; in Adobe's, it became a collaborative dance between intuition and computation; in Unilever, it turned into an ethical system of value translation; and in Spotify, it emerged as emotional storytelling mediated by algorithms. These transitions confirm that creativity and leadership are mutually constitutive in AI-enabled organizations: creativity requires moral leadership, while leadership requires creative interpretation of technology's potential and limits.

The HITL–HOTL–HOOTL framework thus functions as both a diagnostic and developmental model. It reveals that organizational maturity in AI is not defined solely by technical sophistication but by the degree of ethical and cultural coherence embedded in leadership practices. Each stage introduces a new cognitive demand—ethical discernment in HITL, trust calibration in HOTL, and moral foresight in HOOTL. When these capacities align, human–AI ecosystems achieve equilibrium between efficiency and empathy.

From a macro perspective, the findings suggest a reconfiguration of power and authorship in creative industries. Authority no longer derives from positional hierarchy or individual expertise but from the capacity to design inclusive, value-driven ecosystems. This shift represents a profound theoretical inflection: leadership becomes a process of *meaning design* rather than control, and creativity becomes the manifestation of collective moral intelligence.

Theoretical Implications for Leadership and Creativity

Redefining leadership in intelligent organizations

Traditional leadership theories—transformational, servant, and ethical leadership—provide useful but partial explanations for the new reality. Transformational leadership emphasizes vision and inspiration, yet in AI contexts, vision must extend beyond human followers to include non-human collaborators. Servant and ethical leadership stress humility and stewardship; these traits remain essential, but their expression now includes designing moral parameters for algorithms. The observed cases reveal an emergent form of meta-leadership, characterized by governance of socio-technical systems rather than direct human subordinates.

In this perspective, leaders act as architects of interactional ethics. They choreograph exchanges between humans and intelligent systems, ensuring that machine autonomy reflects humanistic values. Authority becomes dispersed, relational, and continuously negotiated through feedback loops. The leader's legitimacy stems not from charisma or control but from *curatorial wisdom*—the ability to align technological performance with ethical and cultural purpose.

Extending creativity theory

The evidence also enriches theoretical understanding of creativity. Classical models, such as Amabile's componential theory, framed creativity as the convergence of expertise, motivation, and supportive environment. The contemporary context adds a fourth elementalgorithmic partnershipwhich expands both the cognitive range and ethical complexity of creative work. The creative act now involves translation between human intuition and algorithmic computation. Consequently, creativity should be reconceptualized as *distributed emergence*: originality arises from dynamic interplay among people, data, and code.

This reconceptualization bridges cognitive and moral dimensions. In HITL environments, creativity remains an expression of mastery and control; in HOTL contexts, it becomes exploratory collaboration; and in HOOTL systems, it transforms into ethical imagination, where design choices embody moral intention. These findings invite refinement of creativity theory toward a human-centered augmentation paradigm—a model that views technology as a co-author of possibility rather than a mechanistic instrument.

Integrating leadership and creativity

The intersection of leadership and creativity becomes the crucible of innovation. The cases collectively show that the two cannot be separated in intelligent enterprises: creative breakthroughs depend on leadership's ethical clarity, and ethical leadership relies on creative capacity to envision inclusive futures. This integrative insight extends existing theory by proposing that *ethical imagination* is the binding principle of human–AI collaboration. Leaders who cultivate imaginative ethics foster organizations capable of sustainable innovation; those who neglect it risk moral and creative stagnation.

Managerial and Organizational Implications

Designing human-AI ecosystems

For practitioners, the findings emphasize that AI adoption must proceed as organizational design, not mere technology deployment. Managers should view intelligent systems as living components of culture, requiring governance structures analogous to human teams. Policies on transparency, bias mitigation, and accountability must be established before autonomy scales. Embedding cross-functional ethics committees, as seen in Unilever, institutionalizes responsibility and prevents ethical retrofitting.

Developing new leadership competencies

Leadership development programs should integrate digital, ethical, and cultural literacy. The Copilot and Firefly cases reveal that psychological safety and prompt literacy determine whether employees embrace or resist collaboration with AI. Training should therefore include reflective exercises on bias recognition, interpretive reasoning, and scenario planning. These competencies shift leadership identity from controller to *facilitator of trust networks*.

Managing creativity in augmented teams

Organizations should redefine creative processes as human–machine symphonies. Workflow design must allow iterative feedback between algorithmic output and human judgment. Creative leaders should encourage experimentation while upholding authenticity, ensuring that AI contributes variation without diluting originality. Performance metrics should evolve accordingly—from volume or speed to *quality of insight* and *ethical integrity* of outcomes.

Governance and strategic alignment

Finally, senior leadership must align AI strategy with corporate purpose. Without explicit linkage between values and algorithmic objectives, even well-intentioned systems may produce unintended harm. The case studies indicate that alignment emerges through continuous dialogue between ethics boards, data scientists, and business leaders. This triadic governance model ensures that efficiency gains do not compromise social responsibility. It also transforms compliance from a constraint into a strategic differentiator, reinforcing brand trust in a marketplace increasingly sensitive to ethical transparency.

Cross-Cultural and Ethical Reflections

Cultural intelligence and contextual leadership

Cross-cultural comparison across the cases underscores that cultural intelligence (CQ) is indispensable for ethical AI leadership. While Western organizations such as Microsoft and Adobe emphasize autonomy and creativity as individual virtues, globally integrated firms like Unilever and Spotify operate within pluralistic moral landscapes. Leadership in these contexts must reconcile universal AI ethics with local sensibilities—respect for collective harmony in Asia, privacy sensitivity in Europe, or expressive individuality in North America.

Culturally intelligent leadership treats ethics as dialogue rather than doctrine. It acknowledges that fairness, transparency, and accountability are interpreted through distinct cultural grammars. Therefore, global organizations must design modular governance frameworks—core ethical principles held constant, but implementation adaptable to regional norms. This model supports legitimacy without moral relativism.

Ethical imagination and human dignity

The deeper ethical implication concerns the preservation of human dignity in algorithmic environments. As AI systems assume creative and affective functions, the boundary between assistance and autonomy blurs. The challenge is to ensure that technological efficiency does not erode empathy, privacy, or authenticity. The framework suggests that the safeguard lies in cultivating ethical imaginationthe anticipatory capacity to foresee moral consequences before they materialize.

Leaders practicing ethical imagination design systems that embody respect by default. They question what kinds of relationships technology invites and what values those relationships sustain. This anticipatory moral reasoning differentiates responsible innovation from reactive regulation. In doing so, it transforms leadership ethics from rule compliance into virtue cultivationa developmental journey parallel to the organization's technological evolution.

Sustainability and social justice

A further implication is that human–AI collaboration must contribute to **sustainability and social equity**. Unilever's integration of AI for environmental optimization demonstrates that technology can operationalize planetary stewardship. Yet such applications also demand vigilance against new forms of digital exclusion: data bias can marginalize underrepresented communities, and algorithmic automation may displace vulnerable workers. Ethical leadership thus extends beyond the enterprise to global society. Balancing innovation with inclusion becomes the hallmark of credible governance in the age of intelligent systems.

Emerging Avenues for Inquiry

The theoretical synthesis opens several pathways for continued inquiry:

1. **Empirical validation of the HITL–HOTL–HOOTL continuum.** Longitudinal studies could measure how organizations transition between stages and which cultural or regulatory factors accelerate progression.
2. **Neuro-ethical and emotional dimensions of AI creativity.** Future work may examine how emotional engagement influences trust and originality in AI collaboration.
3. **Cross-cultural leadership models.** Comparative research across collectivist and individualist societies can clarify how ethical norms shape AI governance.

4. **Measurement frameworks.** Developing quantitative indices for creative augmentation, ethical maturity, and trust calibration would extend the model's practical utility.
5. **Policy and education research.** Investigations into curriculum design for ethical AI leadership training could translate conceptual insights into societal benefit.

By addressing these areas, scholars can transform the present conceptual model into a robust empirical foundation for global AI-leadership research.

Concluding Synthesis

The discussion consolidates the chapter's central proposition: human–AI collaboration redefines both creativity and leadership as moral–intellectual partnerships. The HITL–HOTL–HOOTL framework provides a coherent language for articulating this evolution—from supervision to co-creation to stewardship. The cases demonstrate that technological maturity without ethical maturity leads to fragility, while moral coherence enhances resilience and innovation.

Theoretically, the study advances a human-centered augmentation paradigm, positioning leadership as the art of designing trustworthy relationships between intelligence forms. Practically, it suggests that the future of innovation depends less on computational power than on cultural empathy, ethical foresight, and creative imagination. As organizations continue to inhabit digital ecosystems, those that integrate these virtues into their governance will not only lead markets but also shape the moral architecture of the future of work.

CONCLUSION AND POLICY RECOMMENDATIONS

Revisiting the Research Journey

This chapter begins with a central question: How can human creativity and leadership evolve meaningfully in partnership with intelligent systems? To explore this, the study traces a conceptual and empirical journey across three gradations of human–machine collaboration. In **Direct Oversight** (formerly HITL), humans remain fully engaged, actively guiding and intervening in system decisions. In **Supervisory Oversight** (formerly HOTL), humans monitor system operations and intervene selectively when necessary. In **Autonomous Operation** (formerly HOOTL), systems function independently within predefined ethical and operational boundaries, with minimal human involvement. Across these stages, the research examines how autonomy, ethical responsibility, and imaginative agency develop and interweave, highlighting the evolving interplay between human judgment and intelligent system capability.

Drawing upon cases from technology, design, sustainability, and culture—Microsoft Copilot (Microsoft, 2023), Adobe Firefly (Adobe Inc., 2023), Unilever's AI-for-Sustainability program (Unilever, 2022), and Spotify's AI DJ (Spotify, 2024)—it demonstrated that AI's role is not to replace human ingenuity but to amplify and refine it.

At its core, the study found that creativity and leadership have entered a new symbiosis: machines extend the reach of intelligence, while humans preserve its meaning.

The framework developed throughout this chapter affirms that technological progress is sustainable only when accompanied by moral evolution.As systems acquire independence, leadership must acquire conscience; as algorithms gain precision, leaders must deepen empathy.Together, these forces define the contours of augmented leadership—a form of guidance rooted not in control, but in understanding.

The chapter's theoretical contribution lies in reframing human–AI interaction as a maturity of moral imagination, where each level of collaboration reflects a deepening ethical consciousness.The practical contribution lies in demonstrating that effective AI adoption requires more than infrastructure—it requires an environment of trust, dialogue, and value alignment.Ultimately, the future of creativity will not be determined by how intelligent our systems become, but by how intelligently we choose to collaborate with them.

Key Conclusions and Conceptual Contribution

The central insight emerging from this study is that leadership is evolving into a design discipline. No longer confined to motivating human followers, leadership now entails curating relationships among multiple intelligences—human, artificial, and organizational. The HITL–HOTL–HOOTL framework encapsulates this paradigm shift, translating abstract notions of ethics and innovation into a practical model for governing human–machine collaboration.

- **Human-in-the-Loop (HITL):** Leadership centers on *ethical supervision* and *cognitive partnership*. Creativity accelerates through data-driven augmentation but remains guided by human judgment and moral oversight (Dignum, 2019).
- **Human-on-the-Loop (HOTL):** Leaders engage in *co-creation*, balancing algorithmic autonomy with artistic and ethical integrity (Floridi, 2019).

- **Human-out-of-the-Loop (HOOTL):** Leadership transforms into *ethical governance*, designing systems that embed humanistic values even when operating autonomously (Shneiderman, 2022).

Importantly, HOOTL deployment is ethically appropriate only in low-risk, reversible domains such as entertainment, logistics, or design prototyping. It should be avoided in high-stakes decision contexts like recruitment, criminal justice, or healthcare, where moral accountability must remain human-centered (Vallor, 2016).

This continuum forms a maturity architecture for leadership education, corporate governance, and public policy (Brynjolfsson & McAfee, 2017). The study contributes theoretically by integrating ethical imagination into organizational competence, emphasizing that leadership in the AI era is as much about moral creativity as it is about strategic foresight.

Furthermore, the framework extends transformational and servant leadership theories by introducing a fourth dimension—technological empathy, defined as the capacity to understand, contextualize, and ethically guide AI systems as *agentic partners* (Dignum, 2019). It also advances creativity theory by reframing originality as a relational outcome of human–algorithmic interplay rather than an isolated act of individual brilliance (Adobe Inc., 2023). This emergent construct, termed distributed ethical creativity, captures how *purpose, imagination, and moral reasoning* converge within AI-augmented environments (Floridi, 2019).

The proposed framework complements—but does not replace—human-rights-based approaches to AI governance (UNESCO, 2021). Rather, it enriches the discourse on responsible innovation, providing scholars and practitioners with a conceptual compass for navigating the tension between technological empowerment and ethical vulnerability (European Union, 2024).

By grounding future leadership in empathy, transparency, and inclusivity, this model lays the foundation for a truly human-centered AI civilization—one where technology amplifies, rather than replaces, the moral and creative essence of humanity (Shneiderman, 2022).

Policy and Strategic Recommendations

Institutional Level — Integrating Ethical Design and Creative Augmentation

Educational institutions, corporations, and creative enterprises must embed ethical AI literacy into their organizational DNA (Vallor, 2016). Universities should revise curricula to include interdisciplinary modules that integrate leadership ethics, data literacy, and cultural intelligence (UNESCO, 2021). Business schools can strengthen this effort by incorporating AI governance within leadership programs, preparing managers to act as *ethical innovators* rather than passive adopters (Dignum, 2019).

Corporations, in turn, should establish algorithmic-ethics boards that include data scientists, behavioral experts, and ethicists to ensure fairness, transparency, and inclusivity across AI-driven operations (Floridi, 2019). Internal training initiatives must also foster prompt literacy—the ability to critically and creatively interact with generative systems—transforming human–AI collaboration into strategic value creation.

Governmental Level — Encouraging Regulatory Foresight and Cross-Sector Dialogue

Policy frameworks must transition from reactive regulation to anticipatory governance that foresees ethical and social consequences before crises emerge (Dignum, 2019). Governments should convene multi-stakeholder councils involving policymakers, academics, technologists, and social scientists to evaluate potential societal impacts of AI creativity—such as privacy erosion, cultural homogenization, or labour displacement—and to co-develop proactive policy responses (European Union, 2024).

National AI strategies should promote open, inclusive innovation ecosystems where startups, public institutions, and communities co-design ethical standards and oversight protocols (UNESCO, 2021). Fiscal incentives, such as grants or tax benefits, should be explicitly linked to transparency metrics, periodic ethical audits, and demonstrated environmental sustainability in AI deployment (Unilever, 2022).

Societal and Global Level — Preserving Human Dignity and Cultural Pluralism

At the societal scale, AI systems must be designed with cultural sensitivity to preserve human dignity and diversity, particularly within platforms that shape emotions, preferences, and identities (Spotify, 2024). International collaborations could establish a Global Charter for Human–AI Collaboration, guided by frameworks such as UNESCO's Recommendation on the Ethics of Artificial Intelligence (2021) and the EU AI Act (2024), to promote fairness, inclusion, and creative equity (European Union, 2024).

Creative labour should be recognized as moral labour, encouraging artists, developers, and audiences to co-own the ethical dialogue surrounding authorship and originality (Adobe Inc., 2023). Civil society organizations and academic institutions should host interdisciplinary dialogues to ensure that AI-driven acceleration enriches cultural expression rather than narrowing it (Vallor, 2016).

Broader Societal Significance

The broader significance of this work lies in its affirmation of ethical humanism (Shneiderman, 2022). By demonstrating how creativity and leadership can evolve symbiotically with technology, the chapter redefines progress as moral advancement alongside technical excellence.

In an era increasingly shaped by intelligent systems, human meaning must remain central. Whereas the twentieth century celebrated mechanical efficiency, the twenty-first must celebrate conscious efficiency—productivity informed by empathy and guided by fairness (Floridi, 2019). Future leaders will not be those who command machines but those who interpret, align, and humanize technological processes in harmony with collective aspirations.

Ethical imagination, therefore, is not optional—it is a survival skill in a world mediated by algorithms. Embedding this capacity across education, governance, and culture ensures that technology mirrors human values rather than magnifying ambition alone (Vallor, 2016).

Closing Reflection and Future Horizon

The dialogue between human creativity and artificial intelligence has only begun, yet it already reveals profound truths: intelligence—whether organic or synthetic—seeks meaning, and leadership provides that meaning through direction, empathy, and moral purpose (Shneiderman, 2022).

The HITL–HOTL–HOOTL framework proposed here is more than an analytical model—it is an invitation to reimagine leadership as stewardship in an age of intelligent systems (Dignum, 2019). It calls upon leaders, educators, and policymakers to cultivate wisdom that is simultaneously analytical and humane (Vallor, 2016).

Progress without ethics is acceleration without destination. The ultimate task is not merely to humanize machines but to re-humanize leadership in their presence (Floridi, 2019). When creativity and conscience converge, technology becomes a chorus echoing humanity's highest potential—a vision shared by Shneiderman (2022) and Vallor (2016).

Final Reflection: The Soul of Intelligent Leadership

As humanity stands at the threshold of an intelligent age, our challenge is not merely to create smarter machines but to become wiser custodians of the intelligence we create. The measure of progress will no longer be how efficiently algorithms perform—but how deeply they understand and reflect the human spirit.

True leadership in this new epoch will belong to those who can translate conscience into code and transform data into dignity. When empathy becomes a design principle and ethics becomes innovation's north star, technology will cease to be a mirror of our ambitions and become a magnifier of our collective soul.

The ultimate legacy of human–AI collaboration, therefore, is not dominance but co-elevation—a future where intelligence, in all its forms, serves the higher purpose of awakening humanity to its own creative and moral potential.

REFERENCES

Adobe Inc. (2023). Adobe Firefly: Generative AI for creative professionals. https://www.adobe.com/sensei/generative-ai/firefly.html

Amabile, T. M. (1996). *Creativity in context: Update to the social psychology of creativity*. Westview Press.

Amabile, T. M., & Pratt, M. G. (2016). The dynamic componential model of creativity and innovation in organizations: Making progress, making meaning. *Research in Organizational Behavior, 36*, 157–183. DOI: 10.1016/j.riob.2016.10.001

Brynjolfsson, E., & McAfee, A. (2022). The business of artificial intelligence: What it can—and cannot—do for your organization. Harvard Business Review. https://hbr.org/2022/11/the-business-of-artificial-intelligence

Davenport, T. H., & Bean, R. (2022). AI-driven augmentation: How artificial intelligence enhances human performance. *MIT Sloan Management Review*.

Deloitte. (2022). State of AI in the enterprise, 5th edition. https://www2.deloitte.com/us/en/insights/focus/cognitive-technologies/ai-augmentation.html

Dignum, V. (2019). *Responsible artificial intelligence: How to develop and use AI in a responsible way*. Springer., DOI: 10.1007/978-3-030-30371-6

Dinh, J. E., Lord, R. G., Gardner, W. L., Meuser, J. D., Liden, R. C., & Hu, J. (2014). Leadership theory and research in the new millennium: Current theoretical trends and changing perspectives. *The Leadership Quarterly, 25*(1), 36–62. DOI: 10.1016/j.leaqua.2013.11.005

European Union. (2024). EU AI Act: Regulatory framework on artificial intelligence. https://digital-strategy.ec.europa.eu/en/policies/regulatory-framework-ai

Floridi, L. (2019). *The logic of information: A theory of philosophy as conceptual design*. Oxford University Press.

Floridi, L., Cowls, J., Beltrametti, M., Chatila, R., Chazerand, P., Dignum, V., Luetge, C., Madelin, R., Pagallo, U., Rossi, F., Schafer, B., Valcke, P., & Vayena, E. (2018). AI4People—An ethical framework for a good AI society. *Minds and Machines, 28*(4), 689–707. DOI: 10.1007/s11023-018-9482-5

Hofstede, G., Hofstede, G. J., & Minkov, M. (2010). *Cultures and organizations: Software of the mind* (3rd ed.). McGraw-Hill.

Hollan, J., Hutchins, E., & Kirsh, D. (2000). Distributed cognition. *ACM Transactions on Computer-Human Interaction*, *7*(2), 174–196. DOI: 10.1145/353485.353487

Lincoln, Y. S., & Guba, E. G. (1985). Naturalistic inquiry. *Sage (Atlanta, Ga.).*

McKnight, D. H., Carter, M., Thatcher, J. B., & Clay, P. F. (2021). Trust in a specific technology. *ACM Transactions on Management Information Systems*, *12*(2), 1–25. DOI: 10.1145/3447534

Microsoft. (2023). Microsoft Copilot: Your AI-powered productivity assistant. https://www.microsoft.com/en-us/microsoft-copilot

Mumford, M. D., Hunter, S. T., & Vert, A. (2019). Creativity in organizations: A systems perspective. In *The Oxford handbook of creativity, innovation, and entrepreneurship* (2nd ed., pp. 3–22). Oxford University Press.

Northouse, P. G. (2021). *Leadership: Theory and practice* (9th ed.). Sage Publications.

Parasuraman, R., & Manzey, D. H. (2010). Complacency and bias in human use of automation. *Human Factors*, *52*(3), 381–410. DOI: 10.1177/0018720810376052

Puccio, G. J., Mance, M., & Murdock, M. C. (2018). *Creative leadership: Skills that drive change* (3rd ed.). Sage Publications.

Shneiderman, B. (2022). *Human-centered AI.* Oxford University Press.

Shrestha, Y. R., Ben-Menahem, S., & Von Krogh, G. (2019). Organizational decision-making structures in AI age. *California Management Review*, *61*(4), 66–83. DOI: 10.1177/0008125619862581

Trist, E. L., & Bamforth, K. W. (1951). Social and psychological consequences of longwall method. *Human Relations*, *4*(1), 3–38. DOI: 10.1177/001872675100400101

Uhl-Bien, M. (2006). Relational leadership theory. *The Leadership Quarterly*, *17*(6), 654–676. DOI: 10.1016/j.leaqua.2006.10.007

UNESCO. (2021). Recommendation on the ethics of artificial intelligence. https://unesdoc.unesco.org/ark:/48223/pf0000381137

UNESCO. (2023). AI and the future of work. https://en.unesco.org/artificial-intelligence/future-of-work

Unilever. (2022). AI for good: Responsible technology in sustainability. https://www.unilever.com/planet-and-society/technology-and-innovation/

Vallor, S. (2016). *Technology and the virtues.* Oxford University Press.

Westerman, G., Bonnet, D., & McAfee, A. (2021). Leading digital transformation. *MIT Sloan Management Review*, *62*(3), 35–42.

Wilson, H. J., & Daugherty, P. R. (2023). Collaborative intelligence. Harvard Business Review. https://hbr.org/2023/09/collaborative-intelligence-humans-and-ai-as-business-partners

World Economic Forum. (2023). The future of jobs report 2023. https://www.weforum.org/reports/the-future-of-jobs-report-2023/

Yin, R. K. (2018). *Case study research and applications* (6th ed.). Sage Publications.

Zhang, T., Chen, J., & Brynjolfsson, E. (2023). Creativity in the age of AI. *Management Science*, *69*(6), 3212–3235. DOI: 10.1287/mnsc.2022.4532

Chapter 9
Human-AI Collaboration in Creativity, Design, and Innovation

Ardita Aprilia Putri
https://orcid.org/0009-0008-8231-1641
Universitas Esa Unggul, Indonesia

Binastya Anggara Sekti
https://orcid.org/0000-0001-5489-4888
Universitas Esa Unggul, Indonesia

ABSTRACT

This chapter examines human–AI collaboration as an emerging paradigm in creativity, design, and innovation, emphasizing a shift from automation-oriented systems toward human-centered and augmentation-based approaches. The chapter per the authors discusses how advances in generative artificial intelligence enable AI to support ideation, exploration, and iterative refinement rather than replacing human creativity. Key theoretical foundations such as distributed cognition, co-creativity, and human-in-the-loop frameworks are analyzed to explain how creative outcomes emerge through interaction between humans and intelligent systems. Practical applications across creative industries and design practices are explored, along with ethical considerations related to authorship, bias, transparency, and creative responsibility. Overall, this chapter highlights how responsible human–AI collaboration can enhance creative potential and support sustainable innovation in the digital era.

DOI: 10.4018/979-8-3373-7153-5.ch009

1. INTRODUCTION

Figure 1. Conceptual Diagram of Human–AI Collaboration in Creative Processes

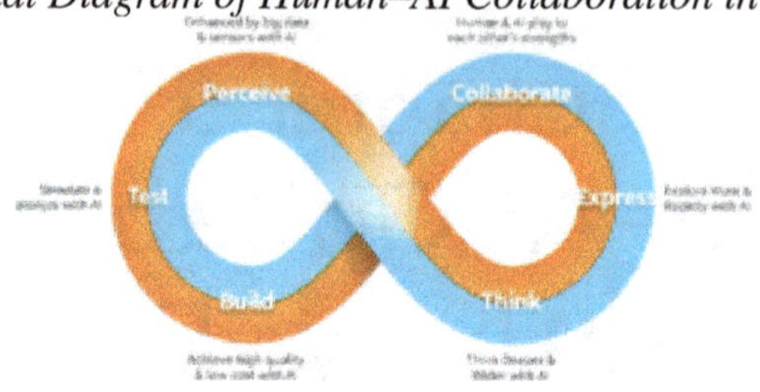

Human–AI collaboration has become an increasingly significant topic in discussions of creativity, design, and innovation in the digital era. Rapid developments in artificial intelligence, particularly in machine learning, deep learning, and generative models, have expanded the role of computational systems beyond automation and efficiency. AI systems are now capable of generating images, music, text, designs, and concepts that resemble human creative output, positioning AI not merely as a tool but as an active participant in creative processes. This shift challenges traditional assumptions about creativity as an exclusively human capability and opens new opportunities for collaborative intelligence between humans and machines.

In creative and design contexts, collaboration between humans and AI is increasingly framed as augmentation rather than replacement. Human creators provide goals, values, cultural context, and aesthetic judgment, while AI contributes computational power, pattern recognition, and generative diversity. This division of roles allows creative professionals to explore broader design spaces, test multiple alternatives rapidly, and overcome cognitive limitations such as fixation or limited exposure to unfamiliar ideas. As a result, creativity becomes a shared process, where human intention and machine intelligence are intertwined in producing innovative outcomes. The rise of generative AI technologies has significantly influenced how creative work is conceptualized and executed. Tools based on neural networks, such as generative adversarial networks (GANs), diffusion models, and large language models, can produce novel content by learning from vast datasets of existing works. These systems do not create in isolation but operate within parameters defined by human users, who curate inputs, refine prompts, and select outputs. This interaction highlights the importance of co-creation, where creativity emerges through continuous feedback loops between human judgment and algorithmic generation (Salma *et al.*, 2025).

Creative industries are among the sectors most affected by this transformation. In visual arts, AI systems assist artists in generating styles, compositions, and visual variations that inspire new directions. In architecture and industrial design, algorithmic tools support form-finding, optimization, and simulation, enabling designers to balance aesthetics, functionality, and sustainability. In media production and storytelling, AI-driven systems help generate scripts, characters, and interactive narratives, reducing production time while increasing personalization. These developments demonstrate that AI is reshaping not only creative outputs but also creative workflows and professional practices. Despite these opportunities, the integration of AI into creative processes raises fundamental questions about the nature of creativity itself. Traditional theories often associate creativity with human traits such as intention, emotion, and consciousness. AI systems, by contrast, operate through statistical learning and pattern generation without subjective experience. This contrast has led to debates about whether AI-generated content can truly be considered creative or whether creativity remains inherently human. In collaborative settings, however, creativity can be understood as a distributed process that emerges from interactions among humans, tools, and cultural systems, rather than residing in a single agent (Barrett *et al.*, 2021).

Human–AI collaboration also introduces complex ethical and legal challenges related to authorship and ownership. When creative works are produced through a combination of human input and algorithmic generation, determining who owns the resulting output becomes unclear. Questions arise regarding intellectual property rights, originality, and the reuse of training data derived from existing creative works. These issues are particularly relevant in commercial contexts, where creative outputs carry economic value and legal responsibility. Addressing these concerns requires new frameworks that recognize shared agency while protecting human creators' rights. Another critical concern is algorithmic bias in creative AI systems. Because AI models learn from historical data, they may reproduce dominant cultural norms, stereotypes, or exclusions present in their training datasets. In creative domains, this can lead to homogenization of styles, marginalization of minority perspectives, and reinforcement of existing power structures. Human oversight and intentional design are therefore essential to ensure that AI-supported creativity promotes diversity, inclusivity, and cultural sensitivity rather than limiting creative expression (Adamakis & Rachiotis, 2025).

The introduction of AI into creative labor markets has also sparked debates about displacement versus augmentation. While some fear that AI-generated content may reduce demand for human creators, others argue that AI primarily transforms creative roles rather than eliminating them. New professions are emerging, such as prompt designers, creative technologists, and AI-curators, who specialize in guiding and interpreting machine-generated outputs. In this context, creativity evolves into a hybrid skill that combines artistic sensibility with technical literacy and ethical awareness.

From a human-centered design perspective, the success of human–AI collaboration depends on maintaining human agency, control, and trust. Creative AI systems must be designed to support transparency, explainability, and user empowerment, allowing creators to understand how outputs are generated and to intervene meaningfully in the process. Human-in-the-loop approaches emphasize continuous human involvement, ensuring that AI remains aligned with human values and creative intentions rather than operating as an opaque or autonomous authority. Cultural perceptions of creativity are also shifting as AI becomes more visible in artistic and design practices. The identity of the "artist" or "designer" is no longer defined solely by manual skill or individual authorship but increasingly by the ability to orchestrate complex systems and collaborations. This transformation challenges long-standing cultural narratives about originality and genius, suggesting instead that creativity is relational, iterative, and socially constructed. Understanding these cultural implications is essential for developing responsible and meaningful human–AI creative ecosystems (Daly *et al*., 2025).

Governance and policy frameworks play a crucial role in shaping the future of human–AI collaboration in creativity. Regulations related to data usage, copyright, transparency, and accountability directly affect how creative AI systems are developed and deployed. At the same time, overly restrictive policies may limit experimentation and innovation, while insufficient regulation may expose creators and audiences to ethical risks. Balanced governance approaches are therefore needed to foster innovation while safeguarding human rights and cultural values (Wong, 2020).

This chapter adopts a forward-looking perspective on human–AI collaboration in creativity, design, and innovation. Rather than focusing solely on technological capabilities, it emphasizes the importance of human-centered, ethical, and culturally informed approaches to AI-assisted creativity. By examining conceptual models, tools, and real-world applications, the chapter aims to provide a comprehensive understanding of how AI can enhance human creative potential without undermining authorship, authenticity, or agency. Ultimately, human–AI collaboration represents a new paradigm of creative practice in which intelligence is distributed across humans, machines, and socio-technical systems. When designed responsibly, AI can serve as a reflective and supportive partner that expands imagination, supports innovation, and enables new forms of expression. This chapter seeks to contribute to ongoing discussions by offering insights into how creative collaboration between humans and AI can be structured to benefit individuals, industries, and society as a whole.

2. CONCEPTUAL FRAMEWORK: HUMAN–AI COLLABORATION IN CREATIVITY, DESIGN, AND INNOVATION

2.1 Defining Human–AI Collaborative Creativity

Human–AI collaborative creativity refers to a creative process in which humans and artificial intelligence systems work together to generate, develop, and refine ideas, designs, or artistic outputs. In this context, AI is not positioned as a replacement for human creators but as a supportive collaborator that enhances human capabilities. Humans contribute intention, meaning, ethical judgment, and cultural understanding, while AI provides computational power, pattern recognition, and generative exploration. Creativity therefore emerges from interaction rather than from a single autonomous agent. This form of collaboration is enabled by advances in artificial intelligence technologies such as machine learning, deep neural networks, natural language processing, and multimodal generative models. These technologies allow AI systems to analyze large volumes of data, learn stylistic patterns, and produce novel combinations of visual, textual, or auditory elements. However, AI-generated outputs do not carry intrinsic meaning on their own. Their creative value depends on human interpretation, selection, and refinement, reinforcing the idea that AI functions as an enabler rather than an independent creator. Human–AI collaborative creativity also emphasizes an iterative and exploratory workflow. Instead of following a linear sequence from idea to final output, creators engage in continuous feedback loops where human input shapes AI generation, and AI output influences human thinking. Through this process, creators can rapidly test alternatives, explore unexpected possibilities, and overcome creative fixation. This iterative interaction expands the creative search space and supports innovation across design, art, and media practices. A key characteristic of collaborative creativity is the principle of human-in-the-loop interaction. Human creators remain actively involved at all stages of the creative process, including goal definition, constraint setting, evaluation, and final decision-making. AI systems respond to human feedback by adapting their outputs, creating a dynamic partnership that balances automation with human agency. This approach ensures that creative responsibility and authorship remain grounded in human control, even when AI contributes significantly to the creative outcome (Hutson, 2025).

From a cognitive perspective, human–AI collaborative creativity can be understood as a form of cognitive augmentation. AI systems extend human imaginative capacity by generating variations, visualizing abstract concepts, and revealing patterns that may not be immediately apparent to human designers. By reducing cognitive load and supporting divergent thinking, AI allows creators to focus more deeply on conceptual coherence, narrative meaning, and aesthetic quality, thereby enriching the overall creative process. In creative and design domains, this collaborative model shifts the definition of creativity from individual originality to relational and system-based innovation. Creativity is no longer seen solely as a personal talent but as a distributed capability emerging from interactions among humans, tools, and cultural contexts. Within this framework, AI becomes part of the creative ecosystem, influencing how ideas are generated, evaluated, and communicated. Understanding creativity in this way provides a more inclusive and realistic foundation for analyzing AI-supported creative practices (Rezwana & Maher, 2025).

Overall, defining human–AI collaborative creativity requires moving beyond technological novelty toward a human-centered understanding of collaboration. Effective creative collaboration depends on aligning AI capabilities with human values, intentions, and ethical considerations. By framing AI as a collaborative partner that augments rather than replaces human creativity, this conceptualization supports responsible innovation and sustainable creative practices in the age of intelligent systems (Henriksen *et al.*, 2024).

2.2 The Need for Human–AI Collaboration in Creative and Design Contexts

Creative and design practices today operate in environments characterized by increasing complexity, speed, and uncertainty. Designers, artists, and innovators are expected to produce original and high-quality outcomes while responding to rapidly changing user needs, market trends, and technological developments. At the same time, creative projects often involve large volumes of information, multiple constraints, and interdisciplinary collaboration. Under these conditions, purely human-centered creative processes may face limitations in terms of scalability, efficiency, and exploration of diverse design possibilities, highlighting the need for collaborative support from AI systems (Desolda *et al.*, 2025).

Human–AI collaboration addresses these challenges by combining human creativity with computational intelligence. AI systems can process large datasets, identify patterns, and generate multiple design alternatives within a short time frame. This capability allows creative professionals to explore broader idea spaces and consider options that may not emerge through human intuition alone. By delegating repetitive or computation-intensive tasks to AI, humans can focus more on conceptual thinking, storytelling, and aesthetic judgment, which remain central to meaningful creative work. In early stages of the creative process, such as ideation and concept development, AI supports divergent thinking by generating diverse and unconventional ideas. These AI-generated suggestions can act as creative stimuli, encouraging designers to question assumptions and move beyond familiar solutions. Rather than dictating outcomes, AI introduces variation and surprise, which are essential components of innovation. Human creators then evaluate, reinterpret, and refine these outputs based on contextual relevance and creative intent, maintaining control over the creative direction. During later stages of design and production, human–AI collaboration also supports convergent thinking and refinement. AI-driven tools can assist in optimizing designs based on functional, aesthetic, usability, or sustainability criteria. In architecture and product design, for example, AI systems help evaluate multiple design configurations against constraints such as material efficiency or environmental impact. This collaborative approach enables more informed decision-making while preserving the designer's role as the final authority over creative outcomes (Almaz *et al.*, 2024).

The need for human–AI collaboration is further amplified by the growing interdisciplinary nature of creative work. Modern creative projects often involve collaboration among designers, engineers, marketers, and stakeholders from diverse backgrounds. AI-powered platforms can serve as shared cognitive tools that facilitate communication, visualization, and alignment across teams. By providing common representations and rapid feedback, AI systems help bridge disciplinary boundaries and support collective creativity and innovation (Leon *et al.*, 2025).

From an economic and professional perspective, human–AI collaboration also responds to pressures for productivity and personalization in creative industries. Audiences increasingly expect customized and interactive experiences, while organizations seek to reduce production time and costs. AI-supported creativity enables scalable personalization without fully standardizing creative output, allowing creators to balance efficiency with originality. This capability reinforces the role of AI as an enabler of sustainable creative practice rather than a substitute for human labor (Gazi *et al.*, 2024).

In addition, the integration of AI into creative contexts supports learning and skill development among creators. By interacting with AI systems, designers and artists gain exposure to new styles, techniques, and perspectives embedded in training data. This interaction can function as a form of reflective practice, where AI acts as a mirror that reveals alternative approaches and inspires creative growth. Such learning-oriented collaboration strengthens human creative capacity over time rather than diminishing it.

Overall, the need for human–AI collaboration in creativity and design arises from the limitations of isolated human or machine-centered approaches. Neither humans nor AI alone can fully address the demands of contemporary creative practice. By integrating human judgment, cultural understanding, and ethical responsibility with AI's generative and analytical strengths, collaborative systems offer a balanced and effective response to the challenges of modern creativity and innovation.

2.3 Models of Human–AI Co-Creation

Human–AI co-creation can be understood through several collaboration models that describe how creative agency, control, and responsibility are shared between humans and artificial intelligence systems. These models help clarify the different ways AI can participate in creative and design processes, ranging from supportive assistance to more autonomous generation. Understanding these models is important for designing collaborative systems that enhance creativity while preserving human agency and accountability.

The first and most common model positions AI as a creative assistant. In this configuration, AI supports specific creative tasks such as idea generation, style exploration, content variation, or rapid prototyping. Human creators define the goals, constraints, and evaluation criteria, while AI generates suggestions that serve as inspiration or starting points. The creative authority remains fully with the human, and AI functions as a productivity and exploration tool rather than an independent creator. A second model conceptualizes AI as a creative partner, where humans and AI engage in continuous interaction and mutual influence. In this collaborative arrangement, AI systems respond dynamically to human feedback, and creative outcomes evolve through iterative dialogue. Humans guide the overall direction and meaning of the work, while AI contributes alternative perspectives and unexpected combinations that may challenge human assumptions. Creativity in this model emerges from the interaction itself rather than from either agent alone. The third model frames AI as a semi-autonomous generator operating within boundaries established by human creators. Here, AI systems may generate substantial portions of creative content, such as design layouts, visual compositions, or narrative structures. However, humans remain responsible for framing the problem, setting ethical and aesthetic constraints, and selecting or modifying final outputs. This model is often used in large-scale or data-intensive creative applications, where AI efficiency is balanced by human oversight (Ziv & Nakash, 2025).

Across all co-creation models, the principle of human-in-the-loop creativity plays a central role. Human-in-the-loop approaches ensure that humans remain actively involved throughout the creative process, providing feedback, making decisions, and retaining creative responsibility. This principle helps prevent over-reliance on automated systems and supports transparency, trust, and ethical accountability in creative AI applications.

Another important dimension of human–AI co-creation models is the balance between divergent and convergent creativity. AI systems are particularly effective at supporting divergent exploration by generating numerous alternatives and variations. Humans, in turn, excel at convergent processes such as evaluation, contextual interpretation, and meaning-making. Effective co-creation models leverage these complementary strengths, allowing AI to expand the creative search space while humans shape coherence and relevance. These co-creation models also highlight that human–AI collaboration is not static but adaptive. As creators gain experience with AI tools, the nature of collaboration may shift over time, with humans learning to better guide AI and AI systems becoming more responsive to human preferences. Designing flexible collaboration models that can evolve with user expertise and creative goals is therefore essential for sustaining long-term creative innovation (Oham & Ejike, 2024).

Overall, models of human–AI co-creation provide a structured way to understand how creativity can be shared between humans and intelligent systems. By clearly defining roles, interaction mechanisms, and boundaries, these models support the development of creative AI systems that enhance human creativity rather than diminish it. They also offer a foundation for analyzing real-world applications and case studies of AI-assisted creativity in design and innovation contexts.

2.4 Theoretical Foundations of Human–AI Collaborative Creativity

Human–AI collaborative creativity draws from several foundational theories that explain how creativity emerges through interaction between humans, technologies, and socio-cultural contexts. Rather than treating creativity as an exclusively human trait, contemporary perspectives view it as a distributed and interactive process supported by tools, environments, and intelligent systems. Understanding these theoretical foundations provides a structured basis for analyzing how artificial intelligence (AI) can meaningfully augment human creativity without diminishing human agency. This study reviews relevant theories to explain the role of AI as a cognitive, interactive, and creative partner in collaborative creative processes, particularly in domains such as design, content creation, and artistic production.

1. Distributed Cognition Theory

Distributed Cognition Theory proposes that cognitive processes are not limited to the human mind but are distributed across individuals, artifacts, and external representations. In creative activities, tools such as sketches, digital platforms, and AI systems actively participate in shaping ideas and problem-solving processes. Within human–AI collaborative creativity, AI functions as an external cognitive component that supports ideation, pattern recognition, and iterative refinement. This allows creators to explore a wider creative space and manage complex creative tasks more effectively, transforming creativity into a shared cognitive process rather than an individual effort (Toumi *et al.*, 2021).

2. Extended Mind Theory

Extended Mind Theory argues that tools integrated into human activity can become part of the cognitive system itself. When creators rely on AI systems for inspiration, generation, or evaluation of creative outputs, these systems effectively extend human thinking and imagination. In creative collaboration, AI serves as a cognitive extension that enhances memory, exploration, and generative capacity. This perspective supports the view that AI does not replace creativity but amplifies human creative potential by expanding the functional boundaries of cognition through technology (Grilli & Pedota, 2024).

3. Co-Creativity Theory

Co-creativity theory emphasizes creativity as a collaborative process involving multiple agents who influence each other over time. In human–AI contexts, creativity emerges through continuous interaction, feedback, and shared control between humans and intelligent systems. AI-generated suggestions, variations, and recombinations shape human decisions, while human judgment, intention, and contextual understanding guide AI use. This reciprocal relationship positions AI as a creative partner rather than a passive tool, enabling the joint production of novel and meaningful creative outcomes (Creely & Blannin, 2025).

4. Human–Computer Interaction (HCI) Theory

Human–Computer Interaction theory provides essential insights into how AI systems should be designed to support creative collaboration. Effective human–AI creativity requires interfaces that promote transparency, usability, and user control. HCI principles emphasize interactive feedback, explainability, and adaptability, allowing creators to understand AI behavior and integrate it meaningfully into their creative workflow. Well-designed AI interfaces enhance exploration and experimentation, ensuring that humans remain active decision-makers throughout the creative process (Xu *et al.*, 2025).

In general, these theoretical foundations illustrate that human–AI collaborative creativity is not merely a technological advancement but a transformative process that reshapes how creativity is produced and experienced. AI enhances creativity by extending cognition, supporting collaboration, and enabling iterative exploration, while humans retain authorship, intention, and evaluative authority. This conceptual framework highlights that the true value of AI in creative collaboration lies in its ability to combine computational capability with human imagination, resulting in creative systems that are adaptive, inclusive, and human-centered.

2.5 Ethics, Authorship, and Creative Responsibility

The increasing integration of AI into creative processes raises important ethical questions related to authorship, responsibility, and creative ownership. As AI systems contribute to idea generation, content creation, and design execution, the boundaries between human creativity and machine assistance become increasingly blurred. This shift challenges traditional notions of creativity that have historically centered on individual human authorship, requiring new ethical frameworks to ensure that human agency and accountability remain central in AI-supported creative practices.

One of the primary ethical concerns in human–AI collaborative creativity is the issue of authorship and originality. AI-generated outputs are typically produced through models trained on large datasets that include existing creative works, raising questions about who should be recognized as the creator of the final output. In collaborative settings, authorship is best understood as shared or layered, where humans provide intent, direction, and evaluative judgment, while AI contributes generative variation and computational exploration. Ethical creative practice therefore requires transparent acknowledgment of AI involvement without diminishing the role of human creators (Das & Kundu, 2024).

Creative responsibility is another critical dimension of ethical human–AI collaboration. While AI systems can generate content autonomously, they do not possess moral awareness or contextual understanding. As a result, humans remain responsible for the ethical implications, cultural sensitivity, and societal impact of AI-assisted creative outputs. Designers, artists, and organizations must actively evaluate AI-generated content to prevent the reproduction of harmful stereotypes, misinformation, or culturally inappropriate representations. This reinforces the importance of human-in-the-loop frameworks where ethical judgment remains a human responsibility rather than an automated function (Chen *et al.*, 2023).

Bias and fairness also present significant ethical challenges in AI-supported creativity. Since AI systems learn from historical and cultural data, they may unintentionally reinforce dominant narratives while marginalizing underrepresented voices. In creative domains, such bias can influence aesthetic norms, storytelling perspectives, and design outcomes. Addressing this issue requires conscious dataset curation, inclusive design practices, and continuous human oversight to ensure that AI-enhanced creativity supports diversity, cultural plurality, and equitable representation rather than limiting creative expression (Zallio *et al.*, 2025).

Finally, ethical human–AI creative collaboration must be guided by principles of transparency, consent, and trust. Creators should understand how AI systems function, what data they rely on, and how outputs are generated. Audiences should also be informed when creative works involve AI assistance, fostering trust and authenticity in creative ecosystems. By embedding ethical considerations into the design and governance of creative AI systems, human–AI collaboration can evolve in a way that respects creative integrity while unlocking new forms of innovation and expression.

3. HUMAN–AI COLLABORATIVE CREATIVITY: THE FOUNDATION OF AUGMENTED DESIGN AND INNOVATION

Figure 2. Human–AI Collaborative Creativity Workflow in Augmented Design and Innovation

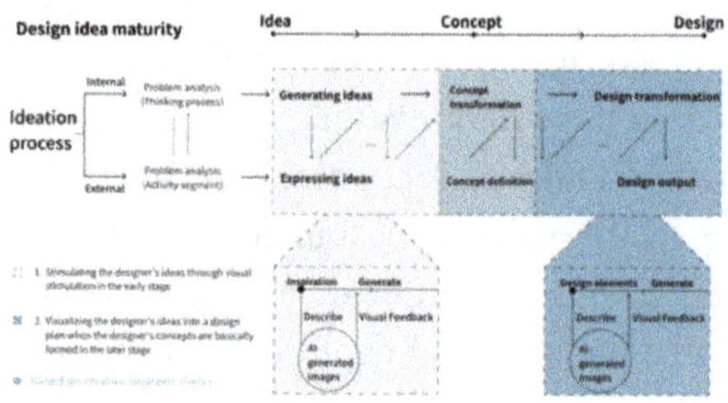

In the evolving landscape of creative industries and innovation-driven design, collaboration between humans and artificial intelligence has emerged as a transformative paradigm. Rather than functioning as autonomous creators, AI systems increasingly operate as collaborative agents that augment human imagination, accelerate experimentation, and expand creative possibilities. This shift reflects a broader transition from tool-based automation toward interactive, human-centered creative ecosystems, where meaning-making, judgment, and intent remain fundamentally human-driven while AI enhances executional capacity and exploration speed.

At the core of human–AI collaborative creativity lies the integration of generative models, machine learning algorithms, and adaptive systems into creative workflows. Technologies such as generative adversarial networks (GANs), diffusion models, and large language models enable AI to produce visual concepts, textual narratives, musical compositions, and design alternatives based on human input. Unlike traditional rule-based software, these systems learn from large-scale data and user interaction, allowing them to generate diverse outputs that inspire, challenge, and extend human creative thinking rather than merely replicating predefined patterns.

For designers, artists, and innovators, human–AI collaboration offers a strategic advantage in managing complexity and creative uncertainty. Creative tasks often involve ambiguous goals, open-ended exploration, and iterative refinement conditions under which AI excels at rapid variation and pattern discovery. For example, in product design, AI can generate hundreds of design variations based on functional constraints, while human designers evaluate aesthetic quality, usability, and cultural relevance. This division of creative labor enables creators to focus on higher-level conceptual decisions while delegating computational exploration to AI systems (Fügener *et al.*, 2022).

In creative industries, human–AI collaboration plays multiple complementary roles. AI supports ideation by proposing unexpected combinations, assists iteration by refining drafts and prototypes, and accelerates production through automation of repetitive creative tasks. Tools such as generative design platforms, AI-assisted image editors, and intelligent writing systems have become integral components of modern creative practice. These systems do not eliminate human creativity; instead, they reshape creative workflows into hybrid processes where authorship emerges through continuous interaction between human intention and machine-generated possibilities. The benefits of human–AI collaborative creativity extend beyond efficiency into strategic innovation. From a performance perspective, AI reduces time-to-concept, lowers production costs, and enables scalable personalization of creative outputs. From an experiential perspective, AI-enhanced creativity allows creators to experiment more freely, explore unconventional ideas, and push beyond cognitive limitations. Furthermore, each interaction with AI generates feedback data that can inform future creative decisions, leading to adaptive and evolving creative systems that learn alongside their human collaborators (Hughes *et al.*, 2021).

However, the integration of AI into creative processes is not without challenges. While AI systems excel at generating variations and recombining existing patterns, they often lack contextual awareness, emotional understanding, and ethical judgment. Creative outputs that rely too heavily on AI risk becoming aesthetically homogenized or culturally insensitive. As a result, human oversight remains essential to ensure that AI-generated content aligns with social values, artistic intent, and audience expectations. Effective collaboration therefore depends on maintaining humans in the loop as curators, critics, and ethical decision-makers. Another critical concern involves authorship and creative ownership. As AI contributes more substantially to creative outputs, questions arise regarding originality, intellectual property, and attribution. In collaborative creativity, authorship should be understood as shared yet asymmetrical: humans define goals, provide meaning, and assume responsibility, while AI functions as an enabling mechanism rather than an independent author. Transparent disclosure of AI involvement and clear governance structures are necessary to preserve trust within creative ecosystems and cultural institutions.

Data ethics and creative responsibility also play a crucial role in human–AI collaboration. AI systems are trained on large datasets that may reflect historical biases, dominant cultural narratives, or unequal representation. If left unchecked, these biases can influence creative outputs and marginalize alternative perspectives. Responsible creative AI therefore requires inclusive dataset curation, continuous evaluation, and ethical design practices that promote diversity, fairness, and cultural sensitivity in creative production. Despite these challenges, the potential of human–AI collaborative creativity continues to expand. Advances in multimodal AI, affective computing, and interactive interfaces are enabling more intuitive and responsive creative partnerships. Emerging systems are increasingly capable of adapting to individual creative styles, responding to emotional cues, and supporting reflective dialogue between humans and machines. These developments suggest a future where AI functions not merely as a generator, but as a reflective collaborator that enhances creative confidence and experimentation (Wei *et al.*, 2025).

From a strategic perspective, human–AI collaboration represents more than a technological innovation it signifies a conceptual shift in how creativity and innovation are understood. Creativity is no longer viewed solely as an individual act of genius, but as a distributed process supported by intelligent systems, social contexts, and digital infrastructures. Organizations and creators who embrace this paradigm position themselves at the forefront of innovation, leveraging AI not as a substitute for creativity, but as a catalyst for deeper, more inclusive, and more sustainable creative practices. Ultimately, the true value of human–AI collaborative creativity lies in its ability to integrate computational power with human imagination, ethical judgment, and cultural meaning. When designed responsibly, collaborative AI systems can expand creative horizons while preserving human authorship and identity. In this sense, human–AI collaboration becomes not merely a method of creation, but a foundation for the future of design, innovation, and creative expression in the digital age (Vinchon *et al.*, 2023).

4. HUMAN–AI CREATIVE ASSISTANTS: ENHANCING DESIGN, INNOVATION, AND CREATIVE PRODUCTIVITY

4.1 Overview

The rapid advancement of artificial intelligence (AI) has significantly transformed creative industries, reshaping how designers, artists, and innovators generate ideas, develop concepts, and produce creative outputs. One of the most influential developments in this transformation is the emergence of human–AI creative assistants AI-powered systems designed to support, augment, and collaborate with humans throughout creative and design processes. Unlike traditional software tools that execute predefined commands, creative AI assistants operate interactively, responding to human input, learning from creative preferences, and generating alternative possibilities in real time (Venkadesh *et al.*, 2024).

Human–AI creative assistants integrate advanced technologies such as generative models, machine learning, computer vision, and large language models to facilitate ideation, experimentation, and iteration. Tools such as Adobe Firefly, Midjourney, DALL·E, Runway, Figma AI, and AI-assisted writing platforms exemplify how AI has become embedded within everyday creative workflows. These systems assist users in producing visual designs, textual narratives, multimedia content, and conceptual prototypes with unprecedented speed and flexibility. In the context of design and innovation, human–AI collaboration shifts the creative process from a linear, labor-intensive activity into a dynamic and exploratory workflow. AI accelerates experimentation by generating multiple design alternatives, while human creators provide direction, judgment, and contextual understanding. This synergy enables individuals and organizations to manage creative complexity more effectively, explore broader design spaces, and respond rapidly to changing market and cultural demands. As creative work increasingly takes place in hybrid and digital environments, human–AI creative assistants play a critical role in sustaining productivity, originality, and collaborative innovation.

4.2 Core Functionalities of Human–AI Creative Assistants

The effectiveness of human–AI creative assistants lies in their diverse and interconnected functionalities that go beyond simple automation. These systems are designed not only to generate content, but also to support cognitive processes such as ideation, evaluation, and refinement. By combining computational intelligence with human intent, AI creative assistants function as collaborative partners within creative ecosystems (Rezwana & Maher, 2023).

Table 1. Core Functionalities and Benefits of Human–AI Creative Assistants

Functionality	Description	Example Tools	Key Benefits
Generative Ideation	Produces multiple creative alternatives based on prompts, constraints, or sketches.	Midjourney, DALL·E, Adobe Firefly	Expands creative exploration and inspiration.
Design Variation & Optimization	Automatically generates and refines design variations according to functional or aesthetic parameters.	Generative Design Tools, Figma AI	Reduces iteration time and supports complex decision-making.
AI-Assisted Prototyping	Transforms ideas into rapid visual, textual, or interactive prototypes.	Runway, Canva AI	Accelerates concept validation and experimentation.

continued on following page

Table 1. Continued

Functionality	Description	Example Tools	Key Benefits
Content Adaptation & Personalization	Adjusts creative outputs to different audiences, contexts, or platforms.	AI Writing Assistants, Branding Tools	Enables scalable and customized creative production.
Feedback & Refinement Support	Suggests improvements, edits, or enhancements based on patterns and user behavior.	Grammarly, Adobe Sensei	Improves quality while preserving human authorship.

These functionalities demonstrate how AI supports creativity not by replacing human imagination, but by extending it. AI systems handle computationally intensive tasks such as generating variations or analyzing patterns while humans retain control over meaning, intent, and aesthetic judgment. As a result, creative workflows become more adaptive, iterative, and collaborative.

4.3 Human–AI Collaboration in Creative Workflows

Human–AI creative assistants fundamentally reshape creative workflows by introducing continuous interaction between human intent and machine-generated possibilities. In traditional creative processes, ideation, production, and refinement often occur sequentially. In contrast, AI-enabled workflows are iterative and non-linear, allowing creators to move fluidly between exploration, evaluation, and revision. For example, in product and industrial design, AI systems can rapidly generate hundreds of design configurations based on material constraints, ergonomics, or sustainability criteria. Designers then evaluate these outputs, selecting and refining those that align with brand identity, user experience, and cultural relevance. This collaborative division of labor allows humans to focus on strategic and conceptual decisions, while AI manages computational exploration. In digital media and storytelling, AI creative assistants support writers and content creators by generating drafts, alternative narratives, or stylistic variations. Rather than final outputs, these AI-generated materials function as creative stimuli, encouraging experimentation and reducing creative blocks. Human creators remain responsible for coherence, emotional depth, and ethical alignment, ensuring that final works reflect human values and intentions (Han *et al.*, 2022).

4.4 Benefits and Strategic Value

From a strategic perspective, human–AI creative assistants offer both operational and innovation-related benefits. Operationally, AI reduces time-to-concept, lowers production costs, and enables scalable creativity across multiple platforms and audiences. Creators can test ideas quickly, adapt designs efficiently, and respond to feedback in near real time. From an innovation standpoint, AI enhances creative confidence by allowing individuals to explore unconventional ideas without excessive risk or resource expenditure. The ability to visualize, prototype, and iterate rapidly encourages experimentation and supports more inclusive creative participation. Moreover, AI systems learn from repeated interactions, enabling adaptive creative environments that evolve alongside their users (Virvou, 2023).

4.5 Challenges, Ethics, and Responsible Use

Figure 3. Ethical AI Principles in Human–AI Creative Collaboration

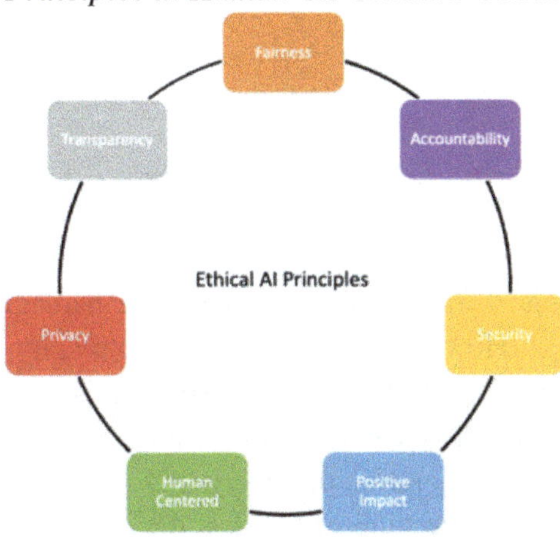

Despite their advantages, human–AI creative assistants introduce significant challenges related to authorship, originality, and ethical responsibility. AI-generated content may reflect biases present in training data, potentially reinforcing dominant cultural narratives or marginalizing underrepresented perspectives. Without careful oversight, creative outputs risk becoming homogenized or culturally insensitive. Maintaining human-in-the-loop oversight is therefore essential. Humans must act as curators, critics, and ethical decision-makers, ensuring that AI-generated content aligns with social values, artistic intent, and audience expectations. Transparent disclosure of AI involvement, responsible dataset curation, and clear governance structures are critical to preserving trust in creative ecosystems (George *et al.*, 2024).

Ultimately, the value of human–AI creative assistants depends on their design and use. When implemented responsibly, these systems function not as autonomous creators, but as augmentative collaborators that enhance human creativity, innovation, and cultural expression. In this sense, human–AI collaboration becomes a foundation for sustainable and human-centered creative practices in the digital age.

5. HUMAN–AI CREATIVE ASSISTANTS: ENHANCING DESIGN, INNOVATION, AND CULTURAL EXPRESSION

Figure 4. Human-Centered AI Framework for Ethical and Responsible Creative Collaboration

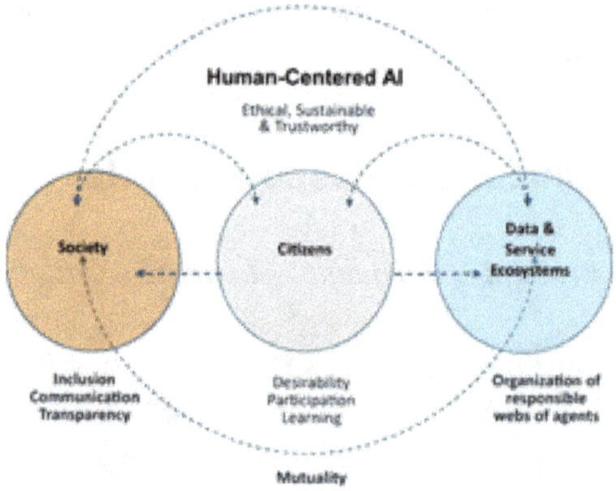

Creative processes have traditionally relied on human imagination, intuition, and experiential knowledge. However, the increasing complexity of design challenges and the demand for rapid innovation have pushed creative industries toward the integration of artificial intelligence as a collaborative partner. Human–AI creative assistants represent a new generation of AI systems designed not to replace human creativity, but to augment it by supporting ideation, experimentation, and iterative refinement. Tools such as generative design platforms, AI-assisted writing systems, and image generation models enable creators to explore a wider range of possibilities while maintaining human control over meaning, intent, and final decision-making. This shift reflects a broader transformation from isolated human creativity toward hybrid creative ecosystems where intelligence is distributed across human and machine actors (Peeters *et al.*, 2021).

At the core of human–AI creative assistants are advanced computational models, including generative adversarial networks (GANs), diffusion models, large language models, and multimodal learning systems. These technologies enable AI to generate visual concepts, textual narratives, design alternatives, and stylistic variations based on human prompts or constraints. Unlike traditional creative software that follows predefined rules, AI creative assistants learn from large-scale datasets and adapt to user interactions, allowing them to produce outputs that stimulate creative exploration rather than merely automate tasks. By rapidly generating multiple alternatives, AI reduces the cognitive and temporal burden associated with early-stage ideation, enabling creators to focus on conceptual depth, aesthetic judgment, and contextual relevance.

The practical applications of human–AI creative assistants are evident across various creative and innovation-driven domains. In product and industrial design, AI systems can generate hundreds of design configurations based on functional, material, and ergonomic constraints, while human designers evaluate feasibility, usability, and cultural fit. In visual arts and media production, AI assists artists by proposing compositions, color palettes, or stylistic transformations that inspire new creative directions. Similarly, in writing and content creation, AI-powered tools support drafting, editing, and idea expansion, helping creators overcome creative blocks and accelerate production cycles. In these contexts, AI functions as a creative catalyst that expands the search space of ideas rather than dictating final outcomes.

The benefits of integrating AI creative assistants extend beyond efficiency gains. From an innovation perspective, these systems enable rapid prototyping, experimentation with unconventional ideas, and scalable personalization of creative outputs. Organizations can reduce time-to-market while maintaining creative quality, and individual creators can explore concepts that may have been cognitively or technically inaccessible without computational support. Moreover, continuous interaction between humans and AI generates feedback loops that allow creative systems to evolve alongside user preferences and styles, fostering adaptive and learning-oriented creative environments (Ren, 2025).

Despite their advantages, human–AI creative assistants introduce significant challenges related to authorship, originality, and ethical responsibility. AI-generated content may reflect biases embedded in training data, potentially reinforcing dominant cultural narratives or marginalizing underrepresented perspectives. Overreliance on AI can also lead to aesthetic homogenization, where creative outputs converge toward familiar patterns. Consequently, maintaining human-in-the-loop oversight remains essential. Humans must act as curators, critics, and ethical decision-makers, ensuring that AI-generated content aligns with social values, artistic intent, and audience expectations. Transparent disclosure of AI involvement, responsible dataset curation, and clear governance mechanisms are critical to preserving trust in creative ecosystems (Dartanto, 2024).

6. INTEGRATION AND SYNERGY OF HUMAN–AI CREATIVE SYSTEMS

Figure 5. Integrated Framework of Human–AI Creative Systems in Design and Innovation

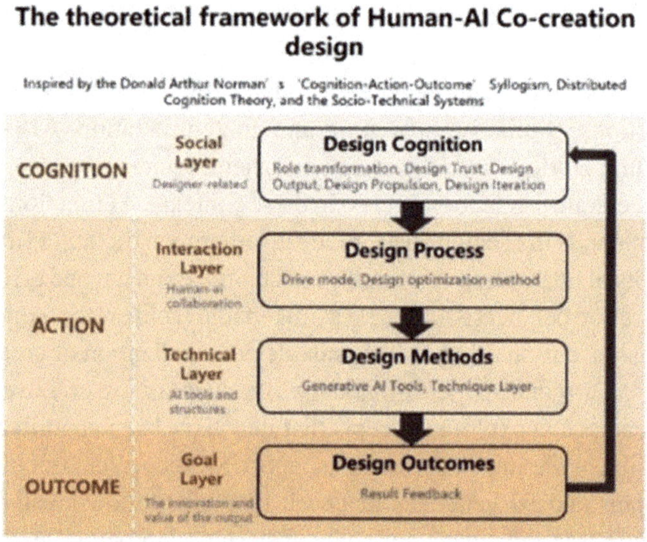

While generative design tools, AI assisted ideation platforms, and intelligent creative support systems each offer distinct contributions to creative practice, their full potential is realized when they are integrated into a cohesive human–AI creative ecosystem. Individually, these technologies address specific phases of the creative process: generative AI expands ideation through rapid variation, intelligent assistants support iteration and refinement, and adaptive systems personalize outputs based on user intent and contextual feedback. However, when deployed in combination, these tools create synergistic effects that enhance creative fluency, innovation capacity, and strategic decision-making in design and creative industries. Rather than operating as isolated applications, integrated human–AI systems transform creativity into an end-to-end, augmented workflow where exploration, evaluation, and execution are seamlessly connected.

In an integrated creative ecosystem, human–AI collaboration unfolds as a continuous loop rather than a linear process. For example, a designer may begin with an AI-powered ideation tool to generate a wide range of visual or conceptual alternatives based on functional constraints and aesthetic preferences. These outputs can then be refined using AI-assisted editing and prototyping systems that suggest improvements in structure, composition, or usability. When creative uncertainty arises, intelligent recommendation systems can introduce new inspirations drawn from diverse datasets, encouraging exploration beyond familiar patterns. Throughout this process, humans remain responsible for defining creative intent, evaluating cultural relevance, and making final design decisions, while AI accelerates exploration and reduces cognitive and operational burden (Shen *et al.*, 2025).

The integration of human–AI creative tools also enables unified feedback and learning mechanisms. Data generated across ideation, iteration, and production stages can be aggregated to provide insights into creative preferences, design performance, and audience reception. By analyzing patterns in human–AI interaction, creative teams can identify which design strategies are most effective, which concepts resonate with users, and where creative bottlenecks occur. These insights allow organizations to refine creative strategies, optimize workflows, and support evidence-informed innovation without constraining artistic freedom. In this way, integrated AI systems do not standardize creativity; instead, they support reflective and adaptive creative practice. From an organizational perspective, the synergy of human–AI creative systems supports scalability and agility in innovation-driven environments. Creative industries often face increasing demands for rapid prototyping, personalization, and cross-platform content production. Integrated AI systems enable teams to manage growing creative complexity without proportional increases in time or labor. Generative models can produce scalable variations of designs, while intelligent systems ensure consistency across formats and channels. This capability is particularly valuable for design studios, media companies, and innovation teams operating under tight deadlines and competitive pressure, allowing them to sustain creative quality while expanding output (Verganti *et al.*, 2020).

Importantly, the integration of creative AI systems reinforces a human-centered approach to innovation. Rather than displacing creative professionals, synergistic human–AI systems redistribute creative labor in ways that preserve human agency, authorship, and ethical responsibility. Humans focus on conceptual framing, emotional resonance, and cultural interpretation, while AI manages computational exploration, pattern recognition, and technical optimization. This balance ensures that creativity remains grounded in human values and social meaning, even as it is amplified by intelligent technologies. Integrated systems thus function as collaborative infrastructures that support, rather than overshadow, human creativity. At a broader level, the integration of human–AI creative tools signals a shift in how creativity and innovation are understood and organized. Creativity is no longer confined to individual tools or isolated moments of inspiration; it emerges from dynamic interactions between humans, intelligent systems, and sociotechnical contexts. Organizations that adopt integrated human–AI creative ecosystems position themselves to respond more effectively to uncertainty, diversity, and rapid change. By connecting AI tools into a coherent creative workflow, they unlock new forms of innovation that are not only efficient, but also inclusive, reflective, and sustainable.

7. ETHICAL, PRIVACY, AND IMPLEMENTATION CONSIDERATIONS IN HUMAN–AI CREATIVE SYSTEMS

As human AI creative systems become increasingly embedded in design, innovation, and creative industries, organizations face growing responsibility to address ethical, privacy, and implementation-related challenges. These considerations extend beyond technical performance and creative efficiency to encompass legal compliance, social responsibility, trust, and organizational culture. Without appropriate governance, the integration of AI into creative workflows may lead to unintended consequences, such as biased creative outputs, unclear authorship, misuse of personal data, and diminished human agency. Addressing these dimensions is therefore essential for organizations seeking to adopt human–AI collaboration responsibly while maintaining long-term sustainability and creative integrity.

Human–AI creative systems frequently process sensitive data, including design drafts, user-generated content, creative prompts, interaction logs, and behavioral feedback. The collection and processing of such data require strict adherence to regulatory frameworks such as the General Data Protection Regulation (GDPR) and the California Consumer Privacy Act (CCPA). Beyond regulatory compliance, organizations are encouraged to adopt privacy-by-design principles, implement robust encryption mechanisms, anonymize personal and creative data where feasible, and ensure informed consent from users. Transparent disclosure regarding data usage, storage, and model training practices plays a critical role in fostering trust among designers, creators, and stakeholders. Regular audits, risk assessments, and incident response strategies are also necessary to protect creative assets and preserve system integrity. Despite their potential to enhance creativity, AI-driven creative systems may inadvertently reproduce or amplify biases embedded within training datasets. Generative models used in design, visual arts, and content creation may favor dominant cultural aesthetics, reinforce stereotypes, or marginalize underrepresented perspectives. Addressing algorithmic bias requires continuous evaluation of creative outputs, diversification of training data, and the integration of fairness-aware design principles. User feedback mechanisms that allow creators to flag biased or inappropriate outputs further support ethical oversight. Proactive bias mitigation not only upholds ethical standards but also ensures that human–AI creative systems remain inclusive, culturally sensitive, and socially responsible (Tariq *et al.*, 2025).

Successful implementation of human–AI creative systems also depends on organizational readiness and human capability development. Designers, artists, and innovators must be equipped with sufficient digital literacy to understand AI-assisted workflows, data governance practices, and system limitations. Seamless integration with existing creative tools and platforms is essential to avoid workflow fragmentation and loss of creative control. Clear ethical guidelines defining human–AI collaboration, authorship responsibility, and decision-making authority are necessary to ensure that AI augments rather than replaces human creativity. Change management strategies including training programs, stakeholder engagement, and continuous technical support play a crucial role in fostering acceptance and effective utilization of AI in creative environments (Patil *et al.*, 2024).

Beyond technical and organizational factors, human–AI creative systems raise broader ethical questions related to autonomy, transparency, and creative ownership. Organizations must consider how AI-generated suggestions influence creative decisions, originality, and the perceived value of human contribution. Ethical deployment requires clear disclosure of AI involvement in creative outputs, preservation of human control in critical design decisions, and responsible governance of creative data. These considerations are particularly important in global and cross-cultural contexts, where sensitivity to cultural values, diversity, and inclusivity directly affects creative legitimacy and public trust (Agbai *et al.*, 2024).

Sustainability and accountability further shape responsible adoption of human–AI creative systems. Organizations must continuously monitor AI performance, maintain transparency in AI-assisted creative decisions, and establish clear accountability for outcomes produced through human–AI collaboration. Iterative evaluation mechanisms enable stakeholders to assess both creative quality and social impact, ensuring alignment with organizational goals and ethical standards. Ethical foresight, supported by adaptive governance frameworks, helps mitigate long-term risks while strengthening trust, innovation capacity, and cultural value creation within evolving creative ecosystems (Perboli *et al.*, 2025).

8. FUTURE DIRECTIONS OF HUMAN–AI CREATIVE SYSTEMS IN DESIGN AND INNOVATION

The continued evolution of human–AI creative systems is expected to significantly transform design and innovation practices across industries. As artificial intelligence advances, creative AI tools will move beyond basic generative functions toward more context-aware, adaptive, and collaborative roles. Future systems are anticipated to support not only idea generation and design automation but also deeper cognitive, emotional, and cultural dimensions of creativity. This evolution positions AI not merely as a tool, but as an intelligent creative partner capable of augmenting human imagination, supporting complex decision-making, and fostering sustainable innovation ecosystems. One prominent future direction lies in the development of emotionally and contextually aware creative AI. Unlike current generative models that primarily rely on statistical patterns, next-generation systems are expected to integrate affective computing and contextual intelligence. By recognizing emotional cues, user intent, and creative frustration or uncertainty, AI systems can adapt their outputs to better support designers during ideation and refinement phases. Such emotionally responsive AI can enhance creative flow, reduce cognitive load, and improve user satisfaction, particularly in collaborative and iterative design environments (Wasosa, 2025).

Another important trend is the integration of human–AI creative systems with immersive technologies such as augmented reality (AR) and virtual reality (VR). These technologies will enable designers, artists, and innovators to collaborate with AI in shared virtual spaces, visualizing concepts in real time and manipulating design elements interactively. AI-driven assistants embedded within AR/VR environments can provide instant feedback, suggest design alternatives, and simulate outcomes before physical production. This convergence of immersive environments and AI-driven creativity has the potential to redefine co-creation by making design processes more intuitive, experiential, and globally collaborative (Gurel, 2025).

Multimodal creative intelligence represents another critical future pathway. Human–AI creative systems will increasingly combine text, image, audio, gesture, and spatial inputs to generate richer and more holistic creative outputs. By interpreting multiple modalities simultaneously, AI systems can better understand creative intent and context, enabling more nuanced and culturally sensitive designs. Multimodal creativity is particularly relevant in design innovation, where visual aesthetics, narrative elements, and user experience must be integrated seamlessly across diverse platforms and audiences (Song *et al.*, 2025).

Personalized and adaptive creative AI agents are also expected to become central to future design workflows. Through continuous learning from user interactions, these systems can adapt to individual creative styles, organizational norms, and project-specific constraints. Personalized AI assistants can anticipate designer needs, suggest contextually relevant inspirations, and proactively support decision-making throughout the creative lifecycle. This personalization enhances efficiency while preserving the uniqueness of human creativity, ensuring that AI supports rather than homogenizes creative expression (Garcia, 2025).

Beyond individual creativity, future human–AI creative systems will increasingly incorporate predictive and strategic intelligence. By analyzing trends, user feedback, and market dynamics, AI can help designers anticipate emerging needs, identify innovation opportunities, and assess the potential impact of creative decisions. Predictive creative analytics enables organizations to align design innovation with long-term strategic objectives, reducing uncertainty and enhancing the sustainability of creative outcomes. When combined with human judgment and ethical oversight, predictive AI becomes a powerful catalyst for responsible innovation (Buhmann & Fieseler, 2021).

9. CONCLUSION

This proposal has comprehensively explored the role of artificial intelligence as a collaborative partner in creative, design, and communication processes, emphasizing a shift from automation-oriented systems toward human-centered and augmentation-based AI frameworks. Rather than conceptualizing AI as an autonomous creator or decision-maker, this study positions AI as an enabling collaborator that supports human creativity, judgment, and strategic intent. Through an integrated discussion of conceptual foundations, theoretical perspectives, system functionalities, ethical considerations, and future trajectories, the proposal provides a structured understanding of how human–AI collaboration reshapes contemporary innovation ecosystems.

At a conceptual level, the proposal establishes that creativity and communication in the digital era are increasingly distributed across humans, intelligent systems, and organizational contexts. Human–AI collaborative creativity emerges not as a substitution of human agency, but as a hybrid process in which humans retain control over meaning, values, and responsibility, while AI contributes computational power, pattern recognition, and generative exploration. This reframing challenges traditional notions of authorship and creativity by highlighting interaction, iteration, and co-creation as defining characteristics of modern creative work.

The theoretical foundations discussed in this proposal further reinforce the view that AI functions as a cognitive and communicative extension of human capabilities. By drawing on perspectives related to cognitive augmentation, social presence, media richness, and collaborative intelligence, the study demonstrates that AI-enhanced systems can support deeper engagement, more adaptive collaboration, and improved decision-making. These theoretical lenses provide an analytical basis for understanding why AI-driven tools are not merely efficiency-enhancing technologies, but transformative infrastructures that reshape how humans communicate, collaborate, and innovate.

Through the examination of AI-powered creative assistants, automated communication systems, integrated AI frameworks, and synergistic tool ecosystems, this proposal illustrates how AI contributes across multiple stages of creative and communicative workflows. AI systems support ideation by generating diverse alternatives, facilitate iteration by refining drafts and prototypes, and enhance execution by automating repetitive tasks. When integrated into cohesive ecosystems, these tools move beyond isolated functionalities to form intelligent workflows that enable scalability, personalization, and global collaboration. Such integration allows organizations and creative practitioners to navigate complexity, manage uncertainty, and accelerate innovation without compromising human oversight.

However, the proposal also emphasizes that the benefits of human–AI collaboration cannot be fully realized without addressing critical ethical, privacy, and implementation challenges. AI communication and creative systems frequently process sensitive data and operate on large-scale datasets that may contain biases or unequal representation. Without appropriate governance, these systems risk reinforcing dominant cultural narratives, marginalizing alternative perspectives, or undermining trust among users. Therefore, the proposal highlights the importance of privacy-by-design principles, algorithmic fairness, transparency, and human-in-the-loop oversight as foundational requirements for responsible AI deployment.

Organizational readiness is identified as another crucial factor shaping the success of AI integration. Effective adoption requires not only technical infrastructure, but also digital literacy, ethical guidelines, and change management strategies that support human–AI collaboration. By clearly defining roles, accountability structures, and escalation mechanisms, organizations can ensure that AI augments rather than replaces human judgment. This alignment between technological capability and organizational culture is essential for sustaining long-term value creation and employee engagement.

Looking toward the future, the proposal outlines several promising directions for the evolution of human–AI collaborative systems. Advances in emotionally intelligent AI, multimodal interaction, immersive environments, and predictive analytics suggest that AI will increasingly support more intuitive, empathetic, and anticipatory forms of communication and creativity. These developments point to a future in which AI systems function not merely as tools, but as reflective collaborators that adapt to individual styles, contextual cues, and evolving creative goals. Such capabilities have the potential to redefine collaboration across industries, cultures, and geographic boundaries.

REFERENCES

Adamakis, M., & Rachiotis, T. (2025). Artificial Intelligence in Higher Education: A State-of-the-Art Overview of Pedagogical Integrity, Artificial Intelligence Literacy, and Policy Integration. *Encyclopedia, 5*(4), 180. DOI: 10.3390/encyclopedia5040180

Agbai, E., Agbai, E., & Oko-Jaja, E. S. (2024). Bridging Culture, Nurturing Diversity: Cultural Exchange and Its Impact on Global Understanding. *Research Journal of Humanities and Cultural, 10*(2), 42–58. DOI: 10.56201/rjhcs.v10.no2.2024.pg42.58

Almaz, A. F., El-Agouz, E. A. E. A., Abdelfatah, M. T., & Mohamed, I. R. (2024). The Future Role of Artificial Intelligence (AI) Design's Integration into Architectural and Interior Design Education is to Improve Efficiency, Sustainability, and Creativity. *Civil Engineering and Architecture, 12*(3), 1749–1772. DOI: 10.13189/cea.2024.120336

Barrett, M. S., Creech, A., & Zhukov, K. (2021). Creative Collaboration and Collaborative Creativity: A Systematic Literature Review. *Frontiers in Psychology, 12*(August), 1–15. DOI: 10.3389/fpsyg.2021.713445

Buhmann, A., & Fieseler, C. (2021). Towards a deliberative framework for responsible innovation in artificial intelligence. *Technology in Society, 64*(December 2020), 101475. https://doi.org/DOI: 10.1016/j.techsoc.2020.101475

Chen, X., Wang, X., & Qu, Y. (2023). Constructing Ethical AI Based on the "Human-in-the-Loop" System. *Systems, 11*(11). Advance online publication. DOI: 10.3390/systems11110548

Creely, E., & Blannin, J. (2025). Creative partnerships with generative AI. Possibilities for education and beyond. *Thinking Skills and Creativity, 56*(October 2023), 101727. https://doi.org/DOI: 10.1016/j.tsc.2024.101727

Daly, S. J., Hearn, G., & Papageorgiou, K. (2025). Sensemaking with AI: How trust influences Human-AI collaboration in health and creative industries. *Social Sciences and Humanities Open, 11*(October 2024), 101346. https://doi.org/DOI: 10.1016/j.ssaho.2025.101346

Dartanto, A. S. (2024). Transforming Curatorial Practices: The Role of AI and Blockchain in Shaping an Ethical Art-Science Paradigm for Public Policy. *International Journal of Creative and Arts Studies, 11*(2), 140–164. DOI: 10.24821/ijcas.v11i2.14388

Das, S., & Kundu, R. (2024). The Ethics of Artificial Intelligence in Creative Arts: A Comprehensive Review. *Interdisciplinary International Journal of Advances in Social Sciences. Arts and Humanities, 01*(01), 27–34. DOI: 10.62674/iijassah.2024.v1i1.003

Desolda, G., Esposito, A., Lanzilotti, R., Piccinno, A., & Costabile, M. F. (2025). *From human-centered to symbiotic artificial intelligence: a focus on medical applications. Multimedia Tools and Applications* (Vol. 84). Springer US. https://doi.org/DOI: 10.1007/s11042-024-20414-5

Fügener, A., Grahl, J., Gupta, A., & Ketter, W. (2022). Cognitive Challenges in Human–Artificial Intelligence Collaboration: Investigating the Path Toward Productive Delegation. *Information Systems Research, 33*(2), 678–696. DOI: 10.1287/isre.2021.1079

Garcia, M. B. (2025). The Paradox of Artificial Creativity: Challenges and Opportunities of Generative AI Artistry. *Creativity Research Journal, 37*(4), 755–768. DOI: 10.1080/10400419.2024.2354622

Gazi, M. A. I., Rahman, M. K. H., Masud, A., Al, , & Amin, M. Bin, Chaity, N. S., Senathirajah, A. R. bin S., & Abdullah, M. (2024). AI Capability and Sustainable Performance: Unveiling the Mediating Effects of Organizational Creativity and Green Innovation with Knowledge Sharing Culture as a Moderator. *Sustainability (Switzerland), 16*(17). Advance online publication. DOI: 10.3390/su16177466

George, A. S., Baskar, T., & Pandey, D. (2024). Establishing Global AI Accountability : Training Data Transparency, Copyright, and Misinformation Partners Universal Innovative Research Publication (PUIRP) Establishing Global AI Accountability : Training Data Transparency, Copyright, and Misinform. *Partners Universal Innovative Research Publication, 2*(3), 75–91. DOI: 10.5281/zenodo.11659602

Grilli, L., & Pedota, M. (2024). Creativity and artificial intelligence: A multilevel perspective. *Creativity and Innovation Management, 33*(2), 234–247. DOI: 10.1111/caim.12580

Gurel, E. (2025). AI-driven experiences in cultural and creative industries: A review of literature and development of a multifaceted framework. *Service Industries Journal, 2069*, 1–40. DOI: 10.1080/02642069.2025.2542822

Han, S., Kelly, E., Nikou, S., & Svee, E. O. (2022). Aligning artificial intelligence with human values: Reflections from a phenomenological perspective. *AI & Society, 37*(4), 1383–1395. DOI: 10.1007/s00146-021-01247-4

Henriksen, D., Mishra, P., & Stern, R. (2024). Creative Learning for Sustainability in a World of AI : Action, . *Multidisciplinary Digital Publishing Institute*, 1–20. https://doi.org/DOI: 10.3390/ su16114451

Hughes, R. T., Zhu, L., & Bednarz, T. (2021). Generative Adversarial Networks–Enabled Human–Artificial Intelligence Collaborative Applications for Creative and Design Industries: A Systematic Review of Current Approaches and Trends. *Frontiers in Artificial Intelligence*, *4*(April), 1–17. DOI: 10.3389/frai.2021.604234

Hutson, J. (2025). Human-AI Collaboration in Writing: A Multidimensional Framework for Creative and Intellectual Authorship. *International Journal of Changes in Education*. https://doi.org/DOI: 10.47852/bonviewijce52024908

Leon, C., Lipuma, J., & Oviedo-Torres, X. (2025). Artificial intelligence in STEM education: A transdisciplinary framework for engagement and innovation. *Frontiers in Education*, *10*(July), 1–18. DOI: 10.3389/feduc.2025.1619888

Oham, C., & Ejike, O. G. (2024). Creativity and collaboration in creative industries: Proposing a conceptual model for enhanced team dynamics. *Magna Scientia Advanced Research and Reviews*, *12*(1), 185–194. DOI: 10.30574/msarr.2024.12.1.0172

Patil, D., Rane, N. L., & Rane, J. (2024). Acceptance of ChatGPT and generative artificial intelligence in several business sectors: Key factors, challenges, and implementation strategies. *The Future Impact of ChatGPT on Several Business Sectors*, *5*(2), 50–70. DOI: 10.70593/978-81-981367-8-7_5

Peeters, M. M. M., van Diggelen, J., van den Bosch, K., Bronkhorst, A., Neerincx, M. A., Schraagen, J. M., & Raaijmakers, S. (2021). Hybrid collective intelligence in a human–AI society. *AI & Society*, *36*(1), 217–238. DOI: 10.1007/s00146-020-01005-y

Perboli, G., Simionato, N., & Pratali, S. (2025). Navigating the AI Regulatory Landscape: Balancing Innovation, Ethics, and Global Governance. Economic and Political Studies. (in press). *Economic and Political Studies*, *13*(4), 367–397. DOI: 10.1080/20954816.2025.2569584

Ren, X. (2025). The Impact of Generative AI-Driven Job Reshaping on Creativity Sustainability. *The Frontiers of Society. Science and Technology*, *7*(7), 5–21. DOI: 10.25236/FSST.2025.070703

Rezwana, J., & Maher, M. Lou. (2023). Designing Creative AI Partners with COFI: A Framework for Modeling Interaction in Human-AI Co-Creative Systems. *ACM Transactions on Computer-Human Interaction*, *30*(5). Advance online publication. DOI: 10.1145/3519026

Rezwana, J., & Maher, M. Lou. (2025). An Exploration of Mental Models of AI in Human-AI Co-Creativity: A Framework and Insights. *ACM Transactions on Interactive Intelligent Systems*, *15*(4). Advance online publication. DOI: 10.1145/3769072

Salma, Z., Hijón-Neira, R., & Pizarro, C. (2025). Designing Co-Creative Systems: Five Paradoxes in Human–AI Collaboration. *Information (Switzerland)*, *16*(10), 1–19. DOI: 10.3390/info16100909

Shen, Y., Kang, B., & Münch, F. (2025). Human-Centered AI in Design: Examining Educational Paradigms for Creativity and Responsibility. *Lecture Notes in Computer Science, 15799 LNCS*, 64–76. https://doi.org/DOI: 10.1007/978-3-031-93236-6_5

Song, Y., Zhou, H., Wei, J., & Qin, J. (2025). Research on the Application of Augmented Reality Technology in Museum Navigation System. [ACS]. *Journal OfArts and Cultural Studies*, *4*(1), 257–270. DOI: 10.5220/0013632200004671

Tariq, B., Ashraf, M. R., & Rashid, U. (2025). Ethical Imperatives in AI Design: A Comprehensive Framework for Risk Mitigation and Responsible Innovation. *Ubiquitous Technology Journal*, *1*(2), 61–73. DOI: 10.71346/utj.v1i2.23

Toumi, K., Girandola, F., & Bonnardel, N. (2021). Technologies for Supporting Creativity in Design: A View of Physical and Virtual Environments with Regard to Cognitive and Social Processes. *Creativity*, *8*(1), 189–212. DOI: 10.2478/ctra-2021-0012

Venkadesh, P., Divya, S. V., & Kumar, K. S. (2024). Unlocking AI Creativity: A Multi-Agent Approach with CrewAI. *Journal of Trends in Computer Science and Smart Technology*, *6*(4), 338–356. DOI: 10.36548/jtcsst.2024.4.002

Verganti, R., Vendraminelli, L., & Iansiti, M. (2020). Innovation and Design in the Age of Artificial Intelligence. *Journal of Product Innovation Management*, *37*(3), 212–227. DOI: 10.1111/jpim.12523

Vinchon, F., Lubart, T., Bartolotta, S., Gironnay, V., Botella, M., Bourgeois-Bougrine, S., & Gaggioli, A. (2023). Artificial Intelligence & Creativity: A Manifesto for Collaboration. *The Journal of Creative Behavior*, *57*(4), 472–484. DOI: 10.1002/jocb.597

Virvou, M. (2023). Artificial Intelligence and User Experience in reciprocity: Contributions and state of the art. *Intelligent Decision Technologies*, *17*(1), 73–125. DOI: 10.3233/IDT-230092

Wasosa, H. (2025). Influence of Psychological Well-Being and School Factors on Delinquency, During the Covid-19 Period Among Secondary School Students in Selected Schools in Nakuru County : Kenya. [IJRISS]. *International Journal of Research and Innovation in Social Science*, *VII*(2454), 1175–1189. DOI: 10.47772/IJRISS

Wei, X., Wang, L., Lee, L. K., & Liu, R. (2025). The effects of generative AI on collaborative problem-solving and team creativity performance in digital story creation: An experimental study. *International Journal of Educational Technology in Higher Education*, *22*(1). Advance online publication. DOI: 10.1186/s41239-025-00526-0

Wong, P. H. (2020). Cultural Differences as Excuses? Human Rights and Cultural Values in Global Ethics and Governance of AI. *Philosophy & Technology*, *33*(4), 705–715. DOI: 10.1007/s13347-020-00413-8

Xu, G., Murthy, S. V., & Jia, B. (2025). Enhancing Intuitive Decision-Making and Reliance Through Human–AI Collaboration: A Review. *Informatics (MDPI)*, *12*(4). Advance online publication. DOI: 10.3390/informatics12040135

Zallio, M., Ike, C. B., & Chivăran, C. (2025). Designing Artificial Intelligence : Exploring Inclusion, Emerging Technologies. *AI*, *6*(7), 25. DOI: 10.3390/ai6070143

Ziv, L., & Nakash, M. (2025). Behind the Algorithm: International Insights into Data-Driven AI Model Development. *Machine Learning and Knowledge Extraction*, *7*(4), 122. DOI: 10.3390/make7040122

Chapter 10

Synthetic Culture and Brand Mythmaking in the Age of Generative AI

Nishita Pruthi
https://orcid.org/0000-0002-6094-0972
Amity University, Dubai, UAE

Jihene Mrabet
https://orcid.org/0000-0003-1848-5918
Amity University, Dubai, UAE

Ridhima Sharma
Vivekananda Institute of Professional Studies-TC, India

ABSTRACT

This chapter discusses the ways in which the new branding emerges through generative AI, generating synthetic culture algorithmically generated stories, symbols and personas, and aesthetic spaces that reproduce the brand meaning-making process and way of interaction with consumers. Based on the socio-technical, cultural systems, and mythmaking theories, the chapter explores the role of AI as a cultural co-creator that is able to generate dynamic, adaptive, and hyper-personalized brand myths. It examines the innovative change of human agency in controlling stories to hybrid human-AI cultural production and points to the consequences of authenticity, identity creation, consumer attitude, and narrative management. also relates the managerial, theoretical and ethical issues related to synthetic culture such as transparency, algorithmic bias, authorship, and cultural safety. The chapter offers

DOI: 10.4018/979-8-3373-7153-5.ch010

an in-depth view of AI-mediated mythmaking and outlines the key areas of future research as the concept of computational creativity begins to dominate the cultural imagination of this era.

INTRODUCTION

The rapidly growing development of generative artificial intelligence (AI) has opened a new era where a brand does not simply convey cultural meaning, but it has an algorithmic way of doing it. The emergence of synthetic culture is being experienced both within organizations and across the broader digital ecosystem in general as increasingly organizations are being saturated with machine-generated narratives, personas, and symbolic worlds via AI-based content, simulations, and interactive experiences, instead of having a human-led approach to storytelling. Similar to Geospatial Information Systems (GIS) having reformulated the approach to decision-making based on data-driven spatial awareness through the combination of technological, social, and organizational parameters, generative AI is redefining the epistemology of branding by altering the process of cultural productions, distributions, and consumption. This change is a radical transformation in the cultural logic of markets in which mythmaking, which was the terrain of human invention, is now created through algorithmic procedures that produce indefinite possibilities to create new symbolic variations in real time.

The making of brand myths has traditionally been based on the consistent narrative, shared memory, and long-term cultural associations. But generative AI is a new paradigm dynamic, adaptive mythmaking where algorithms are used to create emotionally resonant archetypes, icons and stories tailored to the micro-segmented consumer psychologies of vast datasets (Belk, 2013). This is reminiscent of the change detailed in the accompanying manuscript, where the advanced technology of AI and cloud-based analytics are changing previously non-moving systems into predictive, adaptive, and participatory systems. Similarly, AI-motivated mythmaking transforms branding into a non-linear message format to a multidimensional, socio-technical framework in which human creativity goes hand in hand with computational recombination. Such examples as the rise of AI influencers, synthetic brand ambassadors, and machine-generated cultural scripts are an illustration of how brands are delegating some of their symbolic production to intelligent systems that have the ability to learn continuously.

On the cultural level, generative AI serves as mythmaker and myth medium, shifting the association among consumers, brands, as well as accounts that hold them together (Latour, 2005). Customers are becoming more active participants in the world of algorithmically created identities, virtual brand worlds, and artificial community experiences (Nieborg and Poell 2018). These shifts are in line with the socio-technical dynamics pointed out in the manuscript which underscores that technological artifacts transform behaviour, institutional norms and processes of making meaning in organizations. With AI to become part and parcel of brand communication systems, it co-creates the cultural value, affecting the perception, influencing the affective experience, and constructing the stories to look like it was personalized but machine-generated. This produces new mythic powers, not myths confirmed according to a tradition but to algorithmic pertinence and emotional accuracy. Nevertheless, there are also some critical tensions originating in this new environment. Similarly to the GIS textual, there are ethical issues, data governance, and possible inequities with regard to technology-based decision-making, generative AI raises the questions of authenticity, trust, cultural manipulation, and who owns meaning. The brands have to find a way around the world where an artificial culture can not only give strength to the creative process but also blur the line between reality and simulation. Deep fakes, artificial images, and content that is generated by algorithms continue to expand, making it more difficult to separate the process of true involvement by consumers in culture and algorithmic influence (Belk, 2013). Such issues require novel governance structures of transparency, ethical branding, as well as responsible AI-mediated cultural production.

Here, the chapter examines how generative AI transforms brand mythmaking through the theoretical context of synthetic culture, socio-technical forces of AI-driven narrative generation, and relevant implications to brand strategy, brand authenticity, consumer psychology, and cultural sustainability. This chapter follows a too holistic approach, inspired by the integrative, interdisciplinary viewpoint of the attached manuscript, where technological, organizational, and human factors meet to determine the systemic results. It places generative AI not as a means of communication but as a cultural agent, which makes up, breaks, and remakes symbolic systems embedded in modern marketplaces. After all, the emergence of synthetic culture marks a paradigm shift of the way brands are told to create an emotional appeal and root themselves in the cultural imagination. Through knowing the workings of the AI-driven mythmaking, organizations can be more critical and imaginative in crafting brand narratives that are not in vain, ethical, and culturally responsive in a time when algorithms are defining the stories that societies are telling about themselves.

LITERATURE REVIEW

The development of generative artificial intelligence (AI) has changed the culture of cultural production and brand communication, introducing a new paradigm of interaction of algorithmic systems in the process of creation, reproduction, and distribution of symbolic meaning (Bansal et al., 2022). This process is consistent with more general technological changes outlined in the chapter attached where sophisticated digital platforms are transforming how decisions are made, knowledge produced, and how organizations are run in all spheres. In branding, big data AI technologies, such as large language models (LLMs), diffusion models, and artificial audio-visual tools, acts as cultural agents, which can generate stories, personalities and mythic frameworks in scale never seen before (Saini and Bansal, 2025). It has led to the emergence of synthetic culture, a digitally created cultural ecosystem in which, representations, emotions and stories are produced by computational processes, not necessarily solely by human creativity (Escalas, 2004).

ARTIFICIAL INTELLIGENCE: AN ENGINE OF MYTHS AND CONVERSATIONS

Initial branding studies considered the process of mythmaking as a human-based activity that was based on cultural archetypes, communal recollection and symbolic narratives (Holt, 2004). Nevertheless, generative AI transforms the mythic formation process to utilize huge datasets to identify the cultural pattern and synthesize it with the help of algorithms (Shankar et al., 2001). This transformation reflects the change suggested in GIS literature in which descriptive mapping was turned into predictive, real-time analytics with the incorporation of AI and machine learning technologies. Equally, generative AI turns the branding approach, which is a fixed narrative system, into a dynamic ecosystem, where myths are modified to respond to contextual, behavioral, and emotional signals.

AI-based brand virtual influencers or actors represent the transition to computational identity web development where the brands use autonomous narrative carriers to mediate relationships with their consumers (Ao et al., 2023). These online personalities, who can mimic emotion, expertise and human interaction, combine marketing communication with machine personalization. According to literature on synthetic media, the AI constructs in question tend to be more consistent, predictive, and scalable than human influencers which in turn increases their usefulness in the formation of parasocial bonds (Bansal et al., 2024).

THE ARTIFICIAL CULTURE AND THE ALGORITHMS MAKING

Synthetic culture is digital development of emotional moods, symbolic references and community experience that replaces the cultural practices that enhance the understanding of the organically evolved space (Csikszentmihalyi, 1997). Just as participatory GIS facilitates shared representations of reality by facilitating geospatial data co-production among users, generative AI facilitates shared cultural engagement through co-creation of stories between users through prompts, interactive dialogues, and personal stream of content. It means that it has a major impact on brand communications as consumers begin to interact in AI-curated cultural spaces as a result of feedback loops between human input and machine output (Bansal et al., 2023).

Moreover, the synthetic culture allows the brands to generate hyper-personalized mythic worlds, where the stories can respond to the identities. The algorithmic mythmaking uses behavioural prediction, sentiment analysis and psychographic cues, similar to the predictive modelling capabilities which have made GIS more of a forward-looking decision system than a description system (Bansal et al., 2023). Generative AI is currently used by brands in simulating cultural futures as well as testing symbolic scenarios and developing consumer meaning-making via proactive narrative design.

TECHNOLOGY: SOCIO-TECHNICAL DYNAMICS OF AI-MEDIATED BRANDING

GenAI is not a monolith that exists without any connection with organizational, social, and ethical systems - a tenet echoed in socio-technical frameworks that were cited in the chapter attached. Branding research, in its turn, also admits that AI-based culture production is entrenched in the multifaceted data governance ecosystems, managerial choices, institutional legitimacy, and user expectations. With the use of generative AI tools in brands, there are issues that are related to authenticity, transparency, algorithm bias, and cultural manipulation.

According to the literature of technology adoption models (e.g., UTAUT, Diffusion of Innovations), the adoption of AI-mediated brand narratives is determined by the perceived ease of use, perceived value, social influence and trust - the same constructs suggested to predict digital system uptake in the GIS field. The relevance of consumer trust is especially critical when the synthetic identity and machine storytelling leave the distinction between real and fake meaning indistinct. Research shows that brands should strike a balance between automation and human control, since these elements may put the brand at risk of reputational damage and symbolic loss.

ETHICS AND GOVERNANCE ETHICS OF SYNTHETIC MYTHMAKING

The spread of AI-generated cultural work presents the challenges of governance equally to those posed by geospatial technologies, namely, the aspects of privacy, data ethics, bias, and social inequality. The GIS book cautions the high technologies can easily strengthen the power hierarchies or neglect sensitive data without proper approval systems. According to the scholars, AI-mediated branding should also include ethical principles, transparency policies, and participatory cultural activities to make sure that synthetic culture facilitates empowerment and not manipulation.

RESEARCH GAP

Although the literature on the topics of AI-mediated branding, synthetic culture, and automated storytelling has been growing at a rapid rate, some research gaps are critical, and many of them are similar to the structural gaps within the chapter on GIS and sustainability that can be found in the attached chapter. First, generative AI, cultural theory, and brand mythmaking are not connected by any integrated theoretical framework. Much of the available literature takes AI as an instrument of technology or a communication system but seldom as a culture capable of influencing systems of symbolic meaning (Firat & Venkatesh, 1995). This disjointure is also reflected in the criticism of GIS literature, which still lacks a cross-sectoral, holistic synthesis of research, which is very domain-specific. Consequently, researchers have not defined a holistic model that describes the process of synthetic culture creation, distribution, and integration into the overall brand system or how AI-generated myths are redefining consumer-brand relationships on cognitive, emotional, and cultural levels. Second, there is a dearth of empirical studies on how consumer interpret, engage, and internalize AI-generated myths in reality. Although key theories and perspectives on synthetic identities, virtual influencers, and artificial accounts narrated by AI bots are starting to be discussed theoretically, there is no empirical study that tries to analyze the meaning-making mechanisms used by consumers, as well as the experience of trust or psychological reaction to algorithmic cultural creation. This is reflective of the gap identified in the attached chapter according to which it is reported that there is no empirical analysis on the actual ground covering the influence of GIS-based decisions with long-run sustainability performance outcomes. In the absence of empirical basis, the field does not have clarity as to whether synthetic culture refines, distorts or destabilizes brand meaning among consumer segments. Third, the ethical, governance, and transparency concerns are seriously under-researched, despite the fact that generative AI is getting an increasingly significant role in the cultural fabrication. These issues (like in the GIS environment where ambiguity remains on privacy, power imbalances, and data control) are also manifested in AI-influenced myth-making, questions of authenticity and information disclosure, the responsibility of algorithms, ownership of artificial stories, cultural appropriation, and vulnerable audience protection. However, there are not many studies that suggest governance structures or ethical frameworks that brands should adopt in order to apply generative AI in a responsible manner. The risks of such a lack of structure as an opportunity to do some opaque cultural manipulation and destroy consumer trust. Fourth, a significant gap is in the little known about human-AI co-creation in the cultural systems. Synthetic culture does not appear as a result of AI itself but as a result of active relationships between human willfulness and machine-generated information. Nevertheless, academic interest has extensively surrounded human creativity or automation of AI individually. Such oversight reminds of the socio-technical imbalance covered in the provided chapter, in which organizational, human, and institutional factors receive little attention, despite them being the core of technological results. The field therefore does not have finer understanding of the way humans and AI co-operate in mythmaking processes, how power is allocated between creators and algorithms and how co-creation constructs authenticity, authorship and cultural identity.

Lastly, the longitudinal researches investigating the temporal development of AI-generated myths are entirely lacking. Machine learning systems keep on updating the narratives on the basis of new information, changing trends, and feedback mechanisms. This implies that synthetic culture is fluid in nature, but no studies have charted the life cycle, stability, or transformative process of AI-generated brand myths. Consequently, researchers are not informed as to whether synthetic narratives persist, disintegrate, and swiftly evolve- and in what way these changes affect brand equity in long-term periods. All these gaps would demand immediate interdisciplinary, empirically based, ethically centered, and globally knowledgeable studies to identify the complexity of synthetic culture in era of generative AI.

THEORETICAL FOUNDATIONS

To make sense of the synthetic culture and brand mythmaking in the era of generative AI, the multi-layered theoretical foundation is necessary to address the interaction of technology, culture, narrative systems, and consumer meaning-making. As in the integrative theoretical approach chosen in the attached chapter of the GIS (the integration of systems theory, socio-technical systems, and decision-support models to describe technological change in a sustainability setting), the chapter is based on four complementary theoretical perspectives, including Cultural Systems

Theory, Socio-Technical Systems (STS) Theory., Narrative and Mythmaking Theory, and Technology Acceptance and Diffusion Theories. All these structures collectively contribute to understanding how the generative AI creates artificial cultural space, crafts the story of brands, and interferes with human meaning and interaction.

CULTURAL SYSTEMS THEORY

The Cultural Systems Theory gives a theoretical basis of conceptualizing the functioning of a brand as a symbolic system that exists within the wider social, ideological, and cultural frameworks. Cultural meaning in conventional surroundings is passed on by common narration, rituals and common memory. Nevertheless, with the emergence of generative AI, culture ceases to be created in a natural way and is designed in an algorithmic manner (Arnould and Thompson, 2005).

Similarly to how GIS provides the model of integrating divergent environmental, social and economic data layers to put the one systemic interdependencies in the context of sustainability, the way generative AI suggests multimodal data sets into language corpora, visual archives or behavioral patterns, it generates synthetic manifestations of culture. Such artifacts generated by AI do not merely reflect culture; they actively manipulate the categories of culture, aesthetics and values by producing new symbolic associations in scale. The Cultural Systems Theory can therefore be used to clarify how synthetic culture is formed as a result of a network of algorithms, and user interactions and contextual information and not as a result of purely human social processes.

SOCIO-TECHNICAL SYSTEMS (STS) THEORY

Technological systems do not exist on their own; they are integrally embedded within social, organizational and ethical systems as the attached chapter highlights. To comprehend how generative AI can be used to make brand myths, the Socio-Technical Systems (STS) framework is thus critical. STS theory points out that human and algorithmic interaction produce synthetic culture. As the implementation of GIS needs managerial support innovations, training, governance systems, and stakeholder coordination to achieve effective sustainability results, generative AI-mediated branding also necessitates governance systems, human supervision, and ethical considerations to provide responsible narrative generation. It is also based on this theory that the effectiveness and genuineness of AI-created brand myths should be determined by organisational culture, the ability of leaders to adapt, and consumer trust.

NARRATIVE AND BRAND MYTHMAKING THEORY

The brand mythmaking theory suggests that it is the power of a brand to introduce itself into culturally resonant narratives, archetypes, and collective symbolic meanings. These myths have traditionally been built out of deliberate narration brought about by human imagination and cultural understanding. Nevertheless, with generative AI, mythmaking is being automatized, customized, and expedited.

By making comparisons to the predictive and scenario-modeling of GIS, whereby complex futures of an environment can be simulated using real-time analytics, AI allows brands to simulate cultural pathways, project identity scripts, and dynamically modify stories in accordance with behavioral patterns. This theoretical perspective places generative AI not only as a means of communication but as a mythmaking machine that is capable of both generating new cultural logics.

THE THEORY OF SYSTEMS AND FEEDBACK LOOPS

Another theory that is very popular in describing the interrelationship that exists within the processes of sustainable development is the Systems Theory that is considered essential to analyze the synthetic culture. Generative AI models continuously improve on what they write in response to user behaviour, social trends and optimization of their algorithms. Systems Theory aids in the conceptualization of synthetic culture as a self-correcting system that responds to changes in the contributions of technology and consumer reaction and results in a recalibration of the brand myths.

TECHNOLOGY ACCEPTANCE/DIFFUSION THEORIES

The acceptance of AI-generated myths by the consumer is crucial to their spread. Technology Acceptance models including UTAUT- which is also reviewed in the GIS chapter to introduce into the discussion the adoption of digital tools can introduce some insights as to how people assess cultural content generated by AI. Diffusion of Innovations Theory can also be used to explain thc spread of synthetic culture among consumer groups, cultures, and markets. The patterns of adoption are based on perceived compatibility with the existing cultural values, the visible nature of AI-generated content, and the extent of complexity of understanding or trusting the algorithmic mythmaking.

Collectively, these conceptual bases offer an end-to-end prism through which to conceptualize the transformative generative AI as a means of creating synthetic culture and a novel redefinition of brand mythmaking. Through its appeal to cultural theory, socio-technical analyses, systems thinking, narrative theorization, and the economic analysis of the adoption of technology, and by basing the discussion on the conceptual parallels of the GIS chapter to the issue of technological change and governance, the chapter provides a firm conceptual foundation on the emerging forces of AI-based cultural production.

ROLE OF GENERATIVE AI IN SYNTHETIC CULTURE AND BRAND MYTHMAKING

Artificial culture and brand mythmaking in the era of acclaimed AI has a transformative impact on renegotiating brand definition and create identity alongside developing emotional concordance in digital ecologies. Synthetic culture is algorithmically generated and generated as opposed to traditional culture, which is naturally formed as a result of shared human experience and experimented under conditions that place this human experience within a novel context of interaction with different systems that naturally embodies a new culturally mediated phenomenon in humans (Berger, 2021). The brands can create cultural artifacts through these AI-generated cultural artifacts, including virtual influencers and synthetic spokes characters, immersive brand worlds and personalized storytelling, which enable the brands not only to act as meaning communicators, but also as creators of cultural reality. Generative AI combines enormous amounts of cultural representations, consumer habits, and beauty preferences to create stories that will appear personalized, emotionally connected, and culturally sensitive. This places brands to be beyond passive following the cultural trends, and acquire the active way of creating cultural mythologies that appeal to different groups of consumers.

The artificial culture has been especially important in developing brand mythmaking, a process where brands take root in symbolic discourses and archetypal discourses which make them resonate with more emotional resonance. Mythmaking in previous times has mostly relied on human imagination and linear narrative, whereas data-driven adaptive, iterative and generative AI allows mythmaking. Consumer interactions are analyzed in real time by the AI systems, and the stories change the direction, and the resulting story can vary in tone, imagery, and symbolic content. This mythic feedback resembles the systems thinking of feedback found in the attached chapter of GIS where socio-technical environments are in a state of development as a result of interaction between the tools, the users and the contextual data. Equally, brand myths within synthetic culture are dynamic and continuously changing, so that the brand maintains its cultural and emotional relevance in an environment that is in a state of rapid change. Besides, generative AI allows brands to create hyper-personalized myths in correspondence to the identities, goals, and emotional environments of individual consumers. Synthetic cultural artifacts are not homogenous; it is custom-crafted symbolic experiences produced out of the examination of individual histories, psychographic indicators, and signals of behaviour. Such a strong level of personalization will make it more emotionally connected, impact the perceived authenticity, and raise the chances of long-term interaction. Simultaneously, the capacity of the AI to replicate human-type communication and emotional displays erases the line between real and artificial cultural communication. Consequently, artificial brand images are able to exert a considerable amount of social power, acting as the mythological figures of our time, which can only influence the consumer perception and behaviour in a very accurate way.

Synthetic culture is also essential to the further diversification of the creative opportunities of branding, which allows the brands to experiment with narrative forms, aesthetics, and symbolic vocabularies without adhering to human restrictions. Generative AI can be prototyped to create mythic worlds in a short period, test symbolic stories and exercise other cultural realities- similar to state-of-the-art GIS systems, which simulate a given environmental or planning scenario to be optimized. This makes the innovation process quicker as it allows on-going experimentation and real-time adjustment so that the brands can be prompt in changing according to the cultural changes and new expectations of consumers. Synthetic culture at the societal level transforms the dynamics of power of cultural production. The brands that will have AI-powered cultural engines will be more engaged in creating the imagination of the people, shaping the collective identities, and coordinating symbolic experiences to the global audience. This creates critical ethical concerns of transparency, authenticity, cultural safety, and governance of the algorithms of stories. Unless appropriately controlled, synthetic culture will be used to support prejudices, affect the emotional reaction, or homogenize the cultural variety via algorithmic optimization. This is similar to the raised concerns in the GIS field regarding the issue of data control, privacy and the likelihood of inequality in case of implementing advanced technologies without proper ethical standards.

Essentially, the contribution of synthetic culture and brand mythmaking to the era of generative AI is complex and intricate. It reinvents a new meaning of how brands are constructed, turns consumers into coauthors of algorithmically constructed narratives, increases cultural change, and creates new grounds of creativity and influence. Meanwhile, it brings about the necessity of the prudent regulation and moral thought to make sure that the AI-mediated cultural creation adds more, not less, to the richness and variety of human experience.

MANAGERIAL IMPLICATIONS

The advent of artificial culture and AI-offered brand mythmaking bears far-reaching consequences and challenges the managers to reconsider the process of how brands conceptualize the identity, produce content, and involve consumers in the digitally mediated setting. Managers have to understand that generative AI is not a creative tool but rather a cultural engine that can create meaning, shape consumer behaviour, and create symbolic universes within which brands exist. This leaves strategic responsibility on the leaders to make sure that AI-made stories do not contradict the core values of the organisation, its long-term brand vision, and position in the market. Instead of using individual intuition or traditional branding playbooks, the managers should adopt data-driven cultural strategy and leveraging AI-generated knowledge to predict new cultural trends, dynamically reshape brand narratives, and remain relevant in dynamic digital ecosystems (Mittal and Bansal, 2023). The other significant implication is that organizations need to develop resolute socio-technical infrastructures that enable cultural production through AI mediation. With the investments in talent, training, governance structure and cross-functional cooperation, as it has been mentioned in the discussion of technology integration and organizational readiness in the attached chapter, the successful adoption of advanced systems necessitates investments. Managers should accessibly, therefore, develop multidisciplinary teams with artificial intelligence knowledge, cultural brilliance, ethical management, and innovative strategy. New posts, including AI brand supervisors, synthetic culture designers, and algorithmic governance officers, might need to be created to manage the responsible implementation of the generative AI tools. In the absence of appropriate competencies and governance processes, organizations will be driven out-of-shape between the outputs of technologies and brand integrity, which can lead to a reputation loss.

The fact that synthetic culture has ethical and regulatory aspects also requires managers to maneuver through them. Similarly to how the implementation of GIS raises concerns in governance, in terms of privacy, the fairness of the data, and an equitable decision-making process, generative AI is associated with issues of transparency, authenticity, the misuse of deep fakes, and cultural manipulation. Consequently, managers should come up with specific ethical principles that regulate AI-created content, including disclosure policies of synthetic influencers, principles regarding an allowed input of data, and policies to avoid the creation of harmful or biased narratives. This type of frameworks can maintain consumer trust, and shield the organization against the risks of lawsuits because more and more regulations on AI-mediated content are forming. Ethical governance is not to be perceived as a burden of compliance but rather as a strategic advantage that portrays brand responsibility in a world where authenticity is an important and disputed concept.

Another implication is that the managers have to accept consumer co-creation and participatory cultural design. Synthetic culture can be formed as a result of the feedback between user behaviour and algorithmic reaction, just as participatory GIS can contribute to decision-making by creating information collaboratively. The managers should therefore view consumers as active participants in brand mythology and not as passive receivers. Such a change necessitates developing platforms, interactive tools, and artificial intelligence systems that will enable consumers to create stories, mythic experiences tailored to them, and shape the development of brand identities. Those brands that embrace co-creation successfully can establish more emotional bonds and community-ownness and be culturally more relevant.

THEORETICAL IMPLICATIONS

The emergence of synthetic culture and AI-based brand mythmaking creates a number of significant theoretical implications that contribute to the development of modern knowledge on branding, cultural production, and human-technology interaction. To begin with, this chapter adds more dimensions to the cultural theory by proving that culture is no longer a production only of humans but more of a hybrid system created through the work of algorithms. It complicates the historical anthropological and sociological assumptions about the newly understood cultural meaning of depiction only as a working agent of the human infinite, and it is even facing a system where AI is a cultural co-creator seeing the ability to generate symbols, narratives, and aesthetic objects. This is similar to the paradigm shift witnessed in the attached chapter on GIS, which makes digital technologies redefine the interactions and changes of systems in the realms of the environment and social life. Through the theoretical framework of the synthetic culture as the emergent property of human-AI interaction, the chapter extends the cultural systems theory to the computational age. Second, the chapter adds to the narrative and mythmaking theory by redefining myths as not fixed, slow-evolving narratives but as dynamic, data-based, and continuously altering ones. Conventional brand mythmaking is based on archetypal storytelling which has been shaped with human creativity, whereas generative AI ushers in algorithmic plasticity to enable myths to emerge in real-time depending on user behaviour and contextual data. This makes algorithmic mythmaking a novel category of theoretical approaches that are a combination of symbolic anthropology, consumer psychology, and machine learning. It also promotes the rise of synthetic mythic actors like virtual influencers and AI-driven brand personalities that play symbolic and emotional functions once played by human cultural actors (Venkatesh et al., 2012). This re-arrangement of myth breaks the traditional theoretical divisions of fiction, representation and identity.

The third important theoretical implication is that the socio-technical systems (STS) theory has been applied to cultural artifacts and symbolic environments. STS conventionally emphasizes the interaction between the technologies and the social and organizational organization, although the chapter shows that generative AI influences not only behaviour and processes but also the cultural meaning regimes as such. In this way, the ecosystem of branding turns out to be a socio-technical one where human designers, algorithms, cultural values, and user responses all contribute to the creation of synthetic cultural. This is similar to the integrative view in the GIS chapter where it is stressful that the results of technology could not exist outside of the framework of institutions and human beings. The chapter thus also expands the theory of STS by demonstrating that meaning-making and mythmaking are distributed in the human cognition as well as in the computation of an algorithm. Lastly, the chapter is a contribution to the new discourses in the field of ethics and the theory of governance by identifying generative AI as a symbolic power that influences the cultural imagination. This presents emerging theoretical issues of authenticity, cultural safety, the intellectual property of synthetic narratives, and the regulation of the computational meaning-making. In the same way that geospatial technologies develop theoretical issues regarding the concept of privacy, surveillance, and digital inequality in the GIS chapter, generative AI makes scholars reconsider ethical schemas that could manage cultural production. The chapter therefore brings out the necessity of new theories which deal with the manner in which societies negotiate legitimacy, trust and cultural integrity in settings where artificial systems are involved in the production of myth and meaning.

SCOPE FOR FUTURE WORK

The swift development of generative AI and its contribution to the creation of the synthetic culture provide numerous opportunities to conduct future studies that are prerequisite to the enhancement of theoretical, methodological, and practical knowledge of branding and cultural studies. Among the directions is the formulation of compounding theoretical models that bring together the cultural systems theory, the socio-technical systems perspectives and the computational creativity models. As the necessity of holistic frameworks in geospatial sustainability studies, as the chapter attached points out, future research should not be limited to the fragmentary methodology but should develop interdisciplinary frameworks to describe the role of AI in cultural meaning-making, identity-building, and symbolic communication. The other potentially beneficial field of future work is the empirical study of the consumer reactions towards synthetic culture and AI-produced brand myths. Although the conceptual theories of AI-mediated narrative emergence have been described in the literature, there is little empirical data on consumer perceptions and formation of authenticity, emotional bonds, and negotiation of meaning within AI-based cultural spaces. Experimental research, longitudinal research, neuroscience research, and cross-cultural comparison should be included in the future works and research to ascertain the ability of synthetic myths to promote trust, loyalty and behavioral outcomes in various demographic and cultural groups (Holt and Cameron, 2010).

There are also ethical and governance issues that algorithmic mythmaking is prone to and need to be addressed in future research. The issues of transparency, authorship, prejudice, cultural appropriation, and narrative manipulation will only escalate as generative AI is becoming more advanced. Researchers ought to examine regulatory frameworks, models of governance and principles of ethical design that would allow conservation of cultural integrity by incorporating responsible innovation. This can be compared to the appeal in the GIS chapter to conduct more research on ethical information management and fair use of technology. Furthermore, much more can be done in studying the dynamics of human-AI co-creation. Culture synergy is a creation of human creativity and algorithm generation, but there is a paucity of information regarding how such association is realized in the practical branding contexts of the real world. The forthcoming work might explore the intent of utilizing AI tools in creative teams, the distribution of power and transactions between humans and algorithms, and how organizations can build hybrid creative armies that can boost innovation and not sacrifice authenticity. Lastly, longitudinal research on the dynamics of AI-generated brand myths with time is required. Synthetic narratives are dynamic, and constantly updated in a machine learning feedback loop, but there remains very little research on their lifecycle, their diffusion patterns, their longevity and whether they can disrupt culture. Future scholars might be able to follow the evolution of synthetic myths between digital communities, breaking apart, or settling down, and how these evolutionary dynamics affect brand equity, consumer self, and cultural ecosystems in the long term.

CONCLUSION

The rise of generative AI is signifying a radical shift in the meaning creation, identity formation, and consumer interaction of a more digital and algorithmically mediated environment by brands. This chapter has shown that synthetic culture is a new form of culture in which artificial systems are involved in the direct production of the symbolic environments that affect the perceptions and behaviour of consumers. Similar to how the attached GIS chapter shows how digital technologies are changing environmental decision-making and sustainability governance through integrated systems, generative AI too is changing branding into a socio-technical ecosystem in which cultural production is dynamic, participatory and, more crucially, highly integrated with technological intelligence. Brand mythmaking, previously confined to human instincts and imagination, are currently being developed through hybrid mechanisms where algorithms are now co-authors of symbolic meaning so that myths can now develop in real-time based on behavioral feedback, cultural changes and emotions. Another important aspect encompassed in the chapter is the opportunities and challenges of AI-driven cultural innovation. On the one hand, generative AI allows brands to create immersive worlds of narratives, create hyper-personalized worlds of myths, and remove any traditional creative limits. Artificial cultural artifacts like virtual messengers, artificial intelligence plots provide new avenues of brand distinction, feeling connectivity, and community creation. The emergence of synthetic culture, conversely, brings very serious questions of authenticity, transparency, algorithmic bias, and cultural governance. Having no considered ethical principles and organizational controls, AI-produced myths will threaten consumer trust, perpetuate culture inequities, and erase the lines between authentic human narration and AI-based persuasion. Finally, this chapter suggests that the future of branding in the era of the generative AI will be based on the ability to comprehend synthetic culture as not a technological innovation but as a new cultural factor. It demands the adaptability of scholars and practitioners to the interdisciplinary approach relating cultural theory, socio- technical systems thinking, narrative studies, and AI governance. Understanding the relationship between algorithms and humans as a multifaceted process of generating symbolic meaning, organizations will be able to maximize the advantages of generative AI and preserve the cultural integrity and well-being of consumers. The future of synthetic culture is ever-changing, and thus the responsibility of brands is not only to follow it but to be responsible, creative and ethically foresight to ensure that AI-assisted mythmaking only adds to the cultural experiences that make humans connect with one another.

REFERENCES

Ao, L., Bansal, R., Pruthi, N., & Khaskheli, M. B. (2023). Impact of Social Media Influencers on Customer Engagement and Purchase Intention: A Meta-Analysis. *Sustainability, 15*(3), 2744.

Arnould, E. J., & Thompson, C. J. (2005). Consumer culture theory (CCT): Twenty years of research. *The Journal of Consumer Research, 31*(4), 868–882.

Bansal, R., Pruthi, N., Bansal, T., & Chaudhary, A. (2023). Diving into the consumer's mind: Tools, roles, and ethical concerns of neuromarketing. In *Applications of Neuromarketing in the Metaverse* (pp. 206–222). IGI Global.

Bansal, R., Pruthi, N., & Singh, R. (2022). Developing customer engagement through artificial intelligence tools: Roles and challenges. In *Developing Relationships, Personalization, and Data Herald in Marketing 5.0* (pp. 130–145). IGI Global.

Bansal, R., Saini, S., Ngah, A. H., & Durga Prasad, T. (2024). Proselytizing the potential of influencer marketing via artificial intelligence: Mapping the research trends through bibliometric analysis. *Cogent Business & Management, 11*(1), 2372889.

Bansal, R., Shukla, G., Gupta, A., Singh, A., & Pruthi, N. (2023). Optimizing augmented reality and virtual reality for customer engagement. In *Promoting Consumer Engagement Through Emotional Branding and Sensory Marketing* (pp. 24–35). IGI Global.

Belk, R. W. (2013). Extended self in a digital world. *The Journal of Consumer Research, 40*(3), 477–500.

Csikszentmihalyi, M. (1997). *Creativity: Flow and the psychology of discovery and invention*. HarperCollins.

Escalas, J. E. (2004). Narrative processing: Building consumer connections to brands. *Journal of Consumer Psychology, 14*(1–2), 168–180.

Firat, A. F., & Venkatesh, A. (1995). Liberatory postmodernism and the reenchantment of consumption. *The Journal of Consumer Research, 22*(3), 239–267.

Holt, D. (2004). *How brands become icons: The principles of cultural branding*. Harvard Business School Press.

Holt, D., & Cameron, D. (2010). *Cultural strategy: Using innovative ideologies to build breakthrough brands*. Oxford University Press.

Latour, B. (2005). *Reassembling the social: An introduction to actor–network-theory*. Oxford University Press.

Mittal, G., & Bansal, R. (2023). Driving force behind consumer brand engagement: The metaverse. In *Cultural Marketing and Metaverse for Consumer Engagement* (pp. 164–181). IGI Global.

Nieborg, D. B., & Poell, T. (2018). The platformization of cultural production. *New Media & Society*, *20*(11), 4275–4292.

Saini, S., & Bansal, R. (2025). Parasocial relationships and self-disclosure: Strengthening brand image through brand attitude in premium cosmetics. *Journal of Promotion Management*, *31*(2), 337–366.

Shankar, A., Elliott, R., & Goulding, C. (2001). Understanding consumption: Contributions from a narrative perspective. *Journal of Marketing Management*, *17*(3–4), 429–453.

Venkatesh, V., Thong, J. Y. L., & Xu, X. (2012). Consumer acceptance and use of information technology: Extending the unified theory. *Management Information Systems Quarterly*, *36*(1), 157–178.

Compilation of References

Abidin, C. (2018). *Internet celebrity: Understanding fame online.* Emerald Publishing., DOI: 10.1108/9781787560765

Abuali, T., & Ahmed, A. A. (2025). Challenges and Opportunities in Implementing E-Learning in Developing Countries. *The Open European Journal of Social Science and Education (OEJSSE)*, 1-12.

Adamakis, M., & Rachiotis, T. (2025). Artificial Intelligence in Higher Education: A State-of-the-Art Overview of Pedagogical Integrity, Artificial Intelligence Literacy, and Policy Integration. *Encyclopedia*, *5*(4), 180. DOI: 10.3390/encyclopedia5040180

Adobe Inc. (2023). Adobe Firefly: Generative AI for creative professionals. https://www.adobe.com/sensei/generative-ai/firefly.html

Agbai, E., Agbai, E., & Oko-Jaja, E. S. (2024). Bridging Culture, Nurturing Diversity: Cultural Exchange and Its Impact on Global Understanding. *Research Journal of Humanities and Cultural*, *10*(2), 42–58. DOI: 10.56201/rjhcs.v10.no2.2024.pg42.58

Aggarwal, D., Rabby, F., Fahlevi, M., Muttaqin, A., & Bansal, R. (2024). Mapping the history, trajectory, and anatomy of slow and sustainable fashion: A bibliometric analysis. *Cogent Business & Management*, *11*(1), 2423058.

Ajani, O. A., Gamede, B. T., & Bansal, R. (2024). Challenges and opportunities of integrating industry 5.0 and emerging technologies in higher education for enhancing employability skills. *Industry 5.0 and Emerging Technologies: Transformation Through. Technology and Innovation*, •••, 217–230.

Almaz, A. F., El-Agouz, E. A. E. A., Abdelfatah, M. T., & Mohamed, I. R. (2024). The Future Role of Artificial Intelligence (AI) Design's Integration into Architectural and Interior Design Education is to Improve Efficiency, Sustainability, and Creativity. *Civil Engineering and Architecture*, *12*(3), 1749–1772. DOI: 10.13189/cea.2024.120336

Amabile, T. M. (1996). *Creativity in context: Update to the social psychology of creativity*. Westview Press.

Amabile, T. M. (2020). Creativity, artificial intelligence, and a world of surprises. *Academy of Management Discoveries*, *6*(3), 351–354.

Amabile, T. M., & Pratt, M. G. (2016). The dynamic componential model of creativity and innovation in organizations: Making progress, making meaning. *Research in Organizational Behavior*, *36*, 157–183. DOI: 10.1016/j.riob.2016.10.001

Anghel, D. (2023). New Perspectives for Human and Artificial Intelligence Interactions for Leadership e-Recruitment. *Societies (Basel, Switzerland)*, *13*(3). Advance online publication. DOI: 10.3390/soc13030055

Ao, L., Bansal, R., Pruthi, N., & Khaskheli, M. B. (2023). Impact of Social Media Influencers on Customer Engagement and Purchase Intention: A Meta-Analysis. *Sustainability*, *15*(3), 2744.

Arnould, E. J., & Thompson, C. J. (2005). Consumer culture theory (CCT): Twenty years of research. *The Journal of Consumer Research*, *31*(4), 868–882.

Atchley, P., Pannell, H., Wofford, K., Hopkins, M., & Atchley, R. A. (2024). Human and AI collaboration in the higher education environment: Opportunities and concerns. *Cognitive Research: Principles and Implications*, *9*(1). Advance online publication. DOI: 10.1186/s41235-024-00547-9 PMID: 38589710

Babashahi, L., Barbosa, C. E., Lima, Y., Lyra, A., Salazar, H., Argôlo, M., Almeida, M. A. D., & Souza, J. M. D. (2024). AI in the Workplace: A Systematic Review of Skill Transformation in the Industry. *Administrative Sciences*, *14*(6). Advance online publication. DOI: 10.3390/admsci14060127

Bansa, R., Bansal, T., & Pruthi, N. (2024). Demystifying the Benefits and Challenges of Virtual Learning for Differently Abled Students. In *Virtual Lifelong Learning: Educating Society with Modern Communication Technologies* (pp. 70-84). Bentham Science Publishers.

Bansal, R., Pruthi, N., & Singh, R. (2022). Developing customer engagement through artificial intelligence tools: Roles and challenges. In *Developing Relationships, Personalization, and Data Herald in Marketing 5.0* (pp. 130–145). IGI Global.

Bansal, R., Pruthi, N., & Singh, R. (2022). Developing Customer Engagement Through Artificial Intelligence Tools: Roles and Challenges. In *Developing Relationships, Personalization, and Data Herald in Marketing 5.0* (pp. 130-145). IGI Global.

Bansal, R., Pruthi, N., Bansal, T., & Chaudhary, A. (2023). Diving Into the Consumer's Mind: Tools, Roles, and Ethical Concerns of Neuromarketing. In *Applications of Neuromarketing in the Metaverse* (pp. 206-222). IGI Global.

Bansal, R., Martinho, C., Pruthi, N., & Aggarwal, D. (2024). From virtual observations to business insights: A bibliometric review of netnography in business research. *Heliyon, 10*(1). PMID: 38163120

Bansal, R., Pruthi, N., Bansal, T., & Chaudhary, A. (2023). Diving into the consumer's mind: Tools, roles, and ethical concerns of neuromarketing. In *Applications of Neuromarketing in the Metaverse* (pp. 206–222). IGI Global.

Bansal, R., Saini, S., Ngah, A. H., & Durga Prasad, T. (2024). Proselytizing the potential of influencer marketing via artificial intelligence: Mapping the research trends through bibliometric analysis. *Cogent Business & Management, 11*(1), 2372889.

Bansal, R., Shukla, G., Gupta, A., Singh, A., & Pruthi, N. (2023). Optimizing Augmented Reality and Virtual Reality for Customer Engagement. In *Promoting Consumer Engagement Through Emotional Branding and Sensory Marketing* (pp. 24–35). IGI Global.

Barrett, M. S., Creech, A., & Zhukov, K. (2021). Creative Collaboration and Collaborative Creativity: A Systematic Literature Review. *Frontiers in Psychology, 12*(August), 1–15. DOI: 10.3389/fpsyg.2021.713445 PMID: 34434151

Becker, G. S. (1994). Human capital revisited. In *Human capital: A theoretical and empirical analysis with special reference to education* (3rd ed., pp. 15–28). The University of Chicago Press.

Belk, R. W. (2013). Extended self in a digital world. *The Journal of Consumer Research, 40*(3), 477–500.

Bender, E. M., Gebru, T., McMillan-Major, A., & Shmitchell, S. (2021). On the dangers of stochastic parrots: Can language models be too big? *Proceedings of the 2021 ACM Conference on Fairness, Accountability, and Transparency*, 610–623. https://doi.org/DOI: 10.1145/3442188.3445922

Berryman, R., & Kavka, M. (2017). Crying on YouTube: Vlogs, self-exposure and the performance of emotional labour. *Journal of Gender Studies, 26*(3), 278–292. DOI: 10.1177/1354856517736981

Bishop, P., Hines, A., & Collins, T. (2007). The current state of scenario development: An overview of techniques. *Foresight, 9*(1), 5–25. DOI: 10.1108/14636680710727516

Black, P., & Wiliam, D. (2018). Classroom assessment and AI: Emerging challenges. *Assessment in Education: Principles, Policy & Practice*, *25*(3), 299–314.

Blaurock, M., Büttgen, M., & Schepers, J. (2025). Designing Collaborative Intelligence Systems for Employee-AI Service Co-Production. *Journal of Service Research*, *28*(4), 544–562. DOI: 10.1177/10946705241238751

Boden, M. A. (2004). *The creative mind: Myths and mechanisms* (2nd ed.). Routledge., DOI: 10.4324/9780203508527

Boden, M. A. (2016). *AI: Its nature and future*. Oxford University Press.

Brahmi, M., Hussain, Z., Majeed, M. U., Khan, A., Qureshi, M. A., & Bansal, R. (2025). Corporate Social Responsibility's Influence on Brand Image in the Automotive Sector: The Corporate Reputation and Product Quality Role. *Administrative Sciences*, *15*(4), 121.

Brown, P., Hesketh, A., & Wiliams, S. (2003). Employability in a knowledge-driven economy. *Journal of Education and Work*, *16*(2), 107–126.

Bryan-Kinns, N. (2024). Reflections on explainable AI for the arts (XAIxArts). *Interaction*, *31*(1), 43–47.

Brynjolfsson, E., & McAfee, A. (2022). The business of artificial intelligence: What it can—and cannot—do for your organization. Harvard Business Review. https://hbr.org/2022/11/the-business-of-artificial-intelligence

Brynjolfsson, E., & McAfee, A. (2012). *Race against the machine: How the digital revolution is accelerating innovation, driving productivity, and irreversibly transforming employment and the economy*. Brynjolfsson and McAfee.

Brynjolfsson, E., & McAfee, A. (2017). *Machine, platform, crowd: Harnessing our digital future*. W. W. Norton.

Brynjolfsson, E., & McAfee, A. (2019). *The second machine age: Work, progress, and prosperity in a time of brilliant technologies*. W. W. Norton.

Brynjolfsson, E., & Mcafee, A. N. D. R. E. W. (2017). Artificial intelligence, for real. *Harvard Business Review*, *1*(1), 1–31.

Brynjolfsson, E., & Mcafee, A. N. D. R. E. W. (2017). The business of artificial intelligence. *Harvard Business Review*, *7*(1), 1–2.

Bryson, J. M., & George, B. (2020). Strategic foresight and public value. *Public Administration Review*, *80*(4), 565–574.

Buhmann, A., & Fieseler, C. (2021). Towards a deliberative framework for responsible innovation in artificial intelligence. *Technology in Society, 64*(December 2020), 101475. https://doi.org/DOI: 10.1016/j.techsoc.2020.101475

Buolamwini, J., & Gebru, T. (2018). Gender shades: Intersectional accuracy disparities in commercial gender classification. Proceedings of Machine Learning Research, 81, 1–15. https://proceedings.mlr.press/v81/buolamwini18a.html

Carter, L., & Bélanger, F. (2022). Ethical considerations for AI adoption in the public sector. *Government Information Quarterly*, *39*(3), 101664. DOI: 10.1016/j.giq.2022.101664

Chamberlain, R., Mullin, J., Scheerlinck, E., & Wiggins, G. A. (2021). Perceptions of creativity in human versus AI-generated art. *Psychology of Aesthetics, Creativity, and the Arts*. Advance online publication. DOI: 10.1037/aca0000435

Chen, X., Wang, X., & Qu, Y. (2023). Constructing Ethical AI Based on the "Human-in-the-Loop" System. *Systems, 11*(11). Advance online publication. DOI: 10.3390/systems11110548

Chesney, R., & Citron, D. K. (2019). Deep fakes: A looming challenge for privacy, democracy, and national security. *California Law Review*, *107*(6), 1753–1819. https://www.californialawreview.org/print/deep-fakes-a-looming-challenge-for-privacy-democracy-and-national-security

Christensen, C. M., Horn, M. B., & Johnson, C. W. (2011). *Disrupting class: How disruptive innovation will change the way the world learns*. McGraw-Hill.

Clark, A., & Chalmers, D. (1998). The extended mind. *analysis, 58*(1), 7-19.

Collins, A., & Halverson, R. (2018). *Rethinking education in the age of technology: The digital revolution and schooling in America* (2nd ed.). Teachers College Press.

Colton, S., & Wiggins, G. A. (2012). Computational creativity: The final frontier. In *ECAI 2012* (pp. 21–26). IOS Press.

Colton, S., & Wiggins, G. A. (2012). Computational creativity: The final frontier? *Proceedings of the European Conference on Artificial Intelligence*, 21, 21–26. https://doi.org/DOI: 10.3233/978-1-61499-098-7-21

Comunian, R., Taylor, C., & Smith, D. (2014). The role of universities in the creative economy: Comparative perspectives from the UK and the US. *Creative Industries Journal*, *7*(2), 117–135. DOI: 10.1080/09654313.2013.790589

Couldry, N., & Mejias, U. A. (2019). *The costs of connection: How data is colonizing human life and appropriating it for capitalism.* Stanford University Press., DOI: 10.1515/9781503609754

Creely, E., & Blannin, J. (2025). Creative partnerships with generative AI. Possibilities for education and beyond. *Thinking Skills and Creativity, 56*(October 2023), 101727. https://doi.org/DOI: 10.1016/j.tsc.2024.101727

Crootof, R., & Ard, B. (2022). The data we breathe: Reconsidering "publicly available" data and AI. *Washington Law Review (Seattle, Wash.), 97*(1), 167–222.

Csikszentmihalyi, M. (1997). *Creativity: Flow and the psychology of discovery and invention.* HarperCollins.

Csikszentmihalyi, M. (1997). Flow and the psychology of discovery and invention. *HarperPerennial, New York, 39*, 1–16.

Cunningham, S., & Craig, D. (2019). Social media entertainment: The new intersection of Hollywood and Silicon Valley. NYU Press. https://nyupress.org/9781479846894/

Daly, S. J., Hearn, G., & Papageorgiou, K. (2025). Sensemaking with AI: How trust influences Human-AI collaboration in health and creative industries. *Social Sciences and Humanities Open, 11*(October 2024), 101346. https://doi.org/DOI: 10.1016/j.ssaho.2025.101346

Danto, A. C. (1981). *The transfiguration of the commonplace: A philosophy of art.* Harvard University Press.

Dartanto, A. S. (2024). Transforming Curatorial Practices: The Role of AI and Blockchain in Shaping an Ethical Art-Science Paradigm for Public Policy. *International Journal of Creative and Arts Studies, 11*(2), 140–164. DOI: 10.24821/ijcas.v11i2.14388

Das, S., & Kundu, R. (2024). The Ethics of Artificial Intelligence in Creative Arts: A Comprehensive Review. *Interdisciplinary International Journal of Advances in Social Sciences. Arts and Humanities, 01*(01), 27–34. DOI: 10.62674/iijassah.2024.v1i1.003

Dator, J. (2019). *Alternative futures at the Manoa School.* Springer.

Davenport, T. H., & Bean, R. (2022). AI-driven augmentation: How artificial intelligence enhances human performance. *MIT Sloan Management Review.*

Davenport, T. H., & Kirby, J. (2016). Just how smart are smart machines? *MIT Sloan Management Review, 57*(3), 21.

Dellermann, D., Calma, A., Lipusch, N., Weber, T., Weigel, S., & Ebel, P. (2021). The future of human-AI collaboration: a taxonomy of design knowledge for hybrid intelligence systems. *arXiv preprint arXiv:2105.03354*.

Deloitte. (2022). State of AI in the enterprise, 5th edition. https://www2.deloitte.com/us/en/insights/focus/cognitive-technologies/ai-augmentation.html

Desolda, G., Esposito, A., Lanzilotti, R., Piccinno, A., & Costabile, M. F. (2025). *From human-centered to symbiotic artificial intelligence: a focus on medical applications. Multimedia Tools and Applications* (Vol. 84). Springer US. https://doi.org/DOI: 10.1007/s11042-024-20414-5

Devi, K. S. (2019). Constructivist approach to learning based on the concepts of Jean Piaget and Lev Vygotsky An analytical Overview. *Journal of Indian Education, 44*(4), 5–19.

Dignum, V. (2019). *Responsible artificial intelligence: How to develop and use AI in a responsible way*. Springer., DOI: 10.1007/978-3-030-30371-6

Dinh, J. E., Lord, R. G., Gardner, W. L., Meuser, J. D., Liden, R. C., & Hu, J. (2014). Leadership theory and research in the new millennium: Current theoretical trends and changing perspectives. *The Leadership Quarterly, 25*(1), 36–62. DOI: 10.1016/j.leaqua.2013.11.005

Dron, J., & Anderson, T. (2014). Learning and teaching with social media. In *Ubiquitous learning environments and technologies* (pp. 15–29). Springer Berlin Heidelberg.

Duffy, B. E., & Hund, E. (2015). "Having it all" on social media: Entrepreneurial femininity and self-branding among fashion bloggers. *Social Media + Society, 1*(2), 1–11. DOI: 10.1177/2056305115604337

Duffy, B., & Wissinger, E. (2017). Mythologies of Creative Work in the Social Media Age: Fun, Free, and "Just Being Me". *International Journal of Communication, 11*, 4652–4671.

Duin, A. H., & Pedersen, I. (2023). *Augmentation technologies and artificial intelligence in technical communication: Designing ethical futures*. Routledge.

Edmondson, A. C. (2018). *The fearless organization: Creating psychological safety in the workplace for learning, innovation, and growth*. John Wiley & Sons.

Edwards, R., & Fenwick, T. (2016). Digital analytics and educational ethics. *Learning, Media and Technology, 41*(2), 246–259.

Elgammal, A., Liu, B., Elhoseiny, M., & Mazzone, M. (2017). CAN: Creative adversarial networks — Generating "art" by learning about styles and deviating from style norms. *Proceedings of the 8th International Conference on Computational Creativity (ICCC)*, 97–104. https://doi.org/DOI: 10.48550/arXiv.1706.07068

ElSayary, A. (2023). The impact of a professional upskilling training programme on developing teachers' digital competence. *Journal of Computer Assisted Learning*, *39*(4), 1154–1166.

Emery, F. (1980). Designing socio-technical systems for'greenfield'sites. *Journal of Occupational Behaviour*, **•••**, 19–27.

Engelbart, D. C. (1962). Program on human effectiveness. *Reprint in: Nyce, James M./Kahn, Paul (1991)(Hg.)(1962)*, 237-244.

Erstad, O., & Voogt, J. (2018). The twenty-first century curriculum: Issues in education and technology. *Journal of Educational Technology & Society*, *21*(1), 1–4.

Erzed, N., Laksana, R. P., Hasanudin, H., Yuhefizar, Y., Anwar, N., Gunawan, H., Sekti, B. A., & Ichwani, A. (2025). Exploring the metaverse: Foundations of social interaction and community building. In *Unveiling Social Dynamics and Community Interaction in the Metaverse* (pp. 1–25). https://doi.org/DOI: 10.4018/979-8-3693-8628-6.ch001

Escalas, J. E. (2004). Narrative processing: Building consumer connections to brands. *Journal of Consumer Psychology*, *14*(1–2), 168–180.

European Commission. (2021). *Ethics guidelines for trustworthy AI.* https://digital-strategy.ec.europa.eu

European Union. (2024). EU AI Act: Regulatory framework on artificial intelligence. https://digital-strategy.ec.europa.eu/en/policies/regulatory-framework-ai

Facer, K. (2011). *Learning futures: Education, technology and social change.* Routledge.

Faqihi, A., & Miah, S. J. (2023). Artificial intelligence-driven talent management system: Exploring the risks and options for constructing a theoretical foundation. *Journal of Risk and Financial Management*, *16*(1), 31.

Firat, A. F., & Venkatesh, A. (1995). Liberatory postmodernism and the reenchantment of consumption. *The Journal of Consumer Research*, *22*(3), 239–267.

Fitzgerald, R., & McCarthy, J. (2020). Preparing school leaders for AI. *Journal of Educational Change*, *21*(2), 167–186.

Flick, C., & Worrall, K. (2022). The ethics of creative AI. In *The language of creative AI: Practices, aesthetics and structures* (pp. 73–91). Springer International Publishing.

Florida, R. (2002). The economic geography of talent. *Annals of the Association of American Geographers*, *92*(4), 743–755.

Floridi, L. (2014). *The ethics of information*. Oxford University Press., DOI: 10.1093/acprof:oso/9780199641321.001.0001

Floridi, L. (2019). *The logic of information: A theory of philosophy as conceptual design*. Oxford University Press.

Floridi, L. (2019). Translating principles into practices of digital ethics: Five risks of being unethical. *Philosophy & Technology*, *32*(2), 185–193.

Floridi, L., Cowls, J., Beltrametti, M., Chatila, R., Chazerand, P., Dignum, V., Luetge, C., Madelin, R., Pagallo, U., Rossi, F., Schafer, B., Valcke, P., & Vayena, E. (2018). AI4People—An ethical framework for a good AI society. *Minds and Machines*, *28*(4), 689–707. DOI: 10.1007/s11023-018-9482-5

Frau-Meigs, D. (2024). Algorithm literacy as a subset of media and information literacy: Competences and design considerations. *Digital*, *4*(2), 512–528.

Fügener, A., Grahl, J., Gupta, A., & Ketter, W. (2022). Cognitive Challenges in Human–Artificial Intelligence Collaboration: Investigating the Path Toward Productive Delegation. *Information Systems Research*, *33*(2), 678–696. DOI: 10.1287/isre.2021.1079

Furendal, M., & Jebari, K. (2023). The Future of Work: Augmentation or Stunting? *Philosophy & Technology*, *36*(2). Advance online publication. DOI: 10.1007/s13347-023-00631-w

Gallagher, S. (Ed.). (2011). *The Oxford handbook of the self*. Oxford Handbooks Online.

Garcia, M. B. (2025). The Paradox of Artificial Creativity: Challenges and Opportunities of Generative AI Artistry. *Creativity Research Journal*, *37*(4), 755–768. DOI: 10.1080/10400419.2024.2354622

Gaut, B. (2010). The philosophy of creativity. *Philosophy Compass*, *5*(12), 1034–1046. DOI: 10.1111/j.1747-9991.2010.00351.x

Gazi, M. A. I., Rahman, M. K. H., Masud, A., Al, , & Amin, M. Bin, Chaity, N. S., Senathirajah, A. R. bin S., & Abdullah, M. (2024). AI Capability and Sustainable Performance: Unveiling the Mediating Effects of Organizational Creativity and Green Innovation with Knowledge Sharing Culture as a Moderator. *Sustainability (Switzerland), 16*(17). Advance online publication. DOI: 10.3390/su16177466

George, A. S., Baskar, T., & Pandey, D. (2024). Establishing Global AI Accountability : Training Data Transparency, Copyright, and Misinformation Partners Universal Innovative Research Publication (PUIRP) Establishing Global AI Accountability : Training Data Transparency, Copyright, and Misinform. *Partners Universal Innovative Research Publication*, *2*(3), 75–91. DOI: 10.5281/zenodo.11659602

Gervais, D. (2020). The machine as author. *Iowa Law Review*, *105*(5), 2053–2106. https://papers.ssrn.com/sol3/papers.cfm?abstract_id=3359524

Gill, R., & Pratt, A. (2008). In the social factory? Immaterial labour, precariousness and cultural work. *Theory, Culture & Society*, *25*(7–8), 1–30. DOI: 10.1177/0263276408097794

Glăveanu, V. P. (2014). Distributed creativity: what is it? In *Distributed creativity: Thinking outside the box of the creative individual* (pp. 1–13). Springer International Publishing.

Goodfellow, I., Pouget-Abadie, J., Mirza, M., Xu, B., Warde-Farley, D., Ozair, S., Courville, A., & Bengio, Y. (2014).

Gorski, A. T., Gligorea, I., Gorski, H., & Oancea, R. (2023). Navigating the disruptive challenges and opportunities of digital transformation in the labour market: Upskilling and reskilling for the fourth industrial revolution. In *International conference Knowledge-Based Organization* (Vol. 29, No. 3).

Grilli, L., & Pedota, M. (2024). Creativity and artificial intelligence: A multilevel perspective. *Creativity and Innovation Management*, *33*(2), 234–247. DOI: 10.1111/caim.12580

Guilford, J. P. (1950). Creativity. *The American Psychologist*, *5*(9), 444–454. DOI: 10.1037/h0063487 PMID: 14771441

Gunkel, D. J. (2018). *The machine question: Critical perspectives on AI, robots, and ethics*. MIT Press., DOI: 10.7551/mitpress/8975.001.0001

Gurel, E. (2025). AI-driven experiences in cultural and creative industries: A review of literature and development of a multifaceted framework. *Service Industries Journal*, *2069*, 1–40. DOI: 10.1080/02642069.2025.2542822

Han, H., Liu, Z., Li, J., & Zeng, Z. (2024). Challenges in remote sensing based climate and crop monitoring: Navigating the complexities using AI. *Journal of Cloud Computing (Heidelberg, Germany)*, *13*(1), 1–14.

Han, S., Kelly, E., Nikou, S., & Svee, E. O. (2022). Aligning artificial intelligence with human values: Reflections from a phenomenological perspective. *AI & Society*, *37*(4), 1383–1395. DOI: 10.1007/s00146-021-01247-4

Hasan, M., Haque, M. A., Nishat, S. S., & Hossain, M. M. (2024). Upskilling and reskilling in a rapidly changing job market: Strategies for organizations to maintain workforce agility and adaptability. *European Journal of Business and Management Research*, *9*(6), 118–126.

Hemmer, P., Schemmer, M., Kühl, N., Vössing, M., & Satzger, G. (2025). Complementarity in human-AI collaboration: Concept, sources, and evidence. *European Journal of Information Systems*. Advance online publication. DOI: 10.1080/0960085X.2025.2475962

Hemmer, P., Westphal, M., Schemmer, M., Vetter, S., Vössing, M., & Satzger, G. (2023). Human-AI Collaboration: The Effect of AI Delegation on Human Task Performance and Task Satisfaction. *International Conference on Intelligent User Interfaces, Proceedings IUI*, 453–463. https://doi.org/DOI: 10.1145/3581641.3584052

Henriksen, D., Mishra, P., & Stern, R. (2024). Creative Learning for Sustainability in a World of AI : Action, . *Multidisciplinary Digital Publishing Institute*, 1–20. https://doi.org/DOI: 10.3390/ su16114451

Hesmondhalgh, D., & Baker, S. (2011). 'A very complicated version of freedom': Conditions and experiences of creative labour in three cultural industries. Variant: cross currents in culture, 41, 34-38.

Hesmondhalgh, D. (2021). *The cultural industries* (4th ed.). SAGE Publications.

Hesmondhalgh, D., & Baker, S. (2013). *Creative labour: Media work in three cultural industries*. Routledge.

Hines, A., & Bishop, P. (2015). *Thinking about the future: Guidelines for strategic foresight* (2nd ed.). Hinesight.

Hodgkinson, G. P., & Healey, M. P. (2011). Psychological foundations of dynamic capabilities. *Strategic Management Journal*, *32*(13), 1500–1516.

Hofstede, G., Hofstede, G. J., & Minkov, M. (2010). *Cultures and organizations: Software of the mind* (3rd ed.). McGraw-Hill.

Holford, W. D. (2019). The future of human creative knowledge work within the digital economy. *Futures*, *105*, 143–154.

Hollan, J., Hutchins, E., & Kirsh, D. (2000). Distributed cognition. *ACM Transactions on Computer-Human Interaction*, *7*(2), 174–196. DOI: 10.1145/353485.353487

Holt, D. (2004). *How brands become icons: The principles of cultural branding*. Harvard Business School Press.

Holt, D., & Cameron, D. (2010). *Cultural strategy: Using innovative ideologies to build breakthrough brands*. Oxford University Press.

Howkins, J. (2002). The creative economy: How people make money from ideas. Penguin UK.

Huang, M.-H., & Rust, R. T. (2021). https://uk.sagepub.com/en-gb/eur/the-cultural-industries/book250830

Huang, Y., & Wang, H. (2025). Chinese engineering students' perceived emotional experiences in AI-mediated education: An expectancy-value theory (EVT) perspective. *Learning and Motivation*, *92*, 102180.

Hughes, R. T., Zhu, L., & Bednarz, T. (2021). Generative Adversarial Networks–Enabled Human–Artificial Intelligence Collaborative Applications for Creative and Design Industries: A Systematic Review of Current Approaches and Trends. *Frontiers in Artificial Intelligence*, *4*(April), 1–17. DOI: 10.3389/frai.2021.604234 PMID: 33997773

Hutchins, E. (1995). *Cognition in the Wild*. MIT press.

Hutson, J. (2025). Human-AI Collaboration in Writing: A Multidimensional Framework for Creative and Intellectual Authorship. *International Journal of Changes in Education*. https://doi.org/DOI: 10.47852/bonviewijce52024908

Ivcevic, Z., & Brackett, M. (2015). Emotional creativity: The generation and experience of novel emotional responses. *Creativity Research Journal*, *27*(1), 1–8. DOI: 10.1080/10400419.2015.992676

Jenkins, H. (2006). Convergence Culture: Where Old and New Media Collide. NYU Press. https://www.jstor.org/stable/j.ctt9qffwr

Johannessen, J. A. (2020). *Artificial intelligence, automation and the future of competence at work*. Routledge.

Kahneman, D., Lovallo, D., & Sibony, O. (2011). Before you make that big decision. *Harvard Business Review*, *89*(6), 50–60. PMID: 21714386

Kant, I. (2000). *Critique of the power of judgment* (Guyer, P., Ed.). Cambridge University Press. (Original work published 1790), DOI: 10.1017/CBO9780511804656

Kasparov, G. (2021). *How life imitates chess*. Random House.

Kattel, R., Lember, V., & Tõnurist, P. (2020). Collaborative innovation and human-machine networks. *Public Management Review*, *22*(11), 1652–1673.

Kaufman, J. C., & Glăveanu, V. P. (2019). A review of creativity theories: What questions are we trying to answer?.

Kirkby, A., Baumgarth, C., & Henseler, J. (2025). Welcome, new brand colleague! A conceptual framework for efficient and effective human–AI co-creation for creative brand voice. *Journal of Brand Management*, *32*(5), 385–399. DOI: 10.1057/s41262-025-00387-y

Kolb, D. A. (2014). *Experiential learning: Experience as the source of learning and development*. FT press.

Korzynski, P., Kim, S., & Egan, T. (2024). Bridging human resource development processes through generative Artificial Intelligence. *Human Resource Development Quarterly*, *35*(3), 247–256. DOI: 10.1002/hrdq.21551

Kozma, R. B. (2011). Transforming education: Assessing and teaching 21st century skills. *Journal of Educational Technology & Society*, *14*(3), 1–3.

Krinkin, K., Shichkina, Y., & Ignatyev, A. (2023). Co-evolutionary hybrid intelligence is a key concept for the world intellectualization. *Kybernetes*, *52*(9), 2907–2923.

Kumar, A., Palta, P., Palta, A., Dhanka, S., Bansal, R., Fahlevi, M., Rabby, F., & Aljuaid, M. (2025). Dielectric characterization of sugar mill wastewater and its impact on soil properties in the khadar and bangar regions. *Scientific Reports*, *15*(1), 20802. PMID: 40595184

Lakshmi, S., Durgude, U., & Chitra, V. (2024). THE ROLE OF UPSKILLING AND RESKILLING FOR TALENT TRANSFORMATION IN THE ERA OF AI; THEORETICAL FRAMEWORK AND FUTURE RESEARCH DIRECTIONS. *Weser Books*, 198.

Latour, B. (2005). *Reassembling the social: An introduction to actor–network-theory*. Oxford University Press.

Lee, J., Kim, J., & Lee, H. (2025). Diffusedesigner: Sketch-based controllable clothing image generation. *Fashion and Textiles*, *12*(1), 26.

Leon, C., Lipuma, J., & Oviedo-Torres, X. (2025). Artificial intelligence in STEM education: A transdisciplinary framework for engagement and innovation. *Frontiers in Education, 10*(July), 1–18. DOI: 10.3389/feduc.2025.1619888

Leong, W. Y. (2025). Ethical and philosophical perspectives on artificial intelligence-generated art. *International Journal of Social Sciences and Artistic Innovations, 5*(2), 7–20. DOI: 10.35745/ijssai2025v05.02.0007

Leon, R. D. (2023). Employees' reskilling and upskilling for industry 5.0: Selecting the best professional development programmes. *Technology in Society, 75*, 102393.

Li, C., Wang, J., Zhang, Y., Zhu, K., Hou, W., Lian, J., . . . Xie, X. (2023). Large language models understand and can be enhanced by emotional stimuli. *arXiv preprint arXiv:2307.11760.*

Li, L. (2024). Correction to: Reskilling and Upskilling the Future-ready Workforce for Industry 4.0 and Beyond (Information Systems Frontiers, (2024), 26, 5, (1697-1712),). *Information Systems Frontiers, 26*(5), 1713. https://doi.org/DOI: 10.1007/s10796-022-10308-y

Licklider, J. C. (2008). Man-computer symbiosis. *IRE transactions on human factors in electronics*, (1), 4-11.

Liestøl, G. (2021). Situated simulations and augmented reality: Design principles and empirical studies. *Digital Creativity, 32*(4), 227–244. DOI: 10.1007/978-1-4614-0064-6_14

Li, L. (2024). Reskilling and upskilling the future-ready workforce for industry 4.0 and beyond. *Information Systems Frontiers, 26*(5), 1697–1712. PMID: 35855776

Lincoln, Y. S., & Guba, E. G. (1985). Naturalistic inquiry. *Sage (Atlanta, Ga.).*

Liu, Z. (2023). Cultural bias in large language models: A comprehensive analysis and mitigation strategies. *Journal of Transcultural Communication, 3*(2), 224–244.

Luckin, R. (2018). *Machine Learning and Human Intelligence. The future of education for the 21st century*. UCL institute of education press.

Luckin, R., Holmes, W., Griffiths, M., & Forcier, L. B. (2016). *Intelligence unleashed: An argument for AI in education*. Pearson.

Lustig, C., Pine, K., Nardi, B., Irani, L., Lee, M. K., Nafus, D., & Sandvig, C. (2016, May). Algorithmic authority: the ethics, politics, and economics of algorithms that interpret, decide, and manage. In *Proceedings of the 2016 CHI Conference Extended Abstracts on Human Factors in Computing Systems* (pp. 1057-1062).

Mahfouz, J., & Awad, T. (2021). Strategic foresight for school leaders. *Educational Management Administration & Leadership*, *49*(6), 885–905.

Martin, K. (2019). Ethical implications and accountability of algorithms. *Journal of Business Ethics*, •••, 835–850.

McKnight, D. H., Carter, M., Thatcher, J. B., & Clay, P. F. (2021). Trust in a specific technology. *ACM Transactions on Management Information Systems*, *12*(2), 1–25. DOI: 10.1145/3447534

Microsoft. (2023). Microsoft Copilot: Your AI-powered productivity assistant. https://www.microsoft.com/en-us/microsoft-copilot

Mitra, A., Seetharaman, A., & Maddulety, K. (2024). Adoption of Artificial Intelligence Enabling Value Creation in Business. In *2024 4th International Conference on Robotics, Automation and Artificial Intelligence (RAAI)* (pp. 213-220). IEEE.

Mittal, G., & Bansal, R. (2023). Driving Force Behind Consumer Brand Engagement: The Metaverse. In *Cultural Marketing and Metaverse for Consumer Engagement* (pp. 164-181). IGI Global.

Mittal, G., & Bansal, R. (2023). Driving force behind consumer brand engagement: The metaverse. In *Cultural Marketing and Metaverse for Consumer Engagement* (pp. 164–181). IGI Global.

Mittal, G., Bansal, R., Fahlevi, M., & Aziz, A. L. (2025). Mapping the research patterns on fuzzy decision-making trial and evaluation laboratory technique in marketing: A bibliometric analysis. *Social Sciences & Humanities Open*, *12*, 101691.

Mohamed, M., Stankosky, M., & Murray, A. (2004). Applying knowledge management principles to enhance cross-functional team performance. *Journal of Knowledge Management*, *8*(3), 127–142.

Mollah, M. A., Rana, M., Amin, M. B., Sony, M. A. A. M., Rahaman, M. A., & Fenyves, V. (2024). Examining the role of AI-augmented HRM for sustainable performance: Key determinants for digital culture and organizational strategy. *Sustainability*, *16*(24), 10843.

Mould, O., Vorley, T., & Liu, Y. (2020). Rethinking creative clusters: Towards new typologies of geographic assemblages. Environment and Planning A: Economy and Space, 52(2), 305–326.https://www.taylorfrancis.com/chapters/edit/10.4324/9781315712598-9/freelancers-freelancing-creative-economy?context=ubx

Mumford, M. D., Hunter, S. T., & Vert, A. (2019). Creativity in organizations: A systems perspective. In *The Oxford handbook of creativity, innovation, and entrepreneurship* (2nd ed., pp. 3–22). Oxford University Press.

Murthy, Y. S., Rabby, F., Bansal, R., & Chakravorty, C. (2025). Building Resilient Brands: Harnessing Influencers, Evangelists, and Data-Driven Strategies. In *Data Analytics and Influencer Marketing for Cultivating Brand Evangelism and Affinity* (pp. 71-102). IGI Global Scientific Publishing.

Murthy, Y. S., Bansal, R., Chodisetty, R. C. M., Chakravorty, C., & Sai, K. P. (2025). Transforming Minds AI and Machine Learning Applications in Cognitive Neuroscience. In *Transforming Neuropsychology and Cognitive Psychology With AI and Machine Learning* (pp. 107–128). IGI Global Scientific Publishing.

Napoli, P. M. (2019). *Social media and the public interest: Media regulation in the disinformation age*. Columbia university press.

Navarro-Meneses, F. J., & Pablo-Marti, F. (2025). Reimagining human agency in ai-driven futures: A co-evolutionary scenario framework from aviation. *European Journal of Futures Research*, *13*(1), 1–17.

Nguyen, T., & Elbanna, A. (2025). Understanding Human-AI Augmentation in the Workplace: A Review and a Future Research Agenda. *Information Systems Frontiers*. Advance online publication. DOI: 10.1007/s10796-025-10591-5

Nieborg, D. B., & Poell, T. (2018). The platformization of cultural production. *New Media & Society*, *20*(11), 4275–4292.

Nijboer, F. (2015). Technology transfer of brain-computer interfaces as assistive technology: Barriers and opportunities. *Annals of Physical and Rehabilitation Medicine*, *58*(1), 35–38. PMID: 25595535

Nisbett, R. E., & Masuda, T. (2013). Culture and point of view. In *Biological and cultural bases of human inference* (pp. 49–70). Psychology Press.

Nonaka, L., Takeuchi, H., & Umemoto, K. (1996). A theory of organizational knowledge creation. *International Journal of Technology Management*, *11*(7-8), 833–845.

Northouse, P. G. (2021). *Leadership: Theory and practice* (9th ed.). Sage Publications.

OECD. (2022). *AI in education: Ethical and policy challenges*. OECD Publishing.

Oham, C., & Ejike, O. G. (2024). Creativity and collaboration in creative industries: Proposing a conceptual model for enhanced team dynamics. *Magna Scientia Advanced Research and Reviews*, *12*(1), 185–194. DOI: 10.30574/msarr.2024.12.1.0172

Painoli, A. K., Bansal, R., Singh, R., & Kukreti, A. (2021). Impact of Digital Marketing on the Buying Behavior of Youth With Special Reference to Uttarakhand State. In *Big Data Analytics for Improved Accuracy, Efficiency, and Decision Making in Digital Marketing* (pp. 162-182). IGI Global.

Parasuraman, R., & Manzey, D. H. (2010). Complacency and bias in human use of automation. *Human Factors*, *52*(3), 381–410. DOI: 10.1177/0018720810376052

Patil, D., Rane, N. L., & Rane, J. (2024). Acceptance of ChatGPT and generative artificial intelligence in several business sectors: Key factors, challenges, and implementation strategies. *The Future Impact of ChatGPT on Several Business Sectors*, *5*(2), 50–70. DOI: 10.70593/978-81-981367-8-7_5

Peeters, M. M. M., van Diggelen, J., van den Bosch, K., Bronkhorst, A., Neerincx, M. A., Schraagen, J. M., & Raaijmakers, S. (2021). Hybrid collective intelligence in a human–AI society. *AI & Society*, *36*(1), 217–238. DOI: 10.1007/s00146-020-01005-y

Perboli, G., Simionato, N., & Pratali, S. (2025). Navigating the AI Regulatory Landscape: Balancing Innovation, Ethics, and Global Governance. Economic and Political Studies. (in press). *Economic and Political Studies*, *13*(4), 367–397. DOI: 10.1080/20954816.2025.2569584

Peters, M. A., Jandrić, P., & Hayes, S. (2019). The digital university: A new model for the twenty-first century. *Educational Philosophy and Theory*, *51*(1), 1–7.

Plassmann, H., Venkatraman, V., Huettel, S., & Yoon, C. (2015). Consumer neuroscience: Applications, challenges, and possible solutions. *JMR, Journal of Marketing Research*, *52*(4), 427–435.

Przegalinska, A., Triantoro, T., Kovbasiuk, A., Ciechanowski, L., Freeman, R. B., & Sowa, K. (2025). Collaborative AI in the workplace: Enhancing organizational performance through resource-based and task-technology fit perspectives. *International Journal of Information Management*, *81*. Advance online publication. DOI: 10.1016/j.ijinfomgt.2024.102853

Puccio, G. J., Mance, M., & Murdock, M. C. (2018). *Creative leadership: Skills that drive change* (3rd ed.). Sage Publications.

Rabby, F., Murthy, Y. S., & Bansal, R. (2025). Brand Evangelism in the Digital Era: The Impact of Data-Driven Influencer Marketing. *Journal of Open Innovation*, •••, 100552.

Radjou, N., Prabhu, J., & Ahuja, S. (2012). *Jugaad innovation: Think frugal, be flexible, generate breakthrough growth*. John Wiley & Sons.

Rahman, K. T., Bansal, R., & Pruthi, N. (2023). Consumer adoption of technologies: A mindset-oriented approach. In Contemporary Studies of Risks in Emerging Technology, Part B (pp. 243-255). Emerald Publishing Limited.

Raja, M., Swamy, T. N. V. R. L., Das, S., Bansal, R., Fahlevi, M., & Aziz, A. L. (2025). Does human resource information system influence performance management? *Cogent Business & Management*, *12*(1), 2438862.

Rane, N. L., Paramesha, M., Choudhary, S. P., & Rane, J. (2024). Artificial intelligence, machine learning, and deep learning for advanced business strategies: A review. *Partners Universal International Innovation Journal*, *2*(3), 147–171.

Rastogi, S., & Pandita, D. (2025). Driving entrepreneurial success: Navigating AI-driven transformation through workforce agility and sustainability. *Journal of Innovation and Entrepreneurship*, *14*(1). Advance online publication. DOI: 10.1186/s13731-025-00554-0

Ren, M., Chen, N., & Qiu, H. (2023). Human-machine collaborative decision-making: An evolutionary roadmap based on cognitive intelligence. *International Journal of Social Robotics*, *15*(7), 1101–1114.

Ren, X. (2025). The Impact of Generative AI-Driven Job Reshaping on Creativity Sustainability. *The Frontiers of Society. Science and Technology*, *7*(7), 5–21. DOI: 10.25236/FSST.2025.070703

Rezwana, J., & Maher, M. Lou. (2023). Designing Creative AI Partners with COFI: A Framework for Modeling Interaction in Human-AI Co-Creative Systems. *ACM Transactions on Computer-Human Interaction*, *30*(5). Advance online publication. DOI: 10.1145/3519026

Rezwana, J., & Maher, M. Lou. (2025). An Exploration of Mental Models of AI in Human-AI Co-Creativity: A Framework and Insights. *ACM Transactions on Interactive Intelligent Systems*, *15*(4). Advance online publication. DOI: 10.1145/3769072

Rilliard, A., De Moraes, J. A., Erickson, D., Guerry, M., Hönemann, A., Lee, T., & Shochi, T. (2025). Cross-cultural dimensions organizing prosodic attitudes reception. *Journal of Speech Sciences*, *14*, e025012.

Runco, M. A., & Acar, S. (2024). Assessing divergent thinking: recent advances. *Handbook of Creativity Assessment*, 128-147.

Runco, M. A., & Jaeger, G. J. (2012). The standard definition of creativity. *Creativity Research Journal*, *24*(1), 92–96. DOI: 10.1080/10400419.2012.650092

Saini, S., & Bansal, R. (2025). Parasocial relationships and self-disclosure: Strengthening brand image through brand attitude in premium cosmetics. *Journal of Promotion Management, 31*(2), 337–366.

Salma, Z., Hijón-Neira, R., & Pizarro, C. (2025). Designing Co-Creative Systems: Five Paradoxes in Human–AI Collaboration. *Information (Switzerland), 16*(10), 1–19. DOI: 10.3390/info16100909

Samuelson, P. (2023). Generative AI and copyright: A brief introduction. *Communications of the ACM, 66*(7), 23–25. DOI: 10.1145/3609380

Sarkar, S., & Cooper, A. (2022). Creativity in the age of artificial intelligence: User perceptions of human–AI collaboration. *The Journal of Creative Behavior*. Advance online publication. DOI: 10.1002/jocb.632

Sarma, M., Ghahremani, P., Povey, D., Goel, N. K., Sarma, K. K., & Dehak, N. (2018, September). Emotion Identification from Raw Speech Signals Using DNNs. In *Interspeech* (pp. 3097-3101).

Satar, M. S., Aggarwal, D., Bansal, R., & Alarifi, G. (2023). Mapping the Knowledge Structure and Unveiling the Research Trends in Social Entrepreneurship and Inclusive Development: A Bibliometric Analysis. *Sustainability, 15*(7), 5626.

Schwartz, P. (1996). *The art of the long view: Planning for the future in an uncertain world.* Currency Doubleday.

Searle, J. R. (1980). Minds, brains, and programs. *Behavioral and Brain Sciences, 3*(3), 417–457. DOI: 10.1017/S0140525X00005756

Selwyn, N. (2023). The critique of digital education: Time for a (post) critical turn. In *Rethinking sociological critique in contemporary education* (pp. 48-62). Routledge.

Senge, P. (2018). *The fifth discipline: The art & practice of the learning organization* (rev. ed.). Doubleday.

Shankar, A., Elliott, R., & Goulding, C. (2001). Understanding consumption: Contributions from a narrative perspective. *Journal of Marketing Management, 17*(3–4), 429–453.

Shen, Y., Kang, B., & Münch, F. (2025). Human-Centered AI in Design: Examining Educational Paradigms for Creativity and Responsibility. *Lecture Notes in Computer Science, 15799 LNCS*, 64–76. https://doi.org/DOI: 10.1007/978-3-031-93236-6_5

Shneiderman, B. (2020). Human-centered artificial intelligence: Reliable, safe & trustworthy. *International Journal of Human-Computer Interaction, 36*(6), 495–504. DOI: 10.1080/10447318.2020.1741118

Shneiderman, B. (2022). *Human-centered AI.* Oxford University Press.

Shrestha, Y. R., Ben-Menahem, S., & Von Krogh, G. (2019). Organizational decision-making structures in AI age. *California Management Review, 61*(4), 66–83. DOI: 10.1177/0008125619862581

Simon, H. A. (1972). Theories of bounded rationality. *Decision and organization, 1*(1), 161-176.

Simon, H. A. (1983). Why should machines learn? In *Machine learning* (pp. 25–37). Morgan Kaufmann.

Singh, R., Singh, V. P., Rabby, F., Bansal, R., & Gupta, N. K. (2025). The Road to Sustainable Tourism: Financial Mechanisms for Green Project Development. In *Regenerative Tourism for Social Development* (pp. 235-254). IGI Global Scientific Publishing.

Song, Y., Zhou, H., Wei, J., & Qin, J. (2025). Research on the Application of Augmented Reality Technology in Museum Navigation System. [ACS]. *Journal OfArts and Cultural Studies, 4*(1), 257–270. DOI: 10.5220/0013632200004671

Strubell, E., Ganesh, A., & McCallum, A. (2019). Energy and policy considerations for deep learning in NLP. *Proceedings of the 57th Annual Meeting of the Association for Computational Linguistics*, 3645–3650. https://doi.org/DOI: 10.48550/arXiv.1906.02243

Sun, T. Q., & Medaglia, R. (2019). Mapping the challenges of artificial intelligence in the public sector: Evidence from public health. *Government Information Quarterly, 36*(2), 273–282. DOI: 10.1016/j.giq.2018.09.008

Tariq, B., Ashraf, M. R., & Rashid, U. (2025). Ethical Imperatives in AI Design: A Comprehensive Framework for Risk Mitigation and Responsible Innovation. *Ubiquitous Technology Journal, 1*(2), 61–73. DOI: 10.71346/utj.v1i2.23

Toumi, K., Girandola, F., & Bonnardel, N. (2021). Technologies for Supporting Creativity in Design: A View of Physical and Virtual Environments with Regard to Cognitive and Social Processes. *Creativity, 8*(1), 189–212. DOI: 10.2478/ctra-2021-0012

Trist, E. L., & Bamforth, K. W. (1951). Social and psychological consequences of longwall method. *Human Relations, 4*(1), 3–38. DOI: 10.1177/001872675100400101

Tryon, C. (2013). *On-demand culture: Digital delivery and the future of movies.* Rutgers University Press., https://www.jstor.org/stable/j.ctt5hjcmk

Tuomi, I. (2022). Artificial intelligence, 21st century competences, and socio-emotional learning in education: More than high-risk? *European Journal of Education*, *57*(4), 601–619.

Uhl-Bien, M. (2006). Relational leadership theory. *The Leadership Quarterly*, *17*(6), 654–676. DOI: 10.1016/j.leaqua.2006.10.007

UNCTAD. (2022). Creative economy outlook 2022: Trends in international trade in creative industries. United Nations Conference on Trade and Development. https://unctad.org/publication/creative-economy-outlook-2022

UNESCO. (2021). Recommendation on the ethics of artificial intelligence. https://unesdoc.unesco.org/ark:/48223/pf0000381137

UNESCO. (2021). *Recommendation on the ethics of artificial intelligence*. UNESCO Publishing.

UNESCO. (2021). Recommendation on the Ethics of Artificial Intelligence. United Nations Educational, Scientific and Cultural Organization. https://www.unesco.org/en/articles/recommendation-ethics-artificial-intelligence

UNESCO. (2023). AI and the future of work. https://en.unesco.org/artificial-intelligence/future-of-work

UNESCO. (2023). *Guidelines for AI and the futures of education*. UNESCO Publishing.

Unilever. (2022). AI for good: Responsible technology in sustainability. https://www.unilever.com/planet-and-society/technology-and-innovation/

Vaccari, C., & Chadwick, A. (2020). Deepfakes and disinformation: Exploring the impact on trust in news and democracy. *Social Media + Society*, *6*(1), 1–13. DOI: 10.1177/2056305120903408

Vaccaro, M., Almaatouq, A., & Malone, T. (2024). When combinations of humans and AI are useful: A systematic review and meta-analysis. *Nature Human Behaviour*, *8*(12), 2293–2303. DOI: 10.1038/s41562-024-02024-1 PMID: 39468277

Vallor, S. (2016). *Technology and the virtues*. Oxford University Press.

Vaswani, A., Shazeer, N., Parmar, N., Uszkoreit, J., Jones, L., Gomez, A. N., Kaiser, Ł., & Polosukhin, I. (2017). Attention is all you need. *Advances in Neural Information Processing Systems*, *30*. Advance online publication. DOI: 10.48550/arXiv.1706.03762

Venkadesh, P., Divya, S. V., & Kumar, K. S. (2024). Unlocking AI Creativity: A Multi-Agent Approach with CrewAI. *Journal of Trends in Computer Science and Smart Technology*, *6*(4), 338–356. DOI: 10.36548/jtcsst.2024.4.002

Venkatesh, V., Thong, J. Y. L., & Xu, X. (2012). Consumer acceptance and use of information technology: Extending the unified theory. *Management Information Systems Quarterly*, *36*(1), 157–178.

Venugopal, K., Das, S., Gopalakrishna, V., & Bansal, R. (2024). Customer Consciousness Towards Food Wastage in the Indian Hospitality Industry. In *Sustainable Disposal Methods of Food Wastes in Hospitality Operations* (pp. 38–56). IGI Global Scientific Publishing.

Verganti, R., Vendraminelli, L., & Iansiti, M. (2020). Innovation and Design in the Age of Artificial Intelligence. *Journal of Product Innovation Management*, *37*(3), 212–227. DOI: 10.1111/jpim.12523

Vinchon, F., Lubart, T., Bartolotta, S., Gironnay, V., Botella, M., Bourgeois-Bougrine, S., & Gaggioli, A. (2023). Artificial Intelligence & Creativity: A Manifesto for Collaboration. *The Journal of Creative Behavior*, *57*(4), 472–484. DOI: 10.1002/jocb.597

Virvou, M. (2023). Artificial Intelligence and User Experience in reciprocity: Contributions and state of the art. *Intelligent Decision Technologies*, *17*(1), 73–125. DOI: 10.3233/IDT-230092

Waks, L. J. (2018). Massive open online courses and the future of higher education. In *Contemporary Technologies in Education: Maximizing Student Engagement, Motivation, and Learning* (pp. 183–213). Springer International Publishing.

Wang, N., Kim, H., Peng, J., & Wang, J. (2025). Exploring creativity in human–AI co-creation: A comparative study across design experience. *Frontiers of Computer Science*, *7*. Advance online publication. DOI: 10.3389/fcomp.2025.1672735

Wang, W., & Siau, K. (2019). Artificial intelligence, machine learning, automation, robotics, future of work and future of humanity: A review and research agenda. [JDM]. *Journal of Database Management*, *30*(1), 61–79.

Wasosa, H. (2025). Influence of Psychological Well-Being and School Factors on Delinquency, During the Covid-19 Period Among Secondary School Students in Selected Schools in Nakuru County : Kenya. [IJRISS]. *International Journal of Research and Innovation in Social Science*, *VII*(2454), 1175–1189. DOI: 10.47772/IJRISS

Wei, X., Wang, L., Lee, L. K., & Liu, R. (2025). The effects of generative AI on collaborative problem-solving and team creativity performance in digital story creation: An experimental study. *International Journal of Educational Technology in Higher Education, 22*(1). Advance online publication. DOI: 10.1186/s41239-025-00526-0

West, D. M. (2018). *The future of work: Robots, AI, and automation*. Bloomsbury Publishing USA.

Westerman, G., Bonnet, D., & McAfee, A. (2021). Leading digital transformation. *MIT Sloan Management Review, 62*(3), 35–42.

Wilson, H. J., & Daugherty, P. R. (2023). Collaborative intelligence. Harvard Business Review. https://hbr.org/2023/09/collaborative-intelligence-humans-and-ai-as-business-partners

Wong, P. H. (2020). Cultural Differences as Excuses? Human Rights and Cultural Values in Global Ethics and Governance of AI. *Philosophy & Technology, 33*(4), 705–715. DOI: 10.1007/s13347-020-00413-8

Woolley, A. W. (2025). Generative AI and collaboration: opportunities for cultivating collective intelligence. *Journal of Organization Design*. https://doi.org/DOI: 10.1007/s41469-025-00199-z

World Economic Forum. (2023). The future of jobs report 2023. https://www.weforum.org/reports/the-future-of-jobs-report-2023/

Wu, S., Liu, Y., Ruan, M., Chen, S., & Xie, X.-Y. (2025). Human-generative AI collaboration enhances task performance but undermines human's intrinsic motivation. *Scientific Reports, 15*(1). Advance online publication. DOI: 10.1038/s41598-025-98385-2 PMID: 40301425

Xu, G., Murthy, S. V., & Jia, B. (2025). Enhancing Intuitive Decision-Making and Reliance Through Human–AI Collaboration: A Review. *Informatics (MDPI), 12*(4). Advance online publication. DOI: 10.3390/informatics12040135

Xu, X., Arshad, M. A., He, Y., Liu, H., Chen, Q., & Yang, J. (2025). From Skilled Workers to Smart Talent: AI-Driven Workforce Transformation in the Construction Industry. *Buildings (Basel, Switzerland), 15*(14). Advance online publication. DOI: 10.3390/buildings15142552

Yin, R. K. (2018). *Case study research and applications* (6th ed.). Sage Publications.

Yoo, Y., Henfridsson, O., & Lyytinen, K. (2010). The new organizing logic of digital innovation: An agenda for information systems research. *Information Systems Research, 21*(4), 724–735. DOI: 10.1287/isre.1100.0322

Zallio, M., Ike, C. B., & Chivăran, C. (2025). Designing Artificial Intelligence : Exploring Inclusion, Emerging Technologies. *AI*, *6*(7), 25. DOI: 10.3390/ai6070143

Zhang, T., Chen, J., & Brynjolfsson, E. (2023). Creativity in the age of AI. *Management Science*, *69*(6), 3212–3235. DOI: 10.1287/mnsc.2022.4532

Zirar, A., Ali, S. I., & Islam, N. (2023). Worker and workplace Artificial Intelligence (AI) coexistence: Emerging themes and research agenda. *Technovation*, *124*. Advance online publication. DOI: 10.1016/j.technovation.2023.102747

Ziv, L., & Nakash, M. (2025). Behind the Algorithm: International Insights into Data-Driven AI Model Development. *Machine Learning and Knowledge Extraction*, *7*(4), 122. DOI: 10.3390/make7040122

Zuboff, S. (2019). *The age of surveillance capitalism: The fight for a human future at the new frontier of power, edn*. PublicAffairs.

About the Contributors

Fazla Rabby is an accomplished academic and professional with a diverse background in emerging technology, education, management, and AI. Holding a Ph.D. from the University of Southern Queensland, their education includes degrees and diplomas in management, leadership, and information systems from Central Queensland University and the University of Madras. As a Teaching Academic at Macquarie University and Lecturer at Canterbury Institute of Management, Dr. Rabby designs and delivers educational activities, assesses student progress, and contributes to curriculum development. Their role as Academic Director at Stanford Institute of Management and Technology highlights their leadership in stakeholder relationships, business strategies, and HR management. Previously, Dr. Rabby excelled in sales and marketing roles, including Director of Australian Sales and Marketing and Managing Director of Sales Solutions Australia. A prolific researcher and presenter, they focus on blockchain, digital marketing, AI, mental health and well-being and consumer behavior, with upcoming projects on industry innovation and AI in education.

Sweta Thakur is Head of School for School of Information Technology at King's Own Institute. In her role she is looking after the undergraduate and postgraduate courses in Information Technology and Information Systems. She has vast experience of designing and developing new courses in Computer Science, Information Technology, Information Systems and Business Administration with Information Technology specialisation. She is deeply engaged in TEQSA course registration and course accreditation with Australian Computer Society. She is leading the School which requires significant contributions and continuous improvement in teaching and learning ensuring a high standard of education by managing the academic and non-academic staff. Her research areas of interest are Digital Image Processing, Medical Imaging, Machine Learning, Educational Technology, Reflective Practice, WIL for Computing, Big Data in Curriculum etc.,

She is a member of ACS, IEEE, HERDSA and KOI's representative for ACEN and CAULLT.

Shafiqur Rahman is the Head of the Department of Business Administration at the International Open University in The Gambia, working remotely from Australia. Rahman has been teaching all marketing and Management courses. Rahman holds an MBA from Dhaka University, a PhD (Branding and CSR) from Macquarie University, and completed a Post-Doctoral Fellowship at the University Malaysia Perlis, Fundamentals of CaseTeaching from Harvard University. Rahman's significant works include co-authoring with Philip Kotler on 'Essentials of Modern Marketing' and publishing 33 research papers, 11 book/book chapters and presenting 43 conference papers. Rahman has coordinated 32 international conferences, mentored 11 PhD and master's students, and served on several editorial boards as a reviewer of a Q1-ranked journal.

Nishita Pruthi is an Assistant Professor at the Asian School of Business, part of the Asian Education Group, Noida. Awarded with Ph.D. at the Institute of Management Studies and Research, Maharshi Dayanand University, Rohtak, Haryana, she exemplifies academic excellence and scholarly dedication. Dr. Pruthi has an impressive portfolio of nine research papers published in prestigious journals, with six indexed in Scopus, Web of Science, UGCCARE, and ABDC. Her contributions extend to authoring thirteen chapters in edited volumes published by globally renowned publishers such as Emerald, Bentham Science, and IGI Global. Additionally, she has co-edited two books published by IGI Global, USA, reflecting her versatility and scholarly rigor. Her academic journey is further distinguished by her active participation in twelve national and international conferences hosted by premier institutions, including IIM Indore, IIM Jammu, IIM Kozhikode, and Deakin University. Dedicated to fostering a transformative learning environment, Dr. Pruthi inspires critical thinking, ad creativity, ensuring her students are well-prepared to excel in dynamic academic and professional landscapes.

Mukesh Singla, An Academician and prolific researcher, currently working as Dean, faculty of Engineering and Technology and Controller of examinations in Baba Mastnath University Asthal Bohar Rohtak. He has more than 22 years of teaching and research experience in renowned Institutions. His area of research is Computer Network, AIML, Data Science. Dr. Mukesh Singla received his graduation, post graduation and PhD in the field of Computer Science and Engineering. He has published more than 50 research articles in reputed journals including Scopus, UGC Care and more than 30 are presented in National and Iternational conferences. Also 7 patents were registered and has edited no. of books. Eighteen research scholars have awarded with PhD degree under his supervision and some are in progress. He has good network and academic collaboration with many institutions all over the India.

***

Randhir Singh Baghel is an Associate Professor in the Faculty of Science and Humanities at Poornima University, Jaipur, India. With over 17 years of extensive experience in teaching, research, and academic administration, he has established himself as a respected educator and researcher. Dr. Baghel has played a pivotal role in academic events, having chaired numerous national and international conferences and technical sessions across his areas of expertise. His contributions to academia extend beyond the classroom, as he actively engages in various research projects that align with contemporary advancements in his field. An accomplished researcher, Dr. Baghel has authored and published more than 22 research papers in esteemed international journals. His work is widely recognized for its relevance and impact, contributing significantly to knowledge in his domain. In addition to his research and teaching, Dr. Baghel is committed to fostering academic excellence and innovation. His dedication to mentoring students and collaborating with colleagues highlights his passion for education and research. He continues to inspire and guide aspiring scholars, ensuring their active participation in meaningful academic pursuits. Dr. Baghel's multifaceted expertise and commitment to his profession make him an integral part of Poornima University's academic community, contributing to its mission of excellence in education and research.

Rohit Bansal is working as Associate Professor in Department of Management Studies in Vaish College of Engineering, Rohtak. He is a perseverant, passionate academician cum seasoned professional. He obtained Ph.D. in Management from Maharshi Dayanand University, Rohtak. With a rich experience of 16 years, he has achieved growth through robust and proactive academic initiatives. He has authored & edited 30 books with renowned national & international publishers including IGI Global USA, Scrivener-Wiley Publishing, De Gruyter, Weser Books, Scholar’s Press, Germany etc. In addition to, Dr. Rohit has published 150 research papers and chapters in journals of repute including Scopus indexed as well as edited books. He has also presented papers in 50 conferences and seminars. His area of interest includes marketing management, organizational behaviour, services marketing, customer engagement, digital marketing, human resource management and organizational development. He is on Editorial Advisory Board as a member in 110 national and international peer reviewed journals. He has acted as session chair in many international conferences.

Pritam Bhaumik is currently an undergraduate student pursuing a Bachelor of Technology in Computer Science and Engineering at Brainware University, India. His research interests focus on the intersection of advanced computing and user experience, specifically in Artificial Intelligence, Machine Learning, and Human-Computer Interaction (HCI). Beyond his academic curriculum, he is actively involved in developing web-based AI applications that integrate intelligent algorithms into practical software solutions. Mr. Bhaumik also demonstrates a strong entrepreneurial spirit as the founder of an AI-based startup, where he applies his technical expertise to create innovative digital products. His work aims to bridge the gap between theoretical AI research and real-world, user-centric utility.

Avya Singh Chirana is a BBA Marketing student at Christ (Deemed to be University), Delhi NCR. Passionate about branding, digital marketing, and consumer behavior, he focuses on skill growth through projects and industry exposure. Driven, disciplined, and creative, he aims to build a strong professional career in marketing.

Suman Das completed his B.tech in ECE and M.Tech in VLSI and Microelectronics from West Bengal University of Technology. He received University gold medal from West Bengal University of Technology for securing 1st position in M.tech. He completed his Ph.D. in Radio Physics and Electronics from University of Calcutta. He has more than 11 years experience in academia. His research interests lie on VLSI, CMOS and beyond CMOS devices.

Deeksha Gupta Ganguly is an accomplished academician with over 14 years of experience spanning academia and industry. She is currently associated with the School of Business and Management, Christ University, Delhi NCR Campus, India. Her professional journey has been shaped by a strong commitment to teaching, research, and institutional development.

Pratibha Giri brings over 15 years of rich academic experience to her role. She is working as Associate Professor in the School of Business and Management at Christ (Deemed to be University), Delhi-NCR. With a strong foundation in management studies, including an MBA from the prestigious Faculty of Management Studies and a Ph.D Dr. Giri has established herself as a versatile scholar and educator. Her research interests span multiple areas of management, including Marketing, Human Resources, Entrepreneurship, and International Trade. Dr. Giri has authored more than 20 research papers published in reputed national and international journals, demonstrating her commitment to contributing to the academic discourse in her field. An active participant in the academic community, Dr. Giri regularly attends national and international level seminars, conferences and workshops to stay at the forefront of developments in management studies. She has also presented research papers at various national and international conferences, further solidifying her reputation as a thought leader in her areas of expertise.

Piali Haldar earned her MBA from the Institute of Rural Management Anand and completed her PhD at Birla Institute of Technology, Mesra. Her core areas of specialization include rural marketing, rural development, branding strategy, and consumer behaviour. With over 20 years of experience in academia and research, she has published extensively in renowned journals listed in ABDC and Scopus. She has authored one textbook on Marketing and edited three academic books. Dr. Haldar has presented her research at numerous national and international conferences and has contributed more than 50 papers to reputed journals, edited volumes, and conference proceedings.

Akansha Jain is a research-oriented education leader and social entrepreneur working at the intersection of future skills, inclusive higher education, and employability. She is the Founder of EFOS.in (Education Future One Stop), Chairperson of EFOS Foundation, and Director (Academics) at EP Infoways, where her initiatives have facilitated 50,000+ verified opportunities and delivered government-funded skilling leading to 7,000 youth placements. A Gold Medalist (M.Com) with a Ph.D. in Forex Risk Management and PGDBA (Finance) from Symbiosis, Pune, she serves as an approved Ph.D. supervisor, editor, and speaker on women's entrepreneurship, AI-enabled education, and outcome-based learning. Her methodological expertise spans mixed-methods research, policy benchmarking, and impact evaluation, with a sustained focus on NEP-aligned, work-integrated education and AI in vocational/higher education. She is associated with Lamrin Tech Skills University, Ropar (Punjab) as professor in school of commerce and management and specially contributing towards industry-linked, skills-first pathways and curriculum innovation and in research domain. She is also Director of School of innovation and entrepreneurship.

Yusuf Kamal is working as an assistant professor at the Institute of Management, University of Lucknow. He has more than 18 years of Academic and Industrial experience, 5 Patents granted by the Government of India, and authored 1 Book and 13 Articles in Journals of International repute. His earned Ph.D. degree is from the Faculty of Commerce (Major- Marketing & Minor- Digital Marketing). He has also invented many Industrial Designs & Patentable Utilities for Social Causes, free from royalty claims for social upliftment. His research statement includes regard to the changing scenario of the business world and methodology, and he has committed to providing technology-intensive business models by 2030. His 2030 vision includes: 1- Exploring the possible untapped sources of energy. 2- Machine automation and

Digital incorporations of novel electronic systems for business efficiency. 3- Reveal the new domains of Intelligent systems. 4- Innovation in Business Management.

Shikha Khullar is an academic and researcher with expertise in Artificial Intelligence, Machine Learning, and their interdisciplinary applications across domains such as healthcare, finance, and agriculture. She has contributed book chapters and research papers to reputed international publishers, including IGI Global and Wiley–Scrivener. Her research interests include AI-powered fraud detection, intelligent systems, and the ethical dimensions of emerging technologies.

Manjit Kour is working as Professor at University Business School at Chandigarh University. She holds a PhD in Business Management from IK Gujral Punjab Technical University, India. She has a good research record with several research papers published in reputed journals. She is an editorial board member and reviewer of many reputed journals including Scopus and ABDC-indexed journals. Her areas of interest include sustainability, green practices, Fintech, online marketing trends and business ethics.

Chahat Malhotra is a Research Scholar at Guru Gobind Singh Indraprastha University, New Delhi, India Her areas of interest include OB/HR with a special focus on achieving work- life balance of employees in various sectors. She has worked as an Assistant professor in GGSIPU affiliated college. She had experience of working as subject matter expert for UGC NET commerce students at Physics Wallah. She has also presented a paper titled "From Employees Involvement to their Exit": A systematic Review on Quiet Quitting in IIM Kozhikode international conference, 2024. She is working as an assistant Professor at vivekananda Institute of Professional Studies

Kumar Mandal currently serves as an Assistant Professor in the Department of Management at Brainware University, Kolkata. Before this, he worked at ICRA Analytics Ltd and Shriram Finance Ltd. He holds an MBA in Finance and a Bachelor of Commerce degree from Vidyasagar University. Additionally, he has successfully cleared the UGC NET and WB SET examinations in Management.

Raj Kumar Mishra is an Assistant Professor at the Institute of Management Sciences, University of Lucknow, with 14 years of teaching experience. He has also gained valuable experience working at prestigious institutions like PSIT Kanpur and BBD University. He has authored one book, holds one patent, and has published 21 research papers in esteemed national and international journals. With a Ph.D. in Management specializing in Marketing, his current research focuses on the influence of emerging technologies such as AI and Big Data on consumer behaviour and brand engagement. He also explores the effectiveness of personalized and healthcare marketing, as well as the role of ethical advertising in fostering consumer trust.

Ardita Aprilia Putri is an IT professional with expertise in information systems development, web-based application design, and digital solutions that support transparency and organizational efficiency. She has experience in system analysis, software implementation, and database-driven applications, particularly in the development of online platforms for financial and donation management. Her professional work focuses on designing user-oriented systems that enhance accountability, data accuracy, and operational effectiveness. Ardita is especially interested in applying information technology to support social, nonprofit, and organizational governance through transparent and reliable digital systems. She is committed to continuous professional development and aims to contribute to innovative, secure, and sustainable IT solutions that address real-world challenges.

Binastya Anggara Sekti has been a lecturer at the Faculty of Computer Science, Esa Unggul University, Jakarta, since 2016. He is actively involved in the Artificial Intelligence and Information Security Study Group. He holds a Bachelor's degree in Informatics Engineering from the Bandung Institute of Technology and a Master's degree in Information Systems Management from Trisakti University, Jakarta. Prior to entering academia, he accumulated over 25 years of professional experience as an IT practitioner in various companies across Jakarta. His work focused on developing data centers for internet service providers and delivering IT solutions for the manufacturing and oil & gas sectors. His research interests include artificial intelligence, cybersecurity, and the development of IT infrastructure.

Ved Srivastava has more than two decades of work experience comprising both corporate and academic exposure. His specialisation has been in the marketing domain, and he got the opportunity to work for some eminent companies, both Indian and MNCs. As a marketing person, he was a part of some outstanding projects at various locations in the country and in his last corporate stint he functioned as a deputy general manager. He is presently working as an Assistant Professor at the Department of Management, FMS, University of Lucknow, and has published research papers in ABDC and Scopus-indexed journals.

Lintang Tiaraningrum is an independent researcher and technology enthusiast focusing on the intersection of artificial intelligence, software engineering, and digital transformation. With a strong background in informatics and applied computing, she has been involved in various academic and development projects related to AI-driven systems, human-computer interaction, and process automation. Affiliated with Esa Unggul University, Indonesia, she has contributed to several research initiatives and continues to explore the application of emerging technologies in solving real-world problems, particularly in education and sustainable innovation.

Hemadri Ishvarlal Tikawala holds a Ph.D. in Commerce and serves as an Assistant Professor at R.V. Patel and V.L. Shah College of Commerce, affiliated with Veer Narmad South Gujarat University, Surat, India. With over fifteen years of teaching and research experience, she is a recognized postgraduate teacher and heads the Department of Commerce. Her academic expertise spans Business Administration, Management Studies, Marketing, Finance, and Human Resource Management, with a growing specialization in Neuromarketing and Sustainable Branding. She has published more than twenty research papers in peer-reviewed and Scopus-indexed journals and has actively contributed to the design of short-term courses and leadership training initiatives. Her recent research explores human–AI collaboration, ethical leadership, and creative innovation. She integrates managerial science with ethical and spiritual perspectives, reflecting a holistic approach to education and organizational development.

Manya Wadhwa is a passionate and driven student currently pursuing BBA (Hons) at Christ (Deemed to be University), Delhi NCR Campus. With a strong interest in leadership as the current departmental overall coordinator, she aspires to excel in advertising and marketing.

Radna Andi Wibowo serves as an Assistant Professor of Human Resource Management in the School of Business at Woxsen University (India). He holds Master Degree in Management at Dian Nuswantoro University (Indonesia) and holds a Ph.D. in Technological and Vocational Education at National Yunlin University of Science and Technology (Taiwan)

Index

A

B

C

D

E

F

G

H

I

K

L

M

P

R

S

T

U

W

www.ingramcontent.com/pod-product-compliance
Lightning Source LLC
LaVergne TN
LVHW060004031026
849161LV00025B/1414
* 9 7 9 8 3 3 7 3 7 1 5 3 5 *